PENGUIN CANADA

THE NEW CITY

JOHN LORINC is an award-winning journalist who has contributed to *Toronto Life, The Globe and Mail, National Post, Saturday Night, Report on Business,* and *Quill & Quire,* among other publications. He has written extensively on amalgamation, education, sprawl, and other city issues. He is the recipient of four National Magazine Awards for his coverage of urban affairs. His first book, *Opportunity Knocks: The Truth About Canada's Franchise Industry* (1995), was shortlisted for the National Business Book Award. John Lorinc lives in Toronto with his wife, Victoria Foote, and their two sons, Jacob and Samuel.

Also by John Lorinc

Opportunity Knocks: The Truth About
Canada's Franchise Industry

uTOpia: Towards a New Toronto (contributor)

THE NEW CITY

HOW THE CRISIS IN CANADA'S URBAN CENTRES IS RESHAPING THE NATION

John Lorinc

PENGUIN
CANADA

PENGUIN CANADA

Published by the Penguin Group

Penguin Group (Canada), 90 Eglinton Avenue East, Suite 700, Toronto, Ontario, Canada M4P 2Y3
(a division of Pearson Canada Inc.)

Penguin Group (USA) Inc., 375 Hudson Street, New York, New York 10014, U.S.A.
Penguin Books Ltd, 80 Strand, London WC2R 0RL, England
Penguin Ireland, 25 St Stephen's Green, Dublin 2, Ireland (a division of Penguin Books Ltd)
Penguin Group (Australia), 250 Camberwell Road, Camberwell, Victoria 3124, Australia
(a division of Pearson Australia Group Pty Ltd)
Penguin Books India Pvt Ltd, 11 Community Centre, Panchsheel Park, New Delhi – 110 017, India
Penguin Group (NZ), cnr Airborne and Rosedale Roads, Albany, Auckland 1310, New Zealand
(a division of Pearson New Zealand Ltd)
Penguin Books (South Africa) (Pty) Ltd, 24 Sturdee Avenue, Rosebank, Johannesburg 2196, South Africa

Penguin Books Ltd, Registered Offices: 80 Strand, London WC2R 0RL, England

First published 2006

(RRD) 10 9 8 7 6 5 4 3 2 1

LIBRARY AND ARCHIVES CANADA CATALOGUING IN PUBLICATION

Lorinc, John, 1963–
The new city : how the crisis in Canada's urban centres is reshaping the nation / John Lorinc.

Includes index.

ISBN-13: 978-0-14-305604-1
ISBN-10: 0-14-305604-2

1. City planning—Canada. 2. Urbanization—Canada.
3. Canada—Social conditions—21st century. I. Title.

HT169.C2L67 2006   307.1'216'0971   C2005-907768-9

Visit the Penguin Group (Canada) website at **www.penguin.ca**

Special and corporate bulk purchase rates available; please see
www.penguin.ca/corporatesales or call 1-800-399-6858, ext. 477 or 474

For Victoria, Jacob, and Sammy

CONTENTS

THE
NEW
CITY

FOREWORD

The New City: How the Crisis in Canada's Urban Centres Is Reshaping the Nation is about Canada's largest cities and how they are being transformed as a response to extraordinary new pressures and challenges. Sweeping in scope and packed with details, this book is both descriptive—chronicling the problems of Canada's urban regions coast to coast—and prescriptive—setting out policy options for their resolution. The breadth of research and intelligence of John Lorinc's insights distinguish *The New City* as a valuable synthesis of the best current thinking on Canada's urban future.

The timing for this book is ideal. Cities are at long last being recognized as the drivers of regional and national economic performance. Jane Jacobs, who inspired Lorinc along with most modern urbanists, said it first, in the foreword to her 1992 edition of *The Death and Life of Great American Cities*: "Wherever and whenever societies have flourished and prospered, rather than stagnated and decayed, creative and workable cities have been at the core of the phenomenon." But new insights are reinforcing the focus on city-regions. The first such insight is that, in a global economy, the importance of urban regions extends beyond the regional and national spheres. Cities are now the platform for the international export of goods and services. The second insight is that cities are the centres of knowledge and innovation, the places where people, R&D, and high-value services are concentrated in close proximity. Vibrant cities are home to what American academic Richard Florida calls the "creative class," those who work in sectors driven by creativity and intellectual expertise that fuel the innovation so essential to a nation's prosperity. Third, because of intensifying urbanization of both population and economic activities, environmental sustainability—climate change, energy, waste management, water, and so on—is an increasingly urban concern. Recognition is growing of industrial ecology's central importance to sustainable prosperity.

These are the conceptual reasons for the new interest in urban regions. *The New City* brings these intellectual abstractions to life with compelling data and vivid examples drawn from all of Canada's major cities—Vancouver, Calgary, Edmonton, Winnipeg, Toronto, Montreal, and Halifax—and from second-tier cities as well.

In deepening our understanding of the issues troubling our major cities, *The New City* bolsters the voices of advocates for change. In summarizing the key social trends—poverty, health, homelessness— the author paints the picture of a future characterized by "entrenched social ailments that result in youth crime, certain types of health problems, and urban alienation—conditions anathema to a sustained quality of life." Lorinc then asks the hard political question: "If the viability of Canada's hub cities is directly linked to our national well-being, what are the investments we need to make ... [to build] the socially inclusive, healthy cities that are most likely to succeed in a 21st-century, knowledge-based global economy?" His observation that in all developed countries, "housing sits at the intersection between social welfare policy and urban quality of life" is as profound as it is obvious. Yet Canada, unlike most OECD countries, has forgotten what it used to understand, and we have a long way to go to create an adequate national housing program.

Despite what some of us see as a failure of the federal government to follow rhetoric with action on many urban files, Lorinc is optimistic: "No political party that legitimately seeks to govern Canada will ever again be able to ignore its largest cities...." Following a period of 30 years during which Ottawa had no urban strategy and our cities were allowed to deteriorate, we've now arrived at a watershed moment, he suggests, indicated by the establishment of the ongoing federal gas tax transfer, the appointment of a new minister for Infrastructure and Communities, and a newfound federal interest in issues such as homelessness, transit, immigrant resettlement, and affordable housing.

That said, these hopeful signs don't yet add up to the agenda our cities need to adapt to new and growing demands—we've a long way to go.

Thematically organized, *The New City* asks the hard questions on topics as diverse as municipal finance, governance, urban land use and infrastructure planning, culture, and safety. Its answers may help shift the climate of opinion toward one that will support a genuine new deal for cities.

One of the merits of *The New City* is its underlying passion. As the son of Holocaust survivors who fled Hungary during the 1956 Revolution and settled in the stern, puritanical Toronto of that era, John Lorinc displays a particular sensibility to the promise of the new emerging brand of urbanism: "In a nation of immigrants, we can only coexist in our complex urban settings if we respect one another's ways, listen to one another's ideas, and support our neighbours as they navigate that great distance—both geographic and emotional—between old homes and new homes." This optimistic vision of inclusive, healthy, workable, civil, and humane cities animates *The New City*, a book that leaves the reader both better informed and more hopeful about Canada's urban future.

The New City will resonate with all those who have followed municipal politics over recent decades—from veterans of the civic battles in the 1970s to those engaged in the political turbulence of the 1990s. While oriented toward the future, there is enough history to satisfy the nostalgics, enough detail and analysis to engage scholars and policy wonks, and enough relevance to merit the attention of anyone who cares about cities.

Anne Golden, C.M.
Toronto, 2006

INTRODUCTION:
THE NEW CITY

City air makes you free.

—GERMAN PROVERB

n the fall of 1956, my parents, a young Jewish doctor and his wife, decided to flee Budapest during a lull in the Hungarian Revolution. A dozen years earlier, they had survived the Holocaust and the murderous anti-Semitic gangs that overthrew the Hungarian government in 1944. My father had been deported to a labour camp in Yugoslavia, while my mother's family went into hiding. They both lost their fathers during the final months of the war. Now, the populist uprising held disturbing echoes of that earlier time, and their decision to leave was sealed after my father witnessed a revolutionary mob lynch a Community official, chanting, "Kill the Jew." One November day, they boarded a train heading to Hungary's western provinces and disembarked near the frontier. Under cover of night, they hiked across unguarded fields and eventually met an Austrian border patrol, who welcomed them to freedom. From there, they made their way to Vienna to figure out what to do next.

As so many Canadians know first-hand, the experience of emigration is fraught with randomness. It was bitterly cold in Vienna in the waning weeks of 1956. My parents had planned to settle in the United States, but they had heard there were long lines at the U.S. embassy, and those applying for refugee status had to stand outside. Word soon went around their shelter that the Canadian embassy had a foyer inside where one could wait. They knew virtually nothing about Canada and spoke only halting English. My father had a distant relative in Montreal, but my parents had another reason for choosing that city. They had taken up kayaking on the Danube River. In the foyer of the Canadian consulate was a large map of the country. They noticed a river running past Montreal and figured they could resume their paddling once they had settled in. Little did my parents know that the mighty, frigid St. Lawrence, with its ocean-bound freighters, was about a kilometre wide at that point, and anything but suitable for small boats.

Early in 1957, my parents boarded a plane heading from Vienna to Iceland, then to Gander, Newfoundland, and finally on to Montreal. But as the flight approached its end point, the pilot announced an unexpected change of plans. A fierce storm was raging over Montreal, he said, and the plane was being rerouted. A short while later, my parents landed in Toronto. Fate had delivered them to a dot on the map some 600 kilometres west of the city in the middle of the river. And there they stayed.

My parents had fled a continental city which was sophisticated, dense, and cultured, its form reflecting the imperial architectural ambitions that characterized urban planning in Europe in the 18th and 19th centuries. Budapest had a café society ambience, a measure of liberalism, and a self-important intelligentsia. Yet, it also bore the scars of war and vivid reminders of the hate that had swept over the city during the 1930s and 1940s. The North American city in which my parents landed had a population of about a million. Queen's Park had recently established a regional government to manage the rapid development of bedroom suburbs such as Don Mills and Willowdale. A subway along the city's spine—Yonge Street—was being completed. There were also grand plans underway for major highways, shopping malls, and, a few years later, office towers.

For all its prosperity, Toronto presented a stern, puritanical streak cultivated by the Presbyterian Scots and Orangemen who dominated most local institutions. In the late 1950s, there was nothing to do on Sundays but go to church (the municipality even tied up children's swings in city parks to make sure the kids weren't having too much fun on the Lord's day). There was one bookstore, and no cafés. While immigrants—Central and Eastern Europeans, then Italians—had been part of the city's social geography for decades, they were predominantly merchants and labourers who were expected to stay in their own enclaves. Without fear of condemnation, the police routinely harassed young Italian men for the crime of congregating on the sidewalk and speaking a language the police officers couldn't understand. The Toronto General Hospital didn't hire Jewish doctors and made no secret of the fact. The Anglo elites sent their children to the right private schools, lived in certain neighbourhoods, and retreated to exclusive clubs. When, in the late 1950s, municipal officials were looking for a place to dispose of the soil excavated during the subway construction, they didn't think twice about dumping it into a picturesque west end ravine running through a Queen Street West neighbourhood whose once stately Victorian homes had become rundown rooming houses for immigrant labourers.

OVER THE LONG sweep of urban history, 50 years is a blip. Many of today's great international cities have survived centuries filled with war, plagues, city-destroying fires, boom times, cultural flowerings, and economic downturns. In this context, the changes that have transformed Canada's big cities in the six decades since World War II are astounding—rivalling the sudden emergence of Asian megalopolises such as Kuala Lumpur and Singapore, or Las Vegas, North America's fastest-growing urban region. During this brief span, Canadians—80 percent of whom now live in metropolitan areas—have forged a brand of urbanism that can be found in big cities all across the country: at once economically dynamic and reasonably inclusive; global and cosmopolitan in outlook, yet neighbourly and, for the most part, safe. Canadian cities offer a viable choice between the energy of a downtown lifestyle or the creature comforts of suburbia. Middle-class homeowners have created stable neighbourhoods that represent the social bedrock of our large cities. These urban regions, in turn, have become home to millions of newcomers, yet they display little of the anti-immigrant sentiment and alienation that afflict many European cities. Their economies are firing on all engines, but they provide their inhabitants with a reasonably effective social safety net. To paraphrase Sir Peter Ustinov's famous quip about Toronto, our major cities are like Frankfurt, New York, or Hong Kong, but run by Canadians.[1]

Vancouver, founded by loggers and miners, and tied precariously to the rest of the country by a ribbon of steel, is today a gleaming city-state that has learned to take maximum advantage of its natural beauty and westward orientation. No longer a boom-bust resource-industry town known for its lumber barons and penny stock hustlers, Vancouver is architecturally self-confident and highly appealing to young people drawn by its new-economy industries and health-oriented West Coast lifestyle. Waves of Asian immigrants, investors, and philanthropists, meanwhile, have transformed Vancouver into a city with a distinctively Pacific Rim culture—a far cry from the brusque, racist treatment meted out to earlier generations of Chinese and Japanese migrants.

Calgary's per capita gross domestic product during the 1990s climbed to heady levels—40 percent higher than other Canadian cities, with wealth rivalling booming U.S. metropolitan centres.[2] The city is marshalling the extraordinary affluence generated by the oil and gas sector to develop a cosmopolitan urban environment with a highly trained but increasingly international workforce, an economy that's busily diversifying well beyond the oil patch, and a distinctly entrepreneurial arts scene. Where Calgary was once dominated by oilmen and ranching concerns, it's now a city that is focusing on urban issues, including protecting its heritage core and investing in transit. In the 2005 provincial election, a handful of Calgary ridings (and several more in Edmonton) defeated Conservative MLAs—evidence that Albertan city-dwellers no longer see their interests represented by Ralph Klein's red-meat rural political base.

Ottawa, Kitchener-Waterloo, and Saskatoon—which has positioned itself as Canada's Science City—have all reaped the heady economic and social dividends produced by lively research and development sectors. As these cities have discovered, the combination of well-supported university scientists, research labs, technology entrepreneurs, and amenities have yielded rapid changes in the urban quality of life.

Halifax, at the other end of the country, has undergone a 180-degree transformation since the mid-1990s, emerging as the business, cultural, and political capital of Atlantic Canada. Shedding the stereotype of government dependency, the city has been reshaped by its strong commercial ties to Europe and the U.S. northeast, its waning dependence on public sector employment, the amazing flowering of East Coast pop culture, and the wealth flowing from offshore oil drilling. Recognizing the urban and economic role of tourism and recreation, Halifax's civic leaders in recent years have forged ahead with long-delayed plans to stop dumping raw sewage into Halifax harbour.

Montreal, for decades the poster child of Canadian cosmopolitanism, provides further evidence that truly great cities can withstand all sorts of body blows. In 1967, Expo brought iconic pavilions, tourists, and subway construction to an international city with European verve. But the 1970s saw tanks rolling through the downtown to quell a feared FLQ insurgency, the debt and embarrassment of the 1976 Olympics, and then the exodus of thousands of anglophones heading to Toronto to protect themselves from René Lévesque's separatists and their sign laws. Within a generation, though, Montrealers rebuilt the city's economy on the strength of the pharmaceuticals and aerospace manufacturing industries, among others. More research activity—pharmaceutical, aerospace engineering, and more—takes place in Montreal than in any other Canadian city. Montreal is also the destination of choice for thousands of francophone immigrants and students from across the country. It has situated itself as an internationally prominent cultural hothouse for artists, musicians, and computer game designers, winning the admiration of that arbiter of urban cool, American author and academic Richard Florida.

Finally, Toronto now ranks as the world's most ethnically diverse metropolis. Its broad-based economy has turned the GTA into the ninth largest metropolitan region in North America. The city's leading arts institutions are being showily expanded with hundreds of millions of dollars in public and philanthropic funding. The airport has received a $4-billion facelift, the largest infrastructure investment in Canadian history. The downtown university district is fast becoming an international hub for biotech start-ups and venture capital firms capitalizing on the research produced by nine downtown teaching hospitals. Meanwhile, the satellite cities around

Greater Toronto are flourishing as the Greater Golden Horseshoe consolidates into a megalopolis not unlike San Francisco's Bay Area. The Toronto in which my parents settled in the late 1950s—the city that would soon provide my father with a stable position as a hospital pathologist and a comfortable middle-class home—would barely recognize itself circa 2005.

Stepping further back, consider the fact that between 1967 and 2010, Canada's big cities will have hosted three Olympics (Montreal 1976; Calgary 1988; Vancouver 2010) and two Expos (Montreal '67 and Vancouver '86)—a record of civic celebration that much larger nations—Germany, the United Kingdom, France—can't begin to match. (For the record, the United States has had five Olympics in the post-war period.) Toronto hosts literary and film festivals of international renown, as well as North America's leading gay pride parade festitivies weekend. Montreal's annual jazz festival, founded in 1979, is now the largest in the world. Vancouver consistently ranks as one of the world's two most livable cities, according to an annual quality-of-life survey conducted by the multinational human resources firm Mercer Consulting. Calgary's energy giants know their oil sands investments represent a large part of the promise of energy independence for North America. Halifax and Vancouver have become premiere ports of call on the burgeoning luxury cruise circuit.

The health of our cities bodes well for the economy. In 2004, KPMG, an international accounting services firm, ranked Canada as the world's most cost-competitive country in which to conduct business, ahead of all other G-7 nations, including our largest trading partner, the United States.[3] Our cities' convention centres are routinely booked for years into the future by international trade, professional, and academic organizations. Why? Because they are safe, convenient, welcoming, affordable, and lively. Although they may not have ancient cathedrals and magnificent boulevards, Canada's major cities would seem to be a good news story.

Had my parents toughed out that long cold lineup at the U.S. embassy in Vienna in 1956, they would have settled in the midst of a starkly different type of North American urban environment. In the decades since World War II, American cities have been shaped by enormously powerful centrifugal forces that don't exist in Canada: racial strife, white flight, protections for gun ownership, the pre-eminence of property rights, municipal corruption, and the unintended consequences of spending policies, laws, and judicial rulings designed to improve the lot of inner-city minorities. More than any other country in the world, the United States has become a "suburban nation" that has, with a few notable exceptions, forsaken the concentrated urban form in favour of sprawling exurban conglomerations—so-called edge cities—dominated by highway-linked networks of malls, commercial and industrial parks, and subdivisions.[4]

In many ways, suburban America is the logical result of a political culture that places the prospect of home ownership at the emotional core of its ideal of citizenship—a value made concrete with policies such as tax-deductible home mortgages, which have never existed here. This is the fuel that has driven American cities outward with such momentum. While no Canadian cities are as dense as New York, there's also nothing here that compares to sprawling urban regions such as Houston and Atlanta, nor hollowed-out crime-ridden cities such as Detroit.

Befitting its status as the birthplace of the automobile, America is also a frontier country that mythologizes the open road and has let the needs of drivers—as well as the interests of the auto industry—determine the dispersed, transient form of U.S. cities and suburbs. It's a country where car industry executives once lobbied against transit funding and municipal engineers routinely design super-wide residential streets with no sidewalks or curbside trees specifically to accommodate vehicular traffic. Federal highway building programs were responsible for the inner-city expressways that tore through established working-class and visible minority neighbourhoods in almost all large U.S. cities, leaving in their wake irreparable tears in the urban fabric.[5] By sharp contrast, civic leaders in Paris and Rome in recent years have railed against SUVs, threatening outright bans. London mayor Ken Livingstone imposed a toll on cars heading into the downtown. These are political conversations that simply couldn't take place in much of the United States.

American cities have also evolved in direct response to racial conflict and rates of urban violence that remain far higher than almost anything found in Canadian big cities. These urban tensions came to the fore when poor Southern blacks began migrating to work in the factories of the industrial northeast, and exploded at various times in devastating riots in Newark, Detroit, Los Angeles, and Chicago. Developers and real estate marketers recklessly fanned the flames of racial discord, while urban "slum clearance" campaigns—such as those in Chicago in the 1950s and 1960s—masked the racist motives of municipal leaders intent on isolating visible minorities. The flight from the inner city—often to so-called gated communities, with their own security apparatus—is no longer restricted to whites: Middle-class blacks and Hispanics have left the hollowed-out downtown, leaving a devastated landscape of concentrated poverty in cities such as Baltimore and Newark.

The result is that many U.S. cities are staggeringly divided, polarized by wealth, poverty, class, and race. Entrenched desperation has bred urban crime, which tends to be more vicious because of easy access to firearms. Case in point: Rochester, New York, has more murders each year than Toronto, even though it's only a tenth of the size.

Liberal-minded U.S. legislators and judges inadvertently made the situation worse. Electoral boundaries were redrawn to create districts with a majority of black voters, but such measures—intended to provide needed political representation for disenfranchised minorities—have served to racialize urban politics. And judicial rulings from the mid-1950s to the 1970s that sought to desegregate schools—by busing children between white and non-white neighbourhoods—unwittingly triggered a mass exodus from big-city boards of education (although later rulings blocked mandatory busing between suburban and downtown school districts). As of 1990, the 18 largest cities in the northern United States had such heavily concentrated black populations that more than three-quarters of their residents would have had to move in order to achieve a measure of racial balance in urban neighbourhoods.[6] Schools in Los Angeles and New York are overwhelmingly populated by minority students, many from poor families, while the urban middle class chooses to send its children to private or charter schools.

New York, Chicago, Boston, Austin, Seattle, and San Francisco are icons of turbo-charged urbanism. But urban America also reflects many fundamentally anti-urban ideas and conflicts buried deep in that country's genetic makeup: the right to bear arms; that frontier warning, "Don't tread on me"; and the unresolved legacy of slavery. In a world of mass migration and city-states, Canada's constitutional *cri de cœur*— "peace, order and good government"— has turned out to be a much more adroit response to the 21st-century urban condition. These values acknowledge what city-dwellers need to know to survive city life: that the challenge of living together with large groups of disparate strangers means accepting pragmatic constraints on personal freedoms, without which there can be no social peace.

IN 1999, A TORONTO consultant named Joe Berridge began telling a story that resonated with municipal officials across Canada. The British-born former City of Toronto planner had established a thriving private practice, travelling internationally to advise on major development projects, such as London's Canary Wharf. Increasingly, his work was taking him to U.S. and U.K. cities, which, he observed, were seeing a surge of reinvestment. New waterfronts, light rapid transit projects, and urban amenities were turning up in cities such as Baltimore, Cincinnati, and Manchester. The United States appeared to be experiencing an urban renaissance after decades of suburban exodus, while European cities were making major investments in transit and green energy. The New Urbanists—a collection of American architects, planners, and journalists—were railing against the placelessness of exurbia. They set out to reform the worst excesses of suburbia with a return to more traditional ideas about town planning and architectural design. U.S. president Bill Clinton earmarked billions of dollars for urban transportation infrastructure and housing. British prime minister Tony Blair was focusing his government's efforts on tough urban issues such as education, revitalization, and housing. Mayors in Chicago and New York were aggressively cleaning up their downtowns. Boston was burying its waterfront expressway and creating in its path a string of downtown public spaces. For all the futuristic talk about a virtual economy, the new media and computer gaming entrepreneurs of the 1990s and 2000s turned out to be young hipsters drawn to cosmopolitan cities such as Seattle and San Francisco.

Berridge wasn't seeing much of this at home, where cash-strapped Toronto had come to see itself as under siege from a hostile provincial regime and an indifferent federal government. What's more, he had become increasingly conscious of the sort of tools—a potpourri of specialized taxes and grant programs—American municipalities could use to prime the pump of urban revitalization, but which simply didn't exist north of the border. Economists and academics were writing about how city-regions—as opposed to nations—were becoming the real players in the global economy. That profound structural shift didn't square with the financial and political stresses facing Toronto. Nor did the federal government's preoccupation with regional pork barrelling at the expense of big cities. Indeed, Berridge presented voting data showing that Canada's federal electoral system was weighted heavily in favour of less populous rural and small town ridings—the point being that Parliament itself is skewed against urban issues. He wrote up his observations, warning of dire national consequences if Canadian politicians at all three levels didn't begin the arduous task of reinvesting in the country's leading cities. "Managing our decline," was the phrase he used to describe the consequences of the status quo. It was a shot across the bow, heard in big cities throughout Canada.

These trenchant critiques were a commentary on the fiscal conservatism of the 1990s. From the mid-1980s to the early 1990s, federal and provincial politicians were preoccupied with constitutional reform and had tolerated an ultimately unsustainable escalation of the country's cumulative debt. In 1995, then Finance minister Paul Martin accepted the apocalyptic analysis of neo-conservative economists and *Wall Street Journal* editorialists. He broke the back of the deficit by slashing spending and reforming the system of cost-shared social transfers to provincial governments. (For years, Ottawa had paid 50 percent of programs such as social housing and welfare under the Canada Assistance Plan.) By the latter 1990s, however, provincial politicians were discovering that Ottawa's belt tightening had suddenly become a huge fiscal problem. Across the country, provincial legislators, to a greater or lesser degree, began reining in their own budgets and downloading programs—from housing to welfare to transit—to municipalities. Urban mayors had no one (except property owners) to whom they could pass the buck, nor could they run up deficits. They were stuck.

Moreover, troubling social fissures were becoming glaringly apparent in all of Canada's largest cities, despite the festivals and new cultural buildings and buoyant real estate prices. The 1990s saw mounting housing shortages, falling high school graduation rates, and an emerging homelessness crisis. Recent immigrants—the vast majority of whom settle in big cities—have faced an ever tougher time establishing themselves, finding suitable housing, and securing work in the professions in which they are trained. In Western Canadian cities, many Aboriginals live in highly distressed, crime-ridden communities that have assumed the character of American ghettos. Canada's poorest postal code, Vancouver's drug-infested Downtown Eastside, is merely blocks from the gleaming new condo towers in Yaletown and on the north shore of False Creek. Sprawl has gobbled up vast tracts of arable land, fostering energy-gorging suburban cities that grapple with gridlock, bad air, and an epidemic of obesity.

Canada's cities, for the most part, haven't been afflicted by the viral legacies of slavery and colonialism. And they've grown up within the context of a nation whose destiny is to struggle with the difficult business of reconciling ethnic and linguistic difference. The upshot is that we've learned to be both accommodating and prudent, but we are also lucky. There is much to suggest that we shouldn't be complacent.

The emerging cracks in our urban edifice have complex causes, not all of which we can control. But it's clear that many of these problems have much to do with the fact that Canadian cities simply don't register in our constitutional arrangements. The British North America Act of 1867, written when fewer than 1 in 10 Canadians lived in cities or towns, assigned exclusive responsibility for municipal affairs to the provincial governments. The present consequence of Canada's constitutional shrug to cities is that local institutions—from municipalities to school districts, regional health authorities and other agencies—have found themselves operating on a shoestring, and under the thumb of provincial governments, which jealously guard their turf and often turn a deaf ear to the voices of urban communities. This culture of disenfranchisement, in the view of almost all Canadian urbanists, represents a historic mistake in our division of powers, one that puts Canada drastically out of step with a world in which global city-regions have emerged as the arbiters of economic and political power.

THERE HAVE BEEN periods in our history when urban social crises or unruly growth have prompted the upper levels of government to pay attention to cities. But for most of the past three decades, the federal government simply had no urban strategy, no way of thinking about urban affairs without provoking the provinces. By the late 1990s, however, the failure of the constitutional status quo could no longer be ignored. In 2000, senior federal civil servants in the Privy Council Office and other line ministries began quietly inviting leading urbanists to Ottawa to tell them what was going on in the country's cities. Then they embarked on an exercise to view policy making through an "urban lens," meaning that they would actively consider the repercussions of their administrative and policy decisions on cities. That they felt the need to impose this kind of intellectual discipline on their own duties requires no further comment.

Slowly, as the following chapters will show, things began to change, both in Ottawa and in various provincial capitals. By 2003, Paul Martin signalled a tentative interest in shoring up the financial foundations of urban government, through a transfer of the federal gas excise tax and other measures packaged as a "new deal" for cities. Indeed, the establishment of the ongoing gas tax transfer, plus the appointment of a new minister for Infrastructure and Communities and a newfound federal interest in urban issues such as child care, transit, immigrant resettlement, and affordable housing, illustrated that our national leaders were finally realizing that Canada's future depends on the health of its large urban regions. The Liberals weren't the authors of the urban agenda; indeed, they shared in the blame for letting our cities deteriorate. At least they knew enough to heed the warnings. Canada's nascent urban agenda remains a work in progress. But no political party that seeks to legitimately govern Canada will ever again be able to ignore its largest cities in the name of constitutional niceties or ideological bromides that have little to do with the complexities of urban life.

The reason is that the untidy but enervating urban perspective extends into virtually every aspect of what our governments now do … or choose not to do. Whatever else you may think about the rights of gun owners, the fact is that lax federal sentencing laws for handgun possession make urban neighbourhoods unsafe. We all want to save a bit more on our paycheques. But ill-considered provincial tax-cutting promises exacerbate sprawl and make the air unbreathable.

The gay marriage debate in 2004 and 2005 provides another way of seeing these interconnections. Overnight, the Ontario court ruling that sanctioned the issuance of such marriage licences made Toronto a destination for American gay couples. They arrived at City Hall with money to spend on hotels, stores, and restaurants, and took home happy stories of the city's vibrant gay district. At the same time, some opposition to gay marriage came from traditional immigrant communities that have settled in big cities, and whose members haven't been exposed to the four-decade progression of gay rights in North America.

Beyond the back and forth over minority rights and religious values, the gay marriage debate was a parable about city life. When my parents arrived from Hungary in 1957, they settled in a large city that offered new social and economic opportunities, but also the companionship of those who had shared their experience of exile and flight. Indeed, migrants, persecuted minorities, and misfits have long sought refuge in urban neighbourhoods, which afford anonymity but also the possibility of new forms of community—from close-knit ethnic or religious enclaves to derelict warehouses colonized by artists. When working properly, cities transform exclusion into inclusion. If treated pragmatically, and with a healthy scepticism about politicians touting pat solutions, cities also have the *potential* to function like social reaction chambers in which people from vastly dissimilar backgrounds may, or may not, interact with one another.

This is a key point. Because of their dense, diverse nature, our metropolitan regions must provide a multiplicity of options, without which there is merely crowding and uncomfortable conformity. Paradoxically, successful cities also understand the need to collectively negotiate certain limits on the individual freedoms of their residents in order to ensure that urban communities remain livable, safe, efficient, and prosperous. Forward-looking urban leaders, moreover, recognize that constructive, locally driven partnerships between governments, academic institutions, not-for-profit organizations, ethnocultural groups, businesses, and neighbourhoods are much more in tune with the orchestral rhythms of city life than those cacophonous partisan political feuds over archaic jurisdictional boundaries. In fact, one could say that the litmus test of cosmopolitanism is the peaceful coexistence of seemingly irreconcilable differences. "Seemingly," because the close physical proximity of intensely varied human experiences and conflicting aspirations, as Jane Jacobs long ago observed, is the engine that imbues urban life with its particular vitality: the city of opportunities, the city of ideas.

The new city.

PART ONE

THE CITY UNDER STRESS

The story of how Canada's largest cities stumbled into the 21st century begins during the heady years of the mid-1980s. This was an era of turbo-charged capitalism, when greed was good and the stock markets were surging. Toronto was in the throes of an office building boom. Vancouver was gearing up for the 1986 Expo, while Calgary prepared for the 1988 Winter Olympics. Montreal's economy was coming back to life after the exodus of businesses in the late 1970s, and the city's corporate elite had one of its favourite sons—Brian Mulroney—sitting in the prime minister's office.

A handful of pivotal political decisions, taken at the national level over about half a decade, turned out to have enormous but unforeseen implications. Ottawa almost tripled immigration levels and ratified a free trade agreement with the United States—policies that would come to be felt most directly in our largest cities. But Canada's federal and provincial leaders weren't thinking about the health of the country's cities at the time; that was taken for granted. Instead, our politicians focused intently—and almost to the exclusion of everything else—on breaking the Gordian knot of our existential crisis. Yet the two high-profile attempts at constitutional reform—the Meech Lake Accord in 1987 and the Charlottetown Accord in 1992—went up in flames.

When we woke up from our extended constitutional digression, however, things were beginning to look a lot less optimistic in the cities. Real estate markets had buckled. Canada's manufacturers and exporters girded themselves for the brave new world of free trade by casting off thousands of middle managers and closing plants. We had a "jobless recovery," even though Canada's diplomatic missions abroad were processing immigration applications at an unprecedented rate. Meanwhile, the state of the country's public finances began to look increasingly preposterous to international bond rating agencies, whose analysts warned that Canada, with its addiction to multi-billion-dollar deficits, was hurtling toward something economists darkly referred to as a "debt wall."

In 1993, Canadian voters demolished Kim Campbell's struggling Progressive Conservative government and handed Jean Chrétien the reins of power in the first of his three majorities. But it didn't take long for the new Liberal government to suspend most of its Red Book election promises and act on Wall Street's financial warnings. In 1995, Finance minister Paul Martin, Chrétien's former leadership rival, tabled the most fiscally conservative budget the nation had seen in decades, one that eliminated a $40-billion-plus deficit by making drastic social spending cuts. The stage had been set for the wrenching changes—both good and bad—that would soon wash over Canada's largest cities.

GLOBAL CITIES

"Home," of course, was always a village or city in Old China, the place you were raised, where they still wanted you, even dead; where you belonged. For ever.

"Canada no want you," Dai Yee said, matter-of-factly, remembering both her and Mother's welcome-to-Canada three-week confinement together in the "Pig House" customs building in Victoria.

"Canada say, 'Go home, chinky Chinaman!'"

—WAYSON CHOY, *PAPER SHADOWS* (1999)

My own story begins as a young child in another country, one "draped in barbed wire from head to toe" ... The story of that little girl, who watched her parents, her family, and her friends grappling with the horrors of a ruthless dictatorship, who became the woman standing before you today, is a lesson in learning to be free.

—MICHAËLLE JEAN, GOVERNOR GENERAL OF CANADA, INSTALLATION SPEECH, SEPTEMBER 27, 2005

It was one of those quiet passings that tell an important tale. On April 3, 2005, the venerable Wexford Hockey Association, based in the gritty east Toronto suburb of Scarborough, played its last game. Once a lively league with dozens of teams, prominent alumni in the NHL, and as many as 4000 youngsters, the association had gradually shrunk to just 120 players, and its board finally decided to turn off the lights. "Fifty-one years of history is a lot to lose," John Kelloway, Wexford's president, lamented. "It's painful to see. This is not the legacy I wanted to leave."

The problem, as the league's obituary in the *Toronto Star* noted, is that "minor hockey is dying throughout Scarborough." Various reasons were cited, but the most compelling had to do with demographics: two decades of immigration had changed Scarborough's profile; the sprawling post-war community had become home to thousands of newcomers from warm countries where children grew up playing soccer, cricket, and basketball. They simply hadn't tapped into Canada's obsession with its expensive, cold-climate pastime.[1]

As it happened, just a week later, city councillors in Brampton, Ontario, a rapidly growing municipality on Toronto's northwest shoulder, found themselves considering a revised parks and recreation master plan that revealed another tale of urban transformation. Forty years ago, Brampton was a quaint, sleepy town, the place that produced long-serving Ontario premier Bill Davis. Today, it's a sprawling edge city that claims to be Canada's fastest-growing municipality. All around Brampton's historic downtown are vast subdivisions populated by immigrants from South Asia, Africa, and the Caribbean. Of its almost 330,000 inhabitants, more than one in three were born outside Canada; nearly 40,000 immigrants arrived here during the 1990s alone. Brampton officials, the report said, simply hadn't planned for these "demographic" changes, meaning they now had to alter their recreational programming.[2] Here, too, hockey entered the civic dialogue. Even though Brampton's brassy mayor, Susan Fennell, was nationally known as a champion of women's hockey, she couldn't deny that the latest generation of Bramptonians had very different tastes. Which is why the city shelved plans for a two-rink arena in favour of a vast new indoor facility outfitted for soccer, cricket, lacrosse, and kabbadi. Looking out at her community, Fennell realized she now lived in a new Canada.

Despite such episodes, hockey isn't dying in Toronto, or anywhere else, because of immigration. But our national sport now has to share time and resources with other pastimes. Such subtle changes in our collective tastes provide a parable about how Canada's cities are confronting the challenges of the 21st century.

Our large urban centres—lacking the architectural legacy and shared civic mythology that accrue to old cities with deep roots—bear the distinctive traces of the waves of immigrants who settled in ethnic enclaves, launched businesses, opened restaurants, and then watched, sometimes fretfully, as their children moved on. There are Chinatowns of various vintages, Greektowns, and Little Italys; markets whose ethnic composition evolved effortlessly over the decades; aging strip plazas where the merchants come from every corner of the world; teeming Asian malls; and extended suburban districts that have become home to large extended communities of Indian, Chinese, and Russian families. Halifax has a sizeable but low-key Kuwaiti community. Windsor is home to thousands of immigrants from the Middle East. The ethnic diversity in much of Toronto—including some of its high-density, public housing complexes—is so profound that in many communities, no one group dominates, and so the classrooms in local public schools are filled with children who collectively speak a dozen different languages.

Staid brick churches that once served the English-speaking descendants of Scots or Brits now serve congregations of Koreans or Filipinos. Large urban centres typically support thriving ethnic media organizations, and many have come to be associated with colourful festivals and sports tournaments that attract tens of thousands of participants. Some established immigrant communities band together and build dramatic religious structures, while others are content to blend into the urban woodwork and let the past fade. There are Finnish and Armenian and Italian seniors' homes, and parochial schools for the Jewish and Muslim children. Vancouver's architectural renaissance owes much to urban forms found in the Far East, while some of Toronto's landmark buildings (City Hall, the Toronto-Dominion Centre) reflect the city's post-war, international sensibility.

The ubiquitous ethno-cultural diversity that now defines our largest cities represents a daring social experiment in urban globalism that's being watched by countries around the world and has set us on a sharply different course than our continental neighbours. In *Fire and Ice,* a 2003 examination of the widening gap between Canadian and American values, pollster Michael Adams argues that Canadians "are coming to define a new sociological 'post-modernity' characterized by multiple, flexible roles and identities while Americans, weaned for generations on ideals of freedom and independence, have in general not found adequate security and independence in their social environment to allow them to assert the personal autonomy needed to enact the kind of individual explorations—spiritual, familial, sexual—that are taking place north of the border." Despite the fact that both countries were built by immigrants, Adams cites a 2002 Pew Research Center poll of 38,000 people in 44 nations that showed that Canada was the only country in which a majority—77 percent of respondents in fact—said immigrants had a positive influence, well ahead of the 49 percent of Americans who felt the same way of their own country. "Forty three percent of Americans said that immigrants were bad for their nation, more than double the proportion of Canadians (18 percent) who had a negative view of newcomers in their country."[3]

Such attitudes are a powerful testament to the liveability and adaptability of our largest cities. While the late University of Toronto philosopher Marshall McLuhan long ago coined the phrase "global village" to describe how electronic communications had destroyed distances, Canada's largest cities represent the inverse—an ingathering of people from vastly different backgrounds in one place, at one time. Immigrants, of course, arrive with their languages, their customs, and, often, their wounds and animosities. But the vast majority also arrive with skills and a fresh perspective, and, crucially, the desire to be here. Then, having settled in fast-growing cities with very little by way of history or immutable tradition, Canada's older and newer immigrants, and their children, are together confronted with the immense task of forging not just a collective vision of urban citizenship but also a shared language with which to describe it.

What are the hallmarks of this vision? It's about finding ways to adapt, to accommodate, and to make space within the context of bustling urban environments. It's a vision grounded in a forward-looking cosmopolitanism defined by tolerance, educational opportunity, and urban safety. And it's a recognition that the key to Canada's long-term prosperity lies not in Alberta's oil sands or Arctic diamond mines but in the countless links that bind Canada to the world. These ties saturate us with novel commercial opportunities, as well as with new ideas about culture, science, faith, and politics.

But there is a paradox embedded in this way of being a country. The underlying reality of an overwhelmingly urban, multicultural society is that it is bracingly open-ended—a condition that entails an institutionalized undermining of the status quo, and thus functions as a microcosm of the global economy, with its dizzying uncertainties. Immigrants pump a disorderly energy through the veins of Canadian society, compelling its more established groups—the two founding nations and Canada's Aboriginal people, together with previous generations of immigrants and their offspring—to be in a state of constant reflection about Canada's dominant conventions and beliefs. And this is a good thing. As a nation of immigrants lacking any bellicose sense of manifest destiny, we must come to recognize ourselves as a profoundly cosmopolitan country whose citizenry is forever combining and recombining into something unfinished, unknowable, and perhaps even indescribable. It is first about risk and then—perhaps—about reward.

A Nation of Immigrants

The story of how Canada's immigrants are changing the country's cities begins with federal immigration policy, which traditionally reflected the economic and political imperatives of the day, as it indeed still does. In the 19th century, Scottish, German, and Ukrainian immigrants were induced to open up rural areas in Ontario and the Prairies, while large numbers of Central, Southern, and Eastern Europeans came to Toronto in the early decades of the 20th century to work in factories or as labourers. The doors slammed shut at times, for example in the late 1930s, when boatloads of Jewish refugees from Germany were trying to escape from Adolph Hitler's Nazi regime. Then, at the height of the Cold War, they swung open again to allow in thousands of Hungarians and, in later decades, refugees from other Communist-controlled nations. Between 1945 and 1970, Canada admitted 3.5 million immigrants, including many Nazi collaborators.[4] Many European refugees arrived in Canada with academic credentials and technical experience. Unlike previous generations of immigrants, they capitalized on the booming economy and were able to establish themselves professionally, in fields such as engineering, medicine, and the emerging field of computer science.

Post-war economic growth gave rise to a new breed of immigrant entrepreneurs who helped build our cities. Some of the most prominent Toronto-area developers began their careers as bricklayers or carpenters, but rapidly transformed small contracting operations into huge home-building and land development firms during the suburban boom period. Several of Canada's most successful manufacturing giants trace their roots to European immigrants who came here after World War II. Frank Stronach, Austrian by birth, arrived with little more than his machinist training, starting out in his own garage. But he grabbed the wave of car ownership and during the 1970s and 1980s built up one of the world's largest auto parts manufacturing empires. Michael Lee-Chin, a Chinese-Jamaican immigrant, was working on cruise ships and factories in the early 1970s to save enough to attend McMaster University to study civil engineering. After graduation, he ended up in the financial services industry, and his innate salesmanship propelled him up Bay Street's greasy pole. By the time he was in his mid-40s, he had become one of Canada's wealthiest mutual fund dealers.[5]

While we now laud ourselves as a nation of immigrants and point to our tolerance of newcomers as evidence of our social openness, we have often chafed against the presence of "aliens" and visible minority Canadians. The government allowed in Japanese and Chinese labourers at the end of the 19th century to toil on the railways, but also imposed a notorious head tax and, several decades later, interned thousands of Japanese-Canadians living in British Columbia during World War II. In Toronto in the 1910s, a prominent member of the Anglo establishment railed at the growing presence of Jews in the city. Half a century later, Nova Scotia authorities razed Africville, on the edge of Halifax, and dispersed the approximately 400 African-Canadians whose ancestors had called the little community home since the 1840s. (Ironically, many of those forcibly removed from their homes could trace their Canadian roots for generations, yet they were treated as outsiders and pariahs by government agencies.) Italian immigrants in Toronto came in for rough treatment at the hands of the police in the 1950s. In the 1980s, anti-Chinese sentiment in Vancouver expressed itself in neighbourhood campaigns to ban so-called monster homes. Today, racial profiling of blacks by urban police forces remains a tenacious stain on our reputation for tolerance.

Officially, Canada ended one long-standing strain of sanctioned racism in the early 1960s when then prime minister John Diefenbaker repealed the "whites only" admission policy. Over the next two decades, Ottawa embarked on a series of drastic changes in the immigration system, first adopting a "colour-blind," points-based admissions system and then allowing the claims of hundreds of thousands of refugees—Tamils, Somalis, Vietnamese, Ethiopians, Haitians (among them, the young Michaëlle Jean, who would become Governor General of Canada), Central and South Americans—driven from their homes by despotic regimes, civil war, and drought. In the 1970s, prime minister Pierre Trudeau introduced Ottawa's policy of official multiculturalism and then passed long-overdue reforms to the notoriously secretive immigration system, including greater protections for civil liberties and an end to the ban on gay immigrants.[6]

At the same time, however, Trudeau's government kept immigration rates relatively low—84,000 newcomers arrived in 1985—compared with earlier periods of high immigration. "Such cautious, thoughtful management gives the priority to the needs of the country and the welfare of the existing workforce," comments journalist Daniel Stoffman.[7] In his controversial critique of Canada's current immigration policies, *Who Gets In,* he argues that Brian Mulroney came into office in 1984, having seized on the potential partisan advantage of sharply increased immigration. Business groups supported the Tories' plan to increase immigration because it would keep down wages. And demographers backed the higher levels because they would offset Canada's declining birth rate. By the end of Mulroney's second term, Canada's immigration rate had tripled, to 256,000 people. In the run-up to the 1993 landslide that saw Jean Chrétien defeat the Tories, the Liberal Red Book—the party's election platform—upped the ante by promising to hike immigration levels to 1 percent of the population, or about 330,000 newcomers per year.

Canada's Open Door

This broad political consensus, forged over just one decade, represents a turning point in our history and can be seen as the beginning of Canada's urban century.

Over the past decade and a half, 200,000 to 250,000 immigrants and refugees have arrived each year, and in 2005 the Liberal government promised to raise that figure to about 330,000 a year. Today, half of all new Canadians come from just 10 countries (China, India, Philippines, the former Yugoslavia, Sri Lanka, Pakistan, Taiwan, the United States, Iran, and Poland). The federal government has tinkered with the levers of the immigration machinery over the years, adjusting the points systems to deal with labour force shortages, fast-tracking prosperous immigrants from Asia, and increasing the number of family class immigrants (who account for about 40 percent of all newcomers). According to the calculus of immigration policy, if at least half of all new immigrants were accepted under the economic class category, they would collectively generate enough jobs, spending power, and tax revenue to support the family class immigrants and refugees that made up the balance.[8] The bottom line is that immigrants today account for a larger share of the Canadian population than every other OECD (Organisation for Economic Co-operation and Development) country except Australia.[9] What is more, recent immigrants and refugees overwhelmingly settle in our largest urban centres, particularly Toronto, Montreal, Vancouver, Ottawa, and Calgary. The GTA (Greater Toronto Area), in fact, has the highest proportion of foreign-born residents of any city in the world— the next closest being Miami, with its Cuban expatriate community.

In this day and age, it would be difficult to seriously dispute the enormously important social, cultural, and economic role immigration plays in a small, outward-looking, and predominantly urban country like Canada. "Canadian cities have not seen an explosion of racial tension and conflict evident in other countries," notes University of Saskatchewan immigration expert Peter Li. "Canada appears to be sensitive to an integration process that requires immigrants to adapt to Canadian society and Canadian urban centers to accommodate an increasingly multicultural population."[10]

PROPORTION OF FOREIGN-BORN RESIDENTS IN MAJOR CITIES

Census Metropolitan Area	% Foreign-Born
Toronto	43.7
Miami	40.0
Vancouver	37.5
Los Angeles	31.0
Sydney	31.0
New York	24.0
Montreal	18.4

Elizabeth McIsaac, "Immigrants in Canadian Cities: Census 2001—What Do the Data Tell Us?" *Policy Options*, May 2003, 59. Reprinted with permission.

Still, we must ask whether Canada is presently doing its part to ensure that newcomers have the opportunity to thrive and therefore follow in the footsteps of earlier generations of immigrants. Over the past two decades, the Canadian government has enticed hundreds of thousands of people to come here and share in our vision of prosperity and tolerance. But there is mounting evidence to suggest that we're not delivering on our promises—that we've sent out invitations to a great, rollicking dinner party, knowing that we're only really prepared to serve a few stale snacks to those who take us up on our offer.

There is nothing new about the fact that it takes immigrants and refugees several years, and often considerable hardship, to establish themselves. In Canada, traditionally, it took about a decade for a recent immigrant to nose up the economic ladder to the point where his or her income is comparable to what a Canadian-born person with similar skills may expect to earn. But the immigrants who have arrived since 1991 have experienced considerably more trouble closing that gap than previous waves of newcomers. The labour force indicators fill out the picture: A 2004 Statistics Canada study on immigrants in metropolitan areas found that those who arrived after 1991 had lower employment rates and higher unemployment levels than Canadian-born workers.[11] These trends don't apply across the board, however: South and East

Asians are experiencing much more economic hardship than Eastern European immigrants.

What is more, the income gap between racial groups has risen steadily in the last three decades, creating what some immigration experts characterize as the racialization of poverty. Members of visible minorities, according to one report, are three times as likely to be living in poverty and twice as likely to be unemployed.[12]

"We're not doing as well as twenty years ago," observes pollster Michael Adams. "Newer immigrants aren't succeeding as well as the brick-laying Italian immigrants who arrived thirty years ago."[13]

Consider some of the symptoms. In our largest cities, between a third and a half of all immigrants and refugees who arrived between 1991 and 1996 experienced serious housing problems and often ended up paying a far larger share of their income on rent than did non-immigrants. They had to contend with racist landlords, overcrowding, rotting apartments in social housing complexes, or unaffordable rent. Moreover, according to urban geographer Robert Murdie, the latest waves of immigrants have faced more severe housing problems than those who arrived in the 1970s and 1980s. As an April 2000 study by the Canadian Council for Social Development found, about a fifth of immigrants who came to Canada before 1986 live in poverty, while fully a half of those who arrived after 1991 do.[14]

Another symptom: Toronto public health researchers discovered that in high-immigrant downtown neighbourhoods, the mounting economic hardship was increasingly evident in doctors' offices and emergency rooms. With both provincial and federal cuts to welfare, social services, and other support programs in the late 1990s and early 2000s, physicians were treating a growing number of cases of newcomers, especially women and refugees, suffering from stress disorders, depression, and spousal abuse.[15] A 2004 study showed that in inner-city neighbourhoods, immigrants were "significantly" more likely than non-immigrants to be admitted to hospital because they couldn't find family doctors and were more susceptible to the sort of stress-related illnesses that are linked to poverty.[16]

At the heart of this largely unseen crisis is the fact that many recent immigrants haven't been able to reap the benefits of the tremendous wealth that has accumulated in many of Canada's largest cities in recent years. Stoffman and other critics argue that the surge in immigrants in the past two decades has forced thousands of newcomers into dead-end menial jobs that pay low wages and offer little opportunity for advancement.[17] One doesn't need to spend much time in urban Canada to see the human face of these cold statistics. Mass merchandisers such as Wal-Mart, fast-food chains, doughnut stores, pizza outlets, and the hospitality sectors are staffed largely by recent immigrants, the vast majority of whom have come to Canada from South or Southeast Asia, Africa, Eastern Europe, and the Middle East. Certain service sectors have turned into low-wage ghettos for immigrant women—for example, hospitals and especially big-city nursing homes or seniors' residences. Fast-growing private nursing home chains have in recent years become the target of labour-organizing drives—a response to the dismal working conditions and poor wages facing the orderlies and nursing assistants who are overwhelmingly female and tend to be immigrants from regions such as Southeast Asia and the Caribbean.

The nanny economy is a particularly unsavoury feature of the fate of some of the newest cohorts of urban immigrants. With the high cost of city living and an ever-increasing number of women in the workforce, the demand for caregivers has exploded in the past two decades. Many urban parents choose daycare or nursery schools, and in some communities—especially the newer suburban neighbourhoods—there are long waiting lists. Yet a number of affluent urban parents eschew institutional child care and opt instead for live-in nannies. In the late 1970s, Ottawa added a live-in caregiver designation to its immigrant categories. It allowed young women to come to Canada on the condition that they work as live-in nannies for two years, without landed immigrant status. As a result, thousands of young women have flocked to Canada to work in comfortable neighbourhoods in Canada's big cities. These days, these women are overwhelmingly from the Philippines.

According to a 2005 investigation by *Walrus* magazine reporter Susan McClelland, human rights and immigration experts are calling on Ottawa to confront what one Filipina advocacy group describes as the "trafficking in humans." In 2003, a Montreal auction house actually listed nannies on its list of items up for bids—a move that generated intense controversy and promises from federal officials to review the program. But that was only the most outrageous issue on a list that involves verbal and sexual abuse, a dearth of employment rights, and poor pay. Some of the women are threatened with deportation, others shaken down for huge fees to process applications. And all in the dubious service of the pressures of the urban economy. "'There is so much money being made off the backs of foreign women,'" Cecilia Diocson, a Vancouver-based women's rights activist, told McClelland. "'Employers save money by not having to pay childcare fees or having one spouse leave the workforce, employment agencies make domestic workers pay astronomical amounts to pursue their dreams of better lives in the West, and governments like the Philippines deal with the poor and unemployed by sending them abroad.'"[18]

Squandered Opportunities

Here's a very different picture of Canada's immigrant labour force. Every summer, the 500-member Association of Bangladeshi Engineers of Ontario (ABEO), which was formed in 1996, holds a family and professional day: a *prokoushali milon mela*. In 2003, the festivities took place one weekend in July at a large high school in suburban Toronto. For one day, the gymnasium became a bazaar, as families and businesses set up stalls selling clothes, books, and aromatic dishes. In the auditorium, children in traditional costume performed Bangladeshi poetry and musical numbers, while their fathers retired to a classroom for a lively discussion of the challenges they face in their professional lives.

On the face of it, this association's members reflect one of the features of Canada's current immigration system. Two-thirds of immigrants to Canada are now classified as "economic class" (the balance is family members and refugees).[19] As far as the Canadian government is concerned, these are people with skills or entrepreneurial experience who have been chosen, presumably, because they can land on their feet.

Census statistics indicate that the latest wave of economic class immigrants is highly educated. While only 43 percent of Canadian adults have a post-secondary degree, the rate of higher education among immigrants accepted under the skilled worker or business class ranges from 54 to 94 percent. Of the almost 800,000 persons over 15 years of age who came to Canada between 1991 and 2001, three-quarters—equivalent to the population of the city of Vancouver—arrived with post-secondary qualifications in the physical sciences, engineering, the health professions, and business administration.[20]

In many cases, such high-skilled recent immigrants are playing a crucial role in connecting Canadian cities to the global economy. Two suburban cities north of Toronto, Markham and Richmond Hill, have become the destination of choice for thousands of Chinese immigrants. These affluent communities, in turn, have fostered an entrepreneurial class whose members are securing lucrative contracts and business opportunities in mainland China. Alan Lam, a 46-year-old engineer, founded Ecotech International Systems, an environmental services firm that won a $2.85-million contract to install a wetlands-based water purification system in the Chinese city of Wuhan. Such deals represent the "next level" of globalization, as a federal trade official puts it, explaining that small or mid-sized firms wind up with deals through a variety of channels—internet searches and city-to-city twinning arrangements. But these contracts also emerge from the ever denser network of informal personal relationships—*guanxi*—fostered between mainland China and the Chinese-Canadian businesses that have grown up in cities such as Markham, Ontario, or Richmond, British Columbia. It's a story that's been repeated in many urban immigrant communities and one that has knitted Canadian cities into the intricate weave of global commerce.

But during the 1990s, it became apparent that thousands of well-educated immigrants were having great difficulty establishing themselves in jobs that matched the qualifications that got them into Canada. Many immigrants with impressive professional and academic credentials ended up driving cabs, especially in Toronto. This kind of chronic underemployment lay behind a 2005 strike by limo drivers serving Pearson International Airport. Working for $5 to $7 per hour and having struggled through the post-9/11 slump, many cabbies, predominantly Indian, took the driving jobs because they couldn't find work in their chosen fields. Buphinder Momi, 54, came to Canada in the mid-1970s, having been trained as a machinist and a draftsman.

He lost his job during the 1990 recession and was forced to drive a taxi. "There are lawyers working here, there are doctors working here," Momi told a reporter. "You tell me one Canadian-born person who [will] work here for 20 hours a day."[21]

Immigration experts are stumped by this backsliding, and various theories have swirled among networks of policy experts: racial discrimination, language barriers, and a mismatch between the skills immigrants bring with them and the needs of Canada's labour market. (A case in point: While the many engineers who immigrated to Canada in recent years have trouble securing work in their own field, manufacturers are chronically short of skilled machinists and developers scramble to find employees with experience in the building trades.) "One point is clear: the collapse in immigrant earnings performance is real and urgent," Don DeVoretz, a leading Simon Fraser University immigration economist and the co-director of the Vancouver Research on Immigration and Integration in the Metropolis project, warned a parliamentary committee in February 2005.[22]

Despite their advanced education levels, recent immigrants are much less likely to be working in jobs requiring university degrees. The tables on the next page show the percentage of university graduates, ages 25 to 54, working in moderate or low-skilled occupations in six cities. Immigrant women are particularly underemployed in all these regions. (Only Windsor, one of Canada's most ethnically diverse cities, shows a measure of parity between Canadian-born university grads and their immigrant counterparts.)

Between 1991 and 2001, about 1 in 10 recently arrived immigrants went to work in the retail sector—an industry that generally pays low wages and has poor or no benefits. In that 10-year period, the net employment growth in retailing was about 36,400 jobs, but more than 110,000 recent immigrants ended up working in that sector. The numbers tell a story of very high turnover due to a huge surplus of workers compared with available jobs.

One leading culprit has to do with credentials recognition or the vexing requirement that employers demand "Canadian experience" from prospective hires. As Queen's University policy studies expert

Naomi Alboim observes, "Currently, skilled immigrants may find they have to 'start from scratch' in order to practice their specialized field in Canada."[23] Statistics Canada estimates that, six months after arriving in Canada, only 14 percent of immigrants with foreign credentials have had them recognized.

UNIVERSITY GRADUATES WORKING IN MODERATE- OR LOW-SKILLED OCCUPATIONS

Male		
City	% Canadian-Born	% Recent Immigrant
Toronto	10.4	24.8
Montreal	9.7	21.2
Vancouver	12.0	25.0
Calgary	9.5	19.0
Winnipeg	13.3	34.7
Windsor	18.0	19.4

Female		
	% Canadian-Born	% Recent Immigrant
Toronto	13.4	36.3
Montreal	11.5	28.6
Vancouver	13.6	38.5
Calgary	15.1	38.9
Winnipeg	16.5	39.5
Windsor	17.9	38.0

Adapted from Statistics Canada, Grant Schellenberg, *Immigrants in Canada's Census Metropolitan Areas*, cat. 89-613, no. 007 (August 18, 2004), 56. Reprinted with permission

The bottom line is that Canada is on the receiving end of a massive brain gain, yet we're squandering the gift. Take the Bangladeshi engineers living around Toronto who banded together in 1997 to form ABEO. They were motivated by a common dilemma: Even if their English was acceptable, many potential employers refused to accept their degrees as valid and wouldn't consider hiring them because they hadn't worked here. Focus groups conducted by researchers with the Council for Access to the Profession of Engineering, an umbrella organization which includes ABEO, determined that almost half of internationally trained engineers were stuck in jobs that made no use of their professional skills, even though these immigrants were better educated and more conversant in English than earlier waves of newcomers.[24]

Such impediments have become a huge and costly headache for Canada's cities. The Conference Board of Canada estimates that non-recognition of international credentials costs the economy about $3.4 to $5 billion annually. A staggering 340,000 Canadians have unrecognized international degrees. These figures could well continue to rise: By 2011, according to one study, immigration will account for all the net growth in the Canadian workforce.

B.C. immigration economist Don DeVoretz warns that prospective immigrants are beginning to ask tough questions about what awaits them when they arrive in our large cities. A Simon Fraser University research team recently interviewed 500 high-skilled immigrants from the People's Republic of China living in the Greater Vancouver region. What emerged was disillusionment, immigrants who were painfully aware that, in this high-tech era, they still had little option but to work two or three low-paying or menial jobs just to survive. For that reason, they had little time, energy, or money left over to complete the skills training or upgrading they required to find work in their own fields. "[The] numbers of Chinese highly-skilled arrivals have dropped recently because of the robust Chinese economy, and the realization of failures in Canada," DeVoretz says. "Thus, the cost of not attending to the collapse in immigrant economic performance is more pervasive than lost economic opportunity in Canada."[25]

Federal and provincial immigration officials have been scrambling to correct these mounting problems, but some of the proposed solutions—such as boosting immigration levels and bringing in more temporary skilled workers in response to labour shortages facing politically connected industries, such as the home-building sector—miss the mark. One reason Canada's cities haven't seen the emergence of an angry, disenfranchised immigrant underclass, as has been the case in France and the United Kingdom, is that new Canadians are well educated and they're here for the long haul, not on a short-term work visa. The real problem is that we didn't hold up our end of the bargain.

The ramifications will be far-reaching, not just for the social harmony of Canada's large urban centres but also for our international reputation. "The most effective ambassadors for Canada are the immigrants themselves," says Ratna Omidvar, executive director of the Maytree Foundation, an advocacy organization established by Toronto philanthropist and urbanist Alan Broadbent. Working with business and labour organizations, Omidvar, as we will see in a later chapter on Canada's immigration policy, has been looking for new approaches that will remove the barriers that prevent newcomers from establishing themselves in Canada's labour force. And, as she observes, this crisis is a double-edged sword in a country that has staked its future on the economic spinoffs of high immigration: "The word is getting out: Think twice before you come to Canada."[26]

GREYING CITIES

In the early 1970s, long before gardening became fashionable, thousands of Portuguese and Italian immigrants who had settled in Montreal quietly changed the landscape of their adopted city using spades and seeds. Known as guerrilla gardeners, they set up hundreds of community gardens on fallow urban land, where they grew fruits and vegetables in allotment plots. Over the past three decades, Montreal officials got involved in regulating these mini-farms as demand bloomed. There are now over 6600 plots in about 100 locations across Montreal, tended by more than 10,000 gardeners, a significant proportion of whom are over age 55, and neither anglophone nor francophone.[1]

The phenomenon of Montreal's multicultural urban gardening movement—which has since spread to many other large cities—opens a window on the intersection between the two great demographic bulldozers that are dramatically reshaping our cities. One is the mass immigration of the past 20 years; the other is the aging of the population. Over the next 20 years, the proportion of people over 65 living in our large cities will almost double as the baby boomer generation—born between 1946 and 1964—reaches retirement and then old age. The sheer size of this spoiled generation, renowned for its demanding consumer habits, promises to alter all of our expectations about what is entailed by growing old in predominantly urban settings. The impact on how Canada's largest cities function—in terms of housing, employment, health care, recreation, retailing, transportation, even municipal government—will be profound.

In 1998, there were 3.7 million seniors in Canada; by 2031, there will be 9.7 million. Seniors accounted for 9 to 13 percent of the population of Canada's hub cities, with Edmonton, Calgary, and Halifax on the low end, and Montreal at the other. Victoria, Niagara-on-the-Lake, and St. Catharines are already well known as retirement centres, with seniors making up about 17 percent—or one in six—of the population. Twenty-five years from now, almost one in four Canadians will be over age 65. And they will be increasingly urban—a trend already visible in Alberta, where 81 percent of all seniors live in metropolitan areas. Seniors in cities, moreover, tend to be older than their rural counterparts. "As seniors age," according to a Government of Alberta assessment of urban and rural aging, "the percentage that live in urban areas increases."[2]

In Calgary, human resources managers have already had a glimpse of what is to come. Fast-growing firms in the energy, engineering, and high-tech sectors have had to look well beyond Alberta's borders as they scramble to fill the thousands of jobs being spun off by the oil and gas industry. An economic snapshot prepared by the TD Bank predicted that by the next decade, Alberta's workforce will actually begin to shrink—a development the bank deemed to be "a major challenge" for the Calgary-Edmonton corridor. Calgarians who are over age 55 are the fastest-growing segment of the city's population.[3] "While the average age of retirement is higher in Alberta than in other provinces," TD analysts wrote in an April 2003 study, "a large number of Albertans are still opting to retire early—particularly in the education and social services sector."[4]

The Boomers, Act Three

Canadians born during the Depression, and their children, the baby boomers, reaped the benefits of the unprecedented economic prosperity of the second half of the 20th century. The boomers' fixation with health and youth has spawned distinctly urban industries: the workout clubs (martial arts, aerobics, and so on) that virtually didn't exist before the 1980s, health food stores, and wellness clinics offering services such as naturopathy, acupuncture, and therapeutic massage. Urban boomers grew up with strenuous outdoor activities such as cycling, pick-up hockey (for both men and women), and the ubiquitous five-kilometre runs for charity. Their impact on the cosmopolitan flavour of our cities can be seen in the boomer-driven popularity of imported fitness trends such as yoga and tai chi. Middle-aged boomers can be found in clumps in city parks before and after work, chatting and running the much-fussed-over dogs that have taken the place of the children who are growing up and moving on. And their appetite for city-based recreational amenities—from waterfront promenades such as Vancouver's Seawall to the bike paths lining Calgary's Bow River—will only grow as their leisure time expands after they exit the workforce.

The boomers, in fact, are now in the process of reprogramming the very way they live in big cities. In recent years, waves of empty-nesters and seniors—the parents of the boomer generation—have begun selling their single-family homes and moving into condominiums that are closer to the urban core. These housing choices reflect practical concerns—the reduced need for space, a desire to spend less time in cars—but they also underscore a trend that has driven the downtown renaissance visible in many large cities right across North America.

There has also been a proliferation of retirement-geared subdivisions built on the urban fringe: clusters of compact, one-storey luxury homes, perhaps with access to a private three-hole golf course, protected from the outside world by gates and 24-hour sentries. For example, in Kleinberg, northwest of Toronto, Wycliffe Homes has built a pair of exclusive gated enclaves with stand-alone homes in the $800,000 to $1.2 million range. With roads closed to general traffic, these "communities" offer lifestyle amenities such as fitness facilities, tennis courts, paths, and snow-clearing in the winter.[5]

"Tens of thousands of retirees ... are pulling up stakes in suburbia and fashioning their own retirement communities in the heart of the bustling city," *Newsweek* reported in October 2004. "They're looking for what most older people want: a home with no stairs and low crime rates. But they're willing to exchange a regular weekly tee time for a different set of amenities—rich cultural offerings, young neighbours and plenty of good restaurants." As one Texas developer commented, "Who ever thought that suburban flight would be a round trip?"[6]

Real estate developers, in turn, have discovered that some segments of the over-55 set prefer to relocate to the increasingly vibrant downtown areas in older suburbs, such as the Edmonton bedroom community of Sherwood Park, which is developing a $130-million high-density, mixed-use town centre with condos geared to "adult living" and seniors.[7] In the Toronto suburb of North York, older buyers are snapping up units in high-rise luxury condos or townhouses clustered around shopping districts with theatres, bookstores, and fitness centres. Some builders are looking further ahead, linking these luxury condos to so-called assisted-living facilities that offer certain health services, so older residents need not move out of their new high-rise neighbourhoods, allowing them instead to "age in place."

While such demographically motivated changes in residential development trends address some aspects of urban aging, other issues remain unresolved. Our cities have been built around the needs of cars rather than pedestrians and city-dwellers who can no longer drive easily. A young person doesn't think twice about crossing a wide intersection or schlepping shopping bags across a large parking lot. But it's a different story for a senior inching along with a walker. While electric wheelchairs have made the world much more accessible for the disabled, urban public spaces remain a maze of small physical obstacles that younger people barely notice.

As a growing proportion of the population reaches retirement age and beyond, the role of transit will have to undergo a profound transformation. Much transit service is geared to the needs of employees, but seniors and retirees place different demands on such services. An aging population—especially one afflicted by an epidemic of obesity-related diabetes—means far more people with mobility problems, as well as a growing number of elderly people who have lost their driver's licences but not their desire to get around. "Public transit is becoming more and more important as the population ages," says Patricia Raymaker, former chair of the National Advisory Council on Aging.[8] Seniors' advocates point out that decision makers haven't fully grasped the ways in which our urban regions must change in order to accommodate the needs of the growing ranks of the elderly. Adds Judy Cutler, spokesperson for the Canadian Association of Retired Persons, "I can't name any city in Canada that is really senior-friendly."[9]

Old and Poor

With the boomers poised to inherit billions of dollars (a hefty portion of which can be attributed to the extraordinary run-up of real estate values in middle-class urban neighbourhoods since the 1970s), the coming generation of Canadian seniors will enjoy unprecedented affluence.

But while these demographic trends capture a lot of media attention, they hardly provide a complete picture of the realities facing Canada's urban seniors. In many heavily ethnic neighbourhoods, seniors who came to Canada as family class immigrants live with their adult children and grandchildren in conditions that can seem cramped to those who grew up in single-family suburban homes. Having arrived in this country late in life with little or no English, they often find themselves isolated from the urban mainstream.

As has long been the case, these elders step in to play important roles in the lives of their grandchildren. Liberal MP Tony Ianno, who led a prime minister's task force on seniors' issues in 2004, recalled how he boarded with his grandparents in Toronto's Little Italy while his parents built their home in the suburbs. "What I was seeing often was that the children were moving out and leaving parents behind in the city," he said in 2005. Typically, women didn't work outside the home, while their husbands, often labourers, retired with little more than the old-age pension to fall back on. "If it wasn't for children supplying some extra money, it was very difficult for these seniors to maintain their standard of living."[10]

Many don't. According to the 1996 census, more than one in five Calgary seniors was living below the poverty line.[11] Across the country, about a quarter of all seniors spend more than 30 percent of their income on housing. It's true that Canada's main income support programs for those over 65—the Canada Pension Plan, the Quebec Pension Plan, General Income Supplement (GIS), and Old Age Security (OAS)—have "moved seniors away from the bottom end of poverty," according to a TD Bank study.[12] As of 2004, about 8.4 million pensioners collected $47.2 billion from these programs. Canadians tend to be wealthier upon retirement today than in 1970, when over half of all seniors qualified for the GIS (in 2003, the figure was about one-third). This trend has been especially evident in urban regions. In cities with more than 100,000 residents, the proportion of low-income seniors fell from 34 percent in 1980 to 20 percent in 2000.

But for the growing ranks of seniors, urban living is both necessary from a convenience point of view, and increasingly difficult economically because of escalating cost-of-living expenses. Property taxes, in particular, are based on the market value of a dwelling and rise with the assessed value of the home, which poses a daunting problem to elderly homeowners living on fixed incomes. Some municipalities, such as the City of Toronto, have begun offering low-income seniors breaks on their property taxes, while Alberta waives the education portion of the property tax for the elderly. Such moves are well intentioned but problematic: As the number of seniors living in urban areas grows, these age-related exemptions will become an ever more costly line item on municipal budgets, precisely at a time when cities will have no choice but to make accessibility-related investments to address the needs of their elderly residents.

That municipal and provincial governments feel compelled to lessen the financial burden on low-income seniors demonstrates that the current federally funded income supplement levels are inadequate and will not significantly reduce the growing ranks of Canada's poor urban seniors. Such tax breaks should also remind us that Canada's mandatory retirement rules invariably drive some seniors into financial dire straits. The federal government knows the math: In large cities, a senior with no pension other than the OAS and GIS has an income that is $4000 below the official poverty line. In 2002, the after-average-rent income was $7.56 per day, scarcely enough to buy a standard food-court lunch special.[13]

Seniors' poverty appears to have become especially concentrated in high-cost cities in the past decade, according to Ianno's report, *Creating a National Seniors Agenda*. Statistics collected by the City of Toronto show that the proportion of households with residents over 60 years old who depended on food banks almost doubled between 1995 and 2002, increasing from 5 to 9 percent. While a handful of subsidized senior's co-ops have opened up in recent years, there are still 12,600 seniors on waiting lists for affordable housing, while another 400 live in shelters.

In Montreal, a large proportion of poor seniors live in mould- and vermin-infested apartments, according to a 2003 survey by the city's public health officials. Of all Canadian cities, Toronto had the second-highest number of seniors living in rundown dwellings in need of extensive structural repairs.[14]

Or they live on the streets—a hidden and largely ignored urban crisis that clashes mightily with cheery images of prosperous retirees dining in upscale eateries before taking in a show. The figure of the grizzled, alcoholic panhandler is a fixture on the streets of most big cities. But a survey of 90 of Toronto's estimated 500 homeless seniors conducted in 2004 by the University of Toronto's Institute for Human Development, Life Course and Ageing suggests the stereotype is skewed. Low-income single women in Toronto, the researchers found, have become increasingly at risk of homelessness since the early 1990s, especially once they passed the age of 40.

Chris, a 64-year-old Finnish-born architect, found himself drifting on the streets despite all the trappings of a successful life: a broad-ranging education, a solid professional career, a family. He came to Canada in the mid-1970s to teach at a university but succumbed to alcoholism. "I've lost everything," he told *The Globe and Mail*. "I'm living in the moment now."[15] He ended up in the one Toronto shelter geared specifically for seniors. There aren't many such facilities, which function much like retirement homes. One of the first—an eight-bedroom group home—opened in Oakland, California, in 1994 in response to a growing recognition by city officials that traditional homeless shelters—which are typically grim, dangerous, and disease-ridden places—are extremely threatening for vulnerable older people, even those who have toughed it out on the streets.[16]

Cathy Crowe, a Toronto street nurse who has campaigned fiercely to force politicians to confront urban homelessness, says that some homeless seniors consciously choose to live beneath bridges or in makeshift tents in ravines. "Many of them are incredibly proud and independent and have primarily not been shelter users. As the homeless population got younger, starting in the late 1980s, it became a little riskier for older people to be in a shelter. Some are afraid of being attacked or robbed. They feel vulnerable."[17]

Although about half of the men and women in the University of Toronto study reported addiction or mental health problems, many others had slipped down a declining housing spiral, exacerbated by the death of a spouse, evictions, and disabilities. Policy makers have all but ignored the issue, the researchers concluded. "Given that the older homeless population is likely to increase as the baby boomers age and the demand for affordable housing continues to rise, it is important to better understand the needs of this population."[18]

These troubling trends underscore the fact that the cost of living in big cities—especially housing—is significantly higher than in smaller communities, and unexpected increases can severely threaten fixed-income seniors, who may be close to the end of their savings. In New York City, there were some 9000 households of elderly single people living with unrelated adults in 2000. Late in life, they've had no choice but to double up on rental accommodations—often with complete strangers. "Such partnerships," *The New York Times* reported, "are typically accidental, although sometimes anticipated. They can be fleeting or fixed for years. Sometimes, all it takes is a sudden slip on the stairs, and a hospitalization, draining finances and options. Sometimes, all it takes is an eviction notice from a landlord who wants to ride on a hot real estate market."[19]

Are we there yet? Most Canadian seniors don't go broke paying medical bills, yet. But they do face rapidly rising big-city housing expenses, growing drug costs, and the bills associated with delisted medical procedures. Some also risk losing their apartments because of condo conversions. They are vulnerable to fly-by-night telemarketers who persuade lonely, elderly people to hand over their savings. Some seniors are essentially living on the edge. "Cities all have not only homeless [seniors], but potentially homeless," warns Judy Cutler, spokesperson for the Canadian Association of Retired Persons, who feels the definition of "affordable housing" must reflect urban-rural cost-of-living differences. Provincial and federal governments have been extremely reluctant to take this step. Rent supplements, Cutler argues, "have to be based on what is truly affordable."[20]

House Calls

Mark Nowaczynski, a 40-year-old geriatrician with a busy practice, is that rarest of species: a big city doctor who makes house calls. His office looks over the monolithic apartment blocks that sprang up all over the centre of Toronto in the 1960s and 1970s and are now populated by thousands of elderly tenants, many of them widows. His reasons for taking his show on the road aren't simply because he wants to save his frail patients a trip, though that plays a big role. He does house calls because it's the best way to make an accurate assessment of how an elderly person is doing and to take in the sort of critical information that won't emerge in the sterile examining room of a doctor's office.

With his medical equipment tucked in a knapsack, Nowaczynski spends about half his working day visiting housebound 90-somethings whose bodies are failing with age. Some live in their own homes but have gradually moved to the ground floor as the stairs become unmanageable. Many rarely venture outside, have few visitors, and rely on a pet for companionship. They are often widowed, and isolated from relatives. Their family doctors, meanwhile, have retired, but they've been unable to find new medical care, meaning they rely on walk-in clinics or the emergency room.[21]

When he visits his patients' homes, he knows what he's looking for: "You see," Nowaczynski says quietly, "and you smell. You can smell the neglectful personal hygiene and the urine." He looks around to see if his patient is surviving on tea and toast, or if anyone comes by to tidy. He checks to make sure the proliferation of pills are being taken properly. These are the symptoms of medical crises just around the corner: broken hips, malnutrition, dehydration, pneumonia, cascading pharmaceutical side effects. "When you walk into an apartment, it takes 10 seconds to see if this person is in big trouble," he says. "The care I provide for housebound patients is absolutely invaluable."[22]

In the late 1990s, Nowaczynski approached SPRINT, a North Toronto seniors services agency, about a partnership. Among other services, the group offers day activities for seniors with mild dementia and manages two small apartment buildings with supportive housing for frail, elderly people who don't want to be in a nursing home but can no longer live independently. SPRINT has a team of counsellors and personal support workers who visit those residents to help them deal with everything from mild dementia to tasks such as bathing, cooking, and cleaning. Nowaczynski proposed that he come on board as the house doctor, and now he tags along with SPRINT's staff, providing what he calls a "multidisciplinary approach."

What Nowaczynski observes from his elderly patients is that many face a financially strapped health care system that rations home support for seniors or fails to take into account their needs. Elderly female patients, especially those from conservative cultures, balk at having to undress in front of a stranger to take a bath, but he knows that, under Ontario's current rules, those who refuse will be declined home care. "That's disgusting," he says. "It's a dishonest approach to very dire circumstances."[23]

In Ontario, these services are doled out by community care access centres (CCACs), provincially mandated regional agencies that assess patients' needs and then dispense services, which they purchase through a public tendering process. While most of these services used to be delivered by local not-for-profit agencies such as the Victoria Order of Nurses, large private health care conglomerates have crowded into this market aggressively in recent years, elbowing out smaller players. In the early 2000s, several of Ontario's big city CCACs, which are funded by the provincial government, had to contend with severe budget constraints, meaning across-the-board service cuts.

Many seniors' advocates came to view the CCAC budget crises as a cover for another agenda. By nickel-and-diming shut-ins, the CCACs effectively boosted demand for nursing home placements. In the late 1990s, the Mike Harris government ordered the construction of 20,000 new nursing home beds, many of which have been built and operated around Greater Toronto by well-connected private firms that enjoyed close ties to the Progressive Conservatives. A University of Toronto home care expert, by contrast, estimated the actual demand was closer to 7600 beds. The provincial Liberal government inherited the mess, and, as Nowaczynski says, "is desperately trying to fill those beds."[24]

The powerful nursing home industry has earned a well-deserved reputation for shoddy care. Workers are poorly paid, the conditions are often filthy, and there have been a proliferation of incidents of shocking neglect, including the case of an elderly, senile veteran who burned to death in May 2001 in a downtown Toronto nursing home after being left unattended with a lit cigarette dangling from his mouth.

In 2004 and 2005, investigations by both the *Toronto Star* and *The Globe and Mail* revealed numerous disturbing examples of patients left with festering bedsores or deaths due to violent outbursts—pushing, fights, sexual assaults—between senile residents packed into tight rooms with inadequate supervision.[25] Some of these facilities are run by chains Leisure World and Extendicare, and others by community organizations, all of which receive standard per diem funding from the provincial government. (Municipalities also operate homes for the aged.) The private firms must earn a profit, which can mean cutting back on expenses such as fresh food and patient baths, as well as salaries. While nursing home executives say they run more efficient operations, U.S. studies have shown that private facilities tend to have more deficiencies than not-for-profit ones. Extendicare, in fact, lost its licence in some U.S. states because of the poor conditions in its facilities.[26]

TAKEN TOGETHER, the questions raised by these trends are stark and troubling. Will our cities become polarized places where affluent boomers take out reverse mortgages and hang on to their downtown apartments with round-the-clock care, while large numbers of elderly low-income seniors—many of whom immigrated to Canada—must fend for themselves or live out the end of their days in highly institutionalized settings? Or will we figure out how to build cities configured to the needs of older people, cities that can provide a wide range of affordable housing and health care alternatives to nursing homes?

The leading-edge baby boomers and activist ethnocultural community organizations have finally begun to tackle these issues, but from the perspective of advocates and caregivers as they confront their parents' decrepitude. "They don't see themselves," says Nowaczynski. Yet. He takes the long view: "You're not looking at an exotic species in another world. You're looking at your future."[27]

HIDDEN CITIES

When we talk about how generations of immigrants have altered the social profile of Canada's large cities, we often overlook the rapidly growing urban presence of Canada's far-flung Native community. Aboriginals, of course, are neither immigrants nor descended from immigrants, as their leaders are quick to point out. In recent years, thousands of Natives have settled in Canada's large cities to study, take up careers, or tap into the economic opportunities that aren't available in remote communities or on reserves. But their experience of city life is one of deep ambivalence—a mix of opportunity, invisibility, and segregation, accompanied by an internal struggle to carve out an Aboriginal vision of urban living.

Many Canadians simply don't associate Aboriginals with cities—a stereotype perpetuated by some First Nations leaders. While places such as Winnipeg and Saskatoon have predominantly Aboriginal neighbourhoods, most of us link the First Nations with rural images and issues: remote reserves, treaty claims over large tracts of northern land, disputes over fishing rights. We know about the conflicts that exploded in places such as Ipperwash and Oka, the legacy of abuses committed at residential schools, the economic self-determination of the Cree in northern Quebec, and the Nisga'a in British Columbia. Native art and writing are frequently situated in rural communities or wilderness settings. The touchstones of contemporary Aboriginal history seem to be anything but urban.

The demographic reality is quite different, however—so much so that in 2002, a Senate committee decided to shine a spotlight on urban Aboriginal youth and the conditions they have come to face in big cities. Over 18 months, the parliamentarians listened to hundreds of witnesses across the country testify about the mounting sense of danger facing one of the fastest-growing segments of Canadian society.

Though largely overlooked by the media, the Senate committee's 125-page "action plan" was a scorching indictment of the way our decision makers have turned a blind eye on Canada's urban Aboriginals. "Of the nearly $8 billion the government will spend in the 2002–2003 fiscal year [on Aboriginal policies]," states the report, "only $270 million flows to urban and off-reserve programming."[1] What is worse, less than half of that $270 million is delivered by local Aboriginal organizations.

The explanation for this shocking imbalance—one that directly bears on the quality of life of Aboriginals in Canadian cities, especially Winnipeg, Regina, Saskatoon, Edmonton, and Vancouver—has to do with Canada's tense relationship with its First Nations, constitutional turf wars, federal-provincial squabbling, and Aboriginal politics. It may also be linked to the fact that when the Canadian government attempts to tackle Aboriginal issues, it focuses on treaties, self-government, and living conditions on poor reserves. There are sound reasons for these preoccupations, not least of which is a legacy of unresolved land claims. Under the constitution, the federal government has a fiduciary obligation to Aboriginals who qualify for benefits under the Indian Act. Funds administered by the Department of Indian and Northern Affairs—for health care, education, and a range of other programs— have flowed into predominantly rural band councils. But Aboriginals who left their reserves or lost their status under the Indian Act don't qualify, and provincial governments have been reluctant to provide services tailored specifically to the Aboriginals who now live in Canada's largest urban areas.

The problem, as the Senate committee observed, is that Aboriginal rights aren't "portable," meaning that the federal government's financial obligation to First Nations stops at the edge of the reserve. This long-standing policy has given rise to a corrosive dynamic in Aboriginal politics. Huge sums of federal funding to First Nations flow into the coffers of band councils, which means the chiefs and band councillors have a vested interest in seeing that cash continue flowing to the reserves.

This persistent "jurisdictional ambiguity" (in the words of the Canada West Foundation) contradicts the rhetoric of federal politicians who have repeatedly vowed to improve the living standards of Canada's Aboriginals. Unlike immigrants, seniors, and especially middle-class homeowners, urban Aboriginals garner little attention from federal policy makers. Even the 1996 Report of the Royal Commission on Aboriginal Peoples paid scant attention to either the problems or the opportunities associated with urban life.[2]

For critics such as constitutional scholar and Aboriginal rights expert Alan Cairns, the commission's attempt to lay out a framework for Aboriginal autonomy led inexorably toward a romantic vision based on small, rural communities, where citizenship was tied to land rather than ancestry. The road to self-government, in short, did not lead to the city. "This perspective precluded acceptance of a weaker Aboriginal cultural identity as an acceptable cost of economic and other advantages of the urban environment," Cairns remarked.[3]

Leaving the Land

According to the 2001 census, almost half of Canada's 1.3 million Aboriginals (including status Indians, Inuit, Métis, and those claiming Aboriginal ancestry) live in cities with more than 100,000 residents—dramatically up from just 7 percent in the early 1950s.[4] What is more, they are congregating—like recent immigrants and seniors—in the largest urban centres. One in every four Aboriginals lives in either Vancouver, Edmonton, Calgary, Saskatoon, Regina, Winnipeg, Montreal, Victoria, Ottawa, or Toronto.[5] And the Aboriginal birth rate is about one and a half times greater than the Canadian average, meaning that the fast-growing Native communities in these big cities are dominated by young families, children, and youth.

This migration began in earnest after 1951, when Ottawa repealed a provision of the federal Indian Act that prevented Aboriginals from leaving their reserves without authorization. In subsequent decades, growing numbers of Aboriginals moved to big cities in search of jobs and schooling. In response, some municipalities passed bylaws preventing Aboriginals from gathering in groups.

They arrived carrying the scars of the residential schools, racism, loss of culture, and the disenfranchisement that has long stained Canada's relationship with its first peoples. And many also harboured a deep ambivalence about their new homes. Some of Canada's largest cities took root in Aboriginal settlements that long predated the arrival of European colonialists. As recently as 1920, Vancouver authorities forcibly removed the last of the Squamish people from the Whoi Whoi village in Stanley Park.[6] The late Anishnawbe activist and historian Rodney Bobiwash used to give tours of pre-European Toronto, pointing out the numerous ancient burial grounds, locations of former tribal headquarters, and contemporary social landmarks, such as a downtown diner that served as an informal gathering place for Toronto Aboriginals in the 1940s, when there were no Native community institutions. Toronto sat on numerous First Nations trade routes and came to be known as a meeting place for many clans and confederacies. "It was kind of like the United Nations in the sense that all people lived together, maintained their separate identities and got along," he said. "Although the landscape has been irrevocably altered, philosophically [Toronto] is still a gathering place where people of all kinds of cultures meet together."[7]

Cairns has characterized the trade-off between these two worlds: "Various indicators of social breakdown—family breakdown, suicide, sexual abuse, rape, alcohol and drug abuse—are higher for the on-reserve Indian population than [for those who've left]. On the other hand, cultural retention is weaker for the latter, participation in traditional activity diminishes, language loss is greater, intermarriage rates are much higher, and fewer persons with Aboriginal ancestry retain Aboriginal identity." Still, in Cairns's view, "Cities will be crucial to the health and civility—or their absence—of Aboriginal/non-Aboriginal relations in the 21st century."[8]

Today, Canada's increasingly urbanized Aboriginal population mirrors the complexity of our big cities. Urban regions offer economic, educational, and social opportunities that simply aren't available on reserves, which have few jobs and are often dominated by clans with connections to the band council.[9] In large cities, by contrast, the diverse Aboriginal community has grown to include professionals, educators, social workers, business people, and senior policy makers working at all levels of government. Native artists have thrived in urban settings, setting up theatre companies and visual arts spaces where they've been able to connect with broader audiences with an interest in the ethnocultural diversity on offer in big cities.

While average Aboriginal incomes are only about three-quarters of the national average, a 2001 study by the Caledon Institute of Social Policy found that Aboriginal participation in the urban labour force is similar to that of the general population in the major cities, including Toronto, Ottawa, and Montreal. And though Aboriginals are twice as likely to be unemployed as the average city-dweller, they still have a better chance of finding work than in rural areas or on reserves. Their earnings, moreover, are substantially higher than those of on-reserve Aboriginals, in large measure because tens of thousands of Aboriginal youth in recent years have acquired university or community college degrees.[10]

Some First Nations businesses qualify for grants and often rely on federal procurement contracts. Many were—and still are—focused on rural concerns, including everything from the multi-billion-dollar Mackenzie Delta natural gas pipeline project to small tourist-related businesses, such as gift shops and outfitters. In recent years, however, a growing number of Aboriginal entrepreneurs have tapped into lucrative urban markets with economic bases that simply don't exist in small rural communities. Networks of Aboriginal women entrepreneurs have established themselves in St. Catharines and Niagara-on-the-Lake, while a community college in Toronto has begun to offer an entrepreneurship business program geared specifically to Aboriginal students. And in 2004, a group of First Nations businesses in Winnipeg set up Canada's first Aboriginal chamber of commerce. According to Aboriginal Business Canada, an arm of the federal Industry ministry, self-employment among Aboriginals leapt by more than 30 percent between 1996 and 2001—nine times higher than the Canadian average.[11]

One of the veterans of this trend is Roger Obonsawin, who runs the O.I. Group of Companies, a large human resources firm that places Aboriginal employees with large companies and offers benefits and training services. Headquartered on the Six Nations reserve near

Brantford, Ontario, the company he founded in 1983 has corporate clients all over North America.

Obonsawin, a dapper, soft-spoken man, grew up in Sudbury. His brother is a senior provincial government official. His wife is from Central Europe. Obonsawin's reserve is 160 kilometres northeast of Montreal. He came to Toronto in the 1970s to study and then went to do social development work in remote communities, where he witnessed the tide of migration away from the reserves. Today, his business is shaped by two important social currents: the move by many large organizations to outsource human resources management and the growing number of Aboriginals in large urban centres.

Obonsawin belongs to a generation of pioneers who struggled to carve out spaces for the growing Aboriginal communities in Canadian cities. In the 1960s and 1970s, Aboriginal leaders pushed for the estab-lishment of a network of urban "friendship centres," as well as other institutions such as housing co-ops, health agencies, cultural centres, and even First Nations–focused libraries. In Winnipeg, Vancouver, and Toronto, Aboriginal leaders have begun to establish elected First Nations councils with a mandate to represent these large communities, whose members often come from various First Nations and regions of the country. The Aboriginal Peoples Council of Toronto came into being in 2004, with Obonsawin as its first elected chair. It's still in its infancy and intends to serve purely as an advocacy organization for GTA Natives. Obonsawin and his colleagues know they have their work cut out for them. As one of the organization's first policy papers put it, "All too frequently, the face of poverty in Canadian cities (partic-ularly in the West) is Aboriginal."[12]

Canada's Inner-City Ghettos

No one incident brought home the grim isolation of urban Aboriginal ghettos more clearly than the 1990 death of Neil Stonechild, a 17-year-old who lived in a Saskatoon group home. One frigid night, the young man was out drinking, and his noisy behaviour prompted a call to police. He was picked up by two members of the Saskatoon force, beaten, and then dumped in a field on the edge of the city—a practice known within the force and among Saskatoon Aboriginals as "starlight tours." Most victims were left to walk several kilometres back to the city. But Stonechild froze to death in the −28°C temperature that night. His body was found several days later by a construction crew. Although the two officers claimed to have no memory of encountering Stonechild, a $2-million provincial inquiry determined in 2004 that a supervising officer had covered up the incident. While no charges were laid, Stonechild's death exposed the ugly, racially tinged relationship between the city's police force and Saskatoon's poor inner-city neighbourhoods, whose predominantly Aboriginal residents had good reason to believe that the service didn't take their complaints about safety and crime seriously.[13]

Such neighbourhoods are a fixture of the urban landscape of many Western Canadian cities, and they bring to mind uncomfortable comparisons that don't exactly square with the tolerant, multicultural image many Canadians have of their big cities. Thomas Hayden, a Saskatoon-born reporter working in Washington, D.C., compared those "dilapidated" communities with the black, working-class ghettos in the southeast corner of the U.S. capital, neighbourhoods that whites rarely visit: "Like Washington's primarily black South East quadrant, which I've seen only from the safety of a Habitat for Humanity work site, I pass through Saskatoon's largely aboriginal west-side neighbourhoods only to visit St. Paul's Hospital."

"Though I pride myself on knowing my hometown well, I grew up without knowing a single aboriginal family," Hayden continues. "The geographical divide can be just as wide in American cities, but there's a critical difference. In the United States, race is a constant topic of conversation, and the discourse is opinionated, loud, and unmistakable. In the Saskatoon I grew up in, it simply didn't exist."[14]

And these disadvantaged neighbourhoods have grown. With the controversy that accompanied the Stonechild case, it has become increasingly difficult to turn a blind eye to the problems facing these isolated communities and the long-term implications for the health of the cities in which they exist. "Particularly in Western Canada, Aboriginals live [in] ... neighbourhoods that display the characteristics associated with the ghettos of U.S. cities," John Richards, a professor of business administration at Simon Fraser University, commented in a 2001 C.D. Howe Institute report entitled *Neighbourhoods Matter.*[15]

Richards was an NDP MLA in Saskatchewan in the 1970s. He belongs to an emerging group of urban thinkers who have sought to document what they call "neighbourhood effects" as a way of determining what makes communities succeed or fail. Communities flourish when they are socially and economically mixed and provide many opportunities for residents from all walks of life to interact in a range of safe settings, from schools to public spaces, community facilities, and business establishments. Primarily, such neighbourhoods deliver social inclusion—if you live in such a community, you are less likely to be isolated from the rest of the urban fabric.

Distressed neighbourhoods show a very different face. These tend to be isolated urban communities on a downward spiral. In the 1980s and 1990s, many U.S. cities became fixated on the so-called broken windows theory, which holds that the accumulation of neglect—boarded-up buildings, vandalism, petty street crime—is a kind of slippery slope, leading to neighbourhood decay. The reality of poor neighbourhoods is far more complex. Economic desperation breeds crime, a sense of ambient danger, vandalism, and a very real feeling of entrapment for children who grow up in environments where many adults don't have jobs, where gangs prowl the streets, and where there is little apparent benefit in working hard at school.

In a 1996 study on urban poverty, the Canadian Council on Social Development found that more than half of all urban Aboriginals lived beneath the poverty line, compared with 24 percent of the general population.[16] In Winnipeg, Saskatoon, and Regina, the poverty is highly concentrated, especially among the Métis. In Winnipeg, for example, there are more First Nations residents than in all of the Northwest Territories. Almost one in three of the city's estimated 56,000 Aboriginal residents moved in the year prior to the 2001 census. When families or individuals move so frequently, it's often a symptom of underlying social problems: inadequate housing, crime, lack of employment. Children in these circumstances have a far harder time in school, even though urban Aboriginal youth are more likely to graduate than are their counterparts who live on the reserve.[17]

In such communities, family breakdown is another pervasive problem, one strongly associated with poverty. Only half of all Aboriginal children residing in cities with over 100,000 residents live with both parents, compared with 83 percent of Canadian children overall. That's partly because of the stubbornly high levels of teen pregnancy among urban Aboriginals.[18] When the Department of Justice surveyed hundreds of inner-city Aboriginals in four large cities in the early 1990s, the majority of them said they had been sexually molested as children.[19] A 1999 Vancouver/Richmond Health Board study found that the teen birth rate among Aboriginals in the Lower Mainland was 13 times higher than that in the general population. Such babies accounted for a third of low-birth-weight infants and sudden-infant-death cases.[20]

Hard on the heels of such social crises comes crime. Poor and predominantly Aboriginal neighbourhoods have above-average crime rates, statistics show. "As is the case in U.S. ghettos," Richards writes, "the victims of Aboriginal criminal activity are disproportionately members of their own ethnic community. One aspect of this sad fact is the much higher rates of domestic violence suffered by urban Aboriginal women than non-Aboriginal women."[21] "For many, violence is a way of life," federal Justice official Carol La Prairie found in interviews with 621 inner city Aboriginals conducted for a landmark 1994 study of poverty and crime. "A 36-year-old man claimed he saw: 'violence everywhere—in drop-ins, on the street, in my rooming house.' One woman said: 'Fighting (in the inner city) is usually over money, drinks and men jealous of their wives or girl friends." In all, 84 percent of the people she surveyed reported violent victimization.[22]

Such are the grim conditions that await many young Aboriginals who flee the boredom of the reserve in search of the excitement of the city, where they too often end up in gangs, the sex trade, and the drug underworld. In Winnipeg, there are an estimated 2000 members of the dominant Aboriginal gangs, such as Manitoba Warriors and Indian Posse. The Edmonton Aboriginal Youth Gang Task Force in 2003 identified 400 gang members in about 12 groups, while Native teens in downtown Regina come under enormous pressure to join the Indian Mafia Crips, a gang whose leaders recruit members from struggling neighbourhoods and correctional institutions.[23] As these gangs have grown, there's been a troubling recent surge in "extreme violence" as they battle for turf in Regina and Saskatoon, according to 2005 intelligence reports by a network of Saskatchewan law enforcement agencies.[24]

With gangs come the drugs. "A high proportion of the people using needle exchange programs in cities like Edmonton and Vancouver are Aboriginal youth," notes a 2004 study by the Federation of Canadian Municipalities. Many of these kids experience culture shock when they arrive and "discover that there may be a significant gap between their cultural and educational experiences and urban realities."[25]

The drug subculture in Vancouver's Downtown Eastside is heavily Aboriginal, which may explain why Aboriginal women in that city were found to be three times as likely to die from HIV/AIDS as the city's female population as a whole.[26] Not surprisingly, relations between very poor inner-city Aboriginals and law enforcement agencies have long been strained because of well-founded allegations of racism and police brutality. "So much of what we see around us is a kind of dysfunctional Aboriginal world," Gail Valaskakis, research director for the Aboriginal Healing Foundation, told a Senate committee studying the problems of urban Aboriginal youth in 2003. "The Aboriginal gangs ... are in a sense another form of belonging. They are a formation of community."[27]

Franco Buscemi, of the National Inuit Youth Council, turns the issue of severe dislocation on its head. "Imagine how you would feel to be set adrift alone in a kayak in the Arctic Ocean," he told the Senate committee. The attraction of the city, Roy McMahon, youth coordinator for Toronto's Native Canadian Centre, added during that Senate committee's cross-country hearings, "is like looking through a stained glass; the promise of moving to a city is so rich.... The people and youth I have met have come to the city in search of that promise. It is not there."[28]

DIVIDED CITIES

The citizens of Cabbagetown believed in God, the Royal Family, the Conservative Party and private enterprise. They were suspicious and a little condescending towards all heathen religions, higher education, "foreigners" and social reformers....

As Ken hurried south towards his own street he became conscious of the increase in sound. There were more children shouting and crying, more traffic on the narrow streets, more raucous peddlers, and above all this the constant noise of the factories....

The smells were also different. Coal smoke, chemicals, horse manure, wet mattresses, old wallpaper and dirty snow.... But the prevailing smell was one of decay, or old wet plaster and rotting wooden steps, the smell of a landlord's carelessness and neglect.

—HUGH GARNER, *CABBAGETOWN:*
THE CLASSIC NOVEL OF THE DEPRESSION IN CANADA (1950)

Cabbagetown hasn't smelled of "carelessness and neglect" for a very long time. In the past 30 years, this dense downtown Toronto neighbourhood has been lovingly rebuilt by renovation-minded home-owners with a taste for historic architecture. The first were urban pioneers who, in the 1970s, bought up cheap, derelict homes in a rundown neighbourhood that Toronto officials wanted to raze in the name of urban revitalization. There was nothing inevitable about the resurrection of Cabbagetown as a vital inner-city neighbourhood. But this is a story that has played out in many of Canada's large urban centres. We are a nation that watched the emptying out of U.S. cities

and decided that we didn't want to abandon our downtown neighbourhoods. Canada's cities are filled with hundreds of comfortable
older neighbourhoods that have admirably withstood the centrifugal
forces of suburbanization. Property values are good. The public schools
are well run and sought after. Parks and streets are generally safe.
Adults have reasonably rewarding jobs. Families, if they save a bit, can
afford programs for their kids, a cottage vacation, a skiing trip in the
winter. Everyone seems to be renovating or trading up to a slightly
larger place. There is plenty of culture on offer. Thriving retail streets
offer a mix of quirky clothing boutiques, ethnic restaurants, and upscale
food emporiums with specialty cheeses, multigrain bread, and organic
produce. At the beginning of the 21st century, the cosmopolitan urban
lifestyle in Canada has much to recommend it.

At the same time, however, Canadian cities have seen a surge in
poverty in recent years, especially in the inner ring suburbs—those
built in the post-war decades. These are urban communities that have
been caught betwixt and between: As downtown neighbourhoods
became increasingly gentrified, low-income families were forced to look
farther afield to find affordable accommodations, often in the sterile
high-rise apartments or social-housing complexes that were developed
in the 1960s on the margins of post-war residential subdivisions.
Meanwhile, the booming outer suburbs were attracting an increasing
share of new employment growth and development, often at the
expense of their older suburban neighbours. Retail and manufacturing
jobs disappeared, leaving a landscape of abandoned industrial sites,
half-empty malls, and falling property values.

The Cabbagetowns of today, in fact, are communities such as northern Etobicoke, on Toronto's northwest fringe, or the hard-scrabble
neighbourhoods in the far east end of Montreal. They often have large
populations of immigrants and refugees but lack social and recreation
programs. Public housing complexes are rundown, overcrowded, and
often dangerous. They are, moreover, physically isolated from the rest of
the city, separated from more affluent downtown communities by
windswept suburban arterial roads and massive malls. And here's the
disturbing twist: The vast majority of the low-income Canadian city-
dwellers living in such communities aren't wallowing on unemployment

or welfare, because we've spent a decade tightening up our social safety net programs, such as employment insurance, in the name of fiscal probity. Rather, they're working long hours at one or more low-wage jobs, and yet they're still unable to lift themselves out of urban poverty.

What Food Banks Tell Us

In the fall of 2004, the Montreal *Gazette* told its readers the story of a 22-year-old single mother from Latin America with disabled twins. The woman was picking through the stock at a food bank, collecting supplies to carry her to payday. She was taking her high school diploma part time to qualify for a job as a customs official. In the meantime, she worked a 32-hour week at minimum wage as a secretary. The irony of her situation was rich: Her employer was Provigo, one of Quebec's largest supermarket chains.

The woman earned $1000 a month from her job, plus $720 in child benefits from the provincial and federal governments. But that amount was $300 shy of the minimum needed to support a family of four, according to a Montreal-based network of Quebec food banks. Like other food banks in big cities across Canada, Moisson Montréal officials had noticed a steady increase in "business" from the urban working poor. "It's difficult for some people to feed themselves properly every day when fixed expenses have to be paid," Marie-Paule Duquette, of the Montreal Diet Dispensary, said. "So we see mothers going to food banks to get through to the end of the month."[1]

Food banks began turning up in Canada the mid-1980s and now number over 500. In Quebec, over 200,000 people regularly use one. However, Moisson Montréal estimated that on Montreal Island, 154,000 people visited food banks each month—equivalent to more than 70 percent of the provincial total. According to the Canadian Association of Food Banks, about 4 in 10 food bank clients are children. These institutions have media profile. Their directors become household names and some go on to political careers. They solicit corporate support. Not a Christmas or Thanksgiving goes by without a food drive. We have come to accept them as if it's absolutely normal to have thousands of hungry people living in our big cities.

What's the explanation? During the 1990s, median incomes in Montreal, Toronto, and Vancouver all dropped, quite dramatically in the case of the latter two. Throughout the industrialized world, in fact, the gap between the rich and the working poor has widened sharply. The shifts are often most pronounced in Canada's most prosperous cities: Toronto, Vancouver, and Calgary. In Toronto, the median income of the top 10 percent was more than 27 times higher than the bottom 10 percent. Indeed, between 1981 and 2001, the number of poor families in Toronto jumped from 73,900 to 124,700—a whopping 69 percent increase in one generation. Contrary to the promises of neo-conservative economists, rising tides did not raise all the boats in the harbour; quite the opposite, in fact.

While the growth in poverty rates levelled out somewhat during the 2000s, social polarization remains a stubborn feature of our urban geography, and no amount of economic expansion seems to be capable of altering this fact of social life. As a 2003 Federation of Canadian Municipalities study warns, "While Canadian cities have less poverty and show lower levels of crime [compared with U.S. cities], recent changes to Canada's social, education, health and other safety net programs may lead to a greater degree of convergence between the two countries in the future."[2]

This polarization can be traced to the late 1980s and early 1990s, when the country endured a one-two punch: The beginning of the free trade manufacturing shakeout was immediately followed by the 1991 recession and the jobless recovery that lasted until the mid-1990s. An exodus of manufacturing jobs, combined with steep cuts to welfare rates and chronic shortages of affordable housing, produced intolerable pressure for many urban families—especially recent immigrants and visible minorities, who have felt the pinch much more sharply than many other sectors of urban society. Half the children who immigrated to Canada between 1996 and 2001 now live below the poverty line.

The broader explanation of the widening income gap has to do with the way globalization affects urban labour markets and investment capital flows. University of Chicago sociologist Saskia Sassen, one of the world's foremost authorities on globalization and cities, points out that international urban regions have turned into highly specialized strategic command centres that control the deployment of huge sums of capital in various parts of the world. These cities have attracted legions of highly skilled, mobile professionals working in specialized service sectors (accounting, investment banking), as well as those sought-after knowledge workers in areas such as venture capital, R&D, and information technology. They are paid, increasingly, on an international scale (complete with large bonuses, options packages, and relocation perks). And when they go shopping for homes, they are ready to pay prices that reflect the going rate in global cities such as London and New York.[3] With their spending power, this elite segment of urban society has come to demand a high quality of urban living, complete with cosmopolitan amenities such as leading hospitals, cultural and recreational venues, and affluent neighbourhoods.

But the local face of globalization has a darker side. The loss of large numbers of manufacturing jobs to low-cost countries has triggered chronic shortages of reasonably paying jobs in some North American cities (the exodus is more pronounced in the United States than Canada, which remains a net exporter of manufactured goods). In their place, rapidly expanding cities have generated thousands of low-paying retail and hospitality industry jobs, many of which are filled not by employers but HR contractors who provide contract cleaners and clerks to large corporations.[4] These forces have gradually altered the political dynamic of the world's leading cities. "The professional classes can project their lifestyles on urban spaces," Sasken observes. "They capture global capital and this changes the city. But it also displaces the poor."[5]

How? Gentrified neighbourhoods become unaffordable as young families and renovators buy up former rooming houses and convert them back into single-family homes. Employment becomes increasingly concentrated in wealthier core areas and affluent suburban hubs, where there are offices, shops, and high-tech clusters. Mega-malls and mass merchandisers such as Wal-Mart displace the small independent retailers that provided steady jobs and modest investment opportunities. In poorer downtown pockets and older first ring suburbs, employers are thin on the ground, meaning those with jobs have to travel a long way, often by transit, to get to work.

These mighty, swirling forces sweep through urban neighbourhoods like storms. Over the past two decades, the "social character" of modest urban communities has been "altered ... because of large and rising numbers of people with little or no attachment to the labour market," concluded a 2000 study on neighbourhood inequity in Canadian cities. Social transfers to individuals helped blunt these divisive forces, but only by a little bit. "These results," the study observed, "indicate that the relative stability in the distribution of family income observed at the national level conceals important changes in the relative economic position of neighbourhoods in Canada's major cities."[6]

In Toronto, the number of communities with high concentrations of poor families had not only increased since the early 1980s, but those neighbourhoods can now be found in parts of the city that had known little poverty until 1981. That year, fewer than one in five communities was considered to have high or very high poverty; by 2001, however, that figure had skyrocketed to 43 percent—comprising well over half the city's physical area. On the ground, the city was experiencing rapidly escalating concentrations of poverty at the neighbourhood level.[7] And unlike U.S. cities, which hollowed out, urban poverty in our largest urban areas is often found in older suburbs, well away from the vibrant and seemingly prosperous downtowns.

In these communities, many urban families find it increasingly difficult to cover the basic costs associated with city living: food, transportation, and housing. More and more urban households are forced to spend in excess of 30 percent of their total income on rent or mortgage payments—a threshold generally associated with unmanageable financial pressures.

During the latter 1990s, cramped, dingy motel rooms in and around Toronto were filling up with families who had been thrown out of jobs, then their apartments, and had ultimately found they had no place else to go. Some were employed single mothers with small children, others were refugees. "In the parking lots, children play on scorching tarmac," observed *The Globe and Mail*'s Jane Gadd in 1997. "Here, in shabby rooms with hotplates for cooking and garbage bags for cupboards, live hundreds of children and their mothers, single parent families who are losing the struggle to survive and have sunk down, down through society until they now dwell close to the bottom."[8]

Right across Canada, in fact, the number of families forced to use hostels jumped by 76 percent between 1988 and 1996—debunking the stereotype that the homeless are primarily substance abusers or mentally incapacitated.[9] Housing pressures are most severe in economically robust cities, such as Vancouver, Calgary, and Toronto, but also in suburban municipalities, which have seen a steady parade of new customers come to their shelters. In the satellite cities north and west of Toronto, existing shelters are now filled to capacity much of the time. As one municipal housing official told a reporter, "Our estimate is about 1,200 to 1,300 people become homeless in Halton Region [which includes the west GTA cities of Oakville and Burlington] every year."[10] Needless to say, this is no way to grow up. Children living in such transient conditions are exposed to incredible stress, social stigmatization by their classmates, and even elevated risk of respiratory infection because of the tight, under-ventilated conditions.[11]

Indeed, this social centrifuge is nowhere more apparent than in the strikingly divergent opportunities available to affluent and poor urban children. Today's middle- and upper-middle-class city kids have way more going for them than ever before—their lifestyles encompass specialty summer camps, after-school activities, organized sports, music academies, children's museums and arts festivals, kid-friendly restaurants, indoor playgrounds, wave pools, progressive-minded private schools, elaborately themed birthday parties, and urban parks with state-of-the-art, accident-proof climbing equipment. If boredom is the fate of kids in small towns, where there is nothing much to do, the lot of today's urban children is that their parents over-program them, packing their free hours with enrichment activities.

The flip side of this rosy picture can be found in a 2003 report card on Toronto child poverty compiled by a coalition of social welfare organizations called Campaign 2000. It reported that a third of Toronto children are poor, and their ranks swelled by over 21,800, to about 174,000, between 1995 and 2003. In one of Toronto's densest inner-city ridings, half of all children live in poor households. Toronto's child poverty rate is significantly higher than the national and provincial average, and the number of poor children in the ring of new suburbs around the city, though relatively low, has begun to grow at "an alarming rate," indicating social decline in traditional bedroom communities. Finally, according to Campaign 2000, immigrants represent almost 60 percent of Toronto's poor, and the child poverty rate among recent immigrants has risen in each decade since the 1980s. As the report concluded, "Child poverty disproportionately affects Toronto. It has 44 percent of the Greater Toronto Area's children but 57 percent of the GTA's poor children."[12]

Poor kids, moreover, tend to live in pockets of poverty—isolated communities characterized by unsafe social housing projects and little in the way of community services or youth programs. As a 2004 United Way report entitled *Poverty by Postal Code* put it, "The fact that so many more children are being raised in higher poverty neighbourhoods today, that their numbers are disproportionately higher than in the city as a whole, and that they make up a growing proportion of the population of higher poverty neighbourhoods is deeply troubling. It raises concerns about the life chances of these children and the impact on their futures of growing up in disadvantaged communities."[13]

This situation is hardly unique to Toronto. The number of Montreal children living under the poverty line has been growing steadily, and many reside in single-parent households where a welfare cheque is the only source of income. In 2002, Montreal's medical officer of health estimated that 4000 to 5000 teens lived on the streets, while one in six children didn't have enough to eat. As in Toronto, poverty varied dramatically across the island, as the haves and have-nots grew ever more isolated from one another within the confines of one urban region. The 2002 annual report from Montreal's medical officer of health drew particular attention to this social "paradox": "The notion of a modern city brings to mind two distinct images. The first is of a dynamic, cosmopolitan economic, cultural and intellectual hub with lively colourful neighbourhoods. The second image is more unsettling and is one of a concrete jungle, precarious living conditions, pockets of poverty, marginality, polluted air and anonymity."[14]

The widening income gap and the swollen ranks of poor children have become a feature of booming Western Canadian urban centres too. Vancouver's Downtown Eastside—a magnet for runaway teens—remains Canada's poorest neighbourhood. In Calgary, poverty became much more concentrated in the 1990s, leaving a quarter of the city's children and half of all single-parent households—many of whom live in central Calgary—struggling to get by.[15] And in Edmonton, which has seen its fortunes soar because of its proximity to the oil sands projects, one in four children now lives in low-income families. "There's no question our city has growing social problems," said Allan Bolstad in 2004. He had just retired from Edmonton city council, having represented for several terms a ward that included poor neighbourhoods and residents who didn't vote. He had fought hard to get the city to launch a $50,000 school lunch program for poor children and had seen it grow through donations and partnerships. But such measures, though worthy, merely tinkered at the edges of a much broader urban dilemma. "I knew these areas needed help. I felt it was important that I see and hear first hand about the problems these people were facing, and what they thought needed to be done."[16]

No Way Out

In 1989, during Prime Minister Brian Mulroney's second term in office, the House of Commons passed an all-party resolution to eliminate child poverty by 2000—a high-minded parliamentary response to the International Year of the Child. The millennium came and went, but Canada has made little progress in achieving this laudable goal. As of 2004, one in six Canadian children lived in impoverished conditions. According to a 2005 UNICEF report, Canada ranked an unimpressive 19th out of 24 OECD countries in terms of the proportion of children living in households with incomes below 50 percent of the national median (i.e., the dollar figure at which half the population's income is higher and the other half's is lower). On this snapshot measure of relative poverty, we fared somewhat better than the United States, the United Kingdom, New Zealand, and Portugal, but significantly worse than most of the northern European nations, with their social democratic traditions. More revealing, however, was UNICEF's data on how this picture had changed during the 1990s. While overall child poverty rates in the United States and the United Kingdom improved markedly, Canada's remained essentially unchanged, registering a slight (0.4 percent) decrease during a decade capped off by exceptionally robust economic growth.[17]

UNICEF points out that in countries where income support programs are generous, there is far less child poverty compared with nations whose citizens rely primarily on whatever they can earn out in the marketplace. Smart social policy is a big part of the solution, and it takes various forms. In the United States, for example, the child poverty rates fell because of the combined effect of a red-hot 1990s economy and radical welfare reforms, which saw a U.S.$13-billion reduction to social assistance payments to individuals capable of working, accompanied by a six-fold increase in support for working families, to U.S.$66.7 billion. Norway, in turn, cut its child poverty rate by a third by boosting social transfers to poor families with children. As for Canada, UNICEF's analysts trenchantly observed that Ottawa and the provinces have continued to bicker over an official definition of poverty instead of tackling the problem itself. Said UNICEF: "Canada's target year 2000 came and went without agreement on what the target means, or how progress towards it is to be measured, or what policies might be necessary to achieve it."[18]

Hugh Garner's epic novel about growing up poor in Toronto's Cabbagetown reminds us that there is nothing new about children living in urban poverty. Working-class slums defined 19th-century industrial centres, where living conditions became so intolerable that they gave rise to many of the social movements, planning ideas, architectural trends, and technological advances that shaped the 20th century.[19] In the gigantic mega-cities of the developing world, crime-ridden shanty towns spring up in the shadows of gleaming office towers, five-star hotels, and exclusive neighbourhoods defended by security guards. Canadian cities are obviously not in the same league. But we would be wrong to be complacent about the steadily accruing income polarization in our big cities, because these social trends will increasingly define the character of our urban communities and the ways in which city-dwellers relate to one another.

The irony is that while most Canadian cities in the 1960s and 1970s avoided the racial strife and hollowing-out that hobbled so many U.S. cities, we now seem to be segregating ourselves into rich and poor urban neighbourhoods, whose residents have less and less to do with one another. It's a dynamic that could severely undermine the relatively high degree of social peace that has characterized Canadian cities in the past four decades.

The safest, most socially harmonious cities are composed of diverse, reasonably integrated communities characterized by a mix of ethnicities and income levels. By contrast, cities that allow themselves to become highly polarized are criss-crossed by barriers. Affluent neighbourhoods take care to keep out those perceived to be poor and dangerous through various means.[20] Meanwhile, the poverty in have-not neighbourhoods grows ever more concentrated as working families and small businesses flee for safer pastures, leaving behind economically denuded communities with few jobs, leaders, or social supports. They are also gated, except the locks are on the outside.

There is mounting recent evidence that in large Canadian cities with highly concentrated poverty at the neighbourhood level, children are facing much tougher challenges than are those who grew up in low-income but otherwise functioning communities. "Socially isolated and spatially segregated places do not breed new ideas and partnerships, but feelings of despair [and crime]," observes University of Western Ontario political scientist Neil Bradford.[21] As a 2003 study by the Canadian Policy Research Network stated, "Poverty is well known as a multiplier of disadvantage."[22]

Why? Children living in such communities are exposed to many more adults who don't work, who make poor role models, or who place little or no stock in education. Their parents may spend more time during the course of a day in transit because they have to travel longer distances to their jobs. Single mothers, who are much more likely than dual-parent families to be poor, have less time to participate in school activities or neighbourhood projects because they have to do the domestic work of two people. And economic deprivation is the engine that drives a lot of criminal activity, especially among young men who turn to drug dealing and gangs to earn cash. There are drugs and tough kids in every community. But the greater the number, the harder it becomes for straight youth to avoid the threats—and blandishments—of gang members.

What is striking is how these diffuse, hard-to-measure urban influences invariably show up in the way children from such environments fare once they reach school. Verbal ability scores, for example, tend to be lower among children from poor, single-parent households than among youngsters who grow up in households where both parents are present. Behavioural problems are also more common in communities with high unemployment, for the obvious reason: Parents who are struggling to pay the rent or put food on the table function in an atmosphere of relentless, corrosive tension. "Neighbourhood disorder adversely influences children's language development," according to a 2003 study on neighbourhoods by the Vanier Institute for the Family.[23]

In 2000, University of British Columbia researchers divided Vancouver into 23 neighbourhoods and ranked them by affluence. Then they set out to measure whether young children in those communities were ready for kindergarten. In the most well-off neighbourhood, just 6 percent of children were found to be vulnerable in a range of areas, including language and cognitive development, and social, emotional, and physical skills. In the poorest community, by contrast, well over a third of all children experienced these kinds of developmental problems. Suffice it to say that low-income parents have a much tougher time paying for tutors, child psychologists, and extracurricular activities.

Moreover, the relentless daily stresses associated with economic desperation—uncertainty about job security, rising bills, perhaps the threat of eviction—breed family breakdown and crime. Criminologists understand that children who grow up in very poor, broken homes are much more likely to commit crimes in their teens than those who come from stable, although not necessarily affluent, families. This shouldn't come as a surprise. Adolescents in low-income neighbourhoods are drawn into gangs and drug dealing because it's a lifestyle that offers surrogate families, status, and otherwise apparently unattainable economic rewards. These are hardly alien impulses. In every middle-class neighbourhood, homeowners understand what it means to be house-proud. Parents enrol their kids in summer programs or sports teams so they stay out of trouble. The difference is that these communities have the wherewithal to finance the trappings of material prosperity or the opportunities that help their children navigate the shoals of adolescence on their way to adulthood.

The Afflictions of Poverty

Crime is hardly the only symptom of urban poverty. Medical researchers in recent years have begun to meticulously document the ways in which poverty negatively affects health. For instance, U.S. studies of homeless children concluded that they are more prone to asthma, lead poisoning, infection, delayed immunizations, chronic hunger, and obesity than youngsters with stable housing. The National Longitudinal Study on Children and Youth, a long-term tracking study of thousands of Canadians kids, provides corroborating Canadian data: Among children up to age 11, 89 percent who live in decent housing enjoy good health. For those in poor housing—in other words, contaminated with asbestos or mildew, or situated on marginal land exposed to highway fumes, and so on—that figure drops to 72 percent. A third of these children demonstrated aggressive behaviour—three times higher than is the case for youngsters living in well-maintained homes.[24] A nice home doesn't guarantee a child will develop properly, but cramped, rundown living conditions obviously impose an additional layer of domestic pressure on poor families.

The health–urban poverty connection applies to grown-ups as well. Homeless people, drug addicts, and shelter users are highly vulnerable to certain types of communicable diseases, including tuberculosis, hepatitis C, and HIV. If you're poor and isolated from support networks, you will be more susceptible to mental illnesses. In Montreal, the link between neighbourhood poverty and health has been closely charted by the medical officer of health, and the results are disturbing. Compared with affluent West End communities, the residents of low-income industrial neighbourhoods in Montreal's East End have a substantially higher incidence of cancer and suicide (the rate in the West End is 9 per 100,000, but 23 per 100,000 in the poorer neighbourhoods). Across the island, in fact, life expectancy in affluent neighbourhoods is as much as 13 years higher than those in poorer communities.

A few years ago, researchers with the University of Toronto and the inner-city health unit of St. Michael's Hospital decided to test the hypothesis that being poor and urban can actually make you ill—the first study of its kind in Canada. The team collected data on hospital admissions, lengths of stay, medical costs, and household income from the residents of a particularly diverse part of Toronto—a 16-square-kilometre region of the city's southeast quadrant, with a population of over 120,000 people. The area includes wealthy Rosedale and the trendy middle-class neighbourhoods along Danforth Avenue, but also high-immigrant, low-income communities in Riverdale and along Queen Street East. The results were eye-opening: Residents of poor neighbourhoods tended to use local hospitals much more frequently. "The rates of admission and readmission rise consistently with increasing poverty, resulting in significantly increased hospital costs for poor neighbourhoods. These costs are 50 percent more for the poorest neighbourhoods than for the wealthiest, and one third more for neighbourhoods with average income," reports the study.[25]

Other health analysts have found that low-income Canadians with heart disease were less likely to receive treatments, such as angioplasty or bypass surgery, than relatively more affluent patients. The differences are quite striking. A 1999 study published in the *New England Journal of Medicine* reports that "rates of cardiac treatment were 23 percent higher and waiting times were 45 percent shorter among those with the highest incomes compared to those with the lowest incomes."[26] And all this within Canada's universally accessible health care system, the study's authors note pointedly. Canadian welfare recipients, meanwhile, appear to be more likely to suffer from conditions such as general feelings of ill health, depression, heart disease, and obesity, according to the authors of a 2004 article published by the *Canadian Journal of Public Health*.[27]

The question hovering over all these health trends is whether certain public policies have actually undermined the health of poor urban Canadians and triggered higher health care costs. Physicians, social workers, and other community organizers who were working in Toronto's poorest neighbourhoods during the late 1990s had few reservations about making the connection. They were dealing with patients or clients living on the edge, juggling the threat of eviction, steep welfare cuts, and rising grocery prices, as well as the loss of publicly financed programs—from recreational activities for kids to drop-in centres—that made city living a bit more bearable. Fiscally conservative social policies of the late 1990s, many critics said, took aim at the so-called community determinants of health: affordable housing, public education, food security, employment, and so on. "Health refers both to the health of individuals and communities," comments Dennis Raphael, a University of Toronto public health expert. "When considering individuals, health is the presence of physical, social and personal resources that allow the achievement of personal goals. When considering communities, health is the presence of economic, social and environmental structures that support the physical, psychological, and social well-being of community members."[28] The two go hand-in-glove.

Societies where there is less of a gap between the rich and the poor tend to be healthier; the infant mortality rates are lower and life expectancy is longer. In other words, if you live in a country where the relative spending power of the wealthiest segments of society isn't dramatically greater than those of the poorest, your chances of living a longer life are greater. "Health is powerfully affected by social position and by the scale of social and economic difference among the population," wrote University of Nottingham social epidemiologist Richard Wilkinson in his 1996 treatise *Unhealthy Societies: The Affliction of Inequality.* "In the developed world, it is not the richest countries which have the best health, but the most egalitarian." Wilkinson asserts that while medical science can ward off, cure, or manage illnesses, an individual's general health is the product of his or her social environment—which includes everything from earnings to prevailing local attitudes toward smoking, drinking, and fitness. "The quality of social life is one of the most powerful determinants of health and this, in turn, is very closely related to the degree of income inequality," says Wilkinson.[29]

These trends are increasingly evident in American cities. "U.S. metropolitan areas with greater income inequality also have significantly higher mortality rates than metropolitan areas with more equal income distributions," concluded a 2000 study published in the *British Medical Journal.* Interestingly, the authors couldn't establish the same connection for Canadian cities, where the gap between rich and poor still tends to be much less pronounced than it is for urban regions south of the border.[30]

When we add all this up, a troubling picture of our urban—and, indeed, national—future begins to emerge: If our fast-growing, ethnically diverse cities become ever more polarized along economic lines, they will increasingly display the sort of entrenched social ailments that result in youth crime, certain types of health problems, and urban alienation—conditions anathema to a sustained quality of life. These dynamics, in turn, raise hard political questions: If the viability of Canada's hub cities is directly linked to our national economic well-being, what are the investments we need to make to ensure that we are building the sort of socially inclusive, healthy cities that are most likely to succeed in a 21st-century, knowledge-based global economy?

EXPOSED CITIES

When we talk about cities and urban quality of life, we tend to spend a lot of time focusing on city-dwellers who own their own houses or condominiums.

Homeowners are crucial to the health of cities. They create social stability and invest in their neighbourhoods. For most of us, our homes are our primary asset, a nest egg for the future, a place to raise children, and a source of financial certainty in an uncertain world. Homeowners have every reason to protect their property's value. Economists and central bankers, in turn, keep a close eye on the consumer habits of homeowners because they buy appliances and shop around for the best mortgages. Politicians, especially local politicians, pay attention to them because they vote.[1]

Residential developers, in turn, have virtual carte blanche to turn farmers' fields into subdivisions with gleaming new houses. Thriving older neighbourhoods become desirable and may even confer all sorts of values and collective personality traits on their inhabitants. In our cities, equity is king, and with good reason.

Yet, most urban homeowners would probably be surprised to discover that they represent barely half of the population of Canada's largest cities. Indeed, if the two solitudes in the new Canada is the yawning urban-rural divide, there is a parallel social schism within cities, according to University of Toronto housing expert J. David Hulchanski: tenants and owners (see table on the next page).

Despite their numbers, tenants tend to wield little political clout compared with their assertive land-owning neighbours, who take a more activist role, establishing residents' organizations that can lobby

CANADIAN HOUSEHOLDS BY TENURE, 1999 CENSUS METROPOLITAN AREAS

Census Metropolitan Area	Owners	Renters	Total	Tenants (%)
Toronto	940,000	780,000	1.72 million	45
Montreal	690,000	820,000	1.51 million	54
Vancouver	450,000	390,000	840,000	46

J. David Hulchanski, "A Tale of Two Canadas: Homeowners Getting Richer, Renters Getting Poorer," *Finding Room: Policy Options for a Canadian Rental Housing Strategy*, ed. J. David Hulchanski and Michael Shapcott (Toronto: CUCS Press, 2004), 82. Reprinted with permission.

City Hall to keep away unwanted developments, from high-rises to group homes. What is more, tenants appear to be on a financial slippery slope. Hulchanski and other housing analysts have tracked the changes in the assets, income, and demographics of Canada's tenants over the past two decades, and the picture that emerges draws a crisp line linking the widening income gap we saw in the previous chapter on poverty to failures in government policy and the dynamics of an urban real estate industry that has ceased to produce affordable housing on its own steam.[2]

Between 1984 and 1999, the median income of Canadian homeowners grew by about $2100, to $43,500. For tenants, the figure actually dropped slightly, by $600, to $20,850. So while homeowner income didn't exactly soar, it didn't shrink either, as tenant income did. The figures for net worth, however, dramatically illustrate what most homeowners know instinctively: that even with a heavy mortgage, in the long run, it's still better to buy than rent. That is, if you can afford the down payment.

The numbers don't tell the whole story, of course. The tenant market is highly fluid, and at any given moment it includes many people who will, in all likelihood, become homeowners within a few years. University and community college students who live away from home, for example, are overwhelmingly tenants. After they graduate, they will continue to live in rented accommodations in their 20s as they establish themselves in their careers or travel or even return to school to improve their credentials. Few people buy a house the moment they graduate. By their 30s, however, they may have saved, borrowed from parents, or inherited enough money to enter the market.

MEDIAN NET WORTH BY OWNERSHIP STATUS, 1999 CENSUS METROPOLITAN AREAS

	Net Worth Owners	Change 1984–99 (%)	Net Worth Tenants	Change 1984–99 (%)
Toronto	$248,400	+ 43	$3,300	−23
Montreal	$142,300	+ 33	$2,112	−51
Vancouver	$243,600	+ 27	$5,000	−10
Canada	$145,200	+ 24	$2,060	−48

J. David Hulchanski, "A Tale of Two Canadas: Homeowners Getting Richer, Renters Getting Poorer," *Finding Room: Policy Options for a Canadian Rental Housing Strategy,* ed. J. David Hulchanski and Michael Shapcott (Toronto: CUCS Press, 2004), 83. Reprinted with permission.

Yet, there are many more renters for whom homeownership is financially out of the question. A great many are recent immigrants and refugees, thousands of whom arrived in Canada within the last decade. Some immigrants, especially those who qualify under the business class, come to Canada with the wherewithal to buy houses or condos. But for thousands of others, housing, or the lack of it, becomes a major impediment to successful integration into urban society. Many of Toronto's giant low-cost apartment buildings—dense 1960s-era complexes such as St. James Town and Flemingdon Park—are overwhelmingly populated by recent immigrants. In the Horn of Africa, "Dixon Road" has become synonymous with "Canada," a reference to a row of overcrowded, isolated high-rises on the suburban arterial of that name that became home to hundreds of Ethiopian and Somali families.

Discrimination—against visible minorities, families with small children, gays and lesbians—is an enduring, unattractive feature of the apartment market, and there is evidence that recent non-white immigrants from developing countries have endured a tough time finding suitable, affordable apartments. In contrast to the Italian and Portuguese immigrants who settled in Canada in the 1950s and 1960s and managed to establish themselves in row houses in downtown working-class neighbourhoods, newcomers from Latin America, Asia, and the Middle East have encountered considerable difficulty finding decent housing, even in the ethnically diverse cities of Toronto and Vancouver. University of Toronto researchers who interviewed dozens of recent immigrants from Poland, Jamaica, and Somalia found that the Poles had the least trouble, while Somali families frequently ended up spending more than half their household income on rent. As a TD Bank housing study noted, "Households paying 50 percent or more of their income [on housing costs] are almost certainly living from pay cheque to pay cheque or from transfer payment to transfer payment and are unlikely to have a pool of savings built up."[3]

Moreover, the Canada Mortgage and Housing Corporation (CMHC) has found that during the 1990s, a disproportionate number of the most recent immigrants and refugees were relegated to apartments in need of minor or major renovations—everything from better appliances to structural renovations. During the same period, moreover, the ranks of renters paying at least 30 percent of their income on housing increased steadily and now represents about a third of all tenants. These trends present further evidence that Canada has failed to think through consequences of the sharply higher immigration levels introduced in the mid-1980s—consequences borne primarily by the newcomers who came here looking for a better life.

They often end up with just the opposite. Living in overcrowded, substandard, or unaffordable housing is linked to all sorts of short- and long-term health problems, such as mould-related asthma and malnutrition. And the resulting stress contributes to family breakdown: The Children's Aid Society of Toronto determined that inadequate housing is a factor in almost one in five child-removal court orders.

Under the normal laws of economics, the response to rising demand for a given product triggers increases in the supply of that good until some kind of equilibrium is reached. Or so the textbooks tell us. The problem with the rental housing market, observes Hulchanski, is that the collective economic power of all those new customers—recent immigrants with meagre incomes and little in the way of savings— simply isn't sufficient to ignite the apartment development sector, especially in large urban regions, where land, construction, and labour costs are high and the seductions of the condo market—a quick-in-quick-out business with very lucrative rewards—are almost impossible to resist.

Between 1991 and 1996, the net increase in all rentals across Canada was 186,000 units. From 1996 to 2001, by contrast, the apartment development business lurched almost to a halt, with a net growth of just 2000 units. Toronto alone lost more than 17,000 apartments to condo conversions and demolitions. Not surprisingly, the vacancy rate plummeted, even in traditionally relaxed markets such as Montreal. While vacancies have risen somewhat during the 2000s, the improved conditions accrued mainly to the upper end of the apartment market because high-rent units are essentially competing with starter homes and condos whose carrying costs aren't much different. And while a significant proportion of condos are rented out as income properties, they tend not to help the low-income households most urgently in need of decent, affordable accommodation. Indeed, if you happen to be a building manager renting cheap apartments, everything is trending in your direction: Demand continues to grow and supply remains tight, which means you're in the driver's seat as far as rental rates go. Little wonder that so many recent immigrants, with little by way of choice, end up paying such a hefty chunk of their incomes on rent.

None of this is a secret. The CMHC itself estimated that for the balance of this decade, Canada needs to build about 45,000 new rental units a year (with half geared to the lower end of the market) just to catch up with demand. That is akin to building enough apartments to house the entire population of Edmonton—in less than a decade.

The consensus about the extent of Canada's urban housing crisis cuts across ideological lines, from left-leaning housing activists to right-of-centre business groups. Drummond states that "the public policy case for addressing the problem of affordable housing couldn't be more transparent."[4] "Of all the deficiencies of big cities," asserts Pearson-era social policy expert Tom Kent, "none needs more urgent correction than the shortage of affordable housing close to jobs."[5]

The Politics of Affordable Housing

During the 1997 civic election in Toronto, mayoral candidate Mel Lastman, a veteran of local politics with a flair for salesmanship, boasted to reporters that there were no homeless people in North York, the suburban Toronto municipality he had run for years. It was a claim he knew would play well politically with suburban homeowners.

Days after his remark, a homeless woman turned up dead under a bridge in North York, shattering the candidate's credibility on social issues. The chastened Lastman narrowly won the election and then empanelled urbanist Anne Golden to chair a taskforce to find solutions to the crisis.

Urban homelessness is a complex phenomenon that defies simple explanations. A generation ago, for example, mental health experts persuaded politicians to deinstitutionalize a large proportion of non-violent psychiatric patients, but many of these people simply ended up on the streets because governments didn't provide funds for supportive housing. The glamour of city life, in turn, has attracted many teens from troubled rural backgrounds, but they too can quickly end up on the streets, where they're easy prey for pimps and drug dealers.

Yet, Canada's urban housing shortage—and the tragedy of chronic urban homelessness—is an indictment of short-sighted political decision making that put too much faith in a highly market-driven housing system and thus failed to take into account the wrenching social changes our cities have experienced since the early 1990s.

In contrast to many OECD nations, we have failed to provide suitable, affordable accommodation for 1.7 million Canadian low-income households, as well as the 35,000 to 40,000 individuals who sleep on urban streets on an average night. Most other OECD countries recognize these specifically urban housing dynamics and have invested in their social programs accordingly. In the Netherlands, 40 percent of all housing falls under this category, and social housing organizations are regarded as agents of urban regeneration. About 15 percent of households in Germany and France live in affordable housing—a rate three times higher than Canada's. And in the United Kingdom, with its high immigration levels, Tony Blair's Labour government invested Can$2.5 billion per year between 2002–3 and 2005–6 to arrest what it described as the "continuing decline" of the provision of both social and private housing as a means of improving the "sustainability" of cities and towns.[6] The common denominator in all these countries is a recognition that housing sits at the intersection between social welfare policy and urban quality of life.

We used to understand this. Following the devastating urban hardship caused by the Depression, federal politicians established a modest national housing program in 1949. Within the next decade, a post-war suburban building boom was in high gear, but housing shortages persisted. In the 1960s, Ottawa moved to significantly expand its support of public housing, resulting in the construction of 200,000 new units. (By 1993, Canada had half a million such apartments, compared with just 12,000 in 1963.)

At the same time, the CMHC, which underwrites mortgage insurance, adopted a variety of financing policies that stoked the construction of high-rise apartment buildings. The result was a sudden expansion of the supply of both public and market-based rental housing in urban areas. These were hardly neutral policies in terms of the built form of core areas. The suburban exodus of the 1950s had threatened many older neighbourhoods, which seemed to be in a state of long-term decline. One Toronto social planning map from that period categorized vast tracts of the city's downtown neighbourhoods according to their apparent state of deterioration; even Rosedale was targeted. Apartment developers—armed with financial incentives and the encouragement of municipal planners fixated by urban renewal schemes—embarked on massive land assembly campaigns in declining residential neighbourhoods, with an eye to replacing neglected 19th- and early-20th-century working-class homes with forests of modern high-rise apartments. Some got built. But large-scale downtown redevelopment plans ran into opposition, shifting most of the apartment construction farther afield.

Meanwhile, many of the public housing projects from the 1960s and early 1970s turned out to be social disaster zones—not just in Canadian cities but also in large urban regions throughout the United States, the United Kingdom, and Continental Europe. From the late 1970s, however, a new and much more benign form of affordable housing began to appear on the urban landscape—non-profit housing co-op projects, which were financed with a combination of private and public funding and operated independently of the increasingly crime-ridden public housing projects. Such ventures also turned on the availability of matching grants from provincial governments. Generally smaller in scale and geared to a mix of income levels, they represent the most stable and socially integrated type of affordable housing.

During Brian Mulroney's term as prime minister, Ottawa began to pare back federal programs that provided capital subsidies for social and co-op housing projects. It was the era of Margaret Thatcher and Ronald Reagan, and both these leaders unleashed sweeping reforms that cut back earlier generations of urban housing programs. Seizing on this political opening, Canadian developers lobbied the Mulroney government to get out of the housing business altogether, while critics of subsidized housing programs—especially those aimed at fostering the development of mixed-income co-ops—claimed they were benefiting middle-class downtowners rather than those in real need. Responding to pressure from developers who didn't want to be in competition with the government, Ottawa declared that its social housing policies were missing the mark and announced its intention to come up with more targeted programs.

In 1990, a Liberal housing taskforce led by then Opposition MPs Paul Martin and Joe Fontana accused the Mulroney government of abandoning its responsibilities for housing. Asserting that all Canadians have a right to adequate housing, they promised to bring in dramatic reforms should their party form a government, including more funding for co-ops and supportive housing, income supplements for the working poor, and additional federal transfers to pay for a so-called shelter allowance for welfare recipients. But when the Liberals defeated the Tories in 1993, they let that promise sit on the shelf. And in 1995, when Martin turned his guns on the deficit, he didn't bump up federal transfers for provincial social programs such as housing; instead, he slashed them.

In short, by the mid-1990s, there was very little left of Ottawa's housing programs, except for the ongoing $2-billion-a-year expenditure on subsidies to public housing projects built prior to 1993. Developers shunned apartment projects because changes in federal tax and mortgage insurance policies had made them less financially lucrative than condos (the legislation legalizing condo ownership dates to the 1970s). And so capital funding for the construction of multi-unit rental residential projects had ground to a halt. Martin's 1995 budget cuts signalled a completely new era in federal-provincial relations, based on a Faustian bargain: The feds were offering less cash transfers to their provincial partners. But in return, they were prepared to lower their policy expectations. It seemed like a reasonable trade-off yet clearly represented an inversion of the traditional he-who-pays-the-piper dynamic of federal-provincial relations. In fact, by freeing up the provinces to determine their own social welfare policies, Ottawa was creating a country in which the practical availability of a commodity as basic as housing depended heavily on one's address and the political orientation of the provincial regime—a spectacular and opportunistic abandonment of the concept of national welfare.

Drastic inconsistency is the result. In British Columbia and Quebec, on the one hand, progressive-minded governments chose not to withdraw from affordable housing and were somewhat less aggressive about reducing welfare rates than other jurisdictions. Municipalities have also played their part. The City of Vancouver even has a policy that compels condo developers to allocate a quarter of all new units as affordable. Developers acquiesced because they were keen to put up towers and knew they had to play ball with the city.

In Ontario, on the other hand, the developer-friendly Harris Tories subscribed to the neo-conservative idea that the government should stay out of housing altogether, especially subsidized housing, which was seen to promote laziness among welfare recipients. They repealed tenant protection laws and cancelled co-op housing grants. Moreover, they wanted to cut income taxes to middle-class homeowners, so they downloaded financial responsibility for social housing to the municipalities, marking the almost complete abandonment of housing by both Queen's Park and Ottawa.

Such political decisions forced many low-income families into shelters or onto the street. And it backfired in many other ways. Nishnawbe Homes, for example, is a not-for-profit housing organization founded in Toronto in the mid-1980s by a group of Aboriginal community leaders. Their idea was to create a network of affordable drug- and alcohol-free apartments for the Aboriginal young people flocking to study in Toronto. It started with one shared house but expanded gradually into a network of homes and a small east end apartment building with 16 units. In 1995, the organization was preparing to open a new 40-unit building with funds from Queen's Park, but those plans foundered after the Harris government downloaded social housing to cities. "Municipal government doesn't understand Native people," asserts Nishnawbe's executive director Frances Sanderson. "Now municipal government is in charge of Native housing. That's not the way it's supposed to be."[7]

By the time then Toronto mayor Mel Lastman appointed urbanist Anne Golden to unravel the causes behind chronic homelessness in 1998, Canada's housing and income support policies had all but seized up. The Toronto Disaster Relief Committee declared the situation to be a national state of emergency. The waiting lists for social housing were huge, rent increases and evictions had risen in tandem, shelters were packed, and overcrowding had become the status quo in many apartment complexes in high-immigrant suburbs and downtown enclaves. Homeless people were dying of exposure. Urban Aboriginals, who account for nearly a fifth of the homeless population, faced particularly dire circumstances. Says Sean Goetz-Gadon, a long-time housing advocate and former policy advisor to Toronto mayor David Miller: "There was virtually no community in the country that wasn't facing a crisis of homelessness."[8]

The 1999 Report of the Mayor's Homelessness Task Force, which Golden chaired, goaded the federal Liberals into action, sort of. Amid much sound and light, the Chrétien government unilaterally announced a $753-million homelessness initiative in 1999, and then, just a year later, a $1-billion fund to build an estimated 35,000 affordable housing units over a decade.

Ottawa has ploughed millions into homeless shelters since launching the National Homeless Initiative, including $87 million in Alberta alone, where the booming economy hasn't been able to generate housing for the thousands of economic migrants who have gravitated to Calgary only to discover extreme housing shortages.[9] But new shelters attack the symptoms, not the cause, which is the stubborn mismatch between supply and demand. Moreover, those new affordable-housing grants were only for the physical construction of new projects, not for ongoing operating costs—a critical but little understood distinction that made it extremely difficult for housing agencies and not-for-profit organizations to take advantage of the gesture.

Indeed, because of the decentralization of social policy in the post–federal deficit era, Ottawa was riding along on a wing and prayer, hoping the premiers would cooperate by approving new operating subsidies for affordable housing. The Quebec government had few qualms about entering into such an arrangement. The Mike Harris Tories, on the other hand, remained ideologically opposed to social housing and refused to provide the matching funds, meaning almost none of the new money ended up being spent in Ontario. It was a sparkling example of politicized policy making that may have produced a public relations dividend without helping solve the problem.

Lost amid all the politicking and posturing was the fact that our large cities were becoming increasingly uninhabitable for a significant segment of our population. At the beginning of a new century, Canada's hub cities are ringed with vast subdivisions of brand new luxury homes, but they offer only dregs to those Canadians and recent immigrants who can't begin to afford the dream of a $199,000 three-bedroom house. What is more, urban homeowners, having benefited hugely from low-interest monetary policies, have seen property values continue to press upward in large cities right across Canada. It's all cold comfort to the thousands upon thousands of urban families who were languishing on waiting lists for subsidized housing. In Greater Toronto alone, the figure exceeded 100,000 as of 2003.[10] Thanks to an almost entirely deregulated housing market, they have little choice but to make do, sifting through a meagre selection of rotting public housing complexes, overcrowded high-rises, and damp basement apartments.

LEARNING CITIES

If healthy neighbourhoods are the building blocks of cities, strong public schools are the glue that holds diverse urban communities together. Besides their core educational function, the public school system remains the only institution in our society where children, teens, and adults from vastly different cultural, ethnic, and socio-economic backgrounds can come together in a non-commercial environment for extended periods, during which they'll learn at least as much from one another as they will from their teachers. Their parents may be set in their views, comfortable with their prejudices, and resigned to their limits. Not so for their children: Canada's urban schools are social combustion chambers brimming with the energy that has long typified the cosmopolitan culture of international trading cities.

Nor can their role as public spaces be underestimated. School playgrounds and sports fields double as local parks. Community associations, ethnocultural organizations, and adult education programs will use the facilities in the evenings for their own programs. Youth groups rent their gymnasiums and swimming pools. Some school libraries provide public internet access. Parents form networks, webs of casual social relationships that exist somewhere between friendship and nodding acquaintance. (It was a network of outspoken parent activists, People for Education, that played a pivotal role in toppling the Mike Harris regime, with its stridently anti-public-education policies.) Schools bring neighbourhoods out for fun fairs, concerts, musicals, sporting events, cleanup days. Local businesses proudly sport signs showing that they've donated to a school fundraising drive. Children gather in the auditorium to listen to a local police officer, firefighter, or public health nurse. In short, a lot goes on in and around big city schools besides schooling, and their well-being is intimately connected to their surrounding neighbourhoods.

So how are we doing? From a distance, Canada's education system seems to be serving us well. In recent years, Canada has turned in top grades in international rankings of how school-children fare on standardized achievement tests. In 2005, the OECD's program for international student assessment found that, compared with 31 other countries, Canadian kids ranked second, fifth, and sixth in reading, math, and science respectively, with only Finland placing consistently higher.[1]

Canada's urban students, moreover, can boast of "significantly better" reading achievement than rural students, according to a 2002 Statistics Canada study. Its authors attributed the reading gap to the fact that rural children grow up in communities where there are fewer high-skill jobs and generally lower education levels than in big cities.[2]

Immigration also plays a critical role in producing these outcomes. When researchers for the National Longitudinal Survey of Children and Youth monitored the school performance of the children of immigrants between 1994 and 1998, they found that, on average, this group tended to "do at least as well as the children of Canadian born along each dimension of school performance. The children of immigrants whose first language is either English or French have especially high outcomes." The study found that while children with another first language tend to have somewhat lower scores in reading and writing, they do just as well as Canadian-born children in math, and in fact tend to pull even in reading and writing over time.[3]

Lastly, while they have their share of safety problems, our big-city schools aren't guarded by phalanxes of security guards manning metal detectors—yet. For these reasons, they continue to serve a vast majority of the population. As of 2003, about 93 percent of Canadian school-children and teens attended public schools,[4] and there is little doubt that one consequence of our continued support for this institution is the measure of social cohesion in our largest cities. By contrast, between 70 and 85 percent of all students attending public schools in major U.S. cities, including Houston, Los Angeles, New York, and Chicago, come from low-income homes and poor neighbourhoods—an astonishing statistic that reveals just how completely the American middle class has abandoned inner cities since the 1950s.[5]

Canadian big cities don't have to contend with the legacy of slavery, racial segregation, and white flight. But as we saw in previous chapters, they do show the troubling symptoms of growing income polarization and the proliferation of urban neighbourhoods segregated according to class and ethnicity. This long-term reordering of our urban geography could eventually undermine our school system.

There are already plenty of warning signs. Large numbers of young children begin kindergarten lacking readiness-to-learn skills because they've spent the so-called early years—that intensely formative first half-decade of a child's life—staring at a television or attending daycare facilities that fail to provide the sort of preschool curriculum programs that are almost universally available in many European nurseries. A 2004 study of five-year-olds in Peel, a fast-growing suburban region west of Toronto, showed that as many as 30 percent lacked physical, emotional, social, and linguistic skills needed for grade one.[6] Meanwhile, despite almost three decades of declining high school dropout rates, the proportion of kids failing to graduate has risen steadily in Alberta, Quebec, and Ontario. In Quebec alone, the graduation rate fell from 74 to 66 percent between 1998 and 2004.[7]

A growing number of big-city schools in low-income neighbour-hoods are moving to set up surveillance cameras and identification card systems, while the private school sector is expanding quickly—in Ontario between 1995 and 2003, enrolment in private schools jumped by 32,000 students. As troublingly, school boards in big cities such as Edmonton and Toronto have been struggling to adjust to a long-term decline in attendance as homeowners pull up stakes and head out to the suburbs.

In older urban cores, meanwhile, there is considerable evidence of the emergence of a two-tier public school system. Well-meaning, concerned parents in middle- and high-income neighbourhoods have the contacts and savvy to generate tens or even hundreds of thousands of dollars with sophisticated fundraising techniques, while schools serving low-income neighbourhoods struggle to bring in a few hundred through bake sales. In affluent communities, what is more, parents can afford to hire tutors to help those children who struggle with the curriculum. The net effect is that, in comparison with the growing number of low-income urban communities, the schools in prosperous urban neighbourhoods not only are better equipped (with computers, learning resources, playground equipment, and so on), but they also operate in an environment where networks of privately hired tutors function like an extension of the teaching system.

Heading into Canada's 21st century, our urban schools are being called upon to fulfill a role that will be indispensable for the country's future. They must forge an entirely new concept of multi-cultural citizenship: tolerant and internationally oriented, but also rooted in Canada's civic values. In this light, what is happening in big-city classrooms is an experiment without precedent.

The Challenges of Classroom Diversity

In early 2004, the 2300 students attending Turner Fenton Secondary held their first annual Diversity Day. Located in the ethnically diverse Toronto suburb of Brampton, Turner Fenton is filled with students from all over the world. Many have a first language other than English, and about half the student population is South Asian. Some of the grade nines, daunted by the transition to a huge school, were banding together in ethnic cliques, and problems began to brew. There were name-calling incidents and fights broke out between East Indian and black students.

Working with school liaison officers assigned to the regional police force, the school's administrators began to develop cross-cultural activities, including a "Students without Borders" club, dance programs, and a week-long cultural festival. The racial incidents have disappeared. "The same problem exists in most high schools," principal Bob Garton told the *Toronto Star*. "Ignorance starts when you don't know about the individuals. That's when the education and learning come in."[8]

Toronto, Vancouver, and Montreal are among the world's most ethnically diverse cities, and a social transformation is taking place in their classrooms. The kids attending these schools must literally learn to speak one another's language before anything else can happen. As

Toronto Star reporter Andrew Duffy notes in his 2003 examination of immigration and education in Canada, "Those speaking English as a second language make up 20 to 60 percent of the student population in large cities like Vancouver and Toronto." A quarter of all Toronto's schools, he continues, have "enrolments made up of students who have arrived in Canada within the last five years."[9]

If schooling is partly about transmitting a nation's values from one generation to the next, there is no doubt that the children and teens who attend urban schools emerge with a keen sense of just what it means to live in a multicultural society. There are no "foreign-sounding names" to kids who begin kindergarten in classes where their classmates are called Kamica, Taslim, or Ravi. In some schools, a white-skinned child qualifies as the visible minority, while in many others there is no dominant racial group. And where the celebration of a wide range of religious holidays in schools may appear to homogeneous communities like political correctness run amok, children growing up in these urban educational settings see for themselves that some of their friends may be fasting for Ramadan, while others have to beg off Halloween parties because their families consider such events to be excessively pagan.

The practical challenges of running such schools are daunting. As with many professions (e.g., the media, elected political officials, police), Canada's teachers and principals still don't reflect the ethnic diversity of the classrooms they supervise. In most school libraries, there are few bilingual books, even though literacy research shows that children who are acquiring a second language are more successful when they can use so-called dual track readers.

Urban teachers, in turn, face classes filled with immigrant and refugee children who may have survived war, famine, genocidal regimes, and extreme poverty. If parents speak little or no English or French, they find themselves unable to participate in home and school associations, yet funding for translators and community liaison officials has dried up because it's considered to be a non-classroom expenditure. Teachers and school staff are often left struggling to communicate with parents who aren't conversant in either official language and may not understand newsletters, forms, report cards, homework assignments, and textbooks.

The single most pressing issue, from the perspective of urban class-rooms, is language. Classrooms made up of children who collectively speak a dozen languages are commonplace. Many recent immigrant and refugee children may require ESL (English as a second language) classes, sometimes for as long as seven years. The communications barriers within individual classrooms arouse concerns among parents whose children were raised in English- or French-speaking households. In some urban neighbourhoods, a growing number of non-immigrant middle-class parents are directing their children to either specialized public school streams (the most common being French immersion) or private schools, where there tend to be fewer ESL students and the perception is that teachers can spend more time teaching and less on juggling linguistic problems.

The fact is that Canada's school system is failing to address the needs of students whose first language isn't English—a staggering oversight considering our immigration levels. In Nova Scotia, there is no earmarked funding for ESL training at all, even though the provincial government is now trying to attract new immigrants.[10] In British Columbia's Lower Mainland, where 73 percent of all students speak neither French nor English at home, six big-city school boards (Vancouver, North Vancouver, Surrey, Burnaby, Richmond, and Coquitlam) banded together in 2002 to lobby both the federal and provincial governments for additional funding to meet the huge demand for ESL courses.[11]

These boards have 90 percent of all ESL students in British Columbia. In the 1980s and early 1990s, most immigrant children came from Hong Kong, the Philippines, and Taiwan, and already had school experience. But beginning in the late 1990s, these school boards began to see a sharp increase in immigrant students with "lower English skills than used to be the case," according to British Columbia's ESL Consortium. A growing number of immigrants to the Greater Vancouver area were from China, as well as Pakistan and Korea. Teachers in the region's schools were dealing with an ever-increasing number of teens who had come to Canada with little formal schooling, as well as a surge of refugee children demonstrating behavioural problems related to post-traumatic stress disorder and other special education needs, as well as language issues.[12]

When the parents' group People for Education surveyed the state of ESL in Ontario, it discovered that more than four-fifths of urban elementary schools have ESL students, but barely half employ qualified ESL teachers. Worse, it found that the number of urban schools with ESL programs fell by almost a quarter between 1997–98 and 2003, despite a 13.5 percent increase in the number of immigrants in these cities.

The problems with the ESL programs in big-city schools shines an unflattering light on the disrepancy between federal immigration policies and provincial education spending decisions. While Ottawa has long funded language-training programs for adults, the government never took steps to make sure that big-city boards had the wherewithal to deal with the pressures in the classrooms. In fact, Jean Chrétien, in his waning days as prime minister, pushed through a staggering $850-million multi-year spending package for French-language training coast to coast and French immersion instruction.[13] But funding dedicated specifically for ESL teachers in urban schools has never appeared anywhere on the federal New Deal agenda because education is a provincial responsibility.

The long-term repercussions of this linguistic blind spot are serious. In his investigation of education and immigration, *Toronto Star* reporter Andrew Duffy cites the work of a trio of Calgary academics—David Watt, Hetty Roessingh, and Lynn Bosetti—who discovered alarmingly high long-term dropout rates among ESL students in one Calgary high school. "The results of our study indicated an overall drop out rate of 74 percent for ESL students in high school—a figure more than double that of the general high school population," the study found. It's a trend that began to register on policy makers' radar screens in the late 1980s in Ontario and Alberta.[14]

When Roessingh's team interviewed the immigrant students who had left the school, they were confronted with the grinding economic conditions facing many of the immigrants and refugees who arrive in Canadian cities: Lacking the language and needing work, these teens often drifted out of school in frustration. Some took up low-paying menial jobs in factories that employed large numbers of immigrants, while others ended up working in service jobs that allowed them to develop their English and earn some money at the same time. For these teens, there was no future promise associated with attending Canada's big-city schools. "Rather than reporting a sense of increasing accultur-ation, many felt trapped in diminishing circles of social interaction," the researchers found.[15]

In too many cases, the potential of these new Canadian citizens is squandered. The Calgary research team tells of a young Lebanese teen "who arrived in Canada as a teenager with an intact educational back-ground and hopes for academic success in Calgary. She spoke of wanting to attend university. A socially gregarious, ambitious teenager, she was stunned when she was not permitted to re-register in high school due to the newly imposed age restrictions." This young woman dropped out to take a job in a trucker's restaurant, where she developed her English but abandoned her hope of attending university. "While she had resigned herself to her likely long-term situation, she seemed to grieve the loss of her academic potential.... She lives between and, in a sense, within two cultures—she believes that she cannot return home, and yet she is not living to her fullest expectations here."[16]

The Underfunding of Canada's Big-City Schools

Beginning in the mid-1990s, right-of-centre provincial politicians across the country declared war on big-city schools. In Toronto, Ottawa, Vancouver, Halifax, and Edmonton, school boards found themselves either in receivership, under the threat of provincial takeover, or in open conflict with their political masters. Ugly political battles pitted trustees and urban parents against provincial politicians who were storming ahead with a packed agenda that included sweeping reforms to curricu-lum, testing, school board governance, and education funding. Eager to balance the provincial budget, Alberta premier Ralph Klein led the way with draconian cuts to education budgets, and Ontario's Mike Harris followed suit with a Machiavellian agenda that called for manufacturing a crisis in the education system so his tax-fighting government could slash spending, then wrest control of the system from the school trustees and the teachers unions.[17]

Between 1998 and 2004, the Toronto District School Board (TDSB)—Canada's largest, with 300,000 children—lost $300 million in annual funding, almost 15 percent of its overall budget. At one point, the TDSB trustees narrowly refused to approve what was called a compliance budget—that is, an imposed spending plan that corresponded to the value of the provincial education grants being transferred to the TDSB. The Tories had set the stage for political conflict, removing school boards' taxing authority and passing an education governance law that provided for jail terms for trustees who refused to do the provincial government's bidding. After the trustees decided to stare down the government, Queen's Park stripped them of their remaining political powers and installed a slash-and-burn auditor to find $90 million in savings.

A similar test of wills played out in Edmonton, where the local board of education, much admired among educators, lost its right in the mid-1990s to levy property taxes. The school board fought the decision in court and lost. "Now, we rely on the government to provide us with money," says Bill Bonko, a former Edmonton school trustee elected as a provincial Liberal MLA in 2004. "We have to be dependent on them. So there are no new schools being built because of the limits on funding."[18]

In 2003, the simmering tensions erupted when Learning minister Lyle Oberg put Edmonton's school board under review because of what were perceived to be out-of-line teachers' salaries. Facing the threat of major funding cuts, the Edmonton Public School Board warned that 350 teachers could lose their jobs and valued programs would be put at risk. Tory MLAs countered with threats of amalgamation and school closures. Oberg, in turn, pushed forward a law limiting the Edmonton board from offering adult education programs and issued audits showing the need for millions in cost-cutting. Eventually, parents and students took to the streets. "We're working from textbooks that say some people think oil reserves will run out by 1992," Hayley Grundy, a grade 10 student said at one rally. "In English classes, we're working off photocopies of *Romeo and Juliet* because there are not enough books. The principal comes to school every morning worrying about when the roof will start leaking because they don't have enough money to fix it."[19]

Provincial decision makers justified their actions by saying that education spending was out of control. But that's a myth. By 2001,

Canada ranked an unimpressive 19th out of 30 among OECD countries on education spending, allocating 3.4 percent of the gross domestic product (GDP) on schools. The OECD average is 3.8 percent. Most Western European countries, as well as the United States, the United Kingdom, Mexico, and Korea, are investing considerably more in their school systems. The Canadian Teachers' Federation also found that the education share of GDP per capita had fallen from 24.9 percent in 1995 to 20.3 percent in 2000.[20]

In fact, some of our international competitors were heading in the opposite direction. In the United Kingdom, Prime Minister Tony Blair took an active personal interest in the push to reform public schools. Urban schools in Britain were filled with children from council housing and immigrant or working-class families, and these institutions simply weren't succeeding. He appointed an elite team of education experts, including Michael Fullan, the globe-trotting former dean of the Ontario Institute for Studies in Education, to oversee a dramatic overhaul of the system, focusing on setting targets for gains in literacy and numeracy scores and improved principal and teacher training. Several years after the reforms were introduced, there is clear evidence that British school-children are turning in much-improved results.[21]

Now consider what happened in Canada over the same period. In several provinces, conservatives branded the teachers unions as public enemy number one, causing years of labour strife. Throwing money at a problem doesn't necessarily solve it. The impact of budget cuts, nevertheless, became increasingly difficult to ignore. Besides the ESL shortfalls described above, classes were getting too large, especially in fast-growing suburbs where the construction of new schools lagged behind new home construction. Schools in older neighbourhoods were crumbling. Library, sports, and fitness programs were eliminated. In Vancouver, boards faced huge additional costs associated with retrofitting their schools to make them earthquake proof.

According to a 2003 report on urban schools prepared by People for Education, about two-thirds of Ontario's children attend schools in cities with populations of over 300,000.[22] But in 2002-3, these large urban boards received an average of $7,609 per student, well below the provincial average of $8,134. Some northern boards received as much as

$15,000 per student, while the Greater Essex Board—serving Windsor, which, despite its relatively small size, receives a very large number of immigrants—received the lowest amount of per-pupil funding, $6500.

The People for Education report—based on surveys distributed to schools across the province—shows that the urban-rural inequities go well beyond money. It found that 22,000 children in large cities were waiting for special education services, but the number of urban elementary schools with psychologists fell 36 percent in the previous six years. There has been a similar drop-off in the ranks of guidance counsellors, social workers, and youth workers. Moreover, three-quarters of English classes in urban secondary schools are above the government-mandated average class size, which is 10 percent more than the provincial average.

In 2000, a provincially appointed education commission reiterated what numerous previous studies had all acknowledged: "The issues facing the large urban centers deserve special attention."[23] The dilemma at the heart of these battles stems from the differences between urban and rural schools. Provincial education funding rules, according to many critics, fail to distinguish between urban and non-urban environments. "The more diversity you have, the more difficult it is for the teacher to adapt to the individual differences of the kids in that class," says Charles Pascal, a former Ontario deputy minister of education and executive director of the Atkinson Foundation. "You have to have a different approach to urban settings."[24]

The question is, how? Until the mid-1990s, most provinces allowed school trustees to levy local property taxes. This fiscal power represented a de facto advantage for large and economically prosperous municipalities. In those cities, school boards could squeeze the commercial and industrial property tax base to raise enough revenue to deal with the greater demands of delivering education in complicated urban neighbourhoods.

But this system produced mounting inequities—and a regionally tinged politics of envy—because children growing up in economically sluggish cities or rural areas were at an obvious disadvantage in their access to educational resources. Given that education is a universal social program, the uneven playing field was difficult to justify.

The alternative, however, turned out to be equally problematic. In the late 1990s, Ontario's Conservative government attempted to reform the education funding system, ostensibly to put children across the province on an equal footing. Provincial officials came up with a highly complex funding formula—it ran to almost 150 pages of intricate calculations and multipliers—for allocating to school boards grants for a range of expenditures: a basic per-pupil amount plus separate allocations for administrative overheads, transportation costs, and funds for the upkeep and maintenance of school buildings. Rural and remote boards received extra funds, but there was little in the formula that recognized particular pressures of big-city boards. The one-size-fits-all formula simply failed to recognize the differences between urban, suburban, and rural boards.

The result was chaos. Scores of schools in downtown areas were closed because the boards hadn't been given enough money to maintain them. Post-war suburban schools were stuck with rotting, overcrowded portables. And out in the fast-growing suburbs, thousands of families bought homes in new subdivisions where no schools had been built because of lack of funds, meaning children had to be bussed. All kinds of programs, from ESL and remedial reading to breakfast and lunch programs, educational assistants, and stay-in-school initiatives, were cut. A provincially appointed expert panel eventually recommended the establishment of a $400-million Learning Opportunities Grant, to be distributed to (mainly urban) boards serving communities with large numbers of at-risk kids living in low-income neighbourhoods. But then the Tories ignored their own panel's advice and allocated only a third of the amount required.

Neutralizing Canada's Urban School Boards

In 1996, New Brunswick embarked on a radical, but short-lived, experiment in public school governance. As part of a sweeping education reform agenda, Frank McKenna's Liberal government eliminated democratically elected school trustees and replaced them with a network of parent councils.

New Brunswick's lieutenant-governor at the time was the prominent education advocate Margaret Norrie McCain, and there was much talk in education circles of empowering parents and principals as a means of countering bureaucratic control over the education system. New Brunswick wasn't alone. Across the country during the latter half of the 1990s, provincial governments redlined the authority of school trustees, leaving Canada with what amounts to a political phantom limb. While school boards enjoy constitutional status, their elected representatives emerged from the 1990s having lost their taxing power and most of their administrative clout. As mentioned above, Ontario served up the final indignity by legislating jail terms or massive fines for elected trustees who refused to do the provincial government's bidding.

Where crusading school trustees in the 1970s championed causes such as parent involvement, multicultural education, after-school programs, alternative schools, and special-ed services for inner-city kids, school boards today are minutely controlled by provincial bureaucrats. Few people vote for trustees and fewer still understand what role trustees actually play or what they stand for. "Accountability," in the new lexicon of education politics, means reporting school-by-school standardized test scores administered by provincial officials.

To paraphrase the rallying cry of American revolutionaries, Canada's hapless school trustees have come to symbolize a gutted political office in which there is representation without taxation.

The political reaction against school trustees wasn't entirely undeserved. While no one disputes the universal social benefits of education, only about a third of the population deals directly with the school system at any point in time. Consequently, few people vote for trustees, and that means the office can be easily captured by special interests, used as a springboard for aspiring politicians, or manipulated to direct the financial resources of the board for purposes that have little to do with education, such as the construction of luxurious head offices. In some cases, boards were targeted by teachers and other public sector unions with the organizational ability to win riding-level elections. In other cases—most famously, Surrey, British Columbia—Christian fundamentalists took control of boards with stealth candidates, who tried to impose their views on curriculum and teaching resources. Problems also arise when boards are dominated by union-backed trustees who may be less than impartial at contract negotiation time.

But the pendulum swung too far in the other direction in the late 1990s and early 2000s—a period during which parents and community organizations saw their ability to influence education decisions wane dramatically. The pressure became such that in 2000, New Brunswick's Conservative leader Bernard Lord ran on a promise to reinstate elections for "district education councils," which were assigned a range of formal responsibilities, including budgets, operations, and flexibility in determining local curriculum. The reforms took place in 2001.

Most other provinces did not go as far as New Brunswick, but across Canada, the power of school board trustees remains extremely limited; parents still find themselves waging an uneven battle against large and remote bureaucracies whose officials are accountable primarily to provincial education ministries.

This state of affairs runs counter to the principle of local control of local institutions and has the potential to create a pronounced skew in outcomes. Affluent urban parents have the means and connections to guarantee that resources flow to their children's schools. Yet in many other urban schools, educators are contending with a growing number of ethnically isolated or disenfranchised communities whose members lack the lobbying savvy and personal wealth to ensure that their kids' schools are effective and accountable.

Far-sighted investments in public education in the 1960s played a central role in providing previous generations of immigrant and refugee children with an opportunity to share in Canada's prosperity and participate in our ever-evolving social diversity. Yet, these were also hugely important investments in the well-being of our cities and their neighbourhoods. The all-too-visible emergence of a two-tier public school system in recent years is an indictment of the centralization of education funding, unnecessarily aggressive budget cuts, and the orchestrated demise of political control over local schools. From the point of view of the future well-being of Canada's big cities, such developments are disturbing because they point to a future in which our public schools serve to reinforce, rather than break down, the social divisions that have become a feature of our urban landscape.

UNBOUNDED CITIES

Y ork Region is a 1776-square-kilometre swath of suburbia north of Toronto that's bursting at the seams. At some point in the early 1990s, growth in this rapidly urbanizing part of Central Canada switched into overdrive. Subdivisions with thousands of homes, big-box stores, and industrial parks sprang up in farmers' fields and former wood lots, with the result that the area's once discrete municipalities—Markham, Richmond Hill, and Newmarket among them—were bleeding into one another, creating a suburban mega-city with nerve-wracking traffic problems. Indeed, between 2001 and 2005, York's population grew from 759,000 to more than 900,000—a jump of nearly 20 percent. That's like grafting on a city the size of Saint John, New Brunswick, in just four years.

In 2001, York officials calculated that commuting times had ballooned 50 to 60 percent over the previous five years. Stressed-out drivers were growing old just waiting to make a left. Arterials that were rural side roads scarcely a decade earlier became household names across the GTA because they appeared with such frequency on the traffic reports. The problems became so bad that traffic congestion turned into a pressing election issue. "There's no question we have a major commuting problem across the GTA," York Region chair Bill Fisch said in a 2001 interview. "We're about to reach our limit. If we don't solve the transportation problem—or at least know that a solution is down the road, so to speak—it will reduce the confidence people have in the GTA."[1]

Sprawl and Its Discontents

Urban sprawl, by definition, is what happens when a city's physical boundaries grow at a faster rate than its population.[2] Suburbs, in general, take up a lot more space than older downtown areas. In subdivisions, the streets are wider because of engineering standards that cater to large vehicles. Lots are larger to meet consumer demand for more space. There are fewer blocks and intersections because of the winding layout of residential culs-de-sac—features that discourage walking and cycling. Malls and commercial or industrial buildings are surrounded by moats of manicured lawns and ample parking lots, often required by the municipality as part of the development approvals process. Major arterial roads and highways are abutted by generous rights-of-way in the expectation of future expansion.

Toronto's pre–World War II neighbourhoods had densities ranging from 28 to 36 housing units per hectare. But for the post-war suburbs, that figure dropped to 10 to 15 units. By contrast, Montreal's downtown Plateau district has a density of 75 units per hectare, and Vancouver's West End—with its high concentration of apartment buildings—supports 133 units per hectare—a figure that puts this part of the city's downtown in league with parts of San Francisco and New York.[3]

But in recent decades, sprawl switched into higher gear because many suburbs evolved from 1950s-style bedroom communities into high-growth employment hubs in their own right. Suddenly, thousands of city-dwellers didn't need to head into transit-accessible downtown areas to their office jobs; instead, they were doing suburb-to-suburb commutes, which explains why the congestion is so much worse the farther out you go. Indeed, in many Canadian cities, downtown residents have taken to doing a reverse commute, driving long distances to fast-growing industrial and commercial hubs, dubbed "edge cities" by former *Washington Post* reporter Joel Garreau.

This dynamic has been playing out on the fringes of almost all large North American cities, with similar results: terrible traffic, elongated commute times, and deteriorating air quality. Sprawl also diminishes our sense of place as cookie-cutter development eradicates the rural landscape and delivers death blows to small towns that become engulfed by malls and tract housing. Such development patterns have triggered a vicious cycle: The outward expansion gives rise to more gridlock and anti-development backlash, which leads to the construction of new highways, which in turn produces more sprawl.

If we aspire to build sustainable, healthy cities, York Region–style sprawl is evidently the wrong way to go. Given that much of Canada's population growth is taking place in suburban municipalities, there may be good reason to expect that endless sprawl—and all its symptoms— has become the unavoidable destiny of our large urban centres, rendering them increasingly indistinguishable from cities south of the border.

But such predictions fail to take into account the very distinct social and political forces that drove—and continue to drive—sprawl on either side of the 49th parallel. In many U.S. cities, suburban development has been fuelled by white flight, inner-city racial tension, mandatory bussing orders, financial inducements such as tax-deductible mortgages, cheap gas, anti-transit lobbying campaigns by the car makers, and massive federal spending on highway construction.[4] In 1990, in fact, the United States reached a watershed demographic moment: For the first time anywhere in the world, more than half the population was living in the suburbs. All but 3 of the largest 10 metropolitan areas in the United States had densities of less than 2880 residents per square kilometre. Sunbelt cities covered enormous tracts of land. Atlanta, the fastest-growing city in the United States, had come to be regarded as the poster child of urban sprawl, while Phoenix at the end of the century was physically as large as Los Angeles but had only a third of the population.[5]

Urban sprawl in Canada is the product of an entirely different set of influences. Canadian homebuyers, of course, do leave the downtown in pursuit of a suburban lifestyle that is perceived to offer better schools, safer neighbourhoods, larger backyards, and easier access to work. But they have not been as heavily subsidized as those in the United States to vacate the downtown. Nor are they fleeing inner-city chaos and racial tension. Rather, many Canadian city-dwellers and thousands of recent immigrants have settled in the suburbs because traditional downtown neighbourhoods became unaffordable. Consequently, some of Canada's most socially and economically complex communities can be found in the suburbs, especially post-war neighbourhoods that have become, over the course of just two decades, extraordinarily multicultural. The new inner city can be found in suburbs such as Burnaby and Scarborough. In effect, the dynamic driving Canadian sprawl is the inverse of what has occurred in the United States, and that fact raises the question of whether a more urbanized, cosmopolitan form of city living will take root in the ethnically diverse suburbs around this country's largest cities.

More than 80 percent of Canada's population lives in metropolitan areas with more than 100,000 residents. When Statistics Canada compiled a list of Canada's 50 fastest-growing municipalities, based on population growth between 1991 and 1996, it became apparent that the satellite communities ringing our hub cities were the ones taking the lion's share of this growth. These included the north shore Montreal bedroom community of Blainville (30.5 percent); the Ottawa high-tech suburb of Kanata (28.6 percent); the Greater Toronto Area's so-called 905 cities of Richmond Hill (26.9), Newmarket (25.6), and Vaughan (19 percent); and B.C.'s Lower Mainland municipalities, surrounding Vancouver, of Richmond (17.6), Surrey (24.2), and Langley (14 percent).[6] Calgary is considered to be Canada's fastest-expanding metropolitan region, but 80 percent of recent population growth has occurred in the newest suburbs.[7]

Economics, obviously, plays an important role in such trends. Developers and home builders have mastered mass production construction techniques that allow them to create very large subdivisions quickly and efficiently. Moreover, the 1990s real estate boom came at a time when there was plenty of demand but almost no price inflation because of low interest rates. The single-family home, in effect, has become a commodity, mass produced and priced to move on the Wal-Mart formula: Generate profit by selling in volume and keeping the price down.

The mall-based suburban retail sector, with its mega-malls and big-box stores, is the by-product of the development of large subdivisions, where all those new families need groceries and furniture and kids' clothes as soon as they move in. They can't wait for more congenial retail strips to be built. Consequently, very little traditional main-street retail space finds its way to the suburbs, and that dearth, in turn, means consumers will be travelling by car to shopping plazas.

Newer edge city commercial centres sprang up as large companies, such as banks and insurance companies, moved their back-office operations out of pricey downtown office towers and into low-cost suburban office complexes. Meanwhile, in the manufacturing sector, companies sought out large sites with easy highway access and the space for state-of-the-art distribution facilities geared to a just-in-time economy.

The decentralization of urban jobs to outlying areas with poor transit service accounts for the exponential jump in car use and commuting times since the 1990s. According to a 2005 Statistics Canada study, the farther from the core someone works, the less likely he or she is to take transit (see table below). "Between 1996 and 2001, the number of jobs within 5 km of the city centres of census metropolitan areas rose increased by 156,000," the report revealed. "On the other hand, the number of jobs outside 5 km rose by 733,200."[8]

COMMUTERS TAKING PUBLIC TRANSIT BY DISTANCE OF JOB FROM CITY CENTRE, 2001

%	<5 km	5 to 10 km	10 to 15 km	15 to 20 km	20 to 25 km	<25 km
Quebec	14.8	10.4	6.9	2.9	1.5	2.6
Montreal	44.7	24.3	14.1	10.1	7.6	2.7
Ottawa-Hull	29.1	13.4	12.2	8.9	5.5	2.1
Toronto	53.3	28.7	22.6	16.7	9.9	5.7
Winnipeg	18.4	10.1	11.3	2.6	0.6	0.5
Calgary	19.2	10.9	7.6	6.2	3.1	0.5
Edmonton	17.0	8.1	6.4	1.7	0.2	0.8
Vancouver	25.2	11.6	8.2	7.3	4.8	2.3

Adapted from Statistics Canada, Andrew Heisz and Sébastien LaRochelle-Côté, *Work and Commuting in Census Metropolitan Areas, 1996 to 2001*, cat. 89–613, no. 007 (June 1, 2005), 52. Reprinted with permission.

But contrary to the claims of developers, manufacturers, and mega-retailers, there is much more to suburban sprawl than economics and the mythology of single-family homes on large lots. Of particular importance is the fact that in the post-war decades, suburban planners across North America insisted on strictly segregating residential areas from commercial or light-industrial zones—a technical constraint that played a vital role in making suburbs dependent on cars. In older urban areas, there is a far greater mix of land uses—residential neighbour-hoods abut retail streets, industrial zones, and warehouse districts, while apartment buildings sit adjacent to office towers—and the result-ing proximity reduces automobile traffic. While the planning profes-sion has become more accepting of mixed-use zoning, many suburban councils continue to approve status quo development. There are other technical culprits: Over time, engineering standards governing road widths have expanded to accommodate traffic congestion, vehicle size, and safety considerations. The result, however, is that a four-lane street in an older part of a city takes up a lot less space than a four-lane street in a newer suburb. Though such standards are upgraded ostensibly to improve traffic flow, the net result is just the opposite.

Still, in spite of half a century of car-oriented planning orthodoxy and the clout of the development industry, there is clear evidence that sprawl-style growth occurs quite differently in different cities. It appears that unsustainable development patterns are as much a product of the local political culture as anything else.

In Montreal, for example, the provincial government between 1958 and 1976 "blithely constructed 400 kilometres of expressways on and around the island," according to Annick Germain and Damaris Rose, professors of urban studies with the Institut national de la recherche scientifique at the University of Quebec.[9] While the city in the same period built a subway system, it wasn't enough to staunch the exodus.[10] Attempts by various provincial regimes to contain sprawl—including laws passed by the Parti Québécois in the late 1970s to limit highway construction and protect farmland near Montreal—have had relatively little effect. After a slowdown in the 1980s, the off-island suburbs grew by almost 240,000 people, to 1.5 million, between 1987 and 1994, while the population of the city proper remained stagnant.[11] The polit-ical instability after the 1995 referendum drove away even more Montrealers. As the *Washington Post* reported in 1996, "The city that once was Canada's financial and cultural centre is in serious trouble. Its tax base is eroding, poverty is increasing, roads are deteriorating and, most important, citizens are leaving."[12] The telling detail is that during the 1990s, 32 public schools on the island of Montreal were mothballed, while 41 opened in the suburbs.[13]

In Metro Toronto, by contrast, suburban expansion in the 1960s and 1970s was carefully managed through far-sighted regional planning policies that relied on municipal infrastructure investments to direct development. But by the 1980s and 1990s, satellite municipalities such as Mississauga, Markham, and Richmond Hill were rubber-stamping massive, low-density housing developments and luring businesses away from the core with cut-rate property taxes. The provincial government, which regulates property taxes, chose not to step in and resolve this beggar-thy-neighbour approach. Then, during the late 1990s, urban sprawl turned into a runaway train after the Mike Harris government slashed provincial transit funding and altered planning rules dramatically in favour of the development industry.[14] If sprawl continues along its present course, Greater Toronto within a few decades may well become the hub of an uninterrupted suburban expanse stretching from Fort Erie to Waterloo to Lake Simcoe and Peterborough.

Calgary and Edmonton, with their overheated economies, are also feeling the pressure. Their population densities—about 900 and 1000 persons per square kilometre respectively—are low even by U.S. standards, and there are few geographic impediments to their growth. The 2001 census found that the rate of transit use in both cities (13 percent in Calgary and 9 percent in Edmonton) is well below the national average. "Developers are absorbing rural lands at such a fast clip that Alberta Agriculture recently cited development along Highway 2 [the north-south corridor that connects the two cities] as the largest pressure facing agricultural lands," observes a 2003 TD Bank study on the two cities. "While traffic congestion in medium-sized cities such as Calgary and Edmonton remains nowhere near that experienced in bigger cities such as Toronto and Montreal, the worsening trends of gridlock are worrisome. In fact, residents of Calgary have already indicated that traffic gridlock is their number one concern."[15]

British Columbia's Lower Mainland has experienced its fair share of urban sprawl, as the dense, old, and urbanized parts of Greater Vancouver—the cities of Vancouver, North Vancouver, and Burnaby— watched the rapid emergence of low-density satellite suburbs. But sprawl in Vancouver has been mitigated by the Lower Mainland region being sandwiched between the U.S. border and the Rockies. As well, regional planning decisions favouring the downtown have played an important role in containing and focusing growth. What is more, the city's residents have consistently opposed extensive highway construction. In the late 1960s, homeowners blocked a downtown highway that would have damaged existing neighbourhoods and promoted a suburban exodus. That mindset spread outward as the city grew: In subsequent decades, Greater Vancouver municipalities created a greenbelt to contain sprawl and then enacted land-use policies to encourage high-density mixed-use development in the downtown.

It's worth noting that the B.C. government heeded public opinion in Vancouver and elected not to bankroll large highway projects into the city in the early 1970s. Precisely the same thing happened in Toronto in the late 1960s, when downtown residents, led by Jane Jacobs, succeeded in persuading the Ontario government to block plans by the regional municipality to build the Spadina Expressway. Three decades later, however, memories have faded and urban highway building has returned to some cities, including Hamilton, where a major new expressway is being driven through neighbour- hoods and an environmentally sensitive river valley.

Roads versus Transit

While local development policies and consumer housing preferences play an important role in driving sprawl, major transportation infra- structure decisions determine a city's outward trajectory more than any other single factor. Much of the sprawl we see today at the edges of our hub cities reflects the fact that local and provincial governments in many parts of Canada lost sight of the critical need to balance highway projects with strategic transit investments.

Between the 1960s and the 1980s, we seemed to have a better grasp of the need to preserve this equilibrium. The Ontario government set up the GO Transit commuter transit network, linking, in part, Toronto's financial core to the fast-growing bedroom communities springing up around the city's edges. It also committed to pay for 75 percent of the capital costs and 50 percent of the operating budget of the Toronto Transit Commission (TTC), the city's subway, bus, and streetcar system. Ottawa-Carleton developed a highly efficient bus rapid transit service. In the west, Alberta put up almost $120 million for light rail transit lines in Edmonton and Calgary. British Columbia, meanwhile, invested billions in an elevated rapid transit network in the run-up to the 1986 Expo.

In the early 1990s, the Ontario government, under NDP premier Bob Rae, signalled its intention to underwrite a pair of new subway lines in Toronto, the first to be built in nearly a generation. But those plans were severely scaled back when Mike Harris's Progressive Conservatives cancelled all provincial transit funding and downloaded financial responsibility for GO Transit. Why, Harris asked, should homeowners in North Bay pay extra income tax just to help someone in Toronto take the subway to work?

In the years after Harris slashed transit funding, the TTC racked up hundreds of millions of dollars in debt. In fact, throughout much of Canada, new transit spending all but dried up during the 1990s, with one notable exception: British Columbia. There, the NDP government created a Greater Vancouver transit authority and provided the new agency with a range of revenue sources. The province then kicked in billions to expand SkyTrain, the elevated rapid transit network serving parts of the Lower Mainland. Today, it is supporting further expansion, including a rapid transit line linking Vancouver, the airport, and Richmond, which is being built by a private-public partnership and due to open in 2009.[16]

If transit spending took a hit in the 1990s, there was no shortage of new highway projects in and around our big cities. In recent years, huge sums have been invested in regional highway expansion schemes, often as a reward for political support in the suburbs. Between 2000 and 2002, for example, Ontario's Tory government invested $3 billion in highways around Greater Toronto. The McGuinty Liberals are continuing in the same vein, with plans to build a new generation of GTA highways (tellingly, they are referred to as "economic corridors" on planning documents), ostensibly to expedite truck traffic to border crossings at Fort Erie and Windsor.

Ottawa, what is more, has increasingly insinuated itself into the highway building game in recent years, despite ample evidence from south of the border that federally funded urban highway programs are destructive. As part of its "strategic infrastructure fund," Ottawa has helped provincial governments bankroll hundreds of millions of dollars worth of highway and road projects, including the twinning of the Trans-Canada Highway between Halifax and Moncton, and large-scale expansions to the bridge network linking Montreal and its fast-growing south shore. In May 2003, Ottawa and the Klein government in Alberta announced two massive undertakings: ring roads around Calgary and Edmonton, worth half a billion dollars in total. As with Montreal's bridges, the objective, according to the federal press release, is to "reduce congestion." The result will be just the opposite. New suburban highways attract and concentrate traffic, which is why they clog up so quickly once they are built. The irony is that when former Vancouver mayor Mike Harcourt co-chaired the federally appointed National Round Table on the Environment and the Economy, the group recommended that Ottawa cease all federal funding of highways, except for the Trans-Canada.[17]

Paying the Price

The long-term consequences of such development patterns is that we're building wasteful, unhealthy, and inefficient cities that are virtually programmed to squander that ultimate in non-renewable resources: time.

The calculus of sprawl-induced waste isn't difficult to understand. Take the case of two neighbourhoods with an identical number of homes, one with 6-metre-wide lots, the other with 12-metre-wide lots. For the latter, garbage trucks have to travel twice as far to gather the same amount of trash. The pipes bringing in water and taking away sewage need to be twice as long. You need twice as much pavement for the roads, and the snow clearance equipment has double the area to cover. And so on. More generally, municipalities provide only so many community centres, libraries, parks, and schools for a given population, so in low-density neighbourhoods, these amenities are farther apart. Water has to be pumped farther, arterial roads have to extend over greater distances, police and firefighters have to patrol larger areas and expend more gasoline in the process. Transit is disadvantaged from the start because the sprawling suburban layout makes it uneconomic for municipal agencies to provide timely and affordable service.

Since the mid-1950s, in fact, economists on both sides of the Canada-U.S. border have been documenting the incremental cost to the public purse associated with urban sprawl, and the numbers are nothing if not sobering. In 1974, a landmark U.S.-government analysis, "The Cost of Sprawl," found that the overall per-unit costs for low-density subdivisions could be as much as 40 percent greater than for high-density neighbourhoods. In 1994, the Canada Mortgage and Housing Corporation (CMHC) measured the savings that would have resulted if one of Ottawa's typically developed suburban neighbourhoods had been built out in a more compact fashion. The result: a 16 percent savings on the capital expenditures associated with development. The CMHC also discovered that if homes were clustered rather than evenly spaced throughout a subdivision, the cost of providing municipal services would drop by 15 percent.[18] The paradox is that in a landscape dedicated to consumerism, suburban municipalities—and builders— have consistently failed to take advantage of the clear economies of scale associated with higher-density development. If municipalities were private corporations, their shareholders would have turfed the managers long ago for failing to squeeze the most value out of costly assets such as water pumping systems and roads.

Dire warnings about sprawl's financial cost to taxpayers were the focus of the Greater Toronto Area Task Force, which delivered its report to the Ontario government in 1996, and several studies since then, by various government agencies, banks, and think-tanks. The conclusions are strikingly similar and were summed up by the Pembina Institute, an Alberta-based environmental think-tank, in 2003: "There has been increasing concern among local governments regarding the long-term costs and sustainability of the infrastructure associated with the region's current forms of development. These require the extension of sewer and water systems, roads, and other infrastructure over greater and greater distances, while providing a tax base inadequate to support this infrastructure's construction and long-term maintenance. It has been estimated that $55 billion in new infrastructure will be required in the GTA over the next 25 years if present development patterns continue, with an additional $14 billion required in operating costs."[19]

It's not just a public finance issue. Steadily worsening traffic congestion in the suburbs takes a troublingly large bite out of the urban economy. Gridlock translates into lost work hours by stressed-out employees who have seen their driving time rise by as much as 25 percent because of chronic traffic jams and long commutes (see table below).

DENSITY, CAR OWNERSHIP, AND DRIVING PATTERNS

	Toronto: Core	Core Ring	Inner Suburbs	Outer Suburbs
Residential density (persons per square kilometre)	7340	5830	2810	1830
% of households with one or more cars	49	75	87	96
Travel by car (kilometre/person/ day)	7.5	10.2	15	25.6

Ken Ogilvie, *Air, Soil and Water Quality* (Toronto: Neptis Foundation, 2003), 7. Reprinted with permission.

For industry, the consequences can be equally extreme. In today's just-in-time, truck-oriented manufacturing environment, export-minded companies rely on timely shipments of goods and parts, while mass merchandisers depend on the massive distribution depots that have become a common feature of suburban industrial districts. All of these firms require ready access to efficient arterial roads and highways. They contribute to sprawl themselves because the ubiquitous concrete-pad-and-steel frame warehouses they utilize require large swaths of serviced real estate. Municipalities and provincial governments are loath to place land-use constraints on such private investments because they want to promote economic activity and job creation. Yet, there is clearly a cost that hasn't been taken into account. As TD Bank economists have estimated, GTA companies alone lose $2 billion annually because of shipping delays, and they warn that similar problems await Calgary firms if that city's congestion continues to worsen.

If sprawl inflicts a steep price on public and private sector activity, it also takes a toll on the household finances of families who have settled in increasingly car-dependant suburbs. With world oil shortages pushing up the price of gas, the car-oriented suburban lifestyle has become an economic millstone. Because transit is much less viable in outlying areas, suburban families typically maintain two or more vehicles, which tend to be large and well used because the distances between home, work, school, recreation, and shopping are so great. The newer the suburb, the greater the car-related expenses, because more recent subdivisions are even more dispersed and disconnected than those built in the 1960s and 1970s. Similarly, the enticingly spacious suburban home—which is promoted as less expensive per square foot than comparably priced downtown dwellings—is in fact costlier to operate over the long run: Electricity and gas bills tend to be higher because there is more space to heat or cool.

Add it all up, and the financial burden of suburban living starts to look a lot less appealing. In 2002, for example, the average vehicle cost almost $6300 a year to operate (including payments, maintenance, insurance, and fuel)—equivalent to 12 cents per kilometre. And because fuel costs are the largest—and fastest-rising—component of vehicle-related ownership expenses, it's obvious that people who do a lot of driving will pay more as energy prices rocket upward. The relationship between cars, suburbia, and personal finances was laid bare in a study about low-density Houston. There, the average family devoted 22 percent of the total household budget to vehicle costs, while only 16 percent of spending went to shelter expenses such as mortgage payments and renovations. So far, Canadians haven't become nearly that financially indentured to their automobiles. A 2001 Canadian study found that 19 percent of family expenditures went into housing, while vehicles gobbled up 13 percent and food costs represented another 11 percent.[20] But if suburban sprawl continues unabated and gas prices remain stratospheric, Canadian families will face a future of daunting, Houston-style car bills.

Breathing Space

The case against urban sprawl becomes even more damning when we begin to consider its deleterious effects on our health. For much of the 20th century, however, suburban living was seen in precisely the opposite light. The earliest Garden City suburbs were developed to provide families with a healthy and wholesome environment in which to raise children. They offered respite from the polluted, chaotic downtowns of 19th-century industrial cities, which had no greenery, bad air, contaminated water, and excessive crowding.

But each wave of outward development made city-dwellers that much more dependent on cars, and we have finally reached a point where our extreme reliance on automobiles has produced unexpected health afflictions that are increasingly tied to sedentary urban and suburban lifestyles.

The indicators are disturbing. A 2003 survey of 1400 Ontario adults by the University of Toronto's Centre for Addiction and Mental Health found that the incidents of road rage were "more likely" to occur in the Greater Toronto Area, with its heavy traffic. Individuals with underlying cardiovascular conditions are almost three times more likely to have a heart attack while they're weaving through gridlock or immediately afterward, according to a study of German drivers conducted between 1999 and 2001.[21] And about 3000 Canadians die in traffic accidents each year. To put that number into context, it's six times the country's total homicide rate. (In the United States, the accident death toll is a staggering 42,000 people). As University of Toronto transportation experts Eric Miller and Richard Soberman point out, "It is inconceivable that we would tolerate this level of carnage from any other piece of technology and yet we do so from automobiles virtually without comment."[22]

Beyond these road safety issues, North American society's driving habits are increasingly linked to what has been described as an epidemic of obesity and diabetes, especially among children and teens. In the United States, about one in three adults is drastically overweight, while in Canada, the rate is 23 percent—somewhat less, but definitely on the rise as we also become an ever more suburban country.

According to Statistics Canada, the proportion of obese children almost tripled between 1979 and 2004.[23] Obesity is associated with heart attacks, diabetes, respiratory and circulatory illnesses, elevated cholesterol, and high blood pressure. In the United States, obesity kills the equivalent of a population the size of Saskatoon's every year. Health experts have begun to predict that Americans may soon see a decline in life expectancy—reversing more than a century of gains.

For many years, physicians and nutritionists associated obesity and poor diet with poverty and low education. It's also connected to inactivity, excessive television viewing, super-sized food portions, and a diet of sugary, fatty junk foods.

In 2004, however, a team of researchers from the University of British Columbia (UBC), Simon Fraser University (SFU), and Atlanta's Centers for Disease Control and Prevention (CDC) estab-lished a strong relationship between urban form and weight.[24] Urbanists and transit advocates had long decried sprawl-oriented land-use planning, while health experts had shown the benefits of walking and cycling. But until then, no one had managed to put it all together. UBC planner Lawrence Frank, SFU geographer Martin Andresen, and CDC nutrition expert Thomas Schmid decided to focus on a city infamous for its sprawl: Atlanta. Their team inter-viewed almost 11,000 people from the Greater Atlanta area, taking care to account for family size, income, and the density of the respon-dent's neighbourhood, measured in households per square kilometre.

Then they crunched property tax assessment data and analyzed the level of "connectivity" in given communities to quantify whether their subjects lived in walkable neighbourhoods with a range of amenities or in areas that required residents to drive most places. They produced two city maps, colour-coded by land-use categories, to demonstrate their point—which wasn't hard to miss, even if you don't happen to be a planner or geographer. The map of the "disconnected" part of the city

showed winding streets and was mostly one hue, the colour correspon-
ding to "single-family residential." The "connected" map—covering an
area the same size as the disconnected one—displayed the more traditional grid pattern, with plenty of intersecting streets, arterials, and small
blocks. As for the land uses, it looked like a quilt made of swatches in all
the colours of the rainbow: single-family homes, apartment buildings,
stores, offices, industrial districts, institutions, parks—all cheek by jowl.
This is what urban geographers imagine when they talk about mixed
use, and you don't tend to find much of it in sprawling suburbs, where
planners have ensured that land uses are rigidly separated.

What these researchers found shouldn't come as much of a surprise.
They showed that as the degree of land-use mix fell, the likelihood of
obesity grew. The team also discovered that the longer someone spent
sitting in a car each day, the greater his or her chance of being overweight. Likewise, the farther someone walked each day, the less likely
he or she was to be obese. Shockingly, over 90 percent of the people
who participated said they hadn't walked at all during the two days
preceding the survey interview. Frank, Andresen, and Schmid admitted
they couldn't directly prove that low-density suburban sprawl on its
own causes obesity. There are, of course, plenty of downtowners who
love their Big Macs. But their research demonstrated what the residents
of more compact downtown neighbourhoods know in their bones:
that if you don't have to take the car absolutely everywhere, you won't,
and you'll be healthier as a result.

The truly curious point about our unabated addiction to sprawl is
that the obvious consequences of these development patterns conflict
with some of our most broadly based civic values. Canadians want their
governments to be fiscally responsible, yet we build cities that squander
public finances. We want a cradle-to-grave public health care system,
but we have created urban environments that encourage unhealthy
lifestyles. And while we say we want to live in clean neighbourhoods,
we have taken to building our cities in ways that devour non-renewable
resources and inflict serious damage to the environment within which
we must exist. It's a picture that makes less and less sense with each
new subdivision.

WASTEFUL CITIES

If suburbia has a defining condition, it is size. The farther away you get from downtown, the larger things get: roads, stores, homes, malls, vehicles, parking lots, factories, even shopping carts. In a large country, the urban frontier, by definition, lacks space constraints, and our consumption habits have expanded accordingly.

In the 1970s, William Rees, the former director of the University of British Columbia's School of Regional and Community Planning, introduced the concept of an ecological footprint to describe the amount of land, water, mineral resources, and energy required to support an individual's lifestyle. He eventually showed a stark contrast between northern and southern nations. "When we compare the ecological footprints of individuals among countries," he said, "they vary by a factor of twenty, from less than a hectare in a very poor country such as Bangladesh, to 10 or perhaps even 12 hectares in a country like the United States."[1]

Canada, as it turns out, has the world's third-largest ecological footprint. Our per capita production of municipal solid waste is 350 kilograms per year—substantially lower than the OECD average of 540 kilograms and less than half of the U.S. figure (760 kilograms).[2] On the other hand, we love to waste water because we have so much of it, and we use a great deal of paper, for the same reason. Energy is another sore point. Canada has one of the world's worst records for energy consumption. But Rees's analysis also proved that the cities with the largest ecological footprints are the least compact. Using a wide range of data (e.g., income, commuting times, and household expenditures), a report by the Federation of Canadian Municipalities pegged the Canadian average at 7.25 hectares per capita.

Yet in low-density cities such as Edmonton, Calgary, Ottawa, and the GTA suburbs of Peel, Halton, and York, the per capita ecological footprint is as much as a third higher.[3]

In other words, sprawl is directly tied to higher consumption levels. That may be good news for economists and manufacturers, but these unsustainable urban development patterns have precipitated a vicious cycle of environmental degradation that is eroding the quality of life in the very places where our economic future will be made or broken.

Not so long ago, environmentalists focused on rural issues such as clear-cutting, habitat loss, and acid rain. But increasingly it has become clear that the future of the environment—even in remote areas such as the Arctic—depends on the way our cities function, or don't. Atmospheric warming is a global dilemma with potentially catastrophic repercussions that extend from the polar ice caps to the flood-prone coastal areas of south Asia. But for most Canadians, the implementation of the Kyoto Protocol—the international treaty that urges signatory nations to reduce their greenhouse gas (GHG) emissions to 5 percent below 1990 levels by 2012—is, in large measure, an urban air-quality issue. Why? Because the lion's share of Canada's GHGs come from the transportation and energy sectors, both of which are directly connected to the growth of our cities.

The National Round Table on the Environment and the Economy has said that "getting cities right" will be Canada's most significant contribution to the cause of global sustainable development. At the moment, however, we are doing anything but.

The New Endangered Species: Water, Rocks, and Soil

Cities can't exist without a reliable source of water. Recent water contamination crises—in Walkerton, Ontario, where seven people died in May 2000 after negligent officials allowed E. coli bacteria to find its way into the drinking water, and also in Saskatoon and on many Native reserves—illustrate the critical importance of professionally managed municipal filtration and purification systems. Such incidents have prompted all levels of government to begin investing billions of dollars in new water and waste water infrastructure.

While such investments are evidently necessary and sell well politically, they deal with only part of our growing water problems.
Hydrologists have begun to understand how sprawl lowers the water
table and places intolerable stress on other water sources and ecosystems. When rural land is converted into subdivisions, malls, and office
parks, a great deal of it is paved over, triggering sharp increases in
surface runoff.[4] Recent U.S. studies have shown that in low-density
car-dependent suburbs, as much as 60 percent of the impermeable
surfaces involve transportation uses (i.e., parking lots, driveways, and
streets). Instead of trickling into the soil where it is filtered and recycled through the ecosystem, rain water runoff, mixed with various
pollutants such as leaking gas, ends up in storm sewers that drain into
nearby lakes, rivers, or oceans.[5] Groundwater levels drop, causing
wetlands and streams to dry up—hydrological symptoms that become
visible after just 10 percent of a given area is paved over.[6]

In the late 1980s and early 1990s, former Toronto mayor David
Crombie, as chairperson of a royal commission on the city's waterfront,
began urging municipalities and provincial agencies to take watersheds
into consideration when making regional land-use planning decisions—a sea-change in how we think about development policy. While
municipalities and other agencies have made some moves in this
direction, business-as-usual suburban development continues to inflict
extreme pressure on hydrologic features.

The mismanagement of gravel-mining operations is another illus-
tration of how sprawl-oriented development practices are gobbling
up non-renewable natural resources. All cities rely on gravel deposits
to provide the key ingredients for the massive amounts of concrete
and asphalt used in road and highway construction and commercial
development. Builders, municipalities, and provincial agencies want
access to low-cost aggregates. In heavily urbanized Ontario, gravel-
mining firms enjoy a virtual carte blanche and face only cursory
regulation,[7] meaning that companies, municipalities, and provincial
agencies can buy aggregate products at artificially reduced prices.
These customers therefore have less financial motive to promote
compact development. Nor is there much incentive to explore ways

of recycling construction debris. In the United Kingdom, where there is a shortage of aggregate and considerably less space, the government has imposed a Can$4 levy on each metric tonne of aggregate, and the industry there plows the money into aggregate recycling programs that ease the pressure on both gravel quarries and municipal landfill sites. In Ontario, the provincial levy is four cents.

If we're taking gravel for granted, sprawl represents an even more direct threat to the Class One farm land that surrounds most large cities. Many Canadians would balk at the proposition that farmland is a scarce resource. After all, there are the Prairies, breadbasket to the Western world. But Statistics Canada, in a January 2005 study, debunked the myth that Canada has unlimited agricultural resources. Only 5 percent of Canada's land mass is arable. Between 1971 and 2001, urbanization gobbled up 152,000 square kilometres of farmland, an area that's three times the size of Prince Edward Island.[8]

The pressures were particularly pronounced in southern Ontario, in British Columbia's Lower Fraser River Valley, and along the Calgary-Edmonton corridor. In fact, Statistics Canada found that urban areas sit atop 7.5 percent of Canada's best agricultural land. Developers know that municipalities tend to rubber-stamp new subdivisions, so they quietly buy up adjacent farmland on the reasonable assumption that they can persuade local politicians to rezone it. Farmers, in turn, have an enormous financial incentive to sell to developers and then retire on the proceeds. It's a cycle of land consumption that's exceedingly difficult to break, but one that makes Canadian city-dwellers ever more dependent on imported food. "Once consumed," the authors of the study warn, "this land is, for all intents and purposes, permanently lost for agriculture."[9]

Gasping for Air

Of all the sprawl-related environmental concerns that have begun to seriously erode urban quality of life, none resonates quite as troublingly as the precipitous decline in air quality. According to some epidemiologists, outdoor air quality has become, quite literally, lethal. In July 2004, Toronto Public Health officials released a study that concluded that five key air pollutants "contribute to about 1,700 premature deaths and 6,000 hospitalizations each year in Toronto."[10] The Ontario Medical Association (OMA) has estimated the provincial air pollution–related death toll to be about 5800 people. The OMA says the cost is now in excess of $1 billion a year because of direct medical expenditures and lost working time.[11]

The health problems run the gamut, from minor eye and throat irritation to asthma attacks, pneumonia, chronic bronchitis, and even cancer. Bad air days exacerbate pre-existing heart and lung conditions such as emphysema. Then there is something particularly insidious called "reduced lung capacity." Spend enough time outside on a bad air day and the tissue in the lungs swells and remains swollen for as long as 24 hours. Even those quintessential urban warriors—the bike couriers—are getting concerned.

Poor air quality, of course, is hardly a new environmental problem for city-dwellers. A century ago, the air in cities was heavy with airborne soot and heavy metals from industrial smokestacks and chimneys. Then, during the post-war decades, thousands of young Canadian families bought their first cars to round out a comfortable middle-class suburban lifestyle. Those automobiles, however, spewed black exhaust laden with toxic pollutants, especially lead. Since the late 1970s, with the introduction of lead-free gas and more effective vehicle exhaust systems, there has been a marked improvement in tailpipe emissions. Between 1979 and 1996, the concentration of nitrogen dioxide and carbon monoxide fell steadily in urban areas, in spite of increases in the numbers of cars.

North Americans, however, spend about 90 percent of their time indoors, often in sealed environments or buildings with ventilation systems that leave much to be desired. Poor urban children are especially prone to respiratory illness because they often live too close to major arterial roads, bus routes, or in substandard housing with mould infestation, rodent droppings, and inadequate ventilation. Overcrowded schools rely on damp portables. And the air inside new homes filled with synthetic textiles can be redolent of chemical fumes produced by volatile organic compounds. Little wonder that the incidence of childhood asthma has been rising steadily.[12]

What is more, in recent years, concerns over outdoor air quality have taken a new twist, one that directly connects global warming to highly urban-specific issues such as sprawl and local energy-consumption trends. Across Canada, the release of air pollutants with suspected respiratory effects jumped by 25 percent between 1995 and 2003. Alberta, with its booming oil and gas sector, actually led the country in 2003 in terms of overall releases.

In this same period, Ontario endured a disturbing 64 percent increase in the release of toxic pollutants.[13] By 2005, Greater Toronto and southwestern Ontario were experiencing an unprecedented number of smog days—not just in the summer but also in the winter. Part of the problem can be traced to emissions from industrialized Midwest states, where power plants burn coal. But Ontario's sprawling urban areas severely exacerbate poor air quality. The proliferation of vehicular traffic is responsible for the lion's share of greenhouse gas emissions, which trap heat in the atmosphere.

The result is a steady increase in smog as well as ground-level ozone, formed when nitrous oxides react with volatile organic compounds in the presence of sunlight. Smog is now considered to be at problematic levels in B.C.'s Lower Mainland, along the entire Windsor–Quebec City corridor, and in the southern parts of Atlantic Canada. Some cities have worse air than others: While Vancouver has seen significant decreases in the presence of air pollutants since 1990, Montreal, with all its heavy industry, experienced a 55 percent increase in airborne lead between 1990 and 1998. The concentration of tiny airborne particles, known as $PM_{2.5}$ and PM_{10}, was dropping until the mid-1980s, but it has held steady ever since. These minuscule particles—a stew of acid aerosols, organic chemicals, smoke, metal fumes, fly ash, dust, and pollen—irritate respiratory systems, but there is not much you can do to avoid them.[14]

Why did urban air quality stop improving in the 1990s? The beginning of the decade marked the moment when minivans and then SUVs became the vehicles of choice for many city-dwellers. The baby boomers were spending long hours on congested roads, ferrying themselves and their young families between work, school, home, and shopping centres. In urban environments with an abundance of parking spaces, wide streets, and few alternatives for getting around, it's hardly surprising that they took to vehicles that made all that drive time a bit more comfortable. There is a reason why minivans are now fitted out with DVD players: The quick dash to the store has given way to long-haul journeys—the commuting equivalent of the trans-Atlantic flight.

Because of a U.S. regulatory loophole, such light trucks were exempted from passenger-vehicle emission rules. But these vehicles are gas guzzlers that emit about 40 percent more greenhouse gases than ordinary cars. And there are, of course, a great many of them in Canada today. Their numbers doubled during the 1990s, to almost 6.5 million. During the same period, our entire vehicle fleet grew by less than 25 percent, and the number of cars actually fell slightly. In slightly more than a decade, in other words, we completely changed our car-buying habits. But there has been a hefty environmental cost to our sprawl-linked consumer choices: Minivans and SUVs accounted for two-thirds of the total growth in GHG emissions from all Canadian vehicles between 1990 and 2002.

Drivers aren't the only culprits, of course. Huge industrial operations continue to pump hundreds of millions of kilograms of pollutants into the air each year and account for about a quarter of Canada's total emissions. But a growing number of companies are installing equipment to reduce the release of traditional smokestack pollutants. The GHG emissions from Canada's manufacturing and construction sector remain at precisely the same level they were in 1990, despite all the post–free trade economic growth. The fact is that if we want someone to blame for bad air, we must look in the mirror. The 80 percent of Canadians who now live in metropolitan areas account for about half of all greenhouse gas emissions, thanks to the vehicles they drive and the power they use. Cars produce more GHGs than Canada's entire manufacturing sector, while minivans and SUVs generate six times as much as the chemical industry (see table on the next page).

Addicted to Energy

Anyone who spends a lot of time stuck in traffic—by choice or neces-sity—grasps the relationship between driving and air quality. Those who

**GREENHOUSE GAS EMISSION SOURCES BY SECTOR
(2002, MEGA-TONNE CO$_2$ EQUIVALENT)**

Canadian total	731,000
Electricity and heat generation	348,000
Fossil fuel industries (refineries, etc.)	129,000
Transportation (all categories of vehicles)	137,000
Cars	50,200
Light trucks (minivans, SUVs)	40,900
Waste incinerators	350
Chemical industry	8,300
Manufacturing industries	49,000

Canada's Greenhouse Gas Inventory, 1990–2002, EPS 5/AP/10, Greenhouse Gas Division, August 2004, cat. no. En49-5/5-10-2-2002E, ISBN 0-66237819-9. Reproduced with the permission of the Minister of Public Works and Government Services Canada, 2006. © Her Majesty the Queen in Right of Canada, represented by the Minister of the Environment 2004. All rights reserved.

live near areas with heavy industry can see, and smell, the smokestacks and the billowing releases. But the connection between electricity use and air quality remains far less well understood. Yet, the fact is that power consumption has emerged as one of the major culprits in the rapid decline of urban air quality.

Why? One answer is that we build cities that function like huge heat sinks: Immense swaths of asphalt pavement and fabricated building materials absorb the sun's rays, while overdevelopment has destroyed natural sources of ambient cooling, such as woodlots and wetlands. Homeowners cut down trees to make room for pad parking on their front yards and then refuse to allow the city to plant replacement saplings because they don't like to rake leaves. Our dwellings are inadequately insulated, meaning that we need a lot of extra power to heat our houses properly. Developers bulldoze everything before putting up tract housing, creating neighbourhoods completely bereft of shade. Absent nature's own cooling and air purification systems (woodlots, wetlands, and so on), our cities crave air conditioning, which drives up electricity consumption.

When our power usage finally noses above the existing supply, as happens with increasing frequency in some larger urban centres, utilities have to import electricity generated by U.S. coal-fired power plants, thus contributing to the endless invisible clouds of smog that drift north across the border.[15] Five of Canada's 10 worst air polluters in 2003 were utilities, according to Pollution Watch.[16] In most parts of Canada, our electricity needs were traditionally met by abundant sources of (relatively) clean power: hydro-electric dams in British Columbia and Quebec, and the combination of nuclear and hydro power in Ontario. But chronic technical failings in Ontario's electricity system had a huge negative impact on air quality in the densely popu- lation parts of southern Ontario in the latter 1990s. In any period of intense economic growth, the demand for electricity grows. Yet, during the late 1990s, several of Ontario's nuclear reactors were laid up. To compensate, provincial power authorities stoked up Ontario's dirty coal-fired power plants. Between 2002 and 2003, Ontario Power Generation saw its pollutant emissions skyrocket by 20 percent.[17]

It's not just an Ontario issue. In the past decade, British Columbia, Alberta, and Quebec also experienced mounting pressure on their ability to supply power to their urban populations, meaning that several provinces grew more reliant on electricity imports—often from polluting coal-fired power plants—since the early 1990s.[18] Runaway demand for electricity has triggered brownouts and appeals from polit- ical leaders that consumers switch off the lights, run major appliances at night rather than during peak daytime hours, and turn down the air conditioner or the heaters. The point is that a commodity Canadians once considered to be clean and virtually limitless has turned out to be anything but—a point brought home most forcefully in August 2003, when a blackout triggered by a malfunctioning Ohio transmission line brought Toronto and much of the Golden Horseshoe to a standstill.

The One-Tonne Punchline

The grim reality is that Canada has been falling behind its international trading partners on air quality. Between 1995 and 2003, the United States saw its air pollution emission levels fall by almost half, while we managed to bring them down by a paltry 2 percent. "In many ways," says Rick Smith of Pollution Watch, "George Bush's America is doing a much better job cleaning up pollution than our own country." For many regions, he continues, "smog days are the new normal."[19]

Our reputation now precedes us. In a 2004 report, the OECD rapped Canada for continuing to tolerate "unacceptable air quality."[20] The report's authors pointed out that our pollution sources—especially the mining and smelting industry—rank among the worst in the OECD. Ontario is routinely fingered as North America's third most polluting jurisdiction. And despite a 1991 Canada-U.S. agreement to reduce ozone levels (the target is to bring it down by 44 percent by 2010), there are no penalties for non-compliance and the government hasn't yet figured out how to measure which parts of the country are making progress and which aren't.

Part of the problem is that our national air pollution laws are essentially toothless. Under the Canadian Environmental Protection Act, the maximum penalty for contravening air pollution regulations is a $1-million fine. South of the border, the Clean Air Act, which was originally passed in 1970, gives federal regulators far more leverage to go after large polluters. In October 2005, ExxonMobil agreed to spend more than half a billion dollars to reduce toxic emissions at its U.S. refineries, as well as pay out almost $20 million in civil penalties and contributions to community projects near its plants. Such hardnosed regulation is virtually unheard of in Canada.

But its absence is not just a symptom of lax legislation. Federal and provincial fuel taxes, though higher than U.S. rates, remain "significantly lower" than those in most developed countries and haven't changed substantially for a decade, according to the OECD.[21] Ottawa has been gradually tightening up regulations on fuel standards and additives, as have many countries. But federal regulations to reduce the emission of harmful substances, such as benzene and sulphur in diesel fuel, are tied closely to those of the United States and lag well behind standards imposed by the European Union. So while the observed levels of noxious pollutants in big cities remain below existing standards, Toronto Public Health officials say these benchmarks are simply too lax when it comes to acceptable levels of ozone, PM2.5, and nitrous oxides.

Our global warming programs are also tainted by tentativeness. In its spring 2005 budget, Paul Martin's Liberal government proposed a $5-billion spending spree designed to help Canada implement the Kyoto Protocol. Fronting the package was comedian Rick Mercer, the face of Ottawa's One-Tonne Challenge campaign. Although the Liberals were aiming for a high-profile celebrity to kick-start a difficult policy initiative, the joke was on us. Ottawa's implementation strategy will do little to get Canada anywhere close to the elusive and unrealistic Kyoto target. It was another strike against Canada's spotty record on improving urban air quality.

Ottawa's approach to Kyoto was marked by hedges. Canada's GHG emissions are 20 percent above 1990s levels and growing, but the federal government, concerned about harming the economy and alienating Alberta, refused to adopt tough-minded measures, such as imposing a "carbon tax" on fossil fuels. Ottawa did succeed in negotiating a cautious pact with the auto industry to reduce GHG emissions by 5.3 mega-tonnes by 2010 (or 4 percent of Canada's total output), as well as improve fuel efficiency. But that target was a good deal less ambitious than the 25 percent reduction originally envisioned in Ottawa's Kyoto plans.

The political reality of the Canadian confederation—which was amply borne out by the negotiations over Kyoto—is that provincial governments control many of the policy levers that determine urban air quality. They build most highways, finance regional transit, regulate urban planning, levy fines on industrial polluters, test vehicles for emission performance, and create conservation strategies. Provincial building codes—hardly a sexy environmental topic—have the potential to bring about meaningful air-quality improvements if they were written to require all new buildings to incorporate state-of-the-art insulation, materials, and energy systems designed to reduce power consumption. But they aren't. Energy rates are another example. Provincial officials exert almost total domination over the electricity system, determining how and where power is produced, and setting rates that either encourage or discourage conservation. There is little question that in some heavily urbanized areas, especially southern Ontario, a generation of ill-considered provincial energy policies have left us gasping for air.

The relentless upward push of energy prices should be telling us that we've reached a turning point in our urban history. Canadians now need to rethink many of the most basic assumptions about urban living, and plan our cities so they become more compact, less wasteful, and thus sustainable in their growth patterns. In fact, contemporary history shows that periods of drastic environmental deterioration have triggered far-reaching reforms in the way cities organize themselves and conceive of their futures. The intolerable air pollution, filth, and disease that characterized 19th-century industrial cities unleashed revolutions in thinking about urban planning, public health, technology, and social reform. At the dawn of the 21st century, Canada's urban environmental crisis focuses on rapidly deteriorating air quality, the localized symptoms of warming, and the overconsumption of energy. The inhabitants of Canada's large cities must respond imaginatively and proactively, or resign themselves to the fact that their urban environments will soon cease to be livable places.

PART TWO

HEALTHY NEIGHBOURHOODS, STRONG CITIES

Like every country, Canada has its foundational myths. Once we were hewers of wood and drawers of water—a cold, remote colony organized around its natural resources and the iconic railroads that transported all those logs, grains, and minerals to industrial cities, with their mills, factories, and ports. The colonizing powers left their descendants with a bifurcated linguistic, legal, and cultural inheritance, dubbed the "two solitudes" in 1945 by Montreal novelist Hugh MacLennan. For all our divisions, we nonetheless eschewed America's revolutionary, religious, and imperial fervour in favour of a pragmatic, if somewhat inefficient, political culture, one calibrated to the needs of our vast, underpopulated country.

As we head into the 21st century, most of the original stereotypes simply no longer apply. The two solitudes are rural and urban as much as French and English. Almost half of the country lives in just six metropolitan regions. Canada's Natives are increasingly city-dwellers. Our large cities trade more with their southern urban neighbours than one another. The two founding ethnic groups have ceded their social pre-eminence in cities that are evolving into relentlessly multicultural, multilingual global hubs whose economic destiny is tied not to the land but to knowledge, commerce, culture, and trade.

Like all small nations perched on the edge of expansionist empires, we've been compelled to develop a hardy survival gene. This takes the form of a bloody-minded determination to carve out an alternative way of conducting our public affairs within the confines of a highly integrated North American economy.

The relative well-being of our big cities is a testament to this independent spirit. But as we saw in Part One, Canada's large urban regions are showing worrisome symptoms of the fraying of the social safety net that has occurred since the early 1990s. At the same time, it's become increasingly clear that quality of life and social cohesion play a vital role in sustaining an urban-based economy. The point, as Canada's federal, provincial, and municipal leaders have begun to recognize, is that we need to forge a new generation of social policies tailored to a heavily urbanized nation, one whose destiny lies more with the abilities of its city-dwellers than with the wealth of its hinterland. Canada's urban agenda, in fact, begins not with finding more money for roads and bridges but by rebuilding the social infrastructure— schools, child care, resettlement services, housing—needed to hold our big cities together.

CONNECTING IMMIGRANTS AND GOOD JOBS

In his home country of Zimbabwe, Tim Simba was a young man on a fast track to professional success. He had attended high school in the United Kingdom and studied microbiology at university in South Africa. After graduation, he worked for two multinational consumer products giants—Nestlé and Unilever—and later rounded out his post-secondary education by obtaining an MBA. He held senior management positions in a Botswana firm and then a Zimbabwean retail chain, where he oversaw marketing and branding. From there, he moved to Uganda and launched a cellular network.

But when the soft-spoken 46-year-old immigrated to Canada, he sent out 3000 applications, got responses to just 10, and no takers. Why? He had no Canadian experience. To make ends meet, he took a position at a call centre in a Toronto suburb—what those who work in the skills training industry colloquially refer to as "survivor jobs."

Thousands of new Canadians living in big cities face precisely the same situation. Many barely eke out a living wage, but not because they are unwilling or unable to work. About 58 percent of working-age immigrants who arrived in 2001 and 2002 landed jobs within two years of arriving, according to Statistics Canada. But a disturbingly low proportion—33 percent—found work in their chosen field within a year of arriving.[1] It shouldn't be so difficult to connect new Canadians with decent jobs, particularly if they are well educated and willing to work and learn. The bottom line is that if our governments want to maintain or increase immigration levels, they will have to work much harder to provide properly funded local settlement and language-training programs, and then devise ways to collaborate with Canadian employers, professional bodies, and academic institutions to bring about a wholesale change in the way we recognize foreign credentials and work experience.

Settlement Services

Immigrants and refugees find one another in big cities: They congregate in certain neighbourhoods, publish newspapers, form community or cultural organizations, and set up schools. This is the social side of immigration. But resettlement agencies—small shoestring organizations that rely on government grants and fundraising to help newcomers get established—have long taken care of the meat-and-potatoes work of connecting immigrant communities to the rest of society. They arrange job skills and language-training courses, mentor partnerships, and even function as small employment agencies. In the blur and confusion most newcomers experience when they land in a foreign city, such organizations play an incredibly important bridging role.

In the late 1990s and early 2000s, however, immigration experts and municipal leaders discovered a strange skew in the federal funding for such agencies. While the GTA was absorbing half of all newcomers to Canada, Ontario received only 38 percent of federal funding for resettlement agencies.[2] Because of a long-standing agreement negotiated by the Mulroney Tories in the 1980s, Quebec's share was far more generous: $3800 per immigrant, compared with $800 for Ontario. "We didn't sign it," then Immigration minister Joe Volpe said of that deal. "It was done in a peculiar environment ... the impending collapse of Meech Lake ... when Brian Mulroney essentially made a deal with the province of Quebec that would leave anybody at any other time scratching their head."[3] In May 2005, after intense political pressure, Ottawa and Queen's Park agreed to a deal to boost funding for settlement agencies to about $3400 per person, thereby closing the gap with Quebec.

There is a lesson here. With Ottawa planning to further boost immigration levels in the near future, some provinces, including Nova Scotia and Manitoba, have begun to devise strategies to entice newcomers, who still overwhelmingly opt to settle in Montreal, Toronto, and Vancouver. Given that low-immigration provinces such as Alberta and Saskatchewan now have the most acute shortages of skilled workers, it's not difficult to imagine that we're about to see some shifts in immigration patterns; in fact, Alberta oil patch firms already recruit abroad to attract skilled workers and engineers. But when this happens, provincial governments will have to push Ottawa to ensure that the local resettlement service providers are properly funded.

This is an investment in the future of our cities, plain and simple. As a 2005 Royal Bank of Canada report entitled *The Diversity Advantage* warned, Canada's failure to "fully realize the potential of immigrants and women in the workplace is significant." How significant? "If foreign-born workers were as successful in the Canadian workforce as those born in the country, personal incomes would be about $13 billion higher each year than at present."[4]

Foreign Credentials

In 2003, Cesar Fabian Rodriguez and his wife, Lina Escorcia, encouraged by the Canadian government's website that appeared to welcome professionals, decided to flee the drug wars in Colombia and immigrate to Canada. Both in their 20s, they were dentists but had degrees in epidemiology and public health as well. They also had a young daughter. But when they arrived in Montreal, they soon discovered they would be allowed to practise only after retaking three years of dentistry courses, which they couldn't afford to do. The family wound up on welfare. They quickly realized they weren't alone. Rodriguez is a member of a group of other recent immigrants in the same straits: "We are about 35 people," he said. "There is an electrical engineer, a veterinarian, lawyers, teachers, photographers. They are from Romania, Chile, Argentina and Colombia. Everyone is very discouraged."[5]

Policy makers have been aware of this problem for years. In the late 1980s, the Liberal government in Ontario appointed a taskforce to investigate why professionally trained immigrants were having such a hard time finding work. York University law professor Peter Cumming, who chaired the taskforce, reviewed the certification requirements of

37 regulated professions and discovered that most had at least one ques-
tionable eligibility criterion—for example, a Canadian undergraduate
degree that culminated in high grades or Canadian work experience—
that served little purpose other than to keep the numbers down and
trained immigrant professionals from obtaining their papers. Another
member of the taskforce described some of these bodies—especially
those governing doctors, dentists, and engineers—as "cartels."[6] The net
effect: chronic shortages of ethnic professionals—lawyers, doctors, and
so on—with the language skills and cultural sensitivities needed to properly serve the rapidly growing ethnic communities in Canada's big cities.

The case of immigrant doctors is especially revealing. At a time when
many small and remote communities are suffering from acute shortages
of general practitioners and specialists, Canada's big cities have become
home to foreign-trained physicians who can't get their certification. In
Western Canada, it's not uncommon to find immigrant physicians
practising in small towns. It's a very different story in Central Canada.
In Ontario, a report written in the mid-1980s predicted an oversupply
of doctors, a finding that led to restrictions on the number of students
entering the medical training system. In 1997, the Royal College of
Physicians and Surgeons of Canada even discontinued the recognition
of post-graduate training programs completed outside North America.
Just three years later, the College of Physicians and Surgeons of Ontario
moved to confront this glaring disconnect by increasing assistance
for the licensing of internationally trained physicians. Despite that
move, foreign-trained doctors still face a severe shortage of residency
positions—just 50 annually for all of Ontario, as of 2001.[7]

There is little excuse for such largely artificial restrictions.
Throughout the 1990s, the question of how to recognize foreign
credentials drew ever more attention internationally. In the early 1990s,
the European Union and UNESCO began working on a convention
that provides for the reciprocal recognition of degrees and diplomas—
an agreement to which Canada is a signatory. The Council of Ministers
of Education, Canada, also set up something called the Canadian
Information Centre for International Credentials, while the federal and
provincial governments set up an intergovernmental working group. A
growing number of professional bodies—representing everyone from

midwives to respiratory therapists and physiotherapists—has established services that assess new immigrants' training gaps, while others, such as the Council for Access to the Profession of Engineering, have sprung up specifically to push their professional bodies to think about immigrant credentials differently. Various industry groups—such as the Canadian Aviation Maintenance Council, a human resources agency established in the early 1990s by Canada's aerospace manufacturers—have also set up credential assessment services.[8]

Just as industry organizations and professional bodies need to become more proactive, federal immigration procedures and foreign-service operations abroad must be reformed so that qualified immigrants are better prepared once they arrive. Canadian diplomatic missions should ensure that prospective immigrants have their qualifications assessed before travelling to Canada, and then begin filling in the gaps while they're waiting for the paperwork to be completed. There is a need for more bridging programs—that is, language training, technical upgrades, and information on Canadian workplace standards. And foreign graduate students should be granted landed immigrant status once they obtain their degrees from a recognized academic institution—a measure Simon Fraser University immigration expert Don DeVoretz describes as "costless" to Canadian taxpayers but one that would help them integrate into the workforce much more easily than if they were still in a bureaucratic queue.[9]

Lastly, Ottawa should be providing newcomers with low-cost loans to cover the costs of those bridging programs, credential assessment services, exam fees levied by professional organizations, and part-time academic upgrading, according to a 2002 report from the Caledon Institute of Social Policy.[10] It only makes sense; after all, Canada lends immigrants money to cover their transportation costs to get to Canada. Why wouldn't we take the next logical step and make sure they've got the wherewithal to upgrade their credentials once they arrive?

Mentoring and Apprenticeship Programs

In 2003, the Maytree Foundation and the Toronto City Summit Alliance launched the Toronto Regional Immigrant Employment

Council (TRIEC), a pioneering experiment designed to dismantle the obstacles facing well-trained newcomers. Headed by Manulife Financial CEO Dominic D'Alessandro and run by Ratna Omidvar, a veteran of one of Toronto's largest resettlement agencies, TRIEC pulled together a vast array of local players—universities and colleges, banks, GTA municipalities, government departments, foundations, unions, large corporations, and tiny social service agencies—to help connect newcomers with decent jobs. It's no accident that banks such as BMO and CIBC are involved: Federally chartered financial institutions have had to conform to employment equity laws for years and consequently have some of the country's most ethnically diverse workforces.

TRIEC has set up mentoring projects, programs designed to help employers recruit immigrants, and partnerships with public sector institutions, such as the City of Toronto, to make its own human resources departments more receptive to immigrants. The results are encouraging, but modest. In 2003–4, according to the organization's annual review, TRIEC found mentoring arrangements for 250 immigrants, and internships for 200 with 77 Toronto area employers. Of those, 85 percent found jobs in their chosen professions. These are good-news stories. Still, it's only a drop in the bucket. Each year, 100,000 immigrants come to the Toronto area, and 40,000 of them have at least one university degree.

Perhaps more importantly, TRIEC has emerged as an effective lobbying force. In the summer of 2004, D'Alessandro issued an open letter to Prime Minister Paul Martin calling for sweeping reforms to the way Ottawa handles immigration and resettlement. His wish list includes enhanced language instruction that prepares immigrants for the workforce, and reforms to the services provided by resettlement agencies, so they focus not just on basic needs but also labour market skills. As well, the organization has mounted public relations campaigns designed to shine a harsh light on Canada's failure to let its well-educated immigrants work in their own professions.

D'Alessandro and Omidvar insist that cities must drive these changes. Local institutions and agencies are closest to immigration-related social problems, while local employers have the clearest understanding of the urban labour force. "Place matters," says Omidvar. "The city-region has to have a clear mechanism for informing the federal government on the profile of the immigrants it needs. [Greater Toronto] desperately needs construction workers, pharmacists and doctors. We should have the capacity to tell the feds that these are the kinds of immigrants we need." Instead, she notes, Ottawa and the Ontario government still operate parallel bureaucracies that offer duplicate language and training programs, with little or no coordination: "We can't seem to get the right services to the people on the ground because we can't make up our minds about who should be responsible."[11]

That's going to have to take place if the federal government increases the immigration flows into Canada by as many as 100,000 newcomers annually, the vast majority of whom will continue to settle in our largest cities. The federal Liberals felt the solution to some of these issues entailed recalibrating the backlog-plagued immigration admission system. The government also wanted to move away from its policy of attracting professionals in order to bring in more temporary workers on visas to fill thousands of blue-collar jobs requiring specific technical skills. But at least as important are improved federal-provincial resettlement agreements, forward-looking sectoral training programs, and the role of multi-stakeholder agencies such as TRIEC in connecting the various players to one another.

Beyond all these measures, there is a critical choice hanging over the debate about how we reprogram our immigration system. Temporary workers are a short-term solution. As many commentators noted in the wake of the Paris riots in late 2005, the French government created a social powder keg in the barren suburbs of its big cities by creating an underclass of disenfranchised and poorly educated migrant workers. If our economic prosperity is tied to the growth of knowledge-based industries, there is little doubt that attracting well-educated immigrants, who value learning for themselves and their children, remains the best guarantee for the long-term social stability of our cities.

MAKING SPACE FOR URBAN ABORIGINALS

In 1998, the federal government made a splashy announcement about its relations with Canada's First Nations. Native issues had attracted Prime Minister Jean Chrétien's attention: An Indian Affairs minister in the 1970s, Chrétien had exempted First Nations programs from Martin's 1995 deficit reduction campaign. Indeed, since 1994, his government had introduced a hodgepodge of spending programs for housing, education, child nutrition, and so on. Then, having finally recognized that tens of thousands of Native Canadians were settling in a handful of large urban centres, federal officials decided it was time to repackage these programs as an "Urban Aboriginal Strategy." Just five years later, a Senate committee exposed the hollowness of this PR campaign when it revealed that just three cents of every dollar aimed at the Aboriginal community ended up in urban or off-reserve programs—a direct consequence of the fact that First Nations rights aren't portable. Aboriginals who leave the reserve for the city leave behind the federally funded programs and services nominally intended for their benefit.

Moreover, this long-standing federal policy has opened up a growing schism between urban First Nations groups, such as networks of Friendship Centres, and the band council leaders who dominate the Assembly of First Nations. In the latter 1990s, for example, Ottawa devolved responsibility for many Aboriginal programs to the Association of Manitoba Chiefs, then under Métis leader Phil Fontaine, as part of a self-government strategy.[1] Urban Aboriginal leaders, including the newly formed Aboriginal Council of Winnipeg, were left out of the negotiations. The Manitoba chiefs supported reforms that would make Indian Act benefits portable, starting with a $100-million, four-year program for child care, nutrition, counselling, and other programs unveiled by Jean Chrétien's Liberals in 1994.[2] But the Manitoba chiefs then decided to slash the value of the newly downloaded grants earmarked for Winnipeg's First Nations community from $6.2 million to $1.2 million. "With the stroke of a pen," commented the *Winnipeg Free Press,* "the federal commitment to aboriginals living in Winnipeg has been configured with no political input from the people who actually live here."[3]

In recent years, however, the legal and political balance of power between urban and non-urban Aboriginals has shifted sharply. In 1999, the Supreme Court issued a landmark ruling allowing off-reserve Aboriginals to vote in band council elections. Legal analysts, government officials, and First Nations leaders have all predicted that the Corbiere ruling will forever alter Aboriginal politics. How? Because the decision points to a prohibition of discrimination against off-reserve Aboriginals by band councils. "Once these elections happen, people who have a right to vote also have a right to expect benefits [and] services ... from their community," said an Assembly of First Nations spokesperson.[4] The Assembly of First Nations' then leader Matthew Coon Come said urban Aboriginals needed to have access to the same sorts of services provided on reserves. As the Senate committee concluded, "The increasing urbanization of Aboriginal people is amplifying these pressures towards the need for a new direction in policy development."[5]

As with the emergence of a new approach to immigrant resettlement, private sector partnerships—between Native organizations, business groups, and academic institutions—are an increasingly vital ingredient in the task of linking urban Aboriginal youth to promising careers and economic development initiatives. But it has also become apparent in recent years that the solutions to urban Aboriginal poverty, crime, and disenfranchisement depend on an integrated network of First Nations–run child welfare agencies, health and social services, and schools. This goal depends on a new approach to funding Aboriginal off-reserve services, as well as greater collaboration between Ottawa, the provincial governments, municipalities, and school boards.

Indeed, the politics of Aboriginal advocacy is undergoing a sea-change. Since 1990, urban-based First Nations councils have sprung up in Winnipeg, Vancouver, and Toronto. Their leaders are seeking to bring urban Aboriginal issues out of the closet and situate them in the middle of the wider debate about the future prosperity of Canada's big cities. Their determination, in fact, was put to the test as Ottawa, the 10 provinces, and First Nations leaders got down to work in late 2005 to begin implementing a five-year, $5-billion plan to improve the standard of living for Canada's far-flung Aboriginal community. The deal can truly succeed only if the two levels of government and the Assembly of First Nations decide to pay close attention to the conditions facing Aboriginal communities in Canada's largest cities.

Native-Run Services

Wayne Helgason has spent a career trying to reverse the social collapse of Winnipeg's Aboriginal community. His father was a military man from Iceland; his mother grew up just outside a reserve in Saskatoon. In 1982, fresh out of Carleton University with a degree in clinical psychology, he became one of the first two Aboriginal case workers at the Winnipeg Children's Aid Society (CAS), stationed at a north end public school in a very poor neighbourhood where many children lived in public housing projects. Ninety percent of the society's cases involved Aboriginals.

He had been hired after a Manitoba judge slammed the practices of the Winnipeg CAS, condemning the agency for scooping up Aboriginal children and sending them for adoption, in many cases, in the United States. "In the 1960s, this would happen regularly and no one confronted it," recalls Helgason, now executive director of the Social Planning Council of Winnipeg. In his job at CAS, he would meet women who had lost their children because they had no lawyer and no power; "15 or 20 years later, these kids started coming back with a history of abuse by the adoptive families."[6]

In his new job, Helgason asked the teachers and public health nurses which Aboriginal children were doing okay. Then he approached their parents and asked if they would be willing to offer up their homes to

Aboriginal children who had to be taken out of abusive domestic environments. Gradually, he built up a network of Aboriginal foster parents—community-oriented people who volunteered at the school and rewarded themselves with an evening of bingo once a week. He'd also have heartbreaking encounters with 15-year-old mothers who told him they couldn't look after their babies. "In many cases, it was an act of love," he recalls. "They were thinking that some capable family would do better. It was two of the hardest years I ever had."[7]

In the period that followed, the Winnipeg CAS was disbanded in an attempt to reform a system that had served Aboriginals so poorly. There was a growing recognition, too, that the extraordinarily high levels of Aboriginal incarceration—accounting for up to 80 percent of inmates in Winnipeg's jails—could be traced to abuses in the child welfare system.

About the same time, the Ontario government passed legislation that paved the way for the establishment in 1988 of Native Child and Family Services of Toronto, one of Canada's first Native-run child welfare agencies serving a large urban area. Besides traditional children's aid services, the organization offers early-years nursery schools and support programs for poor Aboriginal families. There are more than 70,000 Aboriginals in Toronto, and the city is also home to a number of well-established Native-run service organizations whose staff do everything from develop housing to form street patrols.

One is Na-Me-Res, which stands for "Native Men's Residence." The shelter is a smoky, photograph-filled, bunker-like building; the exterior walls are decorated with colourful Native designs and a large sign that cheerfully declares, "Celebrating 20,000 years in the neighbourhood."

The demand for its services has jumped in recent years. In 2002, Na-Me-Res opened a 52-bed youth shelter. It offers a drug- and alcohol-free environment for reserve kids who have drifted to Toronto. When it opened, says Greg Rogers, the former executive director, he anticipated an influx of Ojibwa and Mohawk youth from southern and central Ontario. Instead, Cree teens from distant James Bay showed up in droves. "It's not what we expected," muses Rogers. "That shocked us."[8] The outreach workers fan out in vans searching for Aboriginal street kids and try to persuade them to come to the shelter, where they will receive not only a bed and a safe place to stay but also counselling, leads on housing, education and training programs, as well as information about drugs, HIV, and AIDS.

Urban Aboriginal activists point to a continued dearth of such integrated, culturally sensitive health, housing, and social services as one reason many Native people, especially youth, encounter such difficulty navigating the transition from reserve or rural life to city living. There are life-and-death consequences. A 1995 Canadian Nursing Association survey concluded that language barriers prevented many urban Aboriginals from accessing mainstream health care services.[9] Too often, according to a 1999 assessment of Aboriginal healing services by the Vancouver/Richmond Health Board, community health agencies failed to recognize diseases that are more prevalent among Aboriginals—for example, non-insulin-dependent diabetes—as well as what the report referred to as the "psychological legacy of colonization."[10] In Vancouver, many were clustered around Vancouver's Downtown Eastside, but these agencies don't employ Aboriginals. As one focus group participant told the authors of a study of these services, "I want to walk into a place and see brown faces."[11]

Changing Schools

In Toronto, Victoria, and Montreal, about four-fifths of Aboriginal high school students graduate, a rate that is virtually the same as for the overall student population, and considerably higher than for teens who live on reserves. Yet in poor Aboriginal neighbourhoods in some Western Canadian cities, Native teens are far less likely to graduate because of poverty, family violence, and gang activity. But it also has to do with a dearth of Aboriginal teachers and counsellors. Some boards appoint "equity" committees and tinker with curriculum, trying to make Canadian history lessons less Eurocentric. Still, some traditional public schools haven't served Native children well. Many experience racism from non-Native children, while others lose touch with their language and culture.

In recent years, however, some cities have decided that it is imperative to tackle these problems more directly. In 2003, the director of Aboriginal education for the Edmonton board of education estimated there were about 8000 Native children enrolled in the city's schools. But the fertility rate in the city's Aboriginal community is one and a half times that of Edmonton's average. That means that within a decade as many as one-fifth of the students will come from Aboriginal families.

Since the early 2000s, Alberta's big-city school boards, community foundations, and the provincial government have been at the forefront of innovative new approaches to Aboriginal education, with encouraging results. In Edmonton schools serving neighbourhoods with a high concentration of Native families, educators have rolled out intensive literacy programs that have succeeded in boosting student achievement. There is curriculum geared to Aboriginal languages and customs (including the study of Native writers and artists, environmental practices, and spirituality), as well as Aboriginal social workers and other professional supports. These schools also receive extra funding—a mix of corporate donations, provincial funding, and United Way grants— for full-day kindergarten, a nurse, and a hot-lunch program.

The Edmonton boards are going one step further, opening schools serving only Native children, staffed mainly by Aboriginal educators, offering Cree language courses and even anger-management counselling. (Such schools have opened as well in Saskatoon, Calgary, and Toronto.) While some educators—both Native and non-Native—feel that Aboriginal children can do as well in mixed classrooms, others see a role for separate facilities. "There is a comfort level with being with your own," says Phyllis Cardinal, principal at Edmonton Public Schools' Amiskwaciy Academy, a 250-student facility founded in 1999. "The kids will talk about racism and discrimination and the feelings of isolation."[12]

In just half a decade, what has become apparent in Alberta is that a more targeted and strategic approach to educating Aboriginal children has yielded significantly improved outcomes.

Urban Reserves and Economic Development

Though social services and education are vital, meaningful employment is the key to an improved standard of living for Canada's growing urban Aboriginal communities. There is little question that our major cities now offer the widest variety of jobs, education and career options, and business opportunities.

As with so many ethno-cultural communities whose members have made their homes in Canada's hub cities, thousands of university-educated Aboriginals have melded into an urban labour force characterized by workplace diversity and cultural vitality. But the complexities of urban Aboriginal poverty—especially in Western cities, where ghetto-like neighbourhoods are dominated by poor Native families—call for innovative solutions based on fresh thinking about urban economic development and the sorts of forward-looking sectoral and community partnerships that are helping thousands of new Canadians get a toehold in the urban workforce.

For example, in 2002, Eric Newell, the former CEO of Calgary's Syncrude Canada, launched Careers: The Next Generation, a partnership of 33 First Nations organizations, employers, and community colleges to promote economic and career opportunities for the next generation of Aboriginal young people.[13] Newell sees enormous potential in the synergies between Alberta's resource sector, chronic skilled-labour shortages, and the rapidly growing ranks of urban Aboriginal youth in cities such as Calgary and, especially, Edmonton. "In Alberta's booming economy, many employers will be limited only by their ability to hire people with the right skills," he says. "The way forward as we work together to build a strong and inclusive Alberta is clear."[14]

Property development is another important piece of the puzzle. Band councils in Saskatchewan have been acquiring urban real estate in the province's larger urban centres of Prince Albert, North Battleford, and Saskatoon. In Winnipeg in the mid-1990s, local First Nations leaders decided to acquire the city's grand old railway station, abandoned by Canadian Pacific Railway (CPR) a decade earlier. Aboriginal service-agency officials came up with the plan after they began thinking strategically about the estimated $350,000 First Nations organizations pay each year in rent for offices in the city's core. They figured it would make more sense to own their own property. The CPR station was in the right location, and, as Wayne Helgason put it, the "optics" worked: It was a national historic site refurbished as an urban Aboriginal centre. "We grew warm to the building. It had this old grandeur about it."[15] The project yielded hundreds of construction jobs for Winnipeg's Aboriginal community. More than a decade on, the station has become a hub for the city's large and growing Native population, many First Nations organizations, as well as a 25,000-square-foot Aboriginal health centre.

Yet Saskatoon's successful experiment with "urban reserves" points toward the most promising example of how the economic momentum of hub cities can be harnessed to provide First Nations communities with urban jobs, commercial and non-commercial space, and investment opportunities that aren't tied to the ups and downs of the natural resources sector. Saskatchewan, in fact, is a national leader in the development of urban reserves, an idea that is now slowly spreading to other cities, including Regina, Calgary, Kelowna, Winnipeg, and even Toronto.

In the early 1980s, the leaders of the Muskeg Lake Cree Nation decided to reduce the band's dependence on farming. They were involved in treaty negotiations at the time. Band elder Harry Lafond, who later became chief, proposed to Mayor Cliff Wright that they wanted to lay claim to a 14-hectare parcel of surplus federal land in Saskatoon's Sutherland district. The land was to become part of the Muskeg Lake Cree Nation, subject to its own bylaws, not the city's. Not all such ventures have played out successfully. In Prince Albert, Saskatchewan, a few years earlier, an urban reserve raised the hackles of the city's non-Native population. But Saskatoon's municipal leaders and officials regarded Lafond's idea as promising. It took several years to work out agreements between the city, the federal government, and the band. Lafond's team knew Saskatoon didn't want a casino, and both sides understood that the reserve—because of its urban location—couldn't use property tax breaks to siphon off tenants from adjacent commercial properties. But Lafond and Wright were both visionaries, and they kept the highly complex talks—involving everything from municipal servicing agreements to harmonizing bylaws—on track.

The band invested $3 million in developing the property, now known as the McKnight Commercial Centre. It offers tenants and customers certain tax breaks, including relief from GST. Many First Nations businesses have located at the centre, among them the headquarters of Peace Hills Trust, a First Nations bank. Band-appointed directors sit on the board of a regional development authority, which allows for a new type of dialogue between the city's Native and non-Native communities—an especially significant development at a time when Saskatoon's leaders continue to try to sort out the troubling issues raised by racist incidents of police brutality involving the inhabitants of some of the city's hard-scrabble Aboriginal neighbourhoods. The reserve, observes former city commissioner Marty Irwin, "serves as a reminder that Aboriginal people are engaged in substantial and productive endeavours. This has helped to dispel some of the negative stereotypes regarding the abilities and potential of Aboriginal leaders and their people. The quality and attractiveness of the building development on the reserve to date have enhanced the image of the entire commercial district in that part of the city."[16]

The upshot, says University of Saskatchewan sociologist Michael Gertler, is that urban reserves could completely rearrange the relationships between First Nations, cities, and the federal government. They legally acknowledge that many Canadian cities sit on what was once Aboriginal land; recognize the urban demographics of Canada's Native population; and provide a glimpse of how the focus of Ottawa's obligation to the First Nations can be shifted from reserve-based social services to practical development initiatives linked to dynamics of the urban marketplace. "Urban reserves," Gertler concludes, "subvert the historic urban versus rural dichotomy that has been a hallmark of state policy towards Aboriginal peoples."[17]

CREATING SENIOR-FRIENDLY CITIES

The social changes that have swept over Canada's large cities since the early 1990s—especially those tied to high immigration levels and growing urban poverty—are the consequence of specific political decisions. But the greying of Canada's cities is a different matter. The baby boomer generation will grow old no matter what. As this demographic tidal wave rolls over the coming decades, it will do more to alter the face of our cities than any set of policy moves. Fifty years ago, the family needs of the boomers created suburbia. Twenty years from now, the geriatric needs of this same generation may well be responsible for equally dramatic changes in our urban regions—changes that could bring about more compact, pedestrian-friendly cityscapes, as well as new forms of supportive housing and long-term care tailored to the temperament of a generation weaned on home ownership and consumer-oriented health services.

That's the view from 40,000 feet. Closer to ground level, seniors already account for a substantial proportion of low-income urban households, and that statistic is unlikely to change. Indeed, with the income gap widening, our cities will almost certainly see a growing number of fixed-income seniors experiencing dire financial pressures, such as steep property tax hikes due to rising real estate values, and skyrocketing utility bills. Many will endure hardships finding affordable housing that's geared to the needs of their failing bodies. While these are urban issues, responsibility for alleviating senior's poverty in big cities must not land, by default, at the feet of municipalities. Many cities have taken to offering property tax breaks to low-income seniors, while in senior-friendly Alberta, the province allows seniors to forgo paying the education portion of their property taxes. But such well-meaning and politically popular gestures will prove to be unsustainable as the ranks of urban seniors swell. More to the point, such municipal tax breaks underscore the inadequacy of our federal and provincial income security, housing, and geriatric care programs—all social policies that remain the responsibility of the upper levels of government.

The solutions lie in more realistic and flexible support programs that recognize the high cost of living for urban seniors on fixed incomes. For example, it makes little sense that seniors lose a substantial chunk of their pension benefits after a spouse dies, even though the survivor still has to pay the same utility and housing costs unless he or she moves. For 20 years, old-age security has been—quite properly—indexed to the rate of inflation. Is it enough? Probably not, which is why the upper levels of governments have begun to make tentative changes that reflect current conditions—for example, offering energy rebates for seniors to soften the impact of skyrocketing hydro and natural gas rates.

Ottawa must go even further. For example, the Liberals' 2004 seniors taskforce recommended that low-income pensioners who qualify for the guaranteed income supplement (GIS) should be allowed to earn up to $4000 annually before their benefits are clawed back—a reform that would allow seniors to take part-time work without being penalized.[1] It's a situation not unlike social assistance recipients trying to get back into the workforce without being penalized. "As with the working poor," says TD Bank economist Don Drummond, "seniors at the top end of the low-income threshold are hit with extremely high tax rates."[2]

Federal moves designed to tackle seniors' poverty, however, are only part of the solution. If Canada's hub cities genuinely want to accommodate the coming demographic changes, municipalities have to do their part by becoming more accessible and pedestrian friendly. Transit services will become ever more important, but only if they can be adapted to the needs of customers with mobility concerns. Provincially and regionally managed health care networks, in turn, will have to find new ways to deliver responsive home care to an ethnically diverse urban population. Most of all, our large cities will find themselves on the front lines of a consumer-driven revolution in the seniors' housing industry, one that threatens to topple the dominance of the rapacious nursing- and retirement-home industry and put the breaks on the suburban development that churns out only single-family dwellings.

Senior-Friendly Planning

In the mid-1980s, fitness-minded seniors in mid-sized cities across North America began to take up mall-walking.[3] But with the accelerating downtown migration of older people, the demand for walking opportunities will shift to inner-city areas. For municipalities, that means ensuring that there are tapered sidewalk curbs suited to those with mobility problems, enhanced snow-clearing services, recreation programs suitable for seniors, and accessible open spaces.

Health and safety concerns will drive much of the push for senior-friendly cities. A 2002 Japanese study discovered that easy access to parks, trails, and quiet, tree-lined streets had a "significant predictive value" in the five-year survival rates of 3144 Tokyo senior citizens. "Our findings suggested that if favourably walkable green streets and spaces were provided, the health of senior citizens would be promoted further, regardless of their socio-economic status," the study notes. The researchers address their findings directly to city officials: "Master plans for urban development should pay more attention to maintaining and increasing greenery filled public areas that ... are within easy walking distance of every household."[4]

Retrofitting the physical face of big cities to meet the needs of seniors and the disabled doesn't end with parks. It also entails redesigning busy intersections so they'll be safer for those who can't dash across six lanes. In fact, while the demand for traffic humps on local streets typically comes from parents with young children, seniors' advocates are on the front lines of the fight for measures to recognize pedestrians' rights in cities filled with cars.

In the mid-1990s, Barry Wellar, an Ottawa geographer, began grappling with the problem of why many signalized intersections feel so unsafe for pedestrians with mobility problems. As an urban planner, he was sceptical of the collision statistics traditionally collected by municipalities as a measure of road and pedestrian safety. "When you have a collision, what do you know?" says the gruff 64-year-old. "That something hit something else! What is it that they don't know? They don't know why."[5]

Wellar developed a Walking Security Index (WSI) of 39 criteria (obscured sight lines, poor signage, trip hazards, traffic flow, and so on) that can be used to measure the relative security of a given intersection. Wellar's objective was to give neighbourhood groups a tool with which they can challenge the way municipal traffic engineers manage busy intersections. Word of the WSI has spread across North America among cycling and pedestrian activists concerned about the increasingly poor driving habits of city-dwellers.

In 2004, a network of Toronto seniors who promote pedestrian issues decided to pressure the city to adopt Wellar's methods as a way of reducing accidents (there are about 90 to 100 fatalities, and another 2000 to 2500 injuries, each year). But they slammed into a wall of resistance from Toronto transportation officials, who dismissed Wellar's index as unwieldy. "I don't think many other cities have figured out how to do this," admitted one bureaucrat. "We're still in the learning stages."[6] But as the downtowns of large Canadian cities become increasingly populated by older people, municipal traffic engineers will have little choice but to think differently about their preoccupations.

Bracing for the era when a growing number of seniors stop driving, transit agencies are also beginning to recognize the need for a broader approach to providing accessibility. For example, in Ajax-Pickering, a suburb east of Toronto, the local transit operator in 2005 launched a "flag bus" service—three wheelchair-accessible buses that work a route connecting local seniors' homes, a mall, and a medical clinic. The routes don't have conventional stops; rather, seniors flag the drivers to stop.[7]

Most larger transit operators have run door-to-door wheelchair buses for years, thanks to lobbying by disabled users. But some have been criticized as expensive and slow, especially with the proliferation of wheelchair-accessible taxis. Meanwhile, as an increasing number of agencies convert their fleets to low-floor buses and install elevators on their rapid transit lines, wheelchair bus operations such as Vancouver's HandyDART have come to resemble non-emergency ambulance transfer services, used primarily by the very infirm as they shuttle to and from medical clinics. Indeed, TransLink, the Greater Vancouver Transportation Authority, is asking whether such transportation services should be funded from provincial health budgets.[8]

Beyond such funding details, TransLink officials and Vancouver social planners put their finger on a critical detail: The aging of the urban population means that single-family, car-oriented neighbourhoods will soon house a significant population of seniors who don't view transit as a work-related commuter service. Demographer David Foot, author of *Boom, Bust and Echo,* predicts that Canadian transit operators could even adopt an "old-new" solution from the developing world—privately operated jitneys, mini-buses, or *collectivos* that will pick up riders away from main transportation corridors.[9] The lesson is that as Canada's big cities enter a new era of transit investment, urban demographics will have to play an ever more dominant role in determining the way our big-city transportation networks function.

Home Care

Most seniors want to stay in their own homes as long as possible. That goal requires a sustainable income security system, safe streets, and local mobility options. But as our cities age, it will also depend on dramatic reforms to home care, which continues to occupy a lowly position on a national health care agenda dominated by debates on wait times, drug coverage, and private delivery of medical services.

Between 1989 and 1998, public home care expenditures jumped from $560 million to almost $2.8 billion—a nearly five-fold increase in one decade.[10] These trends reflect the fact that hospitals are discharging patients sooner but also illustrates the growth in the use of home-based medical procedures. Yet, in a heavily urbanized province such as British Columbia, public health insurance covers less than half of all home care spending. Some jurisdictions limit physician billings from house calls, which are important for elderly patients who have trouble getting around. And in Ontario, the home care system has been under financial siege for several years, with the result that community care access centres ration services. The repercussions are felt especially acutely among the elderly who live in large cities without the support systems that are available in smaller, more tightly knit communities.

The federal Liberals in 2005 tried to fill the breech by adding $3.5 billion to the available tax credit for unpaid caregivers, typically relatives who have to devote their own time and resources to look after elderly parents. And recent health deals between Ottawa and the provinces have made vague promises to expand the number of insured home care services.

But the real solution to this kind of policy neglect is not just more money. It also requires a fundamental shift in thinking, one that acknowledges the value of staying out of institutions. For many elderly seniors, especially those living in isolated circumstances in large cities, the difference between independence and institutionalized care can turn on services as basic as assistance with the preparation of nutritious meals.

Victoria-based health policy consultant Marcus Hollander has laid out a compelling economic case for significantly expanded community-based home care for the elderly, with an emphasis on non-medical support services, which are typically excluded from home care programs.

There is an exceptionally high rate of readmission for elderly people who have been discharged from hospitals. Worn down by their illnesses, a third of such frail seniors fare poorly at home and boomerang back to the emergency room. Some urban hospitals serving communities with large ethnic populations have struggled to ensure that elderly immigrant patients, some with halting English or French, are set up with rehabilitation once they leave. But Hollander's research has shown that jut 10 percent of all seniors' home care costs are for medical services, while the remaining 90 percent are for chronic support: the ongoing bathing, cleaning, and meal preparation these seniors need in order to prevent a return trip to the hospital with a case of malnutrition or dehydration. "The real conundrum," he says, "is that these people have medical needs but the adequate response is supportive services."[11]

The data bear him out. When Hollander compared the costs for Winnipeg seniors receiving chronic home care with the costs for those living in nursing homes, he discovered that the services provided to those living in their own dwellings were "significantly less costly"—the savings ranging from 44 to 75 percent. As he concluded, "The current approach to home care is misguided and may well lead to an increasing cost spiral in health care services."[12]

The Decline and Fall of the Long-Term Care Industry

In the early 2000s, the Ontario government, under premier Ernie Eves, signed off on a rapid and unprecedented expansion of the nursing home sector, whose largest operators were also major donors to the Progressive Conservative Party. The decision led to a boom in nursing home construction around Greater Toronto. But for many seniors' advocates, the government's agenda seemed all too clear. By rationing home care, more families would put aging relatives into regulated long-term care facilities or unregulated retirement homes that offer nursing and other medical services as part of their fees.

During this same period, Greater Vancouver headed in precisely the opposite direction. Vancouver Coastal Health, the publicly funded $2-billion-a-year regional health authority, has opted for a more community-based approach. It plans to close almost a thousand nursing home beds by 2007, while boosting home support services and opening more than 1200 so-called assisted-living units (i.e., apartment complexes with onsite nursing care, security, and optional dining facilities). The agency's goal is to alleviate the pressure on acute care hospitals, reduce "inappropriate usage of residential care services" (i.e., nursing homes), and recognize "the fact that most people prefer, where possible, to stay within their own community and receive support in their homes or home-like surroundings."[13]

Greater Vancouver is not the only jurisdiction taking steps to help seniors stay out of nursing homes. Several years ago, Edwards Place, a 149-unit apartment building for low-income seniors in downtown Calgary, hired an onsite community resources coordinator to help tenants continue to live independently by assessing their needs and arranging chronic support services. Within two years of taking that step, the home saw a reduction in the number of its residents moving into nursing homes, as well as a decline in emergency room trips.[14]

Such developments are rooted in common sense. And they reflect mounting public concern over the nursing home sector's well-deserved reputation for substandard care and shoddy conditions.

But they also point to the coming changes in consumer attitudes toward health care and housing. Seniors born in the early 20th century came of age in the Depression. They were accustomed to dealing with deprivation and paying rent. Their consumer-minded children and grandchildren are much less willing to put up with poor service. What is more, both generations profited enormously from the post-war real estate boom, and their approach to protecting the accumulated equity in their homes will topple the current structure of the retirement- and nursing-home industry.

About 8 percent of Canadians over age 75 now live in retirement homes, many of which have traditionally been operated by nursing home companies and charge exorbitant rents, in some cases as much as $4000 per month. Do such fees make sense for a generation that earned enormous returns on real estate?

It's a question that seems to have dawned on Amica Mature Lifestyles, a Vancouver-based firm founded in 1997 by a 34-year-old chartered accountant, Samir Manji. The company owns 18 retirement homes with over 2000 suites and generated $3 million in net income on $47 million in revenues in 2002. Its approximate occupancy rate for fiscal 2002 was an impressive 95.4 percent—well above the industry average. Most of its facilities are in British Columbia, but the company is aggressively expanding into Ontario.

Amica specializes in residences that look and function more like resorts, catering to seniors capable of living more or less independently, even while providing assisted-living floors. They all offer Wellness & Vitality programs, and several amenities, including pubs. Rather than being attached to a nursing home, they tend to be located near malls or other community facilities. Amica's Calgary residence is in the middle of the city's arty Sixth Avenue neighbourhood. Before opening a 124-unit facility in Woodbridge, an affluent, largely Italian suburb of Toronto, Amica conducted focus groups and found that prospective residents wanted common rooms where they could make wine, and an Italian-style courtyard. In 2001, Amica switched strategies, moving aggressively to reduce its direct ownership stake in its residences in favour of condos. For the first nine months of fiscal 2002, the company generated $6.5 million in the sale of condo units—almost three times more than the same period in 2001. Rental revenues, by contrast, grew just 3.5 percent.[15]

Such changes indicate that some urban seniors are turning away from pricey rental accommodations. Reverse mortgages—which allow elderly homeowners to set up annuities drawn against the value of their houses— are gaining acceptance. Ianno's taskforce recommended that the Canada Mortgage and Housing Corporation backstop reverse mortgages for low-income seniors so they can access the equity in their homes.[16]

The so-called life-lease market is another harbinger of things to come. Life-lease is an ownership arrangement in which the resident buys an equity stake in a retirement residence. There are more than 160 such projects across Canada. In Ontario alone there are almost 5000 life-lease units, with prices in the $150,000 range. Most are available in charitable or not-for-profit complexes that also have a range of other housing options, from standard rentals to long-term care beds. Residents agree to purchase a basic service package, which includes meals, security, recreational programming, and some nursing care. Like condos, life-lease units can be sold, and they typically appreciate in value. The financial advantage is undeniable: The service packages can run as low as $600 a month, and the owner, or his or her estate, gets the initial investment back, plus profit.[17]

Even among the very elderly, nursing homes are becoming the residence of last resort, chosen mainly for those who need 24-hour supervision. That's a wholesale change compared with even 20 years ago, when reasonably healthy seniors moved into nursing homes for the security and support.[18] The active, outspoken 50- and 60-somethings who are now colonizing those upscale downtown towers will, in decades to come, begin pressing their condominium corporation boards to think about retrofits or additional in-house services that allow them to hold onto their apartments as they age. In the greying Canadian cities of the 2020s, 2030s, and 2040s, the elderly won't be shunted out of sight in isolated suburban nursing homes. They will be the urban mainstream.

BREAKING THE POVERTY CYCLE

In June 1995, the Quebec Women's Federation organized a huge rally in downtown Montreal to call on the provincial government to get serious about poverty and unemployment. The message resonated in a city that had endured years of economic decline since its post–World War II heyday as Canada's economic capital. The march, however, was the brainchild of a Quebec City Catholic community organization and supported by the labour movement. The Bread and Roses March aimed to make the recently elected Parti Québécois government fulfill the promise of its social democratic traditions. Poverty rates in the province had been running well ahead of those of other parts of Canada for some time, but the provincial Liberals seemed to be in a state of denial about the issue. The organizers wanted something more from Lucien Bouchard's new regime. Representing hundreds of local agencies and grassroots organizations, the coalition members believed they had a clear-eyed understanding of the causes of urban poverty. They were not content to sit by and watch the Bouchard government enact new social programs; they wanted to be directly involved in fashioning and implementing them.

The anti-poverty activism in Quebec was an early volley in the sustained and broad-based backlash against the fraying of Canada's social safety net. The Bread and Roses demonstration took place just months after then federal Finance minister Paul Martin's first assault on the $40-billion federal deficit. That spring, the Liberals pushed ahead with a historic restructuring of Canada's social policy—a shift that marked the end of a national welfare system created in the 1940s.

Until then, Ottawa had transferred to each province about half the actual costs of social assistance and other income support payments (including subsidized daycare) under the Canada Assistance Plan (CAP). Martin replaced CAP with the Canada Health and Social Transfer (CHST).

Under the new system, federal transfers to the provinces were capped. But to compensate for the decline in funding, Ottawa gave the provinces more latitude to fashion their own social programs. This wasn't just deficit-cutting, however. The introduction of the CHST, coupled with increased restrictions on employment insurance payments, signalled the moment when Canada embraced neo-conservative social policies that had the effect of punishing thousands of low-income families in Canada's big cities. As the table below shows quite explicitly, the net effect of Martin's reforms was to boost transfers to health care at the expense of social services and post-secondary education, both of which are closely tied to urban competitiveness and quality of life.

TOTAL FEDERAL CASH TRANSFERS: 1992–93 AND 2002–3 (CONSTANT 2002 DOLLARS)

	1992–93 ($ billions)	2002–3 ($ billions)	Change ($ billions)
Health care	10.55	11.44	+1.29
Post-secondary education	4.28	2.42	−1.86
Social services	8.83	4.84	−3.35
Total	23.66	18.70	−3.92

Greg de-Groot-Maggetti, Public Justice Resource Centre, Toronto 2003. Reprinted with permission.

The specifically anti-urban consequences of Ottawa's decentralization of social policy became glaringly apparent in Ontario during Mike Harris's term as premier. Having swept to office on a tax-cutting platform, the Harris government quickly slashed welfare rates by 21.6 percent and ended rent control—a one-two punch that triggered a tidal wave of urban homelessness. Ontario is also the only province that compels municipalities to pick up part of the bill for social assistance. In a serious economic downturn, Ontario's big cities, with their greater concentration of social assistance recipients, could suddenly face a crushing spike in welfare costs that would drain funds away from other municipal services, from transit to youth programs.

Overly generous welfare payments and unemployment insurance rules erode the financial incentive to work. After all, when state policies fail to encourage the maximum number of capable individuals to participate in the labour force, the government is frittering away its economic ability to finance the rest of its social programs, from education to health care and old-age pensions.

But the inadequacy of post-CHST social assistance and other income support programs has proven to be equally problematic. According to a 2004 analysis by the Edmonton Social Planning Council, a family of four on social assistance would receive about $700 in welfare benefits per month, plus a housing allowance. But they would need to spend about $500 of that on nutritious food. That leaves $200 for all other expenses, including clothing, personal items, and transit; the latter can gobble up most of that $200 by itself. Meanwhile, a two-bedroom apartment in the city's north end goes for about $600, but the shelter allowance is only $482. Even though the numbers don't add up, over 13,000 Edmonton families were enduring precisely these conditions in 2003.[1]

Such bargain basement social policies created macroeconomic conditions that look good from afar but have produced increasing hardship in many low-income urban neighbourhoods. True, the unemployment rates have been steadily falling, the ranks of the labour force have grown, and the welfare rolls dropped because it has become much harder to qualify for social assistance. Yet, despite low welfare rates and more stringent qualifying rules, almost 200,000 Ontarians remain on social assistance, a number that has stubbornly refused to change since 2000.[2]

Meanwhile, for thousands of city-dwellers, there isn't much choice but to hold down poorly paying service jobs. "The depth of poverty"— meaning the difference between household earnings and the official low-income cut-off—"for two-parent low income families has averaged $9,848 since 1989," concluded a 2004 child poverty study from the advocacy group Campaign 2000. "Conditions among low-income couples with children have actually worsened over the past 20 years, and continued to deteriorate through the latest economic boom. By 2001, these families fell, on average, more than $10,200 below the poverty line—that represents the third worst year for these families in the past 20 years."[3]

This is different from the mass unemployment of the 1930s, observes University of Montreal social policy analyst Jane Jenson: "[Today's] labour market works so that there are many people who have a job but do not earn enough to keep themselves and their families out of poverty."[4] As a 2005 TD Bank analysis of the problems with Canada's income security system notes, "Many adults today cannot earn enough to feed their families, pay for childcare, and cover a variety of other expenses, despite having a significant attachment to the labour force—and no association with welfare."[5]

Yet amid the harsh politics of poverty that shaped much of the past decade (including a short-lived and highly contentious "law against poverty" passed by the Parti Québécois government shortly before it was defeated by Jean Charest's Liberals), the outlines of a more humane but pragmatic approach to income support programs and policies has begun to take shape. No one is calling for a return to ruinously expensive social programs that encourage welfare dependency. But it's clear that the tough-love solutions advanced by neo-conservative regimes in the 1980s and 1990s have harmed Canadian cities. In Europe, especially Scandinavia, economic prosperity, robust labour productivity, and fair-minded social programs go hand in glove—a clear recognition of the reality that in highly urbanized societies, cities succeed globally when they aren't constantly grappling with the volatile, and ultimately costly, consequences of extreme poverty.

Mending the Urban Social Safety Net

Entrenched economic hardship has been eating away at the liveability of our large cities. The only way to reverse these trends is to shift away from the every-man-for-himself approach to social programs and create a new generation of income support policies geared to the labour force realities of large urban regions.

Such a move begins with minimum wages. A 2003 report by the Caledon Institute, a social policy think-tank, slammed Canada's provincial governments for tolerating minimum wage levels that, it said, are comparable to the lowest rates in the United States. As of 2001, the national average minimum wage was 60 percent of the pre-tax poverty line in cities with more than 500,000 residents—well below levels in the mid-1970s. In Ontario, that translated into annual earnings of just over $14,000—a meagre amount on which to subsist in a city with a high cost of living and a labour market that sharply favours employers because of large numbers of recent immigrants looking for jobs. "Contrary to what some people believe," the Caledon study notes, "the archetypical minimum wage worker is not a middle-class teenager working after school for pocket money. In Canada and the US, the majority of minimum wage workers are adults.... Four in ten minimum wage workers in Canada work on a full-time basis."[6] As of 2004, Alberta, Quebec, and Ontario had some of the country's lowest minimum wage rates. The McGuinty Liberals introduced the first increases to Ontario's minimum wage in a decade—a period during which inflation grew by 15 percent. The rate will rise from $6.85 an hour to $8 an hour by 2007. But that level merely puts Ontario on par with British Columbia as of 2002.[7]

Some relief for low-income parents is another piece of the solution, above and beyond income tax deductions for caregivers and child care. For many poor single parents, the vast majority of whom are women, the decision to stay on welfare is as much a function of financial practicality as anything else. In 2000, 62 percent of all working low-income single parents earned under $10 an hour—less than $20,000 per year. The combination of low minimum-wage rates, transit expenses, and child care costs often makes working far less profitable than not working—a perverse outcome if there ever was one. In the late 1990s, Ottawa and the provinces began to tackle this conundrum through the introduction of the Canadian Child Tax Benefit, an income assistance program geared to families, combined with a supplementary program known as the National Child Benefit. Between 2001 and 2005, federal support to low-income families grew by 14 percent, from $5.6 billion to $6.4 billion. Ottawa also claims the National Child Benefit, since 2001, has managed to move almost 41,000 low-income families over the poverty line, increasing their disposable income by about $900.

We now need to craft our welfare rules to find a more sustainable medium between overly generous social assistance rates and the punitive methods that took root in the late 1990s. For example, a linchpin of Harris's welfare reforms was "workfare," meaning that able-bodied welfare recipients had to earn their benefits by doing community service or participating in training programs. But under the rules governing Ontario Works, as the program came to be known, welfare recipients earning some extra income saw all or even more of it taxed away. "It's hard to imagine a more powerful disincentive to leaving welfare for work," concluded a TD Bank study of the flaws of the system devised during the Harris years.[8]

Ontario isn't alone in supporting such practices; indeed, many provinces clawed back part of the National Child Benefit and redirected the funds to programs geared to the working poor, including daycare. Anti-poverty groups and children's advocates say that these policies effectively force welfare families to depend even more heavily on food banks.[9] While Ottawa initially tolerated these clawbacks in the name of allowing provincial governments greater freedom to determine their own social programs, it has begun to urge them to end the practice. In mid-2005, Queen's Park changed its welfare rules in order to make the transition between welfare and work smoother. The so-called tax-back rate was reduced, and social assistance recipients were allowed to hold on to some of the benefits associated with welfare, such as drug and dental benefits. New Brunswick has undertaken similar reforms.

The final piece of the puzzle involves an urban-minded approach to tax reduction. The tax cuts from the latter 1990s came with an ulterior ideological motive: to tie the hands of governments that had become fiscally irresponsible. Instead, the cuts often damaged essential public services and produced all sorts of unintended side effects in our big cities. Meanwhile, the actual value of the tax reductions in high-cost-of-living urban areas was almost negligible for the middle class and upper-income earners who were the principal beneficiaries of such moves. The real burden associated with social spending cuts was borne by low-income families, fixed-income seniors, social assistance recipients, and recent immigrants and refugees—all groups that depended more heavily on urban public services (from transit to youth recreation programs) and income support programs.

Given the prevailing economic and labour market trends, the best single way to tackle the widening income gap in our large urban centres is to significantly ease the tax burden on low-income working families, rather than hoping for a trickle-down benefit from tax cuts for large corporations and the wealthiest earners.

In 1999, the federal Liberals took a baby step in that direction when they indexed tax bracket thresholds and the basic personal exemption to the rate of inflation. That technical shift represented one of the first acknowledgments that Canada's tax system must reflect changes in the cost of living. This decision reduced the tax payable for thousands of low-income families (in 2003, the reduction in personal taxes amounted to about $390 per year), and moved many right off the tax rolls. In late 2005, Ottawa proposed a $30-billion package of tax cuts, mainly targeted at Canadian families earning less than $30,000 a year.

Such measures merely tinker at the edges of the problem, however. In November 2004, Tom Kent, an advisor to former prime minister Lester B. Pearson and one of the fathers of Canada's social programs, upped the ante in a widely read essay in the journal *Policy Options*. Ottawa, he argues, should replace the basic personal allowance (about $8200 as of 2005) with a *refundable* tax credit. "If a person's income is too small to be taxed," he writes, "the full amount of the credit becomes a negative tax, a payment from the treasury to him or to her.... A general tax credit of this kind is by far the fairest and most efficient way to supplement low incomes. If over time, as public finances permitted, it was steadily increased, the call on clumsy and intrusive welfare programs would be much reduced."[10]

BUILDING AFFORDABLE HOUSING AND MIXED-INCOME NEIGHBOURHOODS

Beginning in the mid-1980s, right-wing politicians began to realize that they could score points with many suburban and rural voters by disparaging social and affordable housing programs. Subsidized housing, they'd say, was a form of social engineering that fostered delinquency, family breakdown, and indolence. And so those programs disappeared bit by bit in many regions of the country. It didn't take long for the symptoms to appear on the streets of our largest urban regions—even affluent cities such as Calgary. Outspoken and often radical anti-poverty activists rang the alarm bells, but they were soon joined by big-city mayors, mainstream social service agencies, and, finally, bank economists and business groups.

The political reversal at the federal level can be traced to 2002, when Toronto Liberal MP Judy Sgro issued a taskforce report on the federal role in urban issues. It called for a new national housing policy. In January 2005, Joe Fontana, the federal minister of Labour and Housing, began developing a Canadian Housing Framework. A few months later, Prime Minister Paul Martin and NDP leader Jack Layton negotiated a $4.6-billion amendment to the federal budget bill, complete with a $1.6-billion infusion for affordable housing, including a dedicated fund for improved Aboriginal housing.

Overall, Ottawa spends about $2 billion a year to maintain its existing stock of subsidized housing. During the early 2000s, the Liberals also set aside funds for rent supplements for low-income families, homeless shelters, and small renovation loans for inexpensive homes and apartments.[1] The new money—which is not contingent on provincial matching funds—marked the beginning of a return to an earlier era of housing policy that fizzled out in the mid-1990s.

It's catch-up time. The National Housing and Homeless Network has estimated that Canada needs to produce about 20,000 to 25,000 new units of affordable housing each year, equivalent to about $1.1 billion annually … just to get back to the levels of the 1980s.[2] The scale of the shortage is formidable. TD Bank economist Don Drummond has estimated what the poorest 20 percent of households should be paying for rent, and then compared these figures with the average rents in big cities across Canada. For the country as a whole, the average shortfall is $2500 a year. In lower-cost cities such as Montreal and Winnipeg, the affordability gap is $1700, but it skyrockets into the $4000 range for Ottawa, Toronto, and Vancouver. Yet, Drummond warns, job creation initiatives on their own won't buoy income levels enough to make housing affordable for the working poor and social assistance recipients. Nor, in his view, is the existing system of income supplements—a combination of the child tax benefit, old-age security, social assistance, and federal or Quebec pension plans—anywhere close to being sufficient to close that $2500 chasm.[3]

In other words, solutions require action on both sides of the ledger: more flexible income support programs, combined with funding and land-use policies that trigger the development of the types of housing that are in desperately short supply in Canada's big cities, affordable apartments, supportive housing (for the disabled, substance abusers, or the mentally ill), and subsidized housing, especially the sorts of co-op projects that were one of the bright lights of Canada's housing programs in the 1980 and early 1990s.

The new spending, says University of Toronto housing expert J. David Hulchanski, must be divided—part of it going to offset construction costs (which typically make affordable housing developments uneconomic), the balance dedicated to rental subsidies for low-income tenants. "A two-tier subsidy creates socially mixed communities: a construction subsidy reduces the capital cost, bringing all rent levels down; a rent geared-to-income subsidy helps very low-income and destitute/homeless people," he says. "Social housing supply is a necessary complement to private rental supply. Where demand for housing is high, in regions where population and economic growth are highest, the two sectors supply housing to very different markets: one meets the *social need* for housing, the other meets the *market demand* for housing."[4] For the better part of the last decade, most Canadian governments ignored the former and stoked the latter, with the grim results now plainly visible in overcrowded apartments, lengthy waiting lists for subsidized housing, and the rundown condition of our social housing complexes.

Developing Quality Social Housing

Across North America and Europe, large-scale public housing developments built in the post-war era failed spectacularly, at least partly because of ill-conceived experimental design. Poorly built and lacking in commercial space, these massive complexes were often dehumanizing and spatially isolated from their urban surroundings. Over time, the upwardly mobile tenants pulled up stakes and the apartments fell into disrepair at the hands of incompetently managed public housing agencies. Terrorized by gangs and drug dealers, the complexes themselves became urban blights, their law-abiding tenants consigned to a bleak and unsafe existence.

Between the late 1970s and the mid-1990s, the heyday of Canada's social housing movement, there was a shift to smaller-scale mixed-income co-ops that were independent of the lumbering public housing bureaucracies. But the highly successful co-op movement became a victim of its own success when a growing proportion of the apartments wound up being rented by middle-income households. Provincial governments reacted by targeting housing programs to low-income families. But that funding dried up by the late 1990s, except in British Columbia, where the provincial government continued to fund social housing projects in very poor neighbourhoods such as Vancouver's Downtown Eastside.[5]

Vancouver "has somehow continued to produce social housing projects of a very high standard," comments planner and urbanist Lance Berelowitz. He cites the 108-unit Lore Krill Housing Cooperative, built in the Downtown Eastside in 2002, as an example of a solid, well-designed apartment. The architects proposed reducing the size of each apartment by 10 percent and investing the savings in higher construction standards and materials. The smallest units are for welfare recipients, but there are also larger apartments set aside specifically for seniors. This "innovative strategy" met the approval of the co-op board and British Columbia's social housing agency because it means the building will be less costly to maintain in the long run, observes Berelowitz.[6] The City of Vancouver is now pressing ahead with a major redevelopment of the long-abandoned Woodward's department store site, which will have a mix of social housing apartments, market condos, and space for the School for the Contemporary Arts, an expansion of an existing satellite campus of Simon Fraser University.

Other cities are inching back into the development of social and co-op housing. Some public housing complexes have recently received approval to convert themselves into co-ops in order to get out from under moribund bureaucracies. There are now a handful of co-ops geared specifically to seniors in need of affordable housing—a type of project that will become increasingly sought-after as the population ages.

In 2005, Toronto's huge public housing corporation finalized plans for the redevelopment of Regent Park, one of Canada's first social housing complexes, which was built without internal streets and has long suffered from its reputation as a hotbed of violent crime. The plans call for a conventional street grid that's integrated into the surrounding neighbourhoods, but also high-rises designed by leading architects and reserved primarily for subsidized housing. In Calgary in 2004, meanwhile, the city council approved an innovative financing plan that calls for the city to borrow $70 million to upgrade the infrastructure of the East Village, a derelict area that is home to many shelters, low-income apartment buildings, and seedy hotels. The idea is to attract residential and commercial developers whose projects will lift the East Village out of its doldrums.

These projects will create new urban neighbourhoods that are likely to set the tone for future affordable-housing investment in Canadian cities. But it remains to be seen whether they evolve into mature mixed-income urban communities or whether they will further entrench the segregation between rich and poor in the name of urban renewal. In Chicago, home to some of the worst U.S. housing projects, decrepit 1950s-era high-rises infested with drug dealers have been demolished in recent years to make way for mixed-income neighbourhoods in which the condos sit beside very ordinary-looking city blocks lined with adjoined townhouses that are, in fact, public housing units. Each has its own yard, clear property lines, eyes on the street, and pedestrian-friendly public spaces.

These aren't new ideas. The City of Toronto in the 1980s developed just such a neighbourhood on former industrial land in the west end. It's an enclave of low-rise subsidized or co-op apartments and townhouses, complete with parkettes, a nearby seniors' residence, and standard-issue, single-family, market-based semis. There are shops and schools close by, and transit is readily accessible. And there is no evidence of architectural experimentation. Seamlessly integrated into the city's residential grid, this affordable neighbourhood functions in every way like a diverse downtown community. It has no label and thus no stigma.[7]

Second Suites

Since the late 1990s, Canadian cities have unleashed a small torrent of investment in moderately priced rental housing—a market response to the chronic shortage of subsidized housing in large urban areas. Thousands of basement apartments and second suites have been built in homes in cities across Canada. They offer many of the features—and there's a long list—we want in affordable living spaces in large cities. They are energy efficient. They intensify existing residential neigh-bourhoods and make better use of municipal infrastructure. They're found all over the place, even in neighbourhoods nominally reserved for single-family residential dwellings. They generate respectable profits for their owners. And they don't soak up huge amounts of taxpayers' dollars for administrative overheads.

Basement apartments have been around for years. But in most cities, they were traditionally illegal, and therefore frequently substandard, with poor ventilation, frayed wiring, and lacking in adequate fire-safety equipment. Homeowner associations in affluent neighbourhoods, and their municipal representatives, were often vehemently opposed to basement flats, fearing that they would herald the arrival of rooming houses and thus trigger the creeping deterioration of "stable" communities. In 1995, Ontario's NDP government introduced legislation legalizing basement suites, but the bill was immediately repealed when Mike Harris took office: It was too radical.

A decade later, a pair of Tory MLAs from Calgary was pushing the Alberta government and Calgary Council to legalize basement suites as a way of easing the city's chronic housing shortage. Calgary, rarely on the forefront of progressive urban policy making, is hardly alone in this effort, however. Between 1999 and 2005, Ottawa, Toronto, Vancouver, North Vancouver, and Edmonton all passed bylaws allowing basement apartments, granny flats, and second suites over garages. In 1999, Toronto officials estimated there were about 100,000 basement suites—equivalent to about a fifth of all rental apartments in the city—and from 2000 to 3000 new units were being added each year. Vancouver has 25,000 to 30,000. Homeowners don't build in rental units out of a high-minded desire to provide affordable housing. Rather, in high-cost cities such as Toronto and Vancouver, where real estate prices are soaring, the rental income from a basement apartment goes a long way toward making the mortgage affordable. It's a classic example of how, in an urban setting, self-interest yields a social dividend.

By legalizing and then regulating these units, municipalities can ensure they are safe and built to code, which only makes sense. After all, if a basement apartment turns into a fire trap, the city is expected to provide emergency services. In Vancouver, city council in 2004 also approved rules making it *easier* for homeowners to create secondary suites without having to meet an earlier generation of costly regulations that applied only to basement suites in certain parts of the city. Other municipalities have toyed with the idea of providing modest grants to homeowners interested in converting their basements.

Who are the tenants who occupy these apartments? Some are used by aging parents who don't want to live in an institutional setting. University and college students are another large market, and some homeowners actually find their tenants through the housing offices run by post-secondary institutions. And because many basement suites are relatively inexpensive, they end up being rented by low-income families. As the final report of the 1999 Golden homelessness task-force observed, "Rents tend to be lower than for similar-sized units in apartment buildings, making them an important source of affordable housing for lower-income tenants. The creation of second suites has filled the shortfall in rental supply in Ontario for the past 20 years. They are a cost-effective, market driven alternative to new construction and they do not require subsidy."[8]

Mixed-Income Neighbourhoods

The proliferation of basement apartments, though helpful in blunting the housing shortages, is an indictment of municipal planning. Cities once accommodated a wide range of affordable housing types—starter bungalows, semis, duplexes, townhouses, co-ops, walk-ups, flats above stores, and mid-rise apartment buildings. But the residential-building industry has become increasingly narrow in its output, with the result that very little of what goes on the market could be deemed affordable to low-income households.

There are several reasons behind the accumulating shortage of affordable housing in Canada's hub cities, including the demise of social housing programs, weak tenant-protection laws, and the development industry's long-term shift from rental apartments to luxury condominiums. But large municipalities bear some of the blame for failing to adopt or enforce land-use planning and tax policies that encourage a genuine mix of housing types and ease shortages at the bottom end of the market.

In 2001, a taskforce of Ontario building-industry representatives put forward a wish list of small moves which, when taken together, would help reignite the rental-apartment industry. They included relaxed CMHC mortgage financing rules, certain types of income tax deferrals for apartment-building owners who reinvest in new rental buildings, reductions on the GST for construction materials, and equalization of the property tax rates for rental apartments and condominiums. All three levels of government should be giving affordable-housing organizations first dibs on surplus public land—an obvious but often overlooked fix for governments that frequently are too eager to maximize the profit on land sales or pad the pockets of political patrons.[9] The industry taskforce also had a suggestion for municipalities: Ease the parking space requirements for apartments—an environmentally sound move, but one that makes sense only for high-rises built along transit corridors.[10]

There are still other measures available to local councils. For example, minimum floor space requirements for apartment buildings effectively preclude not-for-profit housing organizations from developing very low-cost units. Councils can also adopt policies that require developers to designate a certain proportion of all new apartments to be marketed as affordable units. In Vancouver, local planners, in consultation with neighbourhood associations, have adopted in-fill zoning rules that promote co-ops and low-rise apartment clusters— four- and sixplexes—instead of high-rises, a move that has intensified single-family neighbourhoods without provoking not-in-my-backyard battles.[11] Lastly, local councils can reject redevelopment applications that involve the demolition of older rental buildings populated by seniors to make way for high-rise condos.[12]

In suburban municipalities, which are also experiencing a mounting demand for more affordable housing, councils must phase out archaic post-war zoning rules that strictly separate commercial and residential land uses or allow developers to build only single-family housing in large subdivisions. Such sprawl-inducing policies have meant that fast-growing suburban satellites don't support affordable rental apartments above storefronts—a common and abundant category of housing in older city cores that has all but vanished from the suburban landscape.

Here's where the ugly side of municipal politics rears its head. In all cities, some local politicians have built careers by keeping group homes, shelters, multi-unit residential complexes, and other forms of affordable housing out of their wards, despite an abundance of evidence that pedestrian-oriented, mixed-income neighbourhoods function cohesively and serve as bulwarks against the social disintegration that takes root in highly segregated cities with large concentrations of isolated, low-income housing complexes. Given that we are now witnessing the grim symptoms of Canada's affordable-housing shortage, all three levels of government, not-for-profit housing organizations, and neighbourhood associations need to move beyond the not-in-my-backyard mindset to ensure that large cities and their suburban satellites embrace urban planning principles that encourage a far greater mix of housing than has been built in the past two decades.

INVESTING IN EARLY LEARNING

Child care [is] a must for a modern city.

—CHARLES COFFEY AND MARGARET MCCAIN,
*FINAL REPORT OF THE COMMISSION ON EARLY LEARNING AND
CHILD CARE IN THE CITY OF TORONTO* (2002)

B esides affordable housing, the most distinctively *urban* social program is child care—a service, like housing, that pays little attention to the laws of supply and demand. As far back as the late 19th century, political campaigns to open kindergartens can be traced to locally driven initiatives in larger towns and cities, especially Toronto, the home of Canada's first day nursery. The urban case for accessible and affordable child care programs is even more compelling today than it was when the social reformers and education activists created those early kindergartens. At the beginning of the 21st century, female participation in the Canadian labour force is significantly higher than some of our major trading partners—76 percent compared with just 64 percent for the rest of the Organisation of Economic Co-operation and Development (OECD). That striking feature of Canadian domestic life has steadily boosted demand for child care over the past three decades. But there are other urban factors as well. Canada's hub cities have large numbers of low-income or working poor families that rely on subsidized child care. At the other end of the socio-economic spectrum, both parents in many middle-class families work, partly because of the high cost of city living, but also because professional women now have access to careers in fields once dominated by men.

While Canada's policy of encouraging family reunification means that immigrant families sometimes can rely on grandparents to look after young children, many more urban parents have come to rely on a hodgepodge of arrangements that run the gamut from nannies and neighbours to Healthy Babies programs, daycare, nursery schools, kindergarten, toy libraries, organized after-school activities, and informal drop-in centres. Indeed, for hundreds of thousands of Canadian parents, the workday begins, ends, and is often interrupted by shuttle trips to various paid and unpaid caregivers.

Over the past decade, this confusing system—to the surprise of no one who has had to deal with it—has all but seized up because of underfunding and politicized decision making that paid little heed to the day-to-day needs of urban families. Indeed, our reputation for lacklustre child care and early childhood education has become known internationally—a stain that certainly won't help Canada boost its immigration targets. In 2004, the OECD issued a report card that slammed Canada for tolerating long waiting lists for child care spaces and poor-quality service. "National and provincial policy is still in its initial stages," the report concludes—especially compared with many OECD countries that are "progressing towards publicly managed, universal services focused on the development of young children."[1]

The comparisons are striking. Less than a fifth of Canadian children under age six are in early childhood education programs, while the proportion in European countries including the United Kingdom, France, and Denmark ranges from 60 to 78 percent. Across Europe, a vast majority of nursery-school-age children—four and older—attend some kind of structured early learning program. What is more, E.U. parents pay on average about a quarter of total child care costs, while in Canada, the figure is more like half. The United Kingdom has been boosting its child care funding since 1998. The Netherlands requires employers to purchase child care spaces for their employees, while Finland uses its alcohol taxes for child care programs.

In Canada, by contrast, early learning and child care centres tend to have substandard toys, dated educational materials, and low-rent premises. Most can afford only low wages for their staff. And, as the OECD points out, you get what you pay for: "Economic analyses of government expenditures on ECE&C [early childhood education and care] services broadly concur that the investment pays off handsomely in terms of better health for children, readiness for school, stronger educational results, and additional income for families."[2]

The solutions require not only new money but a sharply different attitude toward child care. Gone are the days when child care could be marginalized as a left-of-centre cause that primarily serves the needs of working-class parents. As it happens, since the late 1990s, there has been a noticeable shift in the way virtually all provincial governments view child care, resulting in the emergence of what amounts to a broad-based consensus on the relationship between early learning programs and the health of cities.

Making Amends

When it comes to federal politics, 2005 will be remembered for the spectacular revelations of the Gomery inquiry into the abuses of Ottawa's sponsorship program. But long after the details of kickbacks and political interference fade, many residents of Canada's large cities may remember 2005 as the year when Ottawa almost delivered on a long-awaited promise to get back into the child care business. Under the provisions of the Liberal-NDP minority budget, Ottawa allocated $5 billion over five years for a new national child care program. In the months after the announcement, one province after another signed agreements with the feds. These were uncontroversial deals that set out mutual expectations, targets for new child care spaces, and other related policies, including a program in Alberta to compensate stay-at-home parents. The money arrived no less than a dozen years after the Liberal Red Book promised that Ottawa would launch a new national child care program once the economy was back on its feet. Within months of those agreements, both the federal Liberals and Stephen Harper's Conservatives were trying to out-do one another with promises of even more child care–related funding during the January 2006 election campaign. The Liberals pledged to extend their national program by another five years, while the Conservatives promised to tear up those 10 federal–provincial child care agreements signed in 2005 and replace them with a new "allowance" to families with young children, worth about $120 a month, to spend as they see fit. Despite these sharply different approaches, both mainstream parties were acknowledging, for the first time, that child care had become one of the basic cost-of-living expenses for urban and suburban families from one end of the country to the other.

As child care experts know, the new funding will go toward making up for what amounts to a lost decade. This was a time when federal spending cuts gave rise to an increasingly incoherent patchwork of child care policies that varied drastically from city to city and province to province. The timing couldn't have been worse. Between 1991 and 2001, the proportion of children under six who were in child care "increased significantly," as did the number of families relying on unregulated care—everything from private nannies to for-profit daycare centres.[3]

In 2003–4, there were more than 745,000 regulated child care spaces in Canada, scarcely enough for a sixth of all children under 12 who are in daycare or nursery school. Of Canada's four most urbanized provinces, in fact, all but Quebec came in under the national average in terms of per capita child care spending. As of 2003–4, the Quebec government was investing over $4800 per regulated child care space, whereas the funding in Alberta, British Columbia, and Ontario ranged from $1100 to $2400. That year, moreover, the total annual public outlay across Canada was $2.4 billion, roughly half of which was spent in Quebec. The figures amply illustrated how great a difference the $5-billion injection of federal funding could have made.[4]

Battles over Circle Time

Beginning in the mid-1990s, child development experts, some politicians, and a growing number of charities began tripping over one another to promote programs geared to the early years—that all-important period between birth and grade one, when children are said to acquire many of the social and cognitive skills that prepare them for school. Seemingly overnight, new parents were bombarded with prescriptive information about smart parenting techniques, while upscale toy stores did a brisk business in educational products geared to the toddler set. Nestled in their thousand-dollar strollers, big-city infants would be exposed to classical music tapes that promised to hasten the development of the circuitry in their young minds.

Behind the hype, however, lay a substantial body of scientific research. In Canada, much of the responsibility for our awareness of the early years rests with J. Fraser Mustard, a former dean of McMaster University's health sciences faculty and co-founder of the Canadian Institute for Advanced Research. In 1999, he and child advocate Margaret McCain, a one-time lieutenant-governor of New Brunswick, released the *Early Years Study*, which painstakingly synthesized an abundance of international and domestic research demonstrating the critical importance of early childhood development programs, both for disadvantaged and low-birth-weight children, as well as those from middle-class backgrounds. Studies in the United Kingdom showed the benefits of exposure to nutrition programs, drop-in centres with parenting support programs, and early childhood education programs that prepare preschoolers to acquire academic skills once they arrive in kindergarten.

It's not that such programs didn't exist. Ontario had its Better Beginnings, Better Futures projects. The United Way chapters in large cities across Canada supported a range of similar initiatives, while others, such as Montreal's 1,2,3 GO, were backed by prominent business executives and leading child development experts. Most of these programs, however, were geared for children growing up in low-income neighbourhoods and aimed to create better links between the often confusing patchwork of child-oriented services for the working poor. The reason: Children from low-income neighbourhoods tend to have a tougher time succeeding in the education system.

But Mustard's study, delivered to the Harris government, cited evidence that Ontario children from all walks of society would have benefited from early learning programs rather than a steady diet of days filled with television, computer games, and inactivity. Mustard and McCain concluded that Ontario needed a universally accessible early learning program for the under-five crowd. His message: Middle-class parents shouldn't be too smug about their own preschoolers' ability to succeed once they enter the education factory.

The *Early Years Study* captured the attention of politicians and policy makers across Canada. One in particular was Dr. Mustard's former colleague at the Canadian Institute for Advanced Research, John Godfrey, a mid-town Toronto MP from a venerable Liberal family. An urbane former professor and newspaper editor, Godfrey was elected during the 1993 Liberal sweep and continued to push his caucus colleagues to make good on their child care promises even after Finance minister Paul Martin slashed social spending. His outspokenness earned him a seat in the backbenches, but it kept the issue alive inside the party. In the wake of the Mustard-McCain report, Godfrey succeeded in pushing Chrétien to launch the National Children's Agenda, which included a $2-billion allocation for early-years programs in the 2001 federal budget. But the post-1995 decentralization of social policy affected this field as well. Some provinces used the funding for child care, while others redirected it. In Ontario's case, the Tories were adamantly opposed to spending the money on early learning programs that involved non-parental care—in other words, nursery schools or regulated daycare centres that require parents to leave their toddlers in the care of others. Instead, Queen's Park in 2002 earmarked $46 million to open one Ontario Early Years drop-in parenting centre in every riding in the province, an evidently political use of the funds that Mustard later condemned. Meanwhile, waiting lists for subsidized daycare spaces continued to grow in large cities, with as many as 3600 names in Toronto in early 2005. "We'd be light years ahead if that money had been well used," said Jane Mercer of the Toronto Coalition for Better Childcare.[5]

Mustard's campaign to focus political attention on early learning exposed a major fault line in child care circles—pitting those groups who see child care as a custodial support service to working parents (especially those with very young children) against those who want Canada to follow Europe, where such programs are primarily educational, and therefore universal in scope.

The Five-Dollar Solution

For many Ontario city-dwellers who endured a decade of frustration with long waiting lists and service reductions, Quebec's experience with forward-looking child care represented the road not taken. In the mid-1990s, the ruling Parti Québécois government launched a wholesale revamping of its education and child care policies. The 1997 reforms created full-day kindergarten for five-year-olds and, by 2000, $5-per-day child care in regulated centres for all parents, with no fee at all for low-income families. As significantly, the government moved to improve the quality of early childhood education, not just with extended kindergarten for four-year-olds but also by requiring a new breed of non-profit child care facilities, known as "centres de la petite enfance" (CPEs), to deliver such programming with qualified educators.

The CPEs were far closer to Mustard's vision than anything Ontario had come up with. They weren't about sitting three- and four-year-olds in rows and trying to teach them to read. Nor were they about glorified babysitting. Indeed, early on, many parents knew very little about early childhood education. When Jennifer Tanyan, a Lachine parent, first enrolled her daughter in a Dorval CPE in 2002, she didn't know what to expect. She soon learned that the program included story periods, arts and crafts, field trips, structured play, drama, music, and easily understood techniques—red-light/green-light signs, for instance—for teaching preschoolers how to cooperate with one another when using toys and books. "That's pedagogy," Tanyan said. "I didn't know it then, but I know it now."[6]

The combination of low universal fees and high-quality educational programs led to an extraordinary expansion of Quebec's child care network. The number of regulated spaces jumped from 82,300 in 1997 to almost 200,000 by 2005. The growth represented, by Canadian standards, an unprecedented and far-sighted investment in the next generation of Quebeckers. As Mustard's research amply demonstrated, money spent on early childhood education is a far more productive use of the taxpayers' money than public funds spent down the road dealing with the long-term problems created when children fail to make a successful transition to the school system.

When Jean Charest's fiscally conservative Liberal Party swept into office in 2003 on a promise to improve the province's balance sheet, the government quickly moved to rein in the $1.2-billion program by boosting the fee to $7 per day, cutting budgets, eliminating some pedagogical consultants, and repealing the previous government's policy of converting for-profit centres to not-for-profit, board-run operations.[7]

Those decisions have proven to be highly unpopular with urban parents in Quebec. Moreover, they fly in the face of a growing body of research about the effectiveness of those 1997 reforms. A 2003 Quebec government report, for example, found that about four-fifths of CPE staff had university or college degrees in early childhood education, while only 40 percent of those working in private daycare centres did. Moreover, a three-year longitudinal survey of 1500 centres and 900 children, "La qualité, ça compte!" (Quality Counts!) found that the non-profit CPEs "generally offered better quality" than other child care options. Indeed, 35 percent of these early childhood development centres were rated as good quality, compared with just 14 percent of private daycare centres. Yet the authors also had a warning about their results: Children from "privileged" backgrounds tended to be enrolled in higher-quality child care facilities, whereas those from low-income families were more likely to be sent to lower-quality or inadequate programs. For child care experts, such skews didn't come as much of a surprise. The study did, however, point out that at the non-profit CPEs, "the children received services that were on average of the same quality, irrespective of the socio-economic status of the families using them." The conclusion: If the government wants to improve child care for disadvantaged families, its best bet is to expand its network of CPEs into low-income neighbourhoods.[8]

Seamless Days

While some politicians, traditionalist parent groups, and a few religious organizations insist on seeing child care debates in ideological terms, most urban parents take a more pragmatic view. For those who are in the workforce by choice or necessity, it means being able to find quality child care in or near the workplace or school. They care about affordability, accessibility, qualified teachers and supervisors, and, increasingly, a commitment to early learning programs. But too often the resources have lagged well behind demand, while jurisdictional turf wars or antiquated policies have given rise to a complicated and fragmented system.

The plight of early childhood education is perhaps the best example of outmoded thinking. Despite compelling evidence from educators and childhood development experts about the long-term benefits, governments have been unable or unwilling to integrate preschool programs into the larger education system—much in the way that Canada's public health care system stops abruptly, and for no really compelling reason, at the gums in our mouths. No one talks about going back to an optional kindergarten system run by a mishmash of private or not-for-profit service providers. But when we're talking about the learning needs of *all* three- and four-year-olds, it's a different story, even though there is solid evidence to suggest that when early learning is left to the vagaries of the market, it's mainly children from middle- and upper-income families who have the opportunity to take advantage of such programs.

Some large urban boards of education solved some of these access problems by, for example, carving out space in elementary schools that can be leased at low cost to nursery schools and daycare centres. Back in the early 1980s, the Toronto Board of Education also began setting up parenting centres at schools. These drop-in centres, staffed by early childhood educators, gave parents access to resources and educational toys, though they didn't offer non-parental care. But they made sense because they could provide new parents, especially recent immigrants, with information about other child support services, and they offered them a social toehold in urban neighbourhoods. They were convenient, too, for parents with older children already enrolled in elementary school programs. For all the benefits, these low-cost resource centres have had to fight for their lives when provincial governments decide they want to slash education spending.

In the late 1990s, Toronto's Atkinson Charitable Foundation, the charity built from the *Toronto Star* fortune, decided to see if it could find ways to crack the silo mentality that afflicted the child care system, challenging community organizations to develop a seamless network of high-quality, accessible daycare and early learning programs under one roof. The City of Toronto and a network of veteran child care experts picked up the gauntlet, using a $3-million, three-year operating grant approved in 2000. In much of Canada, local government has nothing to do with child care. But in Ontario, municipalities pick up a fifth of the cost of regulated subsidized spaces, which meant that Toronto officials could elbow their way into a policy stalemate.

The First Duty pilot project—run in five inner-city schools and five community centres under one governance structure—is, remarkably, the first of its kind to combine kindergarten, parenting services, and early-learning-oriented child care under one roof. It's a rare joint venture between the city, Toronto's two large school boards, public health officials, the Atkinson Charitable Foundation, and some of the provincial Early Years centres. The philosophy is all about flexibility. Parents, for example, can enrol their children full or part time, or on an occasional basis, and they can stay with their youngsters if they choose. What is more, there are seamless connections between the different parts of the program.

While the First Duty project, because of its reliance on municipal funding, could go only so far, news of the experiment has spread to both the provincial and federal governments. Dalton McGuinty's Liberal government announced in the summer of 2005 that it would plough over a billion dollars into a sweeping child care reform program known as Best Start.[9] The guiding principles are strikingly similar to those of First Duty: a focus on "seamless" service, funding for new child care facilities with an emphasis on locating them in schools, and "wrap around" programs so, for example, a child attending junior kindergarten in the morning could move effortlessly into an afternoon program.[10]

Such fixes didn't come a moment too soon for thousands of urban parents who have struggled with the incoherence and underfunding of the child care system and who would much prefer that their public services actually be of service. But this isn't just about improving convenience and breaking down institutional barriers. The future prosperity of Canada's cities will turn on our ability to make important changes across the breadth of the education system, from the infants and toddlers who enter at one end to the 20-something graduates who pop out the other.

PROMOTING DIVERSITY AND ACCESSIBILITY IN URBAN EDUCATION

During the 2000s, education began to move onto the urban agenda, largely because of mounting parental concerns about declining services, falling graduation rates, and growing class sizes. In the 1990s, many reform-minded provincial education officials recast curricula, slashed spending, introduced standardized testing, and eliminated school boards. As a result, heavily urbanized provinces such as British Columbia, Alberta, and Ontario endured years of bitter labour disputes leading to teachers' strikes and lockouts. In recent years, however, governments in British Columbia and Ontario have moved to reinvest in education, bringing down class sizes and repairing some of the damage created when neo-conservative ideology collides with the untidy realities of urban and suburban classrooms serving students from every corner of the globe and every walk of life.

The foundation of Canada's post-war urban prosperity was the viability and inclusiveness of our school system. But in an era of high immigration and rapid globalization, the future social well-being and economic competitiveness of Canada's cities depends even more heavily on the integrity of their education infrastructure. And this is about much more than class size and testing. To succeed in highly diverse cities, schools and other community agencies need to create targeted mentoring and tutoring programs for at-risk students (indeed, Ontario in late 2005 even tabled legislation that seeks to prevent teens from leaving school at age 16). Big-city boards, in turn, must strive to offer a greater variety of choices and flexible programs tailored to heterogeneous urban communities—an institutional recognition of the fact that the one-size-fits-all approach is incompatible with the social reality of our cities.

Most importantly, however, provincial education officials and the federal government must find ways to substantially improve funding for ESL programs for the school-age children of immigrants and refugees. Indeed, as the parent advocacy organization People for Education points out in its 2005 *Urban Schools Strategy,* ESL training should be made a mandatory requirement of all teacher-training programs.[1] It only makes sense, given that so many of Canada's urban classrooms have become multilingual environments. Such diversity-oriented reforms extend beyond high school. If we aspire to build well-educated cities, the provincial and federal governments must introduce policies that significantly improve the accessibility of post-secondary institutions for families who can no longer afford skyrocketing tuition—many of whom are new Canadians struggling to make ends meet. Only when such far-sighted investments are in place will Canada's urban regions be in a position to boast that they are genuinely inclusive learning cities.

Taking the Risk Out of High School

Canada's large cities have seen a surge in the number of poor and increasingly isolated neighbourhoods where children are exposed to gang activity, drug dealing, and the grind of life in public housing projects—all conditions that militate against success in school.

When Toronto's Regent Park was built in the 1950s, it represented the latest thinking about how the city should house low-income families: Its airy, self-contained layout was the antithesis of overcrowded slums. But like so many public housing projects, Regent Park fostered as many problems as it solved and came to be a symbol of misguided social policy.

As of 2004, the average annual income in Regent Park was about $18,000. There are a great many visible minorities, new Canadians, and single-parent families struggling to get by in the high-crime neighbourhood. Families and social workers, moreover, have long recognized an odd short-circuit in the local school system. Almost all children attended the local elementary school, which provided a welcoming and inclusive environment. But after grade eight, Norman Rowen, an educator and health clinic administrator, says, Regent Park kids travelled far outside their community, and their sense of isolation helped create a dropout rate twice the city average. Their prospects were discouraging: homelessness, jail, or low-paying jobs with no future.

In 2001, Rowen started Regent Park's Pathways to Education program, which focuses on the families who live in those rundown apartments. Pathways has come to represent an extraordinary example of how a forward-looking joint venture between universities, the school board, philanthropic organizations, and community organizations can change the lives of vulnerable kids.

The solution has taken many forms. Pathways promotes what Rowen calls "a culture of achievement" by connecting the neighbourhood's high school students with adult mentors and tutors, many of whom are enrolled at the Ontario Institute for Studies in Education of the University of Toronto and at York University. The tutors volunteer once a week, the mentors once every two weeks. The tutoring is compulsory if a student's marks fall below a certain threshold. Counselling for older teens is also available. "There's a need to be present in these kids' lives over the long term," says Rowen.[2] The program aggressively raises funds from the private sector—to provide both the volunteers and participants with transit fares and bursaries for the graduating students who enrol at a college or university.

The results have been impressive. Almost all students in the Regent Park area are enrolled in Pathways, and, after its first four years, the dropout rate has improved substantially. Absenteeism is down, and these high school students are getting more of the credits they need to graduate. As Pathways officials point out, such carefully targeted programs represent huge savings over the long run by transforming future inmates and welfare recipients into self-reliant individuals who earn salaries, buy goods, and contribute taxes to the public purse.[3]

rhoods, and Municipalities

about projects such as Pathways is that it didn't
in Toronto's enormous school board. Like their
ny big city boards, Toronto education officials have
e figuring out how to cut programs, not add them.
ey've become ever more isolated from the urban
rve. Indeed, much of Canada's public school
a serious governance deficit, and trustees in
me increasingly outspoken about gaining back
rs and securing a "new deal" for school boards.
, several big cities have stepped into this
oston, Chicago, Philadelphia, and New York
r state legislatures to grant them direct control
education. New York City mayor Michael
iated his city's handover in 2002, sees municipal
schools in economic development terms. The
gy, he told *The New Yorker*, "is to improve the school system, so
that our children will be able to get the jobs of tomorrow, which
require a higher level of skills." He ended social promotion (the practice
of passing students who haven't mastered their current curriculum),
established leadership training for principals, and closed "dysfunctional"
high schools.[4]

Stanford University professor Michael Kirst concluded there were
some "positive" results from these takeovers, including better budget-
ary control and improved public attitudes toward local schools.
"Proponents justify giving the mayor control of, or an increased role
in, the schools because it provides a single point of electoral accountability, greater integration of children's services with schools, and
better pupil attainment. Such improvements will spur city economic
development, stimulate more middle-class people to live in the city,
and forge a closer alliance between city government and businesses.
Mayors stress that they are in a better position to integrate citywide
services (such as land use, transportation, after-school programs, and
children's social services) with the schools."[5] At the same time, such
takeovers have spurred a trend toward outsourcing the operations of

troubled big-city public schools or entire inner-city districts to for-profit or not-for-profit "education management organizations."[6]

Should Canada's big-city mayors seek to gain control—or some measure of control—over their school districts? Some urbanists think so. "Education should be on the agenda in the debates about how to run Toronto," states University of Western Ontario municipal government expert Andrew Sancton. "The courts have ruled that it's okay for the Government of Ontario to remove the taxing authority of school boards, so it's okay for municipal governments to step in."[7]

But rather than a wholesale administrative takeover, municipalities, big-city boards, and local agencies should begin to reposition local schools as multipurpose community hubs serving diverse urban neighbourhoods. In the 1970s and 1980s, some boards and municipalities built a few combined school–community centres, and it's a concept that deserves to be revived. In British Columbia, where boards and the provincial government support this approach, there are now dozens of "community schools," including several in Greater Vancouver. Community groups make use of school facilities outside school hours, while these institutions—which employ community school coordinators—link up with local organizations that can provide services to students and their families.

The point is that the jurisdictional schism between school boards and other local institutions is artificial and counterproductive. It has resulted in a situation in which our urban public schools are under-utilized and inadequately connected to their surrounding communities. Knitting these local institutions into the broader web of city life represents a vital tool for building social cohesion in diverse urban neighbourhoods.

Choice and Diversity

Of all the many jarring contrasts between public education in Canada and the United States, few are more revealing than our sharply divergent attitudes toward charter schools—those publicly funded academies set up by networks of parents or local organizations to operate independently of the board of education bureaucracy. South of the border, these institutions have come to be seen as a way for low-income minority parents to extricate their children from embattled and barely functioning public schools. Here in Canada, they are viewed by many as a fragmenting influence, eroding the foundations of a public school system that continues to serve over 90 percent of the population. Of all the provinces, only Alberta allows charter schools, but just a few exist, and some of the most high-profile ones were dogged by financial mismanagement. Under the Harris Tories, Ontario tried to launch a variation, offering tax credits for private school tuition. The move aroused widespread public outrage and was soon repealed.

Which is not to say there is no pent-up demand for alternatives. In Ontario, private school enrolment has jumped by more than 30,000 students since the mid-1990s—a trend partially fuelled by years of administrative upheaval in the public system.

But these shifts are mainly driven by the baby boom generation's consumer-oriented attitude toward everything from health care to education. Internet-savvy parents are versed in academic debates on the relative pedagogical merits of whole language versus phonics, the emotional consequences of bullying, and techniques for dealing with developmental problems such as attention deficit disorder. Depending on what parents value, they'll want their kids' schools to deliver arts curricula, heritage-language training, sports training, special education programs, and so on. Some parents and educators are pushing for separate classes for boys and girls in middle schools. Where their parents never questioned what got taught and how discipline was meted out, baby boomers rarely hesitate to intervene in their children's education. Indeed, the publication of school-by-school standardized test scores has added a new dynamic, as education-conscious parents push to get their kids enrolled in high-scoring schools outside their own neighbourhoods.

Immigration has also played a role in our way of thinking about urban schools, as new Canadians bring their own expectations to the education of their children. For decades, private parochial schools served ethnocultural and religious communities. But in some heavily ethnic communities, residents have been asking, quite rightly, whether the public system itself shouldn't be finding ways to accommodate their needs. In 1995, for example, Chinese parents began petitioning the

Richmond School Board, in suburban Vancouver, for the right to set up their own alternative school. This affluent immigrant community opposed multi-grade classes and wanted uniforms and traditional curricula for their children. The Richmond board initially rejected the request because trustees and teachers felt the proposed program was inconsistent with the basic principles of the province's education policy. The parents didn't give up and, over the course of five years, hammered out a compromise program that was consistent with provincial guidelines but relied on the sorts of traditional teaching styles favoured by Richmond's Chinese community.[8]

Nor are these pressures coming only from recent immigrants. Some urban Aboriginal communities and boards have opened all-Native public schools offering traditional learning. More recently, a handful of educators, including Ontario Institute for Studies in Education professor George Dei, have called for all-black schools in Greater Toronto as a means of countering racism and creating an environment more conducive to delivering curricula to children who feel alienated in the mainstream system.

Such controversial ideas raise tough questions and force us to examine what we value about public schools. Do such breakaway programs undermine the education system's ability to inculcate our children with common civic values and expose young people from different backgrounds to Canada's diversity? And, how should parents, educators, and local politicians retool big-city boards to provide genuine choices not just to middle-class kids but across the socio-economic spectrum?

These aren't new issues, of course. In many jurisdictions, schools used to stream children into technical or academic programs, depending on their perceived ability. In the 1960s and 1970s, many urban boards opened progressive alternative schools designed for those kids who simply didn't fit the cookie-cutter mould of mainstream public schools. In the 1970s, boards began to offer French immersion programs and then set up a handful of magnet schools specializing in the arts, science, high-performance sports, or intensive academic programs, such as the international baccalaureate. More recently, there has been growing interest in highly specialized schools—for example, all-girls schools and Canadian studies schools (in Calgary).

Streaming became discredited among educators, while some large boards, especially those facing steep funding cuts, have moved toward greater standardization, cutting alternative schools and programs, and restricting parents from choosing out-of-district schools. And, as the experience of French immersion shows, some of these programs are patronized mainly by middle-class children who grow up in homes where education is highly valued. Indeed, critics fear that by offering parents too much choice, the public system will further fragment along class lines.

If there is a happy medium, Edmonton may have located it. In the early 1970s, the Edmonton board, on the advice of a crusading principal turned superintendent, decided that "one size doesn't fit all, and parents should have a greater voice in their children's education," says Gloria Chalmers, manager of alternative programs for the Edmonton Public School Board (EPSB).[9] Since 1973, the EPSB has allowed parents to send their kids to out-of-district schools and choose from a menu of alternative schools. It has even encouraged them to propose programs. The board has one of North America's best-respected principal recruitment programs, and these school leaders, in turn, enjoy a high level of administrative and financial autonomy.[10] The result is that, today, 15 percent of Edmonton's 80,000 students are enrolled in more than 30 alternative schools, while over half attend schools outside their own communities. No other Canadian school board offers so many options. For its pioneering work, the EPSB, with 209 schools, has become something of a poster child of organizational acumen, demonstrating how a large urban board can manage parental demands for choice without fragmenting the city's public schools. In fact, legislators from several states, including California, Minnesota, and New York, have been beating a path to Edmonton's board, to figure out what it has been doing right.

Chalmers freely admits it's administratively challenging to run a school district where parents can vote with their feet. She notes that the board's motto is "Diversity within neighbourhoods," an apt characterization of the particular challenge of delivering education in urban areas. "Offering choice adds to the complexity of the organization. You have to be flexible and creative and figure things out."[11]

The EPSB moved to an open boundaries system in 1973—meaning that the neighbourhood school no longer enjoyed a monopoly over local kids. But injecting competition into the system required an entirely new approach to managing the local school. That's why, in 1980, the board adopted a "site-based management" approach, providing principals with a lot of added responsibility so they could react to local conditions—"giving them the direction without telling them how," as Chalmers puts it.[12] The board also created a leadership-training program for principals and now supports a culture in which principal—rather than superintendent—is the most sought-after management position.

This radically decentralized board turned out to be highly responsive to middle-class parents' demand for choice, without forgetting its duty to children in disadvantaged neighbourhoods. The EPSB has a small policy shop which fields and then develops parent requests for specialty programs—everything from heritage languages (Ukrainian and German in the 1970s, Arabic and Punjabi in the 2000s) to schools for Aboriginal children, back-to-basics devotees, and Christian academies. In some cases, the EPSB will work with teachers with a specific expertise to develop ideas into viable programs—such as an elementary stream with an orientation toward teaching science through various projects—introduced in a handful of locations in recent years. Chalmers, who has headed this team since 1990, says the board monitors enrolment in its specialized programs and adds sites to meet demand—essentially franchising one successful mini-school (a.k.a. a school-within-a-school) into other locations. A progressive-minded all-girls school, Nellie McClung Girls' Junior High, was introduced for 80 students in 1995; by 2003, it had grown to 500 girls in three locations.[13]

The board, meanwhile, has been careful to locate these alternative stream programs in older downtown schools that are seeing declining enrolment, a nod to the role local schools play within inner-city neighbourhoods in transition. In one older community in the city's southeast, the EPSB in 1999 located L'Académie Vimy Ridge Academy—one of its new programs, this one with a dress code that focuses on Canadian studies and military history—in a school that had seen its enrolment drop from 1500 to 300 during the 1990s.[14]

This long-running organizational overhaul served the EPSB well in 1995, when the Klein government introduced charter school legislation—the only province to do so. In Calgary, where the local board doesn't have this kind of flexibility, eight charter schools have opened up. Edmonton, meanwhile, has organized itself in such a way as to resist this middle-class exodus from the public system. "When we started, it wasn't about market share at all," says Chalmers. "But now it's a factor. Parents have more choices, let's face it. You either respond to that or you don't."[15]

Tuition Blues

If Canadians want their school system to retain its role as a pillar of civic inclusiveness while reversing the disturbing trends in graduation rates, our education officials must find ways to adapt to the evolving demands of urban communities, which means not just testing and smaller classes, but more ESL programs, strategic supports for at-risk youth, improved partnerships with other urban institutions, and administrative nimbleness. Yet none of this will matter if, upon graduation, daunting economic barriers prevent young people from continuing into post-secondary schooling—a life move that is indisputably linked to future material and social well-being.

The picture doesn't look promising. With a growing concentration of low-income families in our large cities, more and more young people are unable to finance university or college, even with student loans. Between the early 1990s and 2003–4—a period when average household income stagnated—tuitions more than doubled, rising at four times the rate of inflation in some provinces (the exception being Quebec, where tuitions have been frozen since the early 1990s). Graduates are leaving university with crushing debt loads, an average of $25,000 in 2003, up from about $10,000 a decade earlier. The costs have risen so sharply that several provinces in recent years introduced tuition freezes. Studies in Canada and the United States have shown, not surprisingly, that such costs deter students from low-income families from pursuing higher education.[16] As former Ontario premier Bob Rae's 2005 commission on the state of post-secondary institutions reveals, 40 percent of children from the top income quartile attend university, compared with only 17 percent from the lowest-income quartile.[17] Accessibility, clearly, has become a major problem.

Internationally, Canada ranks third, after Korea and the United States, in spending as a percentage of gross domestic product on universities and colleges.[18] In the early 2000s, the federal government launched a bevy of heavily hyped programs geared to post-secondary institutions—funding for research chairs so universities could attract top-flight academics and staunch the so-called brain drain; seed money for academic think-tanks geared to high-priority areas such as health; and a new tax shelter incentive designed to encourage families to save for their children's university or college education. Yet, the *actual* spending trends are revealing. Federal cash transfers to Ontario's universities and colleges fell 49 percent between 1992 and 2003, while the total value of Ottawa's research grants and contracts going to Ontario academics jumped by 79 percent. Provincial funding, meanwhile, has shrunk. Here again, as Rae points out, we face one of the enduring trickle-down legacies of the 1995 assault on the deficit: Funding to post-secondary institutions remains lower in real dollar terms in 2005 than it was in 1992, even while developing economies such as China and India are making "unprecedented" investments in this sector.

More than almost any other public institution, Canada's universities and community colleges are, with very few exceptions, urban creatures. They can help cities attract top-flight academics and graduate students. And increasingly, their development offices are establishing R&D partnerships with investors, corporations, hospitals, and a range of other agencies. One need only look at the technology clusters in and around Boston, Waterloo, Toronto, and San Francisco to recognize the way universities can dramatically alter urban economies. But in a more diffuse sense, cities depend on the social and cultural energy created by a steady influx of young people attending post-secondary institutions. Recent policy decisions, however, have placed far more emphasis on the university's economic development role than on its social function, not just in providing higher education but also in serving as a hub of urban vitality.

Rae's diagnosis of Ontario's post-secondary sector should resonate in other provinces, including British Columbia, Alberta, and Nova Scotia, where many universities and colleges have boosted tuitions well beyond the level of affordability. Rae took both the federal and provincial governments to task for failing to properly manage their student loans programs and for underfunding institutions so central to Canada's future economic and social well-being. But Rae points out that post-secondary institutions aren't some kind of "nationalized industry" controlled by provincial bureaucrats. In his view, they must have the flexibility to set tuition, make competitive or strategic decisions about their programs, and tap into other non-governmental sources of revenue. Students, in turn, must share the cost because they benefit in the long run from an investment in their own education.

So what about affordability? The answer isn't just about providing more middle-class parents with access to large student loans, as Stephen Harper promised during the 2006 election campaign. Such measures don't address the very real financial barriers facing low-income families. Rather, Rae's recommendation, which generated considerable controversy among student groups, provides a much more compelling market-oriented alternative to unsustainable increases in public funding, on the one hand, and unregulated tuition hikes, on the other. He calls for a long-term loan repayment system linked directly to a graduate's real earnings, rather than the current system, which has long required graduates to start paying off their debt within six months of leaving school, regardless of their employment status.

"I am convinced," Rae says, "that if we told all students, 'We'll pay for you now, and you can pay us back when you have the money,' then more students would attend—and succeed. Think of these deferred costs as an investment on behalf of students and their parents, to be repaid later as a 'Graduate Benefit'—an investment whose benefits clearly last a lifetime. The Graduate Benefit would be repaid by graduates, but the repayment amount would be linked to income and could even be paid through payroll deductions." In other words, something that looks much more like a mortgage, amortized over many years, than a short-term, financially onerous loan. And, as he points out, "A system that relies on a healthy mix of public and private funding will be more sustainable and successful than one that relies exclusively on either the state or the market."[19]

PART THREE

TOWARD THE NEW CITY

Since the early 1990s, there has been mounting interest among urban experts in the emergence of "world cities," those ultra-dynamic metropolises that function as global leaders in a world increasingly dominated by city-states. These places are large, to be sure, but their power derives from much more than population. Global cities, as it turns out, share a very specific set of characteristics. They regularly host international conferences and provide a base for international institutions. They are serviced by highly sophisticated transportation and transit networks, high-tech communications systems, and major hub airports. Such cities attract head offices, foreign firms, and networks of leading business service providers. They are media centres and cultural destinations, and their academic institutions attract pre-eminent researchers. Most of all, global cities are ethnically diverse and resolutely cosmopolitan in outlook.

The Globalization and World Cities Study Group, a Loughborough University think-tank linked to an international network of prominent urban experts, has established a four-tier ranking: alpha, beta, and gamma cities, plus those considered to be up-and-coming candidates. The alphas include New York, London, Paris, Tokyo, as well as Chicago, Frankfurt, Hong Kong, Los Angeles, Milan, and Singapore. Toronto ranks as a beta city, in the same league as San Francisco and Sydney. Montreal is considered to be a gamma, on par with Rome and Stockholm. Vancouver and Calgary, the only other Canadian cities that make the cut, are in the emerging category.

Forget the G-8. The global city network has become the most powerful of all international clubs.

Why should Canadians care? The reason, quite simply, is that only these cities will be in a position to control their destinies in an unpredictable world. Part Two outlined some of the reforms needed to ensure that our cities remain socially healthy. But in the coming decades, Canada's largest urban regions will have no choice but to keep pace with these world cities. This isn't merely about giving municipalities a bit more cash to fix potholes or buy buses under the rubric of the New Deal. Nor is it about securing showcase international festivals and events. Rather, it entails a wholesale shift in our political culture, one that recognizes the specific requirements of a handful of very large cities whose prosperity has a direct bearing on the national interest. What is more, this shift can be accomplished only if we equip our major city-regions with the tools they will need to attract and manage economic growth, focus development, and create culturally vibrant urban landscapes. Failure to do so will consign Canada to also-ran status, a nation whose time has come and gone.

AUTONOMOUS CITIES

Cities are now the level at which federal and provincial policy initiatives are implemented, including welfare, training, immigration-settlement services, and social housing. Unfortunately, cities have little political, economic, or fiscal manoeuvrability—a reality that conflicts with their growing importance in the global economy.

—ANNE GOLDEN, *THE GLOBE AND MAIL* (2001)

At the cusp of a new century, the leaders of Canada's major cities arrive at work each day and cast their gaze over teeming urban landscapes that are at once deeply troubled, invigorating, fractured, and alive with opportunity. They must reconcile the pressing needs of the poor with the demands of building 21st-century infrastructure. They have to think about daycare and immigrant resettlement in the morning, then turn their attention to state-of-the-art waste management and high-capacity optical networks in the afternoon. They ponder the mysterious relationships between a lively neighbourhood park, climate change, and global networks of researchers; between the machinations of a faraway drug war and the profusion of guns in low-income housing projects. In large cities, as former Toronto chief planner Paul Bedford says, "Everything is connected to everything in some way."[1] We have no choice but to try to make sense of this complex urban web. But the ultimate challenge facing every citizen of the new Canadian city is to marshal the explosive and unpredictable energy released when the global collides with the local.

After a decade and a half of tumultuous political upheaval, three inescapable conclusions should be obvious. First, that Canada's economic and social destiny is being forged in its major cities; second, that certain laws and spending decisions promulgated at the national and provincial levels have had far-reaching and problematic implications for cities; and third, that municipal governments don't have the means to deal with the fallout.

On paper, federal and provincial policies are supposed to be universally applicable. But when provincial governments change rules governing rent control or the hospitalization of the mentally ill, the effect is felt disproportionately on the streets of large cities. When Ottawa boosted Canada's immigration targets in the mid-1980s, it created unprecedented stresses in urban schools, hospitals, and community agencies. In a country as overwhelmingly urban as Canada, as Anne Golden points out, the unintended consequences of a great many political decisions—no matter how important or closely considered—invariably reverberate in our hub cities.

The downloading of federal and provincial services has prompted municipal and civic leaders to call on the upper levels of government to give cities a seat at the decision-making table. At the same time, the rapid expansion of Canada's big cities is forcing policy makers to reconsider the scope of local government itself. After all, large cities encompass multiple municipalities, and their leaders grapple with regional issues—transportation, air quality, economic development—alongside the strictly local ones.

Yet, our constitution, forged at a time when only 10 percent of the population lived in cities and towns, marginalizes municipal government. But as Canada closes in on its 140th birthday, the logic of these interconnected urban trends points inexorably toward the elevation of the formal role of local institutions—not just municipalities but also school boards, health districts, development corporations, port authorities, and quasi-governmental agencies—in the determination of Canada's future. The less remote the decision makers, the greater the chance of implementing flexible, responsive, and fiscally responsible policies that simultaneously recognize local conditions while addressing regional dilemmas such as gridlock and urban air quality.

This isn't just a Canadian problem, obviously. Rapid urban growth has been the defining feature of most industrialized and developing countries. As University of Western Ontario political scientist Neil Bradford observes, "Local governments everywhere today are grappling with economic, social and cultural challenges well outside the traditional municipal box of 'property servicing.'"[2] Among all of Canada's trading partners, the interconnectedness of urban, regional, national, and international issues is best understood in Europe, with its long tradition of urban self-government. As the European Charter puts it, "Local authorities should be entitled to adequate financial resources of their own, distinct from those of other levels of government and to dispose freely of such revenues within the framework of their powers."[3] In countries such as Germany, Sweden, and the Netherlands, leading cities have political clout, financial resources, and a clear sense of their importance in national life.

Canada's hub cities have succeeded in recent years in making a case for gaining access to more predictable revenue sources, and they've put urban issues firmly on the national agenda. But the success of this determined exercise in urban empowerment depends on whether the upper levels approve legal reforms that acknowledge the increasingly important role of local government as well as the legitimacy of local democracy.

To this end, central cities need access to more flexible revenues, and they must be able to exert far more authority over development and land-use planning. Big-city mayors, in turn, have to be granted additional power to implement their mandates and demonstrate their accountability to voters. Meanwhile, provincial governments need to establish regional bodies with a mandate to tackle those urban issues that cut across municipal boundaries. As well, they must relieve the municipal sector of its obligation to fund basic social services, as is currently the case in Ontario and Nova Scotia. Lastly, the well-being of these new city-states will depend heavily on a high degree of intergovernmental collaboration, as well as forward-looking partnerships with the private sector, citizens groups, educational institutions, and the not-for-profit organizations that supplied the social glue that has held our cities together in the face of a decade or more of severe funding cuts.

Unscrambling the Amalgamation Egg

In Montreal and Halifax, the historic city halls are self-important stone and masonry landmarks, architecturally emblematic of a colony's desire to reproduce old-world symbols of power and dominion. But the more revealing image of Canada's relatively brief municipal past is a famous 1886 photograph of a group of stern-faced Vancouver aldermen sitting around a rough-hewn wooden table. Just behind them is a canvas tent, bearing a sign that reads "City Hall." At the time, municipal governments in Amsterdam, London, and Frankfurt had existed in one form or another for centuries, whereas Canada's had only just started. The era of organized local government in Canada can be traced to 1839, when Lord Durham, the governor general dispatched by the British parliament to Canada to investigate the rebellions of 1837, recommended making municipal institutions an order of government. Canada's earliest municipal laws came into effect in 1849, and they put local officials in charge of "issues" such as public drunkenness and profanity, the regulation of cattle and poultry in public places, travelling salesmen, and noise abatement.[4] Scarcely two decades later, the Fathers of Confederation chose to ignore Durham's recommendation and gave the provinces full responsibility to manage municipal affairs, then seen as a minor jurisdiction.[5]

For decades, municipal governments in Canada concerned themselves with the prosaic work of city building—laying pipes and sidewalks, constructing roads and bridges. While visions of more livable cities began to emerge in the second half of the nineteenth century, Canadian cities began to regulate urban development only in the 1920s.

There were glimpses of the expanded future role of local government when public health and works officials in the late 19th and early 20th centuries began searching for solutions to sanitary conditions and to eradicate infectious water-borne diseases in overcrowded slums such as Toronto's Ward (which extended from College Street to Queen Street and from Bay Street to University Avenue) or Montreal's East End. But the fact is that Canada's big cities were shaped in large measure by federal bodies such as the port authorities, the railways, the St. Lawrence Seaway, and the military.

The Depression of the 1930s triggered urgent calls from local leaders for a broad range of social reforms intended to address the grinding misery that had befallen Canada's largest cities—measures that included housing programs, settlement agencies, rules governing working conditions, enhanced parks and recreation facilities, health regulations, planning rules, and public ownership of electrical utilities. In the 1930s and 1940s, Ottawa began creating the welfare state, and national social programs such as unemployment insurance and affordable housing. In 1946, C.D. Howe, the legendary minister of reconstruction in Mackenzie King's government, called for the refurbishment of public facilities and more coherent planning on the "urban fringe."

"The great urban problems of the earlier era were effectively re-defined as subsets of national ones," says Neil Bradford, who sees clear parallels to what has been happening in Canada since the 1990s. "Municipal finances were stabilized but local government was marginalized as a political space and, for public policy purposes, the unique qualities of places fell out of view."[6]

The modernization of municipal politics began in earnest in the 1950s and 1960s, when Ontario, Quebec, Manitoba, and British Columbia all took steps to establish various forms of two-tier metropolitan government in larger urban centres. These reforms were an attempt by provincial governments to manage rapid, haphazard suburban growth. Development pressures were outpacing the construction of infrastructure, and these new regional municipalities were assigned the financial and administrative responsibility to marshal all that new growth by managing regional tasks, such as major roads, water treatment, and policing. Upper-tier governments were established in Montreal, Quebec City, Ottawa-Carleton, and Winnipeg—all of which had far outgrown their original municipal boundaries. But it was Metro Toronto, which came into existence in 1953 and was led for years by a hard-driving, hard-drinking Tory lawyer named Fred Gardiner, that came to be renowned internationally as the state of the art in regional government.

Not all of Canada's big cities followed this route: Calgary, Saskatoon, and Regina grew by steadily annexing the developing areas on their borders. In 1970, Manitoba disbanded Greater Winnipeg and established Metropolitan Winnipeg, an amalgamated upper-tier local government, only 10 years after the introduction of the two-tier structure. Over the next 20 years, the two-tier governments in Quebec and Ontario came under attack and have mostly disappeared, except in the Greater Toronto Area's fast-growing 905 suburbs.

This period also saw a surge of activism at the local level. In downtown Toronto, for example, there were heated battles in the late 1960s and early 1970s between residents groups and Metro bureaucrats intent on building a network of inner-city expressways; the neighbourhood organizations ultimately prevailed—as they did in a similar battle in Vancouver. Metro's credibility as an agent of civic improvement was permanently impaired, while a generation of idealistic, urban-minded reformers—spurred on by the likes of Jane Jacobs and former Toronto mayor David Crombie—infused new energy into local politics.

Through the late 1990s, many of Canada's largest cities were rocked by a new and destabilizing development: imposed municipal amalgamations, which occurred in Toronto, Halifax, Ottawa, Montreal, and Hamilton, often in the face of strident opposition from local voters who were well within their rights to demand to know why provincial governments should be allowed to wipe out democratically elected councils. This wave of forced restructurings—carried out in the name of fiscal probity—held echoes of the anti-government sentiment that swept through the United States and the United Kingdom during the Reagan-Thatcher era. They also ran counter to one of the core principles of the Council of Europe's 1985 Charter of Local Self-Government, which denounced municipal mergers without the residents' approval.[7]

The promised administrative savings never materialized, as critics in the media and academe had predicted all along. Nor did the policy objections to amalgamation come exclusively from the left end of the political spectrum. Robert Bish, an expert in public administration and economics at the University of Victoria, blasted these developments in a wide-ranging study published in 2001 by the C.D. Howe Institute. He decried amalgamation as an "obsolete" 19th-century idea incompatible with the urban complexity of the 21st century. According to Bish, there was no evidence to suggest that one very large municipal government could efficiently deliver the full range of urban services. "Amalgamation," he commented, "tends to eliminate the very characteristics of local government that are critical to the most successful and least costly systems."[8] What large urban regions need is a variety of municipalities, offering residents choices.

Bish's case against amalgamation ventured well beyond economics and took aim at issues that drive right to the heart of the question of how local governments ought to represent their constituents. In his view, large modern cities are such complex places that they defy tidy administrative solutions to anything. "The diversity of metropolitan areas requires close links to citizens and the ability to handle a wide variety of activities on a small scale.... The current weight of evidence is that no single organization can accomplish these tasks."[9] As he warned, presciently, large governments favour well-organized lobbyists and marginalize other segments of urban society that haven't mastered the techniques of manipulating the political process. Large governments tend to reduce, rather than increase, voter turnout. And the sheer cost of winning elected office becomes so high that candidates have little choice but to become reliant on donations from special interest groups and align themselves ever more closely with political parties.

Most city-dwellers spend very little time focusing on the fine points of municipal governance and administration. And in fact, the structure of local government is only one factor in the well-being of urban regions. Cities succeed or fail for many reasons: location (Toronto), architectural innovation (Chicago), natural beauty (Vancouver and Halifax), proximity to natural resources (Calgary and Edmonton), and the blind luck that finds an aspiring entrepreneur such as Bill Gates in Seattle rather than, say, Tulsa.[10]

But local government structures are crucial to the evolution of cities because they control land-use planning, deploy infrastructure, and provide various local social services. Winnipeg, where amalgamation occurred over three decades ago, presents a cautionary tale about the long-term consequences of sweeping reforms to municipal finance and governance. When the provincial NDP eliminated the two-tier system, it did so to equalize taxes across Winnipeg. At the time, Winnipeg expected to become Canada's Chicago, with a projected population of a million people. By the turn of the 21st century, the city was locked in a spiral of decline—more like Cleveland than Chicago—while Saskatoon, though equally remote, is booming.

The 1996 amalgamation in Halifax has played out quite differently. Halifax Regional Municipality (HRM) was created from the former cities of Halifax and its county; the Town of Bedford; and Dartmouth. With more than 350,000 residents, the new city is an awkward amalgam of everything from bustling downtown Halifax to the forested rural regions to the south and west. Nova Scotia initially promised to carry off the merger for less than $10 million, but the final costs exceeded $26 million.[11] The merged council attempted to deal with its regional composition by creating a three-tier property tax system, with separate rates for its urban, suburban, and rural regions—an acknowledgment of the different service levels through the new HRM.

To some extent, the municipal upheaval caused by the amalgamation was overshadowed by the recovery of the Halifax economy, which began to surge in the latter 1990s thanks to a sharp increase in cruise ship tourism and off-shore oil revenues. The politically emboldened HRM found itself in a position to push ahead with solutions to tenacious infrastructure failings that had long bedevilled the city—a cleanup of the Halifax harbour, an innovative region-wide approach to waste management, and plans for the establishment of a light rail transit network.

In 1997, Mike Harris's Tories in Ontario followed Nova Scotia's lead by lowering the amalgamation axe on Metro Toronto and its six lower-tier municipalities, consisting of Toronto's downtown and the surrounding post-war suburbs of Scarborough, North York, Etobicoke, East York, and York. The result was six years of political and administrative upheaval, financial scandal, and wearisome conflict between the new city and the provincial government.[12] The $7-billion-a-year municipal corporation that emerged from this amalgamation is the sixth-largest government in Canada—ahead of all the Atlantic provinces combined. But while the seven former municipalities faced their own budget pressures, the new city is saddled with almost $3 billion in debt and has an annual operating shortfall that exceeds $1 billion, according to a 2005 analysis by the Conference Board of Canada.[13]

Yet, Toronto's amalgamation produced an unforeseen by-product: It focused political attention on the simmering social problems in Toronto's post-war suburbs, which had seen an exodus of manufacturing jobs, rising poverty, and a woeful shortage of community programs. Still, nearly a decade after amalgamation, there remain pressing questions about whether the new City of Toronto can ever be an effective government, given its unwieldy size and entrenched financial problems.

The considerable risks inherent in trying to unscramble the amalgamation egg can be seen in the confusion that has settled like a dense fog over the City of Montreal, which went through a wrenching amalgamation between 2000 and 2002, and then attempted to reverse it two years later. As in Toronto, Montreal's metropolitan government represented only about half the population living in the metropolitan area that encompasses the Island of Montreal, as well as Laval and the fast-growing regions surrounding it on either shore of the St. Lawrence River. In the late 1990s, Montreal's mayor Pierre Bourque began lobbying Lucien Bouchard's PQ government to amalgamate the 28 local municipalities on the island. Bouchard responded by promising legislation that would create a "one-island-one-city" model.[14] Ostensibly inspired by the establishment of the new City of Toronto, Bourque hoped amalgamation would position Montreal as a global city, strengthen the core, and provide the poorer parts of the island with access to the tax bases of wealthier downtown and suburban municipalities. The political subtext was more complex. With the old City of Montreal in dire financial straits, Bourque was eager to gain access to the large reserve funds controlled by affluent island municipalities such as Westmount and Outremont. Then there was language: Bourque's amalgamation plans also revealed a linguistic power play that would put a francophone municipal government in charge of Montreal's predominantly Anglo west end neighbourhoods.

The ensuing battle was as ugly as the anti-amalgamation fight in Toronto. The old City of Montreal was notorious for its bloated bureaucracy, a state of affairs that seemed unlikely to change, given promises that no civil servants would lose their jobs.[15] Anglo residents groups outside central Montreal, fearing that their local services would be dismantled or reduced, attempted to counter the mergers with a

legal challenge that ultimately failed. Two voices emerged to oppose
Bourque's amalgamation: Peter Trent, the bilingual millionaire mayor
of Westmount, and Montreal *Gazette* columnist Henry Aubin, who
provided highly critical coverage of the feared erosion of local democracy.

In 2003, Jean Charest's Liberals defeated the PQ and, responding to
critics such as Aubin, promised legislation allowing "de-mergers." Under
amalgamation, the 28 former municipalities had been transformed into
boroughs, each with its own directly elected mayor but significantly
fewer councillors. The new law permitted these boroughs to re-establish
themselves as independent municipalities, provided that 10 percent of
eligible voters signed a petition requesting a de-merger and 35 percent
actually voted in favour of the move in a referendum. But the legislation
also included mystifyingly complex provisions governing the service
relationships between these de-merged municipalities and the broader
City of Montreal (e.g., with respect to city-wide services like snow-
clearing).

As of 2005, 12 of the 28 municipalities had opted out, and the result
is pervasive confusion. "Amalgamation is one of the greatest fiascos that
ever happened. The whole thing was poorly done from the beginning,"
states Mario Polese, a senior researcher of urbanization, culture, and
society at the Institut national de la recherche scientifique in Montreal.
The cure, however, may be as bad as the disease. "No one knows how
the new system is going to work," Polese notes. "The city's agenda has
been totally overshadowed because of the fiasco of amalgamation and
de-amalgamation. No politician will touch this again for two decades."[16]

Of Canada's three largest urban regions, only Greater Vancouver has
avoided the disruption and confusion inflicted on local government in
these other cities. The reasons trace back half a century, to 1953, when
the B.C. government gave the City of Vancouver its own charter, establishing what would become an enduring and far-sighted tradition of
provincial forbearance in the affairs of its largest city. Less than a decade
later, British Columbia established the Greater Vancouver Regional
District (GVRD)—a weak federation of local municipalities that
encompassed the Lower Mainland, including Richmond, Surrey, and
Delta. Its territory precisely corresponds to the Vancouver census

metropolitan area (CMA)—meaning it extends across Greater Vancouver's true geographic limits, as opposed to artificial political boundaries.[17] British Columbia, in turn, gave the GVRD a pragmatic, limited mandate to perform regional services where it made sense to intervene in the affairs of local municipalities. But it isn't a directly elected government, meaning its decisions are made by a board composed of mayors and councillors from the member municipalities. In other words, local officials are compelled to develop regional solutions. Some governance experts have come to regard the GVRD as Canada's most effective model of local democracy.

The relationships among the GVRD's downtown and suburban municipalities over issues such as transportation policy are at times strained. But they have to work out their differences. In fact, notably absent in British Columbia's otherwise fractious political culture is that provincial compulsion to rationalize local government by merging downtown and suburban municipalities in a bid to eliminate political conflict. Which isn't surprising. After all, two recent B.C. premiers, Mike Harcourt and Gordon Campbell, are former Vancouver mayors. Each represents opposite ends of the ideological spectrum, but both evince a respect for urban government, albeit in different ways. The result is an enviable degree of stability and autonomy. "By Canadian standards," observes Andrew Sancton, a University of Western Ontario political scientist who specializes in city government, "the municipal system of the Vancouver CMA is quite highly fragmented, but the GVRD acts to provide services such as public transit, water and sewage services, garbage disposal, and regional parks. Its [2004] *Livable Regional Strategic Plan* is recognized internationally as a model of its kind."[18]

Greater Toronto, by contrast, can boast of no similarly practical or flexible governance structures. The 1997 amalgamation of the City of Toronto, as Sancton notes, completely failed to address the bigger issue, which was the complete absence of regional planning for the Greater Toronto Area. Why? Toronto, with a population of 2.8 million people, is merely the core of an amoeba-like megalopolis with a population of 6.7 million (the same as California's Bay Area) that sprawls in a large built-up arc from Fort Erie-Niagara to Kitchener-Waterloo, past Toronto and its suburbs, and on east to Oshawa—an area known as the Greater Golden Horseshoe.

In 1995, Anne Golden, then head of the United Way of Greater Toronto, led a taskforce that recommended a Greater Toronto Council not unlike the GVRD. It would consist of delegates from the GTA's local municipalities—including Toronto, Mississauga, and Richmond Hill—and assume responsibility for regional planning and economic development.[19] But the Harris government ignored her prescription and passed planning laws that gutted the power of local councils to dictate growth. The sprawl and air pollution around the GTA today attest to the importance of governance in the evolution of cities, as well as the complexity of urban issues that pay little attention to municipal boundaries. In fact, a decade after Golden's report, the McGuinty Liberals, having come to office on a promise to rein in sprawl, concluded that regional planning around the GTA was too complex to be managed by local politicians. Instead, they passed legislation handing senior Cabinet ministers sweeping powers to direct urban development patterns and make strategic municipal infrastructure investments within the Greater Golden Horseshoe.

New Powers for Cities

The fraught amalgamations of the late 1990s gave rise to a potent force in Canadian politics. Since the late 1990s, big-city mayors began storming the national stage and have come to represent the driving forces behind the New Deal for cities. Their newfound influence is the local echo of an international trend that has seen powerful big-city mayors emerge as key figures in national and supranational politics.[20]

They weren't the only ones calling for wholesale changes in the way cities are governed. In Ontario in the late 1990s, the triple whammy of amalgamation, downloading, and laissez-faire planning so alarmed many prominent urbanists that a group, including Jane Jacobs and philanthropist Alan Broadbent, put together a proposal for a "Greater Toronto Charter." They saw the need for something like an urban constitution that recognizes the region and its municipalities as a legitimate order of government, equipped with broad-ranging jurisdiction, fiscal power, and iron-clad protection from high-handed provincial regimes intent on trumping local democracy. The proposal won the endorsement of a coalition of Greater Toronto mayors, prominent business leaders, and community activists.[21]

The charter was but one volley in a nationwide push by large cities to secure a greater degree of political legitimacy. Provincial legislatures since the mid-1990s have begun cranking out reforms—some incremental, others ambitious—to municipal laws. Alberta, Manitoba, Nova Scotia, and Ontario (twice) all passed legislation handing extra powers to municipal councils. In 1996, British Columbia negotiated a "recognition protocol" with the Union of B.C. Municipalities, which recognized local government as independent, responsible, and accountable. (The municipal sector there even succeeded in extracting a promise from Victoria that Crown corporations and provincial agencies would pay their property taxes—long a thorn in the side of municipal officials.) Seven years later, Manitoba gave Winnipeg its own charter, granting the city additional powers in 14 "spheres" of jurisdiction. Meanwhile, Jean Charest's Liberals in Quebec vowed during the 2003 election campaign to expand the autonomy of municipal councils and give them access to a share of the sales tax.

A key feature of these reforms is that municipal corporations were granted what are known as natural person powers. Traditionally, municipal councils were allowed to do only the things their provincial overseers permitted them to do. Under the new rules, they have, at least in theory, more latitude to take matters into their own hands, provided they aren't trespassing into areas of explicit provincial jurisdiction (e.g., environmental protection). And, in fact, there is little question that new municipal issues have opened up, requiring a more flexible regulatory approach. Cities today deal with issues ranging from environmental cleanup operations to alternative fuels. Some want more flexibility to enter into private-public partnerships, such as the innovative relationship between York Region and a private consortium that is running its new rapid transit service. The caveat is that these expanded powers will be exercised only if municipalities have the wherewithal to act on them, and that depends on bold leadership combined with new sources of revenue, such as hotel occupancy levies or sales taxes.

This debate, however, isn't just about regulatory authority and money. Since the early 1990s, the organizations representing municipalities in both British Columbia and Ontario have been pushing their provincial masters to come clean on how they manage this intergovernmental relationship at the political level. Cities have complained that they are not consulted in advance about important policy decisions, even though they often end up dealing with the fallout.

Reinforcing the expanded political and legislative status that municipalities have acquired, local governments also appear to be getting a slightly better shake from the courts. While the Supreme Courts in both Ontario and Quebec slammed the door on legal challenges to municipal and school board amalgamations, judges in recent years have sided with cities in court cases where their bylaws have come under attack. As Donald Lidstone, a B.C. municipal legislation expert, says, "The courts are willing to imply jurisdiction where powers are not expressly conferred."[22]

One precedent-setting case that went all the way to the Supreme Court involved a lawsuit brought by Calgary cabbies upset over a city bylaw capping the issuance of new licences. In October of 2002, a hundred drivers belonging to the United Taxi Drivers' Fellowship went on a hunger strike, complaining that no new licences had been issued in 16 years. "There should be no restriction for any driver who wants to serve the public in a free enterprise system," said Fellowship secretary Surinder Tut.[23] The cabbies' case against the city was upheld by the Alberta Court of Appeal but overturned in March 2004 by the Supreme Court of Canada. The justices ruled that the licence-capping bylaw was consistent with Alberta's 1995 Municipal Act, which had given cities enhanced regulatory authority. As Calgary's city solicitor told reporters, "This is much more than just a taxi issue. It involves aspects of all operations municipal governments in Alberta are involved in and could also impact other provinces and territories."[24]

All these swirling political forces coalesced in Ontario in the first 18 months of the McGuinty government's term, during which the new Liberal Cabinet hustled through an ambitious agenda of municipal reforms. While the government put itself in charge of regional planning, the Liberals made some key changes in the planning laws designed to reinstate some of the powers municipal councils had lost during the Harris years. At the same time, officials working for Dalton McGuinty and Toronto mayor David Miller embarked on what was to be the icing on this urban cake—legislation giving the City of Toronto and its council extensive new political, administrative, and regulatory powers. Toronto politicians for some time complained about how they had to beg for provincial approval for a wide range of purely local moves—everything from installing speed humps to building new streetcar lines. Miller wanted to liberate the city from the overweening influence of provincial bureaucrats and have Toronto recognized as a full order of government.

The new law, tabled in late 2005, gives Toronto's mayor more administrative clout—a reaction to the peculiar situation where a leader directly elected across Canada's largest municipality still has only one vote on council. But Queen's Park stopped short of creating the kind of "strong mayor" system that exists in some cities, including Chicago, where Mayor Richard Daley used the considerable powers vested in his office to make sweeping improvements to the city's downtown, take over the troubled school board, and bulldoze a small waterfront airport to make way for more green space. Even the Toronto Board of Trade called on the Liberals to give the mayor the power to develop a "long-term strategic plan" for the city and then be held accountable for its implementation.[25]

As for its other provisions, the new City of Toronto Act gives the municipality more independence but falls short of providing Canada's largest municipality with the kind of autonomy Vancouver enjoys. Toronto council was granted "broad permissive governmental powers" that give it the authority to require developers to submit to a design review process; to prevent the conversion of rental housing to condominiums; and to establish "minimum densities" as a means of promoting more compact development.[26] But city council's planning decisions—like those of all other Ontario municipalities, no matter how small—can still be overruled by the unelected members of the Ontario Municipal Board (OMB), a quasi-judicial body that traces its origins to the late 19th century, a period when local councils in Ontario were unsophisticated and susceptible to corruption.

During the Harris years, the OMB became a kind of star-chamber, dominated by patronage appointees who used their powers to impose the Tories' free market ideology on the urban landscape. Municipalities lost virtually all their authority to plan, resulting in sprawling, uncoordinated suburban development and boom times for development lawyers. Under the McGuinty Liberals, the pendulum swung back somewhat, as the provincial government in 2004 and 2005 introduced changes in its planning laws and policies designed to rein in the OMB while giving municipal councils more ability to encourage compact development. According to the government, the reforms give municipalities the power to establish requirements for new residential developments, such as external architectural guidelines for new buildings, transit- and pedestrian-friendly subdivision layouts, and energy-efficient design.[27]

Still, Ontario doesn't yet enjoy the municipal policy conditions driving Vancouver's extraordinary renaissance. In British Columbia, there is no equivalent to the OMB, and it shows. The City of Vancouver, which has a charter but no strong mayor system, wields broad powers to execute a land-use planning vision that has transformed the downtown into a showcase of architectural excellence and urban-minded, compact development driven by principles that go well beyond the bottom line.[28] What is more, since 1999, the provincial government has been providing stable revenue sources for transportation infrastructure projects and has participated in a tripartite agreement with Ottawa to tackle the drug crisis on the Downtown Eastside. Nor do MLAs make a sport out of bashing Vancouver. Indeed, Victoria stays out of the way—an implicit recognition that Greater Vancouver is a mature metropolis whose leaders are capable of managing the region's growth responsibly. As Vancouver's internationally respected chief planner Larry Beasley puts it, "We like to say the city plans the city."[29] The point is that municipal government in large urban areas operates in conditions that compel the elected representatives and their officials to be both accountable and aware of the social and economic implications of their planning policies. As with teenagers, the only way to encourage responsible, mature behaviour is to offer up a measure of trust.

These sharp philosophical differences in urban government systems in Canada's largest city-regions pose a basic question that lurks at the heart of the debate on the new deal for cities: Thrust into the choppy seas of the global economy—with its loss of manufacturing jobs to China and its soaring energy prices—which of Canada's major urban regions is now best positioned to thrive in the future?

As important is the recognition that these rapid changes in the power of local government situate Canada squarely in the mainstream of a dynamic that's long characterized the evolution of cities—that urban economic success breeds a desire for autonomy and political self-determination. In medieval Europe, observe urban historians Richard T. LeGates and Frederic Stout, "it was the economic function of the great trading towns that led inevitably to their growing power and political independence. Having used their wealth to win from the barons the right to self-government, the medieval towns became islands of freedom in a sea of feudal obligation."[30] Sound familiar? Canadians, it must be said, should be relieved to know that their hub cities want control over their own destinies. What remains to be seen is whether our upper levels of government are prepared to take a step back and allow these new players to guide Canada into the future.

SELF-SUFFICIENT CITIES

When Glen Murray became mayor of Winnipeg in the late 1990s, he took command of a city in decline. More than any of Canada's 10 hub cities, Winnipeg had seen the rapid impoverishment of many of its downtown neighbourhoods—communities that had once hummed with urban life and commercial activity. The street life around Portage and Main, Winnipeg's historic central intersection, had been killed off by misguided planning and, according to some local critics, the decentralizing impact of suburban sprawl.[1] In some areas north of the core, main streets were lined with boarded-up storefronts, while homeowners with means abandoned adjacent neighbourhoods in favour of safer subdivisions.

Despite well over three decades of revitalization schemes underwritten by all three levels of government, a cosmopolitan city once renowned for its business acumen and arts scene was locked in the downward fiscal spiral that has afflicted many U.S. cities, including Detroit. How does this process work? Businesses move away from the downtown, taking with them jobs and tax assessment. As the employers leave, their employees follow, leaving behind low-income residents who either can't afford to move or haven't got jobs.[2] Retail businesses fold as their customers leave. Residential real estate values stagnate or fall, causing the tax base to shrink. But municipal expenses don't change. The roads still need to be cleared, the garbage collected, the sewers maintained.

All the while, the residents of these increasingly impoverished, crime-ridden areas grow needier and rely more heavily on public services. They spend proportionally more of their income on housing and food than do middle- and upper-income city-dwellers. The net effect is that the municipality's costs rise while its revenues fall. Local politicians, who tend to be elected by homeowners rather than tenants, come under mounting pressure to redirect municipal spending to the neighbourhoods that pay the bills. Consequently, infrastructure in rundown areas is neglected.[3] Ultimately, the evidence of this neglect (potholes, broken playgrounds, graffiti) serves to discourage home buyers and young families, which is how the cycle feeds on itself.

As a fast-talking, peripatetic, urban-minded mayor, Murray was relentless when it came to promoting Winnipeg. But he soon realized he would need to attack some long-standing assumptions about how the city finances itself in order to bring about a meaningful improvement in Winnipeg's quality of life. Chief among these was the city's reliance on property taxes as its primary means of tax revenue. Murray had his officials undertake a wide-ranging assessment of Winnipeg's costs and its revenue sources, a process that yielded some surprising results.

His officials calculated, for example, that the city's streets simply weren't paying for themselves. They took up a lot of space and consumed a large chunk of the city's budget but failed to generate commensurate tax revenues. As journalist Don Gillmor explained in *Saturday Night*, "[Murray] propose[d] a complete overhaul of an antiquated tax system, which would reflect a closer relationship between taxation and behaviour. Thus, a fuel tax would punish SUVs and trucks and have a marginal effect on fuel-efficient vehicles. According to Murray, 80 percent of police calls are alcohol-related, and so a liquor tax would go toward the police budget. A fee for garbage pickup would have the greatest impact on those who fail to recycle."[4]

In 2002, Murray, Jane Jacobs, and Toronto philanthropist Alan Broadbent founded the C-5, a caucus of the mayors of Canada's five largest cities, to ratchet up the debate about the crisis in municipal financing. The following year, Murray tabled a high-stakes proposal to correct these imbalances with a radical restructuring of the city's finances—a bold stroke that has changed the thinking of urban leaders and city-friendly politicians across Canada.

Murray's "new deal for Winnipeg" was intriguingly simple. He proposed that provincial grants to the City of Winnipeg—$139 million in 2004—be replaced with a share of the provincial income tax. As well, he said Ottawa should transfer to Winnipeg two-thirds of one percentage point of all the GST revenues collected within the city. In the first year, the new arrangement would bring an extra $123 million to the city, to be used for upgrading aging infrastructure. According to an analysis by the Conference Board of Canada, Murray's new deal would bring long-term benefits to the city—a 0.9 percent boost to the city's gross domestic product and an additional 2300 jobs by 2020, thanks to an annual $88-million boost in construction spending. And it would reduce Winnipeg's dependence on property taxes as a principal source of funds. As the Conference Board warned, Winnipeg can't continue to finance its infrastructure under the status quo.[5] It needed new sources of revenue to ward off financial collapse and all the associated urban ills.

How We Measure Up

For well over a decade, Ottawa and most provincial governments have eliminated deficits, paid down debt, and cut taxes. In the process, they slashed funding to municipalities while downloading a host of services to the municipal or local level—everything from airports and ports to transit, child care, waste water financing, and social housing. For instance, British Columbia's transfers to municipalities plummeted from $209 million in 1996 to $90 million just three years later, with much of that money ending up in small cities.[6] Ontario cities were especially hard hit. Since the late 1990s, they have had to spend almost a quarter of their total expenditures on delivering mandated social services such as welfare. "In order to meet emerging local needs, municipalities are forced, by legislation or practicality, to fill the void," comments Donald Lidstone, a B.C. municipal law expert.[7]

Urban voters themselves have contributed to the squeeze, observes Enid Slack, director of the Institute for Municipal Finance and Governance at the University of Toronto's Munk Centre for International Studies: "Pressure for zero property tax increases, which began with Proposition 13 in California and has recently spread to this country, has prevented many municipalities from increasing property taxes to finance growing service demands."[8]

The resulting fiscal squeeze allowed the upper levels of government to reap the financial and political rewards of a booming economy, while local governments were left with mounting debt loads and deteriorating services. There is a poignant irony here. The decline in urban quality of life is occurring at a time when our health care system is gobbling up an ever larger chunk of our public finances. Wouldn't it make more sense to take a proactive, preventative approach by investing in healthy cities?

Many of the world's most globally competitive cities have been the beneficiaries of far-sighted urban-minded reforms. In the United Kingdom, Europe, Japan, and the United States, local governments have gained access to a more stable and broad-based source of revenues than is available to most Canadian cities. In Canada, by contrast, the primary source of municipal revenues is the property tax and service charges, such as parking permit fees. Keen to protect their own taxing power, provincial governments have been careful to limit municipalities to a narrow range of other revenue sources, such as licences, development charges, and debentures.

In fast-growing and complex urban areas, however, property taxes have turned out to be a highly flawed form of revenue. They are regressive (i.e., there is no relationship between a homeowner's tax bill and that person's income) and inelastic, meaning the revenues don't expand in step with economic activity.[9] They provoke inter-neighbourhood conflict and are vulnerable to politicized decision making that distorts urban development patterns. In neighbourhoods with vibrant real estate markets, a growing number of homeowners have had to endure sharp increases to their property taxes because the assessed market value of their dwellings—which forms the basis of the calculation of the tax bill—rises whether or not they're planning to sell. For fixed-income seniors, who will make up an ever larger proportion of our urban population in coming years, such increases are tough to stomach. At the same time, property taxes don't reflect the fact that a large, busy city's infrastructure and services—water, roads, parks—are also used by thousands of visitors: tourists, business people, freight trucks, and so on. Such externalities have much less impact on smaller, quieter cities.

Meanwhile, tenants, who make up a less affluent segment of any urban population, often end up paying disproportionately high property taxes, but those costs are hidden in their monthly rent payments. Municipal politicians may overtax commercial and industrial landowners, for the simple reason that businesses don't vote. In rapidly expanding urban regions, moreover, outlying municipalities will deliberately lure businesses away from the core with cut-rate property taxes—a beggar-thy-neighbour growth tactic closely linked to the deterioration and depopulation of downtowns.

For all its flaws, property tax is being called upon to fund a range of costly urban social services—the legacy of a decade of provincial down-loading. In Nova Scotia, the only province that requires local government to help pay for schools, municipalities pick up 15 percent of the education bill. Ontario municipalities contribute almost a quarter of every dollar spent on social assistance. Affordable housing, certain public health programs, welfare, child care—public finance experts are unanimous in their view that these income redistribution programs ought to be financed by progressive taxes that grow with the economy.

As any corporate CFO knows, declining sales and rising costs are a recipe for trouble. That's why, in 2001, City of Toronto finance officials began calculating how far their own corporation had fallen behind. The results were alarming. While federal and provincial revenues jumped by 42 and 53 percent respectively during the go-go 1990s, the municipality's own income had risen just 6 percent between 1992 and 2001—not even keeping pace with inflation.[10] In terms of total taxes collected, billions more were flowing out of big cities than were coming back in the form of programs and services.

Long-term shifts in the distribution of Toronto's expenditures tell the story of how rapid increases in the cost of provincially mandated social service programs impact other civic departments. Between 1978 and 2003, municipal spending on protection to persons and property, transportation, recreation and culture, planning and development, and general government all fell as a proportion of total expenditures. The two areas that saw significant gains were environmental services (i.e., waste management and water treatment and sewer systems) and social services and housing. The financial burden of funding these social services has increased sharply, from 12.7 to 27.4 percent of all municipal spending. In other words, when cities are forced to use property taxes to pay for income redistribution programs, they have no choice but to cut back on everything from maintaining parks to policing. Such trends fly in the face of international trends that link urban quality of life to economic growth.[11]

Nor is this just a Toronto complaint. In most of Canada's large cities, there is a net outflow of tax revenue, meaning that Canada's major urban regions are essentially subsidizing public services for the rest of the country. In Calgary in 2001, officials estimated that, of every dollar of tax collected inside the city limits, merely eight cents went toward supporting local services. "When you look at the quality of life, we deliver virtually everything other than health care and education," former Calgary mayor Al Duerr said at the time. "It's a massive misappropriation of funds. The wrong people are managing the money."[12]

Big cities, of course, have tremendous advantages, and they have to pull their weight—to a point. But the practical consequences of what many big-city mayors have taken to calling the "fiscal imbalance" is that Canadian municipalities not only face increasing difficulty financing their own services but they now operate at a clear financial disadvantage compared with their counterparts in the United States and Europe (see table below). In New York, Seattle, Dublin, and Madrid, property taxes represent less than 40 percent of municipal revenues, evidence that these cities function in a political environment that recognizes the need for a diversity of revenue sources for large urban regions.[13]

SOURCES OF MUNICIPAL REVENUE

	Local Taxes (%)	User Fees (%)	State/Province (%)	Federal/National (%)
Canada	53	21	18	1
United States	43	40	6	4
Europe	28	19	28	32

Adapted from Joe Berridge, "Cities in the New Canada," *TD Forum on Canada's Standard of Living* (October 2002), 13. Available at www.td.com/economics/standard/full/Berridge.pdf. Reprinted with permission.

The American experience, however, offers limited lessons for Canadian cities. Ever since the 1960s, U.S. urban funding arrangements have been inextricably bound up in the dynamics of racial politics. Meanwhile, many mid-sized municipalities rely on discredited financing ideas to promote local economic development, such as enormous municipal tax breaks designed to attract sports arenas and large factories. The notable exception is tax increment financing (TIF), which a growing number of U.S. cities have tried as a means of revitalizing troubled inner-city neighbourhoods. Using strict criteria, municipal councils designate areas in need of reinvestment and issue bonds that will be used to repair urban infrastructure, improve streetscapes, and even finance training programs. Such moves trigger private sector investment, and the bonds are gradually paid back using the incremental increases in the property taxes within the TIF zone. Some mid-sized U.S. municipalities have misused TIFs, effectively turning them into subsidies for shopping mall developers. But since the mid-1990s, Chicago mayor Richard Daley has turned his city around with the help of dozens of TIFs that generate more than $5 in private investment for each dollar of public financing. In Canada, only the City of Calgary is experimenting with TIFs, in an attempt to spur the redevelopment of the downtown's scruffy east end.[14]

For solutions to the riddle of local government finances, we would be wiser to look to Europe, where several countries have been far more successful in achieving a balance between economic development, sustainability, and urban quality of life. The link between national decision making in Europe and stable local government is a reflection of the fact that municipal institutions in countries such as Germany and the Netherlands predate nation-states by centuries. Unlike Canadian cities, they aren't constantly called upon to prove their legitimacy but are recognized as an accountable order of government.

The funding arrangements follow accordingly. In 1996, 43 large E.U. cities spent, on average, $2100 per capita—almost three times more than in Canadian municipalities. In Sweden, for instance, local governments have been given the cash and responsibility for delivering a wider range of national social programs. At the supra-national level, the European Union's regional development budget—U.S.$175 billion from 2000 to 2006—poured funds into urban projects, especially transit, roads, and water systems. France, in turn, levies a payroll tax on all but the smallest companies located in cities with more than 30,000 people. That money goes back into transit. Frankfurt, Germany's business and financial capital, spent U.S.$4979 per capita in 1997, almost three times more than Toronto, while in Stockholm, the comparable figure exceeds $10,000.[15]

London's mayor Ken Livingstone in the early 2000s imposed a congestion charge—a $20-a-day electronic toll on cars entering a horrendously crowded 21-square-kilometre patch of the downtown during peak hours—which will generate an additional £1.3 billion over 10 years of operation. The proceeds must, by law, be reinvested in London's transport infrastructure.[16] In Stockholm, tolls on a ring road generate U.S.$130 million annually—30 percent of which goes toward transit and bike paths.[17] The Netherlands transfers funds to the country's four major cities—Amsterdam, Rotterdam, Utrecht, and The Hague—for programs proposed by municipal councils, including infrastructure, housing, economic development, and transit.[18] Swedish cities levy their own income tax. German cities automatically receive a 15 percent cut of the federal income tax and 7.5 percent of the state taxes. As a Federation of Canadian Municipalities study notes, "European funding to municipal government supports sustainable development in the broadest sense … E.U. funds increased the competitiveness and productivity of urban regions by supporting investment in infrastructure and human capital."[19]

The Infrastructure Deficit

Much of local government spending goes toward the meat-and-potatoes work of ensuring that a city functions properly—fixing roads and making sure there is somewhere to put garbage; maintaining the network of pipes that bring in fresh water and take away waste; providing emergency services, and operating local recreational facilities. This is as true for New York City as it is for Timmins, Ontario. But in big cities, local government is compelled to underwrite costly long-term responsibilities—those relating to transportation, waste management, social services, law enforcement, and so on—that smaller, more homogeneous communities simply don't have to deal with.

None is more expensive, or more crucial, than municipal infrastructure. Cities that allow their physical assets to crumble are doomed because homeowners, investors, and businesses identify the neglect as evidence of urban decline, and leave.

Canada's municipal infrastructure deficit stands at about $60 billion, according to the Canadian Society of Civil Engineers. This figure, which is a ballpark estimate, is growing at roughly $2 billion annually.[20] In 1984, the infrastructure deficit stood at just $12 billion—meaning we've seen a fivefold jump in one generation. Peel away the big numbers and you find an accumulation of crumbling sidewalks, potholes, neglected city parks, leaking water mains, antiquated buses, faltering subway tracks, and a general dearth of funds for civic improvements.

In the City of Toronto, for example, works officials estimate that it could take almost 200 years—two centuries!—to refurbish century-old sewer pipes at the current rate of replacement. The City of Edmonton, meanwhile, can devote no more than half of what it should be spending to maintain municipal infrastructure, even though the city sits on the edge of one of the world's largest crude oil reserves. Alberta's Recreation and Parks Association estimates that three-quarters of the province's major recreation facilities are in the latter half of their life expectancy. Upgrading them is estimated to cost $270 million. "There is a very broad consensus that the [infrastructure] debt exists, that it is substantial and that it poses a threat to the quality of life and prosperity of Alberta's communities," the Canada West Foundation, a Calgary think-tank, concluded in the fall of 2004. "Tinkering with the status quo will not suffice."[21]

But "tinkering" is an apt description for how the upper levels of government have addressed the issue of the declining infrastructure in Canada's hub cities. In 1994, shortly after taking office, Prime Minister Jean Chrétien announced that his newly elected Liberal government would be setting up something called Canada Infrastructure Works Program (CIWP), a $2-billion program to run through 1998–99. With the country struggling to recover from the early 1990s recession, he said the sight of construction workers on the job in big cities would help restore consumer confidence. The prime minister promised that the funds would create 100,000 new jobs. In short, as generations of politicians have done, Chrétien was seeking to stoke the economy by building roads and bridges. But the money came with a proviso: Every project would be cost-shared evenly between Ottawa, the provincial government, and the municipality. With the defeat of the Charlottetown Accord still fresh in the public's mind and separatist sentiment on the rise in Quebec, the Liberals knew they had to be cautious about wading into provincial jurisdiction. The key point is that Chrétien, the product of small-town Quebec politics, wasn't thinking about urban finances so much as pork barrel job creation schemes.

The CIWP funding yielded all sorts of projects—everything from a $160-million trade and convention centre in Toronto to rural access roads for private golf courses and sidewalk upgrades. The Auditor General expressed reservations about the gap between the CIWP's ostensible purpose and the way the money was actually used.[22]

By the time the program expired in 1999, however, the political landscape had changed dramatically. Paul Martin's campaign, as finance minister, to kill the federal deficit had precipitated severe budget shortfalls at the provincial and municipal level. Moreover, governments hostile to the federal Liberals—especially in Ontario and Alberta— opposed the earlier tri-level infrastructure funding agreements. The Harris government in particular downloaded enormous costs on big cities, including transit and social housing, but blocked hundreds of millions in infrastructure funds for partisan reasons. By contrast, Vancouver and Winnipeg both negotiated tripartite funding arrangements with Ottawa and their respective provincial governments, deals designed to address inner-city social issues and urban renewal projects.

Meanwhile, U.S. president Bill Clinton, during his second term in office, succeeded in establishing a six-year $217-billion fund—the Transportation Equity Act for the 21st Century—to finance transportation infrastructure in partnership with local and state governments. Of that, $41 billion went to transit—an extraordinary and unprecedented investment. The contrast wasn't lost on Canadian municipal leaders. Such a program would have pumped the equivalent of $42 million in annual funding into the GTA alone.

Since the late 1990s, Ottawa has reinvented its municipal infrastructure programs in various guises; first as a $425-million extension to the CIWP, then as the $2.05-billion Infrastructure Canada Program. After that came the Canadian Strategic Infrastructure Program, which was established as a $2-billion fund in 2001 and topped up with another $2 billion in 2003. The government also created a $600-million Border Infrastructure Fund to underwrite investments such as improved crossings for trucks.

Strip away all the labelling and Ottawa's contribution to rebuilding Canada's big-city infrastructure has worked out to about $1 billion a year between 1994 and 2005, with roughly the same amount provided by provincial and municipal partners. That level of funding barely keeps up with the normal deterioration of roads, bridges, and transit systems, and certainly fails to make a significant dent in the backlog.

Over time, however, the politics of Ottawa's infrastructure rhetoric underwent a transformation. The objective was no longer old-fashioned job creation but, rather, urban "sustainability" and "quality of life." Some of the new money found its way into financing green projects such as harbour cleanups in St. John's and Halifax, and transit expansion schemes for Ottawa and Toronto. Yet, the infrastructure dollars also underwrote traditional highway schemes in rural and Western Canada. And these programs continued to fund projects that could only be loosely described as infrastructure, such as a $400-million contribution to a convention centre in Vancouver and a $25-million shuttle bus service for tourists visiting Niagara Falls.

No self-respecting politician is immune from the allure of a feel-good ribbon cutting, and such investments have generated a steady stream of press conferences, where MPs, MPPs, and MLAs can gather to glad hand and have their pictures taken. Behind the smiling faces, however, urban leaders have had to grit their teeth, because they knew how much cajoling, pleading, and lobbying preceded the launch of each new iteration of infrastructure funding. Municipal officials had no certainty about the next round of funding, and so they couldn't press ahead with large, multi-year projects, especially transit.

By the early 2000s, big-city mayors had begun to push Ottawa to adopt a less overtly political approach. They wanted to end the annual dance that required mayors to go to Ottawa with their hands out. One suggested solution was to take a portion of the federal gas excise tax and earmark it for urban infrastructure. The big-city mayors endorsed the scheme, but it aroused the ire of federal finance officials, who disliked the notion of dedicated taxes. It also raised tricky jurisdictional issues, because most provinces, particularly Quebec, don't want to allow Ottawa to intrude on their constitutional turf.

What about the policy case for this idea? The federal gas excise tax has been around since the 1970s. It was set up originally to underwrite transportation infrastructure. The policy as written had a certain tidiness: The tax linked vehicular traffic to the ongoing reinvestment in Canada's roads and bridges. Over time, the reality proved to be far less elegant. Transport Canada, the federal agency in charge of such assets, had real trouble spending the annual $5 billion generated by the tax. Typically, Ottawa allocated about $400 million to highway construction, much of it in Atlantic Canada, where road building remains a favoured instrument of political patronage. The rest was siphoned off for the federal government's other spending plans.

In 2002, Chrétien appointed Toronto MP Judy Sgro to conduct a cross-country fact-finding investigation into the financial plight of cities. Her taskforce recommended national transit, infrastructure, and housing programs. Although her report was cautious, it emboldened other nationally prominent urban advocates—former B.C. premier Mike Harcourt, Toronto-area MPs John Godfrey and Byron Wilfert, and then Winnipeg mayor Glen Murray—to step up calls for reforms. Behind the scenes, Ottawa's powerful mandarins were also starting to recognize that the federal government had fallen behind in its policy thinking about cities. European countries, as we saw earlier, have in recent years made large, strategic investments in urban and regional transit. In the United States, transit agencies received about $29 billion between 2001 and 2006, thanks to a 2.8-cents-per-gallon transfer from the federal gas tax. Even the provincial governments had changed their approach. Quebec had established a 1.5-cents-per-litre transfer to Montreal's transit agency from its provincial gas tax. The B.C. government in the late 1990s set up a Greater Vancouver Transportation Authority and gave it access to a wide range of predictable funding sources, including a 4-cents-per-litre share of the provincial gas tax, worth $79 million per year. Even Alberta was allocating part of its fuel tax to transportation infrastructure in Calgary and Edmonton.[23]

The final two holdout jurisdictions—Queen's Park and the Government of Canada—changed their minds in 2004. Soon after defeating the provincial Tories, Dalton McGuinty's Liberals at Queen's Park approved a $680-million transfer to 78 transit authorities between 2004 and 2007, linked to a gas tax transfer that would ramp up to two cents per litre.[24] Paul Martin, in his 2004 budget, moved to eliminate the GST on municipal purchasing—a $7-billion transfer over a decade. Then, a year later, the newly appointed minister for Infrastructure and Communities, John Godfrey, unveiled the government's much antici-pated New Deal for Cities and Communities. That such an explicitly urban-oriented Cabinet position had been created testified to a shift in the way Ottawa was thinking. Not since the early 1970s, when Pierre Trudeau established the position of minister of state for Urban Affairs, had cities enjoyed so much visibility in Cabinet.

The successor to Ottawa's previous municipal infrastructure programs, the New Deal for Cities and Communities was funded by earmarking a portion of the federal gas tax, up to $5 billion. The funding was contingent on agreements between Ottawa and each province, which were negotiated quickly. The City of Toronto, alone among all Canadian municipalities, cut its own agreement with Ottawa—a precedent in the fraught history of intergovernmental rela-tions in Canada. Finally, the 2005 budget deal between the minority Liberals and Jack Layton's NDP delivered an additional $900 million for green urban infrastructure.[25]

On the surface, these moves seemed to provide Canada's hub cities with greater certainty, and certainly more funding. For example, some of Alberta's share will go to extending Edmonton's light rail transit. And the Toronto Transit Commission used its share to buy new low-floor, wheelchair-accessible buses. But the effectiveness of Ottawa's new infrastructure program was highly limited because the Liberals insisted on spreading the funding among all Canadian municipalities instead of focusing these investments on the handful of large urban regions that needed it the most. As of 2005, the program had a five-year best-before date, meaning that the big-city mayors' goal of truly long-term sustainable funding had not been achieved. The federal Liberals sought to buy themselves some votes in smaller communities, but they demonstrated that they didn't yet understand the urgency of the financial headaches facing Canada's largest municipalities.

Paradigm Shift

In the fall of 2003, Winnipeg's Glen Murray and Toronto's David Miller, who had just been elected to succeed Mel Lastman as mayor, quietly began contemplating a dramatic policy fix that they hoped would go well beyond the limitations of the gas tax transfer. They wanted a guaranteed share of tax revenues that *grew* with the economy—namely, the federal income tax. Manitoba had passed a law that transferred 2.2 percent of the provincial income tax to municipalities—equivalent to $47.3 million for Winnipeg in 2002.[26] The two mayors figured it was time to export this policy to the rest of Canada's big cities, as well as to the federal government. The objective was to further diversify municipal revenue sources and thus reduce their financial risk. It's a strategy familiar to any savvy investor.

Ottawa, they knew, routinely transferred tax points to the provinces. What this means is that a certain percentage of the federal income tax is simply shifted over to the provinces' coffers each year. These transfers are often the by-product of high-level agreements over health care or cost-shared social programs. But once complete, the money moves with a minimum of bureaucratic fuss and publicity, year after year after year. Canada's equalization system works in much the same way. The federal government has a long-standing formula to redistribute some of its revenues among have and have-not provinces. These First Ministers deals are all subject to political debate and review, of course. But unlike the highly politicized infrastructure funds, they drop out of view on implementation, leaving provincial officials to do what is necessary to meet their end of the bargain. It's a way for Ottawa to share the federal government's considerable wealth without throwing around its political or bureaucratic heft. Tax point transfers don't generate photo-ops, and that, as Miller and Murray reckoned, was precisely the point.

Early in 2004, Miller invited Canada's 10 big-city mayors to Toronto for a summit. Miller and Murray decided in advance to propose to their counterparts that they ask for a share of the income tax. Building on what Murray had pitched to the Manitoba government a year earlier, it was a gutsy gambit that upped the ante in the national debate over a new deal for cities. During the two-day summit, they laid out their strategy, both to the other mayors and to senior federal officials. The mayors' communiqué focused on the gas tax but also called on Ottawa to hand over income tax points to Canadian cities. During a press conference, Montreal mayor Gerald Tremblay, a lawyer and former Cabinet minister in Robert Bourassa's Liberal Cabinet, spoke eloquently about the need to reinvest in cities because cities were the source of the economic growth that had so enriched federal coffers. What is good for Montreal is good for Quebec, he said, striking a note he knew would play well with Premier Jean Charest.

Some critics say this sharing of income tax revenues will have the effect of taking cash out of schools and hospitals and putting it into the hands of big-city mayors. But many E.U. nations—which routinely show up at the top of international rankings for productivity and quality of life—have figured out how to share their taxing capacity with their major cities without beggaring social programs.

Moreover, the size and sustainability of the federal surplus suggests we can afford to take this step without abandoning our commitment to federal fiscal prudence. In 2004, Enid Slack, an authority on municipal finance, calculated the cost of various revenue-sharing options. Her conclusion (see table on the next page) was that both levels could transfer small portions of their tax bases to Canada's hub cities without making a serious dent in their own spending capacity. Indeed, the total amount from the federal income tax earmarked for these eight cities adds up to $1.4 billion—less than half of what Martin, as Finance minister, would routinely set aside as a contingency fund and then direct toward Ottawa's accumulated debt.

The federal government has a long track record of deploying its spending powers to promote Canada's economic competitiveness, one which includes giving subsidies to strategic industrial sectors and

ESTIMATED COSTS OF REVENUE-SHARING OPTIONS

	1% Federal Income Tax ($ million)	1% Provincial Sales Tax ($ million)	1-Cent-per-Litre Fuel Excise Tax ($ million)	1% Hotel Occupancy Tax ($ million)
Vancouver	108	82	$19	$4
Calgary	186	N/A*	$16	$2.2
Edmonton	92	N/A	12	2.6
Toronto	447	369	37	8
Ottawa	161	135	14	2.4
Montreal	253	112	28	6
Halifax	61	46	6	1
Winnipeg	110	87	12	1.5

* Alberta does not charge sales tax.

Harry M. Kitchen and Enid Slack, "Special Study: New Finance Options for Municipal Governments," *Canadian Tax Journal*, vol. 51, no. 6 (2003), 2215–75. Reprinted with permission.

R&D. Investing a significant part of that surplus in the financial competitiveness of Canada's hub cities is an integral part of any national economic development policy. The alternative is to risk the decline of the handful of large cities that generate well over half of Canada's wealth.

It's an argument that Martin acknowledged in a speech to municipal leaders in June 2005: "Our cities will lose their effectiveness and their vibrancy if their infrastructure is allowed to deteriorate. There will be implications for our national economy and so too for our international reputation. Our big cities are Canada's signature to the world. We cannot allow them to atrophy."[27] But his soaring rhetoric didn't match his government's tentative actions. Canada's large urban regions were on a more stable financial footing than in the late 1990s, but they remained woefully over-dependent on a form of taxation that no longer met the demographic and economic needs of 21st-century city-states.

COMPACT CITIES

*As we look to the 1990s, we see a compact, transit-oriented
Metropolitan Toronto as the centre of the region, surrounded by
highway-oriented urban sprawl modelled on U.S. cities: Vienna
surrounded by Phoenix.*

—JURI PILL, *TORONTO STAR* (1990)

When Juri Pill, a long-time senior manager with the Toronto
Transit Commission, came out with his famous quip, he put
his finger on one of the major fault lines within Canadian cities: In
many respects, almost all of our major urban centres are a synthesis of
American and European urbanism—sprawling and car-oriented on the
one hand, yet cosmopolitan and vital on the other. In the coming
decades of the 21st century, Canadian cities will experience an epic
tug of war between these different halves of their split personalities.
Which will prevail—the concentrated, conservation-minded European
approach or the decentralized suburban consumerism that has replaced
the frontier mentality of America? More than anything else, our collective decisions about sprawl, transit, energy, and the protection of the
urban environment will determine the future persona of the handful of
large cities that have become home to the vast majority of Canadians.

The Lessons of New Urbanism

In the early 1990s, Ontario's NDP government decided to take on the
worst abuses of suburban planning. Then premier Bob Rae hired

former Toronto mayor John Sewell to oversee a province-wide commission. Its mandate was to recommend reforms to the planning laws, with an eye to encouraging the development of more compact, transit-friendly suburbs. Queen's Park also wanted to test drive its ideas in a new suburb called Cornell, a 970-hectare subdivision on the outskirts of Markham. It was to become a showcase for European-style development in a typical suburban landscape.[1]

Markham is an affluent satellite northeast of Toronto, home to a large Asian community and much of the city's high-tech industry. Cornell was to be designed according to the principles of the New Urbanists, a group of U.S. architects and planners whose members condemned the anti-social design elements of suburbia—indistinguishable, inward-facing homes that turned their backs on streets with little social life or, worse, the gated communities popping up all across America. They bemoaned planning that failed to create the subtle hierarchy of street patterns typical of older neighbourhoods, as well as the demise of institutions such as the corner store. They advocated neo-traditional town planning (squares, grid streets, and so on) and residential architecture featuring front porches, eyes-on-the-street design, and relatively narrow lots.

This Jane Jacobs-esque philosophy appealed to many journalists and urbanists, and it stirred up nostalgic feelings in the hearts of some North Americans who yearned for more traditional urban settings. Developers took note and began promoting New Urbanist subdivisions with the blessing of municipal planners. Similar ventures—featuring main streets, rear laneways, mid-rise apartments, and row-house-style residential design—sprouted in Calgary and Victoria, as well as else-where in Greater Toronto.

For all the hype, New Urbanism failed to short-circuit sprawl because developers and planners focused on residential aesthetics without addressing the more fundamental issue, which was the contin-ued creation of car-dependent subdivisions. But in Markham, the local debate on Cornell whetted the public's appetite for intensification in a traditionally suburban landscape. In the decade since Cornell got started, Markham has begun implementing an ambitious plan that will concentrate thousands of new mid-rise residential units, townhouses, schools, parks, retailers, and offices in a 365-hectare swath of land near the civic centre. The city is developing pedestrian-oriented buildings and access to a new bus rapid transit service linking the area with the rest of the city.

It's hardly the only suburban municipality to take this step. In Burnaby and the GTA suburbs of Mississauga, North York, and Brampton, planners and developers have been gradually creating relatively compact, high-density cores—some centred on older downtown districts and others growing up around shopping plazas. In many cases, these fast-emerging downtowns have a raw quality—they are incomplete cityscapes, dominated by building sites and parking lots at the expense of pedestrian amenities. But they have become substantial employment centres with recreational amenities and high-rise apartments. They are also becoming transit hubs, serving their own suburbs. In a sense, they represent New Urbanism in reverse: The aesthetic and urban design elements will evolve as these commercial hubs, with the snowball-like growth and critical mass of offices, mature over the coming decades.

Downtown Intensification

Canada's hub cities have a huge social and environmental advantage over almost all of their U.S. counterparts. With the exception of a handful of cities, Hamilton and Winnipeg among them, they never hollowed out in response to racial strife, inner-city violence, and poor schools. There is no stigma associated with downtown living. Indeed, in most Canadian cities, the most expensive residential real estate can be found in older core neighbourhoods. The gravitational pull of Canadian downtowns, then, has functioned as a counterweight to the outward momentum of sprawl-style development, which has shifted hundreds of thousands of good jobs to edge-city employment districts.[2] Increasingly, planners in central cities have realized that they will need to find ways of retaining businesses as well as building denser communities, especially in the post-war suburbs most at risk of losing jobs and residents to newer subdivisions farther out.

Some of this intensification has been achieved by planning rules designed to encourage the reuse of so-called brownfield sites (i.e., fallow industrial or commercial land within older urban areas) and infill development. In the mid-1990s, Toronto planners discovered another trigger: They moved to approve residential uses of all the old factory buildings in the downtown garment district, many of which were occupied illegally by artists. That change unleashed a rush of investment on former industrial land that had lain fallow for years, creating highly desirable neighbourhoods in downtown, transit-oriented areas with ample municipal infrastructure.

More recently, the amalgamated City of Toronto pushed even further, adopting a far-sighted plan that projects a population increase of about 700,000 residents within the next 20 years. To achieve that kind of growth in the face of intense competition from the GTA suburbs, city officials have laid down policies promoting fast-track approval of eight-to-twelve-storey, apartment-retail buildings along suburban arterials that have long been dominated by the familiar land-scape of fast-food restaurants and strip malls. Those changes have yet to play out. In the meantime, Toronto's development boom has focused on highly desirable downtown neighbourhoods, such as Yorkville, where developers have snapped up land with the intention of erecting extremely tall condo and hotel towers. The scale of many of these proposed projects has raised the ire of local residents, who are concerned about the impact such huge residential buildings will have on their neighbourhoods. It's a legitimate worry. The problem is that city council is unable to regulate development because builders can appeal most decisions to the Ontario Municipal Board. The irony is that ham-fisted, greed-driven intensification has fostered a political backlash that threatens to undermine an otherwise environmentally responsive approach to urban planning.

The City of Vancouver, for its part, recognized the importance of promoting downtown living in the mid-1990s when it altered the zoning bylaws to allow for high-density residential development in areas that had long been set aside for office towers that failed to materialize. Vancouver's unwillingness to improve automobile access to the core has prompted thousands of Vancouverites to eliminate their commuting problems altogether by purchasing downtown condo apartments or townhouses near their workplaces. As with Toronto homeowners, overdevelopment is a potential obstacle to intensification. But Vancouver planners have far greater control over their development policies, and they were able to work with communities and builders to promote a less intrusive form of intensification, focused on the development of clustered low-rise apartment complexes in residential neighbourhoods and along retail strips.

Whatever the approach, it's clear these downtown development trends are spreading. When Richard White founded the Calgary Downtown Association in the mid-1990s, the idea of living amid the city's soaring office towers held little appeal. Less than a decade later, he surveyed the downtown condo market and calculated that, by 2007, the core will be home to 3000 new residents. They are attracted by arts festivals, restaurants, and the lively street scene on 17th Avenue. "What is the attraction to downtown living?" he asked. "If you read the advertising, it is being able to walk downtown to work. Calgarians are discovering what people in Toronto, Vancouver, Montreal, San Francisco, Boston, and New York have known for years—walking to work is way more fun than driving. Not only is it more environmentally friendly, it is good for your heath, both physically and mentally. It is also good for your pocketbook as you save on gas and parking or transit fees."[3]

What happens when cities and city-regions begin to intensify? There are environmental dividends, of course, but also important changes in lifestyle. Across the GTA, for example, sales of single-family detached homes dropped from 20,000 units in 2002 to just over 5000 in 2005. Meantime, developers have succeeded in selling a steadily growing number of stacked townhouses (which are a more land-efficient form of housing than detached houses), and there has been a slight increase in sales of condos in those European-scale apartment buildings.[4]

The way people get around cities provides another glimpse into the way compact cities affect our lives. According to a 2004 report by the Montreal-based Association for Canadian Studies, the most car-dependent cities in North America—Detroit, Dallas, Houston, and Miami—are also among the most spread out. When it comes to the number of people taking transit to work, New York tops the list, but Toronto and Montreal rank a close second and third, respectively.

The Canadian-U.S. skew becomes even more evident with bicycles. Ottawa tops all North American cities for cycling to work: 2.9 percent of the working population does it. Yet Vancouver, Calgary, Montreal, Toronto, and Edmonton all rank in the top seven; the only U.S. city in the cycling-to-work club is San Francisco. As for walking, the most pedestrian-oriented North American city turns out to be Montreal (7.4 percent of the population hoofs it to work), ahead of even New York, which is tied with Ottawa at 6.7 percent.[5]

MEANS OF TRANSPORTATION TO WORK: CANADA AND THE UNITED STATES

Means of Transportation	Canada (% trips taken)	United States (% trips taken)
Car	80.6	90.8
Public transit	10.4	4.7
Bicycle	1.2	0.4
Walking	6.5	3.0

Canadian and U.S. census, 2000, 2001, as cited in Jack Jedwab, *Gettting to Work in North America's Major Cities and Dependence on Cars* (Montreal: Association for Canadian Studies, 2004), 1. Reprinted with permission.

A few years ago, City of Toronto planners discovered that as many as 4 in 10 downtown residents were walking or riding to their jobs, and many offices now provide shower facilities and secure bike storage areas to accommodate their needs. These are people living in new lakeshore high-rise condos and warehouse lofts. They are working in office towers and the new media districts that sprang up in old downtown factories. Unlike their suburban counterparts, they've broken the codependent relationship with their vehicles.

That's why Toronto, Vancouver, and Ottawa have all been expanding their cycling infrastructure in recent years.[6] Municipalities are establishing bike lanes on major streets, creating new routes through residential neighbourhoods, adding ramps, installing cycling signals and equipping city buses with bike racks. Toronto has deployed thousands of posts where cyclists can lock up their bikes and plans to quadruple its cycling routes, including more than 400 kilometres of new bike lanes.[7] The Greater Vancouver Transportation Authority, or

TransLink, tripled its cycling infrastructure budget between 2002 and 2004 and plans to spend $54 million through 2013 on outlays including additional routes and bike lockers at SkyTrain stations. But cycling activists look to cities such as Munich for the state of the art. There, bicycles account for an amazing 13 percent of all trips taken within the city—four times more than Ottawa. The municipal government has focused on creating a highly interconnected network of bike routes off the main arterial roads. With over 40,000 bike parking spaces, the city says its current dilemma is a *shortage* of spots.[8] When Canadian cities have such problems, they'll know they're making headway in the battle against sprawl.

Smart Growth and Greenbelts

In 1990, the Greater Vancouver Regional District (GVRD), composed of the fast-growing municipalities in the Lower Mainland, took what their leaders considered to be a world-beating step. They adopted a far-reaching strategic plan designed to protect farmland and other natural amenities, provide affordable housing and transit, and set strict targets designed to focus new development around a handful of urbanized nodes—also called "regional town centres"—rather than in the hinterland. The move was a direct response to citizen concern about runaway sprawl in the Lower Mainland. This initiative led, a few years later, to the GVRD's Livable Region Strategic Plan, which established hard urban growth boundaries, a green zone, watershed protection, and targets for high-density infill development.

In some ways, this was a case of what is old is new again. In the early 1950s, the Ontario government established Metro Toronto to marshal post-war development by managing large-scale infrastructure investments in roads, transit, and waste management. Lauded internationally, Toronto's experiment with two-tier local government was widely credited for creating a relatively compact urban environment with high transit usage and excellent municipal services.

Four decades on, it was Greater Vancouver that had moved ahead of the curve. In the mid-1990s, planners, environmentalists, and developers across North America began talking fervently about "smart growth." Recognizing that the solution to sprawl goes well beyond neo-traditional subdivisions, smart growth argued for a region-wide approach that encompassed a host of interconnected elements, including compact mixed-use development linked to transit investments; incentives for the redevelopment of brownfields; the provision of a range of housing styles; the protection of natural heritage features; and urban design policies designed to create lively, pedestrian-scale public environments that offer a sense of place to counteract the anonymity of boilerplate suburban malls, the de facto community centres of many post-war cities.[9]

"What was new," according to an analysis by the Canadian Urban Institute, "was the coalition of many different interests behind the idea that the current way in which cities grow needs to change. Suddenly the Sierra Club and the National Association of Home Builders found themselves using much of the same language and promoting some of the same goals. Federal, state and municipal governments, as well as the private and non-profit sectors rallied around a single cause."[10]

The Clinton administration and progressive-minded states such as Maryland pushed a raft of smart growth initiatives,[11] including billions in new funding for transit, affordable housing, and the rehabilitation of brownfield sites; tax incentives to protect natural heritage and promote downtown revitalization; public-private partnerships geared toward downtown redevelopment; and the introduction of federally under-written "location efficient mortgages"—homeowner loans geared toward households being developed near transit hubs.[12] As a 1997 article in *American City & County* noted, "Growth management is on the agenda of virtually every metropolitan area in the country.... Region after region is moving beyond the question of whether to continue sprawl patterns of the last 50 years or replace them with growth management policies designed to rein in untrammelled development. The question now is how this can be accomplished. And beneath it all lurks the question of who will win and who will lose."[13]

Amid the me-tooism of the smart-growth fad, one city in particular could lay claim to an especially tough-minded form of regional planning, with remarkable results given North American development patterns. Since 1979, Metropolitan Portland had been pursuing a compact-development approach to planning that had, by the late 1990s, turned the region into one of the fastest-growing and most sought-after mid-sized cities in the United States. Built around the resource industries, Portland in the late 1970s was eating up the farms that had contributed to the city's wealth—an alarming development that prompted the city's leaders to establish a strictly enforced urban growth boundary (UGB) designed to contain the next two decades of development. The UGB encompassed the City of Portland plus 24 adjacent municipalities and parts of three counties. Over the next several years, the directly elected regional government—the only one of its kind in the United States—took command of Portland's highly regarded light rapid transit network, as well as parks and waste management, and even downtown parking management. State legislators ensured that development stayed within the UGB. Not coincidentally, Portland's transit use rivals Toronto's, whose transit service is more cost efficient than those in any other North American city including New York.

Rapidly exceeding its population growth projections (the area has 2.2 million people, about a quarter of whom live in the city proper), Portland became a mecca for Americans (especially Californians) looking for a fitness-oriented lifestyle and urban culture without the financial stresses associated with living in New York or San Francisco. Its approach was copied by other U.S. cities, including Minneapolis-St. Paul; Boulder, Colorado; and San José, a high-tech satellite of San Francisco whose residents are eager to avoid Los Angeles's fate.

During the 1990s, Portland finally grew out to the urban growth boundary it had laid down in 1979, and the region faces the difficult question of whether it can continue to mandate compact growth for the next two decades in the face of pent-up development pressures. There was mounting concern that the development taking place at the edges of the UGB was no different from what could be found in suburbs across the United States. Portland residents responded by approving a growth management charter and a 50-year plan for future development that respected the city's priorities, including efficient transit and protection for accessible natural areas. In 1995, the region approved a $135-million bond issue to acquire open spaces.[14]

Portland's lessons have begun to hit home with Canada's municipal and provincial leaders, who face ever-increasing costs associated with sprawl and gridlock. Greater Vancouver's greenbelt has been in place since the mid-1990s. Has it worked? According to a 2003 assessment by the GVRD, regional town centres such as Burnaby's Metrotown, Coquitlam Centre, and Surrey City Centre have all been successful in attracting high-density residential developments and retailers. But as with downtown Vancouver (and indeed most downtowns), office buildings haven't materialized in recent years because many companies prefer the far more affordable low-rise offices and warehouses located in the suburban business parks that fringe most large cities today.

Ontario began inching toward a greenbelt approach to growth management in the early 2000s. In 2002, in the wake of widespread outrage over a massive residential development scheme to build hundreds of luxury homes on the environmentally sensitive Oak Ridges Moraine, the provincial Tories were forced to pass legislation intended to block future development in an area that contains the headwaters for many of the river systems running through Greater Toronto and into Lake Ontario. The moraine contains wetlands, Carolinian forests, and kettle lakes—a natural heritage asset much loved by thousands of local residents who live in the heavily suburban-ized municipality of Richmond Hill.

Scarcely three years later, the McGuinty Liberals created a million-hectare GTA greenbelt explicitly modelled on Portland's urban growth boundary. It is an enormous band of rural land arcing around the western end of Lake Ontario where urban development will not be permitted to occur. The government simultaneously passed new land-use planning laws requiring municipalities within the GTA to direct as much as 40 percent of all new development to the network of regional hubs that are set to become suburban downtowns, as described earlier. These moves firmly established Queen's Park as the body overseeing regional planning for the Greater Golden Horseshoe. McGuinty's prescriptive policies certainly represent a historic shift in Queen's Park's approach to planning. But the measures remain exceedingly cautious. Environmental groups are dubious about the government's ability to promote compact development because the approved boundaries of the GTA greenbelt remain so far from the urban fringe. Nevertheless, these reforms send the message that there must be physical limits to Greater Toronto's outward expansion if this megalopolis isn't to collapse under its own rapidly expanding girth.

Such measures, however, can succeed only if accompanied by far-sighted transportation planning policies and investments designed to gets cars off the highways. Why? Not just to improve air quality and reduce gridlock, although these are important goals. Our hub cities desperately need to take these steps so the trucks that are indispensable to the productivity of a manufacturing-driven, export-oriented economy can get their goods to market on time.

EFFICIENT CITIES

Overall auto usage in our urban areas is becoming pathological in terms of the ever-growing negative impacts. Experience ... throughout the world shows that we cannot build our way out of these problems. In other words, more roads simply lead to more sprawl and more congestion.

—ERIC MILLER AND RICHARD SOBERMAN,
TRAVEL DEMAND AND URBAN FORM (2003)

B y North American standards, Canada's largest cities have a strong track record when it comes to public transit. Toronto and the Ontario government championed far-sighted planning and transit investment policies between the 1950s and 1980s, which led to ridership levels more in line with European cities than with American metropolitan regions. Since the mid-1980s, Greater Vancouver and the B.C. government have made large-scale investments in a regional rapid transit network that have helped consolidate the Lower Mainland's status as one of the world's most livable regions.

Over the long haul, these investments have paid off in spades—environmentally, economically, and socially. About 1.6 million Canadians take transit to work every day, according to a 2004 Statistics Canada study, and as many as one in four residents of Montreal and Toronto. Easy access to a subway station is a huge boost to residential real estate values and serves as a magnet for development activity. In 2004, the Montreal Board of Trade went so far as to quantify the value of the transit dividend with a study showing that transit was responsible for some 13,000 jobs, yielded annual savings of $570 million to commuters, and produced a 45 percent return on investment to the upper levels of government that helped foot the bill.[1]

What is more, viable transit is crucial in a country with high immigration levels. Census data collected between 1996 and 2001 show that recent immigrants living in large urban centres, as well as young people and those earning under $40,000 a year, tend to be the heaviest transit users. Even in low-density suburbs, according to Statistics Canada's analysis, up to a quarter of the recent immigrants rely on transit, even though the service is primarily provided by buses. As the study's authors point out, "A shift in the geographic concentration of immigrants from urban core to outlying areas has implications for where public transit services should be located, especially in [metropolitan areas] with centralized transit systems."[2]

While Canadian city-dwellers are positively disposed toward public transit, governments in many parts of the country squandered all that goodwill with policies that paved the way for rampant sprawl. During the 1990s, we slashed two-thirds of all transit funding, forcing operators to limit their service instead of investing in new transit infrastructure. In 1992, fares for transit agencies across the country covered about 53 percent of all operating costs; by 2000, the figure had jumped to 62 percent.[3] Today, Canada's transit sector, by necessity, is more cost-efficient than those of France, Sweden, and the Netherlands, and is almost in league with transit in densely populated Hong Kong and Tokyo. That's the good news. The bad news is that, because of sprawl and rising ticket prices, transit use dropped sharply in many parts of urban Canada during the 1990s and has only recovered partially in the 2000s. The numbers tell the tale: The total number of transit trips taken each year in Canada went up by 5 percent between 1992 and 2001. Average fares, by contrast, rose by more than 40 percent over the same period.[4]

Despite overwhelming evidence that something was seriously amiss in the transportation systems of Canada's largest urban regions, the federal government as of 2001 had no national transit strategy, setting it apart from virtually every other industrialized country. Ottawa has long regulated rail, air, and sea travel, and owns a chronically underfunded passenger rail service. But transit, according to a fiscally expedient reading of the division of powers in Canada's constitution, was purely a provincial and/or municipal responsibility.

FEDERAL AND PROVINCIAL/STATE SUPPORT FOR PUBLIC TRANSIT (2004)

	Operating Costs (%)	Capital Projects (%)
Canada	5	10
United States	24	67
Europe	15–30	30–100

Canadian Urban Transit Association, unpublished briefing memo, 2005. Reprinted with permission.

Yet, as we've seen, big-city transit is directly linked to a long list of national and regional concerns—a point that may not have been apparent in the 1950s but is impossible to dispute today. Transit and transit-friendly development are closely connected to issues such as environmental stewardship, farmland protection, air quality, the competitiveness of our manufacturing sector, health, and even immigration. Our major trading partners, but especially the world's top-performing city-regions, understand these interrelationships and have invested in modernizing, expanding, and integrating their rapid transit and regional commuter-rail services.

After a lost decade or more, Canada's political leaders finally figured out why transit matters and have unleashed a small gusher of new funding.[5] In the early 2000s, the B.C. government spent $716 billion on a 21-kilometre expansion of Vancouver's Expo-vintage SkyTrain rapid transit line, which opened in 2001, shortly before the GVRD approved the $1.7-billion Richmond-Airport-Vancouver rapid transit line, due to be completed in 2009 under a private-public partnership arrangement. Montreal, in turn, is extending the Métro out to Laval. In Alberta, the LRT (light rapid transit) systems in Edmonton and Calgary will see a $335-million infusion for extensions.[6] In Ontario in 2001, the Harris government partially reversed its anti-transit stance and launched a $3-billion, 10-year expansion of GO Transit—the regional commuter transit agency founded in 1967—with additional service, new lines, and dedicated bus lanes. Toronto is also planning to expand its subway, bus, and streetcar network. Across the country, transit operators are using their new funding to further reduce greenhouse gas emissions, for example, by purchasing buses that run on natural gas or using clean energy to power transit extension projects.

All the renewed political enthusiasm for transit is also ushering in a generation of new rapid transit systems in mid-sized cities. Waterloo and Halifax are pressing ahead with plans for LRTs. In 2004, Ottawa-Carleton, Queen's Park, and the federal government embarked on a $600-million LRT project, the largest transit infrastructure project in that city's history. The city is also expanding its bus Transitway, Canada's only dedicated bus lane network that has served the capital's transit needs effectively since the 1970s.

But difficult questions await our urban leaders. How much of the new funding should go toward existing transit systems that have accumulated a backlog of repair expenses, and how much should be spent on transit expansions, especially in low-density suburban cities? What kind of transit service works in suburban regions? And what else do we need to do to ensure that taxpayers get full value for their investment?

Planning and transportation experts warn that the solutions depend on much more than just transit spending. Our cities need to connect the smart-growth planning policies we saw in the last chapter to strategic decisions about transit infrastructure. We then need to stop building more highways and look for solutions to relieve the traffic on the ones we already have. Most importantly, we need to begin to pay for the full cost of driving our cars.

The True Cost of Driving

Few Canadians would balk at paying for a transit ticket when boarding a bus or subway train. Nor is it an alien experience for many of us. According to the Canadian Urban Transit Association, 19 million Canadians have access to transit, and well over half use the service, regularly or occasionally. So even though transit systems were financed by taxpayers and receive ongoing subsidies from property owners (regardless of whether they take the bus or not), riders accept that there is a fee for service. Users cover an average of two-thirds of the cost of operating the system, with their total outlay linked directly to the number of trips they take. It's Economics 101.

Although highways and urban thoroughfares serve as the circulatory systems of modern urban economies, Canadian governments seem to believe that these infrastructure assets operate outside the laws of supply and demand. Like transit systems, taxpayers financed their construction and pay millions each year for their upkeep. But there is no fee for service, meaning the downtown apartment dweller who has no car pays as much for highway maintenance as the suburban family with a minivan and an SUV. Indeed, downtown apartment dwellers may be paying several hundred dollars a year in transit fares, on top of the portion of their taxes that pays for the highways. This is voodoo economics: Our car-friendly policies have grossly distorted the price mechanism associated with driving. The result is akin to what would happen if a city suddenly decreed that all restaurants be required to offer $5 entrees. The very best eateries would find themselves swamped and unable to manage the demand.

If Canadian politicians are serious about boosting transit use, easing gridlock, improving air quality, and reducing travel delays for trucks, they need to begin introducing "demand management" policies that account for the true cost of driving. These include tolls on all major highways, priced to recoup at least a third of their operating expenses; after all, transit systems continue to receive an operating subsidy of about 30 to 40 percent in recognition of their contribution to the broader good, and it should be the same with highways. For crowded downtown areas, meanwhile, municipalities should establish congestion charges. Municipalities should also be given the power to tax companies that provide free parking spots to their employees, according to the National Round Table on the Environment and the Economy. The rationale is the same as with highways: Cities spend millions each year on road maintenance and traffic signals, so it follows that some of those costs be borne by the drivers who make the most use of them.

There is ample precedent for such fees. U.S. interstates have always been toll roads, while in several European countries, Sweden among them, urban ring roads have tolls. After years of debate, the City of

London in the early 2000s imposed a congestion charge on the heavily trafficked downtown core as a means of discouraging car use. For decades, New York has charged drivers to cross the tunnels and bridges connecting its boroughs. But with the exception of the privatized electronic toll highway, 407 ETR, north of Toronto, transportation infrastructure in and around Canadian cities appears to drivers to be free and is thus drastically overused.

Reforming the road pricing system to reflect the full cost of driving isn't only about tolling car owners stranded at the wrong end of a miserable commute. Another important piece of the puzzle involves car insurance premiums. At present, insurance rates—which are provincially regulated—take into account factors such as location and age but barely recognize the amount driven. Economist Todd Litman, director of the Victoria Transport Policy Institute (VTPI), says the current insurance system favours individuals who drive a lot, although actuarial data suggest that the number of accidents increases with the distance driven. In his analysis, standard insurance policies effectively force low-mileage drivers to cross-subsidize high-mileage, accident-prone drivers. An insurance regulatory regime calibrated to encourage transit use and reduce emissions should reward those who drive less. The VTPI's studies show that "pay-as-you-go" insurance will yield savings of $50 to $100 per year and result in mileage decreases of 5 to 15 percent.[7]

This isn't a theoretical solution. Since 2001, legislation permitting pay-as-you-go (PAYG) insurance has been introduced in Texas and Oregon, while insurers in the United Kingdom, the Netherlands, and Australia—including the insurance giant Norwich Union—have begun offering such premiums to their customers. General Motors' financing arm also began providing mileage-based discounts to owners of vehicles equipped with the OnStar geo-positioning devices.[8] In April 2005, the PAYG movement finally came to Canada, when Vancouver City Council approved a motion to urge the B.C. government to compel the provincial Crown corporation that provides car insurance to offer such packages. As councillor Anne Roberts said, "If we can get people driving 10 to 30 percent less, that would make a significant contribution, both to clearing out some of that traffic congestion, but also reducing greenhouse gases."[9]

If provincial insurance rules can be tweaked to reduce mileage, Canada's tax laws should be changed to promote transit use. For years, the federal tax department has considered a workplace parking spot to be a non-taxable benefit. It's a perk that's built into the suburban land development system, because companies build large parking lots for their employees to use. There is nothing "free" about these sprawl-promoting lots—the land, the pavement, and the maintenance all cost money. But the Canadian government doesn't recognize these expenditures. On the other hand, when employers give their workers a transit pass, such benefits are deemed to be taxable. Not only is the playing field uneven but there is little financial incentive for companies to urge their employees to car pool, cycle, or take transit to work.

As with PAYG insurance, these aren't merely idealistic policy musings. In 1998, the U.S. government amended its tax laws to allow for non-taxable transit passes, and the result, according to Canadian Urban Transit Association statistics, was a 37 to 58 percent jump in transit use at participating workplaces.[10] The very next year, the House of Commons voted 240 to 25 to endorse such a move. Proponents include everyone from left-leaning environmentalists to right-of-centre Vancouver city councillors and Stephen Harper's federal Conservatives. Quebec in its 2003–4 budget changed its tax code to allow such passes to be considered a non-taxable benefit, while some large employers now offer them as an employment perk. Harper promised a tax credit for transit passes as part of his 2006 campaign to attract support among urban voters, especially in Central Canada. Inexplicably, though, the federal government's tax collectors continue to stand in the way of a low-cost, high-impact way of putting urban transit systems on a more sustainable footing.

The point behind such policy changes is that transit will succeed in providing a realistic alternative to driving only if it is convenient but also priced competitively.

More Bang for the Buck

For many politicians, transit projects represent a lasting personal legacy that shines far brighter than much of the abstract work of governing.

They also attract the attention of construction contractors, engineering consultants, and the large firms that make transit vehicles. Consequently, it's not hard to find examples of transit schemes where vested interests prevailed over sound planning. During the late 1990s, Toronto's mayor Mel Lastman persuaded his provincial counterparts to bankroll a $1-billion subway spur along a suburban arterial, terminating after only four stops at a shopping mall. Transit planners had recommended other routes running through denser parts of the city. But municipal and provincial leaders chose the politically expedient route and ended up constructing a subway to nowhere. In 1998, the Parti Québécois government made a similar gaffe with plans to extend Montreal's subway to the suburb of Laval. It promised to build the 5.2-kilometre line for just $179 million. The actual budget more than quadrupled, even though Montreal transit officials insist the cost remains comparable to subway ventures in other cities.[11] Today, it's referred to as "the Big M," an unsubtle reference to Montreal's other great boondoggle, the crushingly expensive Olympic stadium known universally as the Big O.

The point is that building pricey new rapid transit lines can soak up huge sums of public funds without necessarily improving service. In recent years, however, some transit planners have begun to look at ways of boosting ridership on existing transit networks before embarking on costly expansion schemes. This is about better and more efficient service, and it can include measures such as restricting street parking on transit routes that run along major arterial roads; creating dedicated rights-of-way and high-occupancy vehicle lanes for car-poolers, buses, trolleys, and streetcars; and investing in smart-ticketing or swipe-card technology that allows passengers to buy their transit passes in a variety of ways, including over the internet.

Pricing, too, will be critical to making the next generation of transit investments pay a dividend for city-dwellers. In recent years, underfunding and budget cuts have forced some transit agencies to hike fares, often at a pace that considerably exceeds inflation. Meanwhile, jobs in large urban areas have been shifting to the suburbs, where service is poor or non-existent. The result is a drop-off in riders who can choose to take their cars, while lower-income transit users—

often recent immigrants and university students—are stuck carrying the load because they have no alternative.

Recognizing these demographic skews, some adroit agencies have targeted monthly passes to these customer groups. In 2003, for example, the University of British Columbia decided to offer all students the opportunity to purchase a discount U-Pass, an eight-month transit pass that costs less than $200, compared with the estimated $1000 cost of driving to the campus. The program turned on the Greater Vancouver Transportation Authority's willingness to provide volume discounts to the university. Almost overnight, the U-pass program sharply increased transit travel onto campus.

Transit's Next Century

The calculus of transit planning has been forever altered by the rapidly decentralizing employment and land-use patterns of the 1990s and 2000s. In the suburbs, everything is farther apart, and the transit operators know the math as well as anyone else. For $250 million (in 2005 dollars), they can build about one kilometre of a subway line, lay five kilometres of light rail, or purchase 250 state-of-the-art city buses. At the same time, they know that many people avoid traditional bus service because it's considered to be bumpy, inconvenient, and unreliable. And transit experts also understand that the costliest part of building rapid transit isn't the tunnels but the construction costs associated with subway stations.

Greater Vancouver, eschewing the underground approach as unsuitable for a city that sits on a major geological fault line, has opted instead to build the elevated SkyTrain system, supported by a growing network of express buses. Since the mid-1980s, the city and the province steadily extended the regional rapid transit network to the most urbanized sections of the Lower Mainland, knitting together the fast-growing suburban hubs of Burnaby and Surrey, and, later this decade, Richmond.

By contrast, Toronto's subway construction virtually ground to a halt in the 1980s. During the period when Vancouver was undertaking major rapid transit investments, Toronto was watching its own system decay because of underfunding. Today, there is little chance that large-scale core-area subway lines will be built in the foreseeable future unless Queen's Park introduces a significant change in the way transit expansion projects are financed—for example, through the sort of public-private partnerships that have driven SkyTrain. While Toronto politicians continue to pursue plans to incrementally extend existing lines, a more cost-effective approach has emerged as a result of the city's long-standing commitment to streetcars—a clean form of transit that many cities phased out in favour of buses in the post-war decades. The Toronto Transit Commission was poised to eliminate streetcars in the 1980s, but those plans were shelved because of intense local opposition from an outspoken network of streetcar aficionados. A generation later, the long-term benefits of this decision have come to the fore. A key element of Toronto's 2003 Ridership Growth Strategy is to create a network of dedicated streetcar lanes down the middle of selected arterials—both downtown and in the older suburban districts—that are wide enough to support such rights-of-way. The strategy effectively holds out the prospect of a relatively inexpensive version of the sort of surface rapid transit that has proven to be highly effective in many European cities as well as Portland.

Indeed, this approach may prove to be a solution to alleviating suburban traffic congestion. In York Region, that sprawling agglomeration of edge cities north of Toronto, municipal transportation officials have gone well beyond any other suburban region with a new network of luxury-style express buses traversing the highways and major arterials that link the various employment and commercial hubs throughout the region.

York Region was once a bucolic area that included farms, moraine hills, and a handful of quaint towns, Richmond Hill among them. By the early 2000s, its growth had produced crippling traffic problems and pent-up demand for alternatives to car travel. Its political leaders have perhaps the most aggressive transit expansion plan of any suburban city in Canada. The regional municipality first amalgamated all the little old bus companies serving different parts of York, then lobbied furiously to win federal and provincial funding for a $150-million bus rapid transit system to be run by a private operator. Viva, as the heavily branded bus service is known, came into operation in the fall of 2005, complete with priority lanes, high-tech ticketing machines, frequent services (5-to-15-minute wait times), seamless links to other GTA transit services, and state-of-the-art Belgian-made vehicles that even have wireless internet and tables for commuters who want to work en route. They operate along two major axes connecting York's four major town centres and York University, moving on dedicated lanes running down the middle of arterial roads. As transit use grows over the coming decade, the bus routes will be converted into an extensive LRT network, financed partially from contributions from developers willing to put up higher-density buildings along these increasingly urbanized corridors.

York Region Transit's ridership levels have been rising, and its ambitious planners envision continued increased ridership over the next 20 years, from just 8 percent of the area's population to 33 percent. Still, it's important to put the numbers in context. York's entire system carries only about 1.2 million customers per month, compared with almost 35 million for the Toronto Transit Commission—even though the City of Toronto's population is scarcely three times larger than York's. The most formidable challenge, clearly, is to figure out how to provide efficient and reliable transit service to the thousands of people who live in the older central city but have taken to commuting out to the commercial hubs in sprawling places such as York Region.

Making It All Hang Together

In coming years, Canadian governments will expend billions on new transit investments intended to reduce highway congestion, improve air quality, and enhance urban quality of life. But none of it will pay off unless the three levels of government figure out how to coordinate these transit investments with local land-use decisions. Absent such planning, we'll have a suburban landscape littered with pricey white elephants, while the older downtown transit systems deteriorate as their infrastructure continues to age and their traditional peak-hour riders find jobs that can be reached only by car.

There is reason for hope, however. As we've seen, Canada's cities are evolving into very large urban regions composed of high-density core areas surrounded by traditional suburbs, as well as by fast-growing but relatively concentrated regional hubs, such as Mississauga City Centre, in Ontario, or Burnaby, in British Columbia. These 24/7 edge cities have clusters of high-rise offices, condo towers, and public buildings, arrayed around traditional regional shopping centres, entertainment complexes, and recreation facilities. In other words, they have the critical mass required to support transit investments.

There are many places in our low-density suburban cities that will never be well served by transit—for instance, large industrial parks filled with huge, low-slung warehouses. Yet, it's possible to envision a future in which our mega-cities support a series of hub-and-spoke-style transit networks that focus on the new regional centres.

Our traditional approach to transit no longer fits into this kind of landscape. In the Greater Golden Horseshoe, for example, gridlock and noxious air are the direct consequence of two decades of utterly uncoordinated planning. Municipalities competed with one another for low-density development, essentially with the blessing of a provincial government that put a lot of money into highways and failed to invest in long-overdue improvements to its regional transit agency.

In 2005, the Ontario Liberals passed hard-nosed regional planning legislation designed to give Cabinet direct control over the next generation of multi-billion-dollar urban infrastructure investments in the Golden Horseshoe—not just transit, but also roads, highways, water treatment plants, and waste management facilities. In theory, such laws allow provincial planners to ensure that transit spending ends up serving high-density areas. But Queen's Park is continuing to build new highways around the Golden Horseshoe, investments that will further exacerbate sprawl. What is more, it's not clear whether Queen's Park should be interfering so directly in the affairs of these mega-cities.

As a result of British Columbia's philosophy of empowering local government, Greater Vancouver is benefiting from a regionally driven approach to transit and transportation planning. In 1999, the provincial government set up the Greater Vancouver Transportation Authority, known as TransLink, as a sister agency to the Greater Vancouver Regional District. In effect, TransLink coordinates the activities of the various transit operators in the Lower Mainland, including SkyTrain, the municipal bus companies, BC Ferries, and the commuter rail service. The B.C. government transfers a range of revenue sources to TransLink, which is also responsible for determining how to spend the new transit infrastructure funding coming down from Ottawa. (TransLink's $700-million-a-year budget comes from fares, emission testing fees, gas tax transfers, and other sources.) What makes the agency unique in the Canadian context is that it enjoys an exclusive mandate to manage the major road and bridge network throughout Greater Vancouver—an institutional acknowledgment that most transit users also drive, so they have a stake in both networks. The arrangement reveals real foresight. When the new federal-provincial infrastructure funding for transit began to flow to cities, TransLink was all set up and ready to go. The same hasn't been true for either Toronto or Montreal.

The result is that, in Greater Vancouver, local politicians representing the extended urban region have had to figure out among themselves how to balance their collective transportation challenges and allocate resources. There are plenty of subdivisions in the Lower Mainland, and no shortage of SUVs. As in Montreal, the congestion on the two bridges across the Burrard Inlet remains a source of irritation for commuters. For all that, TransLink's political masters have consistently opted to spend the majority of the agency's budget on transit, while the region's land-use planners work hard to direct new development to increasingly dense regional town centres. Between 2004 and 2013, TransLink expects to invest $3.9 billion in capital upgrades. Of that, only a third is going into road maintenance, limited expansions, and a new bridge over the Fraser River. While B.C. has recently proposed new highways for the Lower Mainland, the region is staking its economic future on expanding the freight-oriented rail service that links Vancouver's major container ports with Western Canada.

It's also no coincidence that transit use in the GVRD is going up by leaps and bounds. Ridership, states TransLink's 2004 annual report, rose by 20 percent in 2003 and 2004. TransLink's transit operators, meanwhile, are rolling out innovative services, such as high-speed inter-suburban buses and community shuttles. The moral of the story is that in Canada's sprawling urban regions, responsibility for transportation planning must be delegated to a new breed of regional body that has a mandate to look at the big picture. These agencies need the financial and political clout to short-circuit municipal parochialism, yet they must also take their direction from local communities and their elected representatives. It's a delicate balance, but one that is absolutely essential if urban Canadians are to realize a financial and environmental return on all the infrastructure money now underwriting Canada's 21st-century transit schemes.

ECO-CITIES

E ven though our largest cities occupy a minuscule proportion of Canada's overall land mass, they punch well above their weight when it comes to their overall contribution to climate change, certain types of environmental degradation, and the depletion of the world's energy resources. In Victoria, St. John's, and Halifax, raw sewage was being dumped into their respective harbours for years. Around Montreal and the GTA, unchecked sprawl has gobbled up farmland, altered the local climate, and filled the air with micro-particles spewed out by the SUVs and minivans that clog urban highways. More worrisome, the energy demands of low-density urban agglomerations have placed a crushing burden on some provincial electricity grids. In July 2005, in fact, Ontario energy regulators warned that Greater Toronto "urgently" needs new power-generating facilities over the coming decade just to keep up with current demand. To deal with the shortages, Ontario energy officials in late 2005 recommended a multi-year, $40-billion investment in new nuclear facilities. Without reliable power supplies, manufacturers will pick up and leave. If we want to understand why, we simply need to connect the dots: Urban sprawl has placed intolerable pressure on our electricity grid, and eventually the consequences of our short-sighted planning will boomerang back on us in the form of lost jobs as companies relocate to areas where they don't have to worry about brownouts.[1]

So we need more power, and more sustainable power. But that's only part of the equation. Cities can tackle these problems head on only by changing the way they plan and then ensuring that high-level policies are incorporated into all new development projects. But there will be a payoff in the long run. A Quebec study on the Montreal Metropolitan Region found that a household situated near a Métro station instead of the suburban periphery generates 1050 fewer automobile trips, 15,000 fewer kilometres travelled by car, a 6000-kilogram reduction in greenhouse gases, and more than a thousand additional journeys by transit, bicycle, or foot.[2] Evidently, compact development produces an environmental dividend.

Indeed, writing about "Green Manhattan" in *The New Yorker* in 2004, David Owen argues that, on a per capita basis, the island, contrary to conventional wisdom, is one of the world's most environmentally friendly, energy-efficient cities. Living in a dense urban area entails less consumption of the commodities that imperil the environment: less gas use because car ownership is low, less electricity use because dwellings are smaller, less fertilizer use because of the dearth of lawns. It all translates into fewer greenhouse gas emissions from vehicles and power plants. "Dense urban centers offer one of the few plausible remedies for some of the world's most discouraging environmental ills," he writes. "To borrow a term from the jargon of computer systems, dense cities are scalable, while sprawling suburbs are not. The environmental challenge we face, at the current stage of our assault on the world's non-renewable resources, is not how to make our teeming cities more like the pristine countryside. The true challenge is how to make other settled places more like Manhattan."[3]

Outside Vancouver's West End, parts of downtown Toronto, and Montreal's Plateau district, Canada's cities have a long way to go before they can describe themselves as green. The smart-growth policies and strategic transit investments discussed in previous chapters represent a step in the right direction. But our cities won't be able to claim the environmental high ground until we change the way we think about sewage, municipal garbage, and the opportunities for alternative energy in urban settings.

Water, Water Everywhere ...

Until the 1910s, thousands of Toronto children were dying each year from illnesses caused by water-borne bacteria. But by the 1920s, public health crusaders and strong-willed works officials succeeded in chlorinating the city's water supply and planning a new generation of treatment facilities. Over the past hundred years, in fact, the worst water contamination catastrophes have tended to occur in rural towns—Walkerton, Ontario, among them—or on Native reserves. In our large urban centres, the supply of drinking water has been well managed for years.

The same can't be said of waste water. In older parts of large cities, combined drains and storm sewers carried raw sewage, including fecal matter, directly to nearby water bodies. Toronto's beaches, once a well-loved playground for the city's children, were routinely closed during the height of summer because high coliform bacteria counts rendered them unsafe for swimming. In St. John's, Halifax, and Victoria, meanwhile, municipal sewers drained untreated waste directly into the harbours, and this in a country that has a reputation for both pristine lakes and an engineering industry that specializes in building water purification systems in many parts of the developing world.

Over the past decade, however, some of Canada's leading waterfront cities have made significant strides in reducing this kind of environmental degradation. In 1999, the City of Toronto began building a $57-million network of pipes and holding tanks designed to catch and treat storm water overflows before they get into the lake—a measure that has helped clean up the city's beaches after decades of neglect.[4]

Both Halifax and St. John's tried for years to deal with the pollution in their harbours. As one consultant described the situation in St. John's, "The Harbour is contaminated with potentially pathogenic bacteria. Bacteria levels are high enough that ear and gastrointestinal infection should be expected from bodily contact with Harbour water. There is visual pollution in terms of floating material on the water surface."[5] In Halifax, meanwhile, over 180-million litres of untreated waste water flowed into the harbour each day, killing shellfish and contaminating the sediment on the bottom.

In both cases, money and federal-provincial turf wars stood in the way of workable solutions, with the result that remediation plans drawn up in the 1970s and 1980s gathered dust. But during the 1990s, both cities tried again, this time with realistic and phased plans that turned on intergovernmental cooperation and the involvement of citizens' groups. In both cases, urban quality of life had become a more pressing consideration. Both cities were growing quickly, and, in Halifax's case, the filth in the harbour represented a drag on the tourism that had emerged as a pillar of the city's booming post-naval economy. Ottawa's infrastructure programs kicked in a total of $91 million for both, while the provincial and municipal governments picked up the balance. In Halifax's case, residents voted to approve a plan that would provide the lion's share of the funding—a levy on their water bills. This display of urban self-reliance illustrated the city's sense of optimism about its economic position as the capital of Atlantic Canada.

As of 2005, Victoria remains the only holdout. In 1992, a majority of the city's residents voted to continue to allow the municipality to dump raw sewage into the harbour (city public works officials maintained that the ocean currents dissolve and dissipate the waste material to non-toxic levels). But since then, British Columbia's capital has faced tourism boycotts, threats of regulatory action from Ottawa, and complaints from Washington State. In the 2005 mayoral elections, one of the registered candidates was "Mr. Floatie," a university student who dressed up as a huge turd and campaigned for a sewage treatment plant to end the dumping. Municipal officials responded by finding a technicality to bar him from the race—a decision that merely garnered more negative attention for Victoria. "What the city's trying to do by keeping me off the ballot is avoid talking about the sewage problem," Mr. Floatie, who represents People Opposed to Outfall Pollution, or POOP, told a reporter. "But you know what? I'm not going away until they build us a plant. So, let's get off the pot and do it."[6]

Waste Not, Want Not

Besides sewage, cities produce immense amounts of refuse, and municipal governments handle few more basic tasks than finding ways of disposing of it. When Canada's cities were relatively small and compact, and when governments didn't think much about the environment, waste management was pretty straightforward: The garbage was dumped and buried, or burned outright. For decades, municipal landfills seeped toxic leachate, while incinerators belched poisonous air pollution. When environmental activism became a force in North America in the 1960s and 1970s, older solid waste incinerators began to close down. Then, in the 1980s, a generation of old-style municipal dumps started to fill up. What happened next represents nothing less than a revolution in the way our cities think about the immense amounts of garbage they produce. In a matter of years, municipal waste became a new and potentially lucrative resource.

The turning point occurred in the 1980s, when New York City's waste management officials faced monumental difficulties in disposing of 24,000 tons of urban trash each and every day. Garbage-laden barges floating in New York Harbor came to be seen as a symbol of the city's failure to deal with one of its most basic tasks.

Following the example of many European countries, the Canadian Council of Ministers of the Environment in 1989 set a target of diverting 50 percent of garbage from municipal landfills by 2000. Canadian municipalities and provincial regulators gradually began removing recyclable materials from the waste stream. Blue box programs started with newspapers and then glass, and grew to include a wide range of paper products and consumer packaging, from egg cartons and cardboard boxes to plastic tubs and soft drink bottles. Increasingly, large municipalities were required to collect or separate out hazardous solid wastes such as used paint and batteries. Several provinces introduced pop and wine bottle–deposit return systems— although Ontario, which has had such a system in place for beer bottles for decades, has failed to extend it into other types of beverage containers. Some municipalities modernized the age-old art of scavenging by setting up consumer reuse centres where homeowners can deposit or find used furniture and other goods. Construction debris is thoroughly sorted so salvageable material such as pipes, timber, and drywall can be resold. Most waste management operations now separate out so-called e-junk (discarded computers, cell phones), which recycling companies dismantle for the reusable components.[7]

Provincial regulators, in turn, are much more finicky about landfills. No longer stinking dumps, they became meticulously "engineered" landfills with liners and systems for capturing toxic leachate and escaping methane gas created by garbage sludge. Municipalities are required to lay down sand-and-gravel coverings, while landfill crews work to fill sequences of "cells" rather than just randomly bulldozing the trash into huge heaps. The result is that state-of-the-art landfills—while hardly popular with their neighbours—aren't nearly as smelly and seagull infested as they once were.

In recent years, several larger cities have progressed from promoting backyard composting to collecting yard waste and organics—everything from kitchen scraps to dog feces. Some municipalities process this material into feedstock for commercially sold compost, while a few—including Toronto and Newmarket, Ontario, a fast-growing GTA satellite—have experimented with anaerobic digestion, a technology far more popular in Europe than North America. Considered to be an effective means of reducing the worst kinds of garbage-related greenhouse gases, anaerobic digestion involves the accelerated decomposition of biodegradable waste in special facilities equipped to convert garbage-produced methane gas into energy and carbon dioxide.

The supply of recycled goods hasn't always grown in step with demand. But rapid advances in recycling and sorting technology have produced new end uses, as well as sources of feedstock—for example, recycling used french fry oil into new types of fuel additives. In an era of rapidly increasing energy costs for manufacturers, the benefits are hard to ignore. As one waste management study based on 1996 Environment Canada data points out, "Aluminum is the best example of energy saved. It takes 96 percent less energy to manufacture aluminum from recycled aluminum than from virgin material. The relative energy intensity is less dramatic for other materials, but is still significant."[8]

Some cities and provinces have adopted a much more proactive approach to these changes than others—often because they had no choice but to act fast. In 1994, Edmonton waste management officials devised a 30-year strategic plan that minimized the need for landfills and established the city as a solid-waste leader. The city and TransAlta, the provincial utility, set up a $12-million materials recovery facility on a 200-hectare piece of land in the mid-1990s. At the plant, "blue bags" filled with recyclables are opened and their contents manually separated, while biodegradable organic waste and the bio-solids from the city's

EXAMPLES OF ENERGY SAVINGS RESULTING FROM USING RECYCLED RATHER THAN VIRGIN FEEDSTOCK IN MANUFACTURING OPERATIONS

	Energy Requirements Using Virgin Material (MJ/t)	Energy Requirements Using Recycled Material (MJ/t)	Reduction in Energy Requirements, Recycled Compared with Virgin (%)
Unbleached coated boxboard	71,321	40,483	43
Linerboard	73,552	41,203	44
Corrugated medium	55,274	40,111	27
Aluminum	241,688	9,668	96
Glass	15,686	11,503	27
Steel	22,774	19,637	14

Perspectives on Solid Waste Management in Canada: An Assessment of the Physical, Economic and Energy Dimensions of Solid Waste Management in Canada, prepared by Resource Integration Systems Ltd. for Environment Canada, March 1996. Cited in *Federation of Canadian Municipalities, Solid Waste as a Resource: A Review of Waste Technologies* (Ottawa, n.d.), 41. Reprinted with permission.

waste water plant (i.e., the waste from toilets and sewer sludge) are turned into compost at a $150-million co-composting facility that was built in 2000. The entire operation has been fitted out with a research lab and enough space to accommodate private recycling companies on site.[9]

Halifax undertook a similarly sweeping overhaul of its waste management systems in the late 1990s. As of 1996, after Nova Scotia created the Halifax Regional Municipality, the city relied on 70 leaking dumps and 20 open burning sites in nearby forests. The city looked into building a new incinerator in Dartmouth. But an environmental assessment panel rejected the plan because it was too expensive and didn't promote more progressive approaches. The city then undertook a wide-ranging public consultation that led to the establishment of an ambitious waste diversion program. The program included user fees on residential garbage bags to promote waste reduction; recycling; disposal bans on reusable materials; a household hazardous waste program; the establishment of compost farms; and front-end processing—a mechanical separation system installed in transfer stations where bulky items and recyclable materials can be removed from the waste so they don't end up in a landfill. Organics were banned from the garbage stream. As in many cities, Halifax recognized that its citizens wanted the opportunity to participate in a more sustainable approach to dealing with their own waste. It also knew that such changes don't come cheap.

The results have been impressive in both cities. Edmonton's program claims to divert up to 80 percent of the collected waste headed for its landfill, while Halifax has achieved a 56 percent rate.[10] Before it began its reforms, Halifax's diversion rate was a mere 5 percent. But the fact that such programs were working in these mid-sized cities didn't mean they had been successful in larger municipalities. Greater Vancouver operates a relatively new landfill in a rural area a few kilometres south of the city that's going to last for decades: While the city wants to divert 60 percent of its residential waste by 2008, its rate remains stuck in the 40 percent range. Montreal has had far less success in reshaping its waste management practices, despite a 1998 provincial government decree that municipalities reach 65 percent diversion by 2008. As of 2002, less than 20 percent of Montreal's trash was being diverted from its landfills, including a quarry on the island and others north of the city. The city continues to grapple with the mechanics of organic waste collection.[11]

Toronto, during the 1990s, faced the same story. The city's enormous Keele Valley landfill was due to close in the early 2000s, and attempts to secure a new location—which cost the city and the provincial government almost $200 million—had come up empty. In the late 1990s, a well-connected consortium pitched the City of Toronto on a far-fetched 20-year scheme to ship Toronto's garbage by rail to an abandoned mine near the town of Kirkland Lake, in northern Ontario. According to its backers, the mine would be equipped with pumping and filtering systems to prevent leachate from seeping into the groundwater. But environmentalists and hydrogeologists heaped scorn on the untested technology, while left-leaning city councillors, led by Jack Layton and David Miller, exposed the fiscal time bombs in the proposed contract between the consortium and the city. After a dramatic showdown during the fall of 2000, Toronto council rejected the Kirkland Lake scheme, approving instead a long-term deal to ship the city's waste by truck to a private landfill near Detroit, Michigan, at a cost of about $50 million annually.[12]

As with New York in the 1980s, Toronto's enormous garbage problem gets a lot of attention, and deservedly so. The city's decision to ship its trash to Michigan precipitated a tense U.S.-Canada trade dispute, as both state and federal legislators have put forward legislation designed to keep Toronto's garbage from crossing the border. Indeed, Toronto's dependence on the Michigan landfill exposed an ugly double standard. Had a private firm established a landfill on the Canadian side of the border and began importing U.S. trash, there would almost certainly be cries of outrage from Canadian politicians. More generally, Toronto's out-of-sight-out-of-mind approach is environmentally indefensible.

As of 2004, about 150 trucks were driving each day between Toronto and Michigan. That means approximately 55 million additional vehicle-kilometres travelled by heavy-duty diesel trucks along Highway 401 each year—equivalent to half the total annual mileage logged by Toronto's city buses.[13] That's a lot of exhaust and diesel fuel. As former Toronto councillor Richard Gilbert points out, "Each truck's return journey generates a tonne of carbon dioxide and large amounts of locally acting pollutants that affect hundreds of thousands of people living along the route to the landfill site. This export of waste shows shameful disregard for the health and well-being of residents of Michigan and southwest Ontario."[14]

Apart from all the additional diesel fumes on the highway, Toronto's arrangement with Michigan underscores the practical limits of waste diversion. Even the most progressive municipalities are stuck with "residuals" after most of the recyclables and organics have been removed—used toothbrushes, mattresses, plastic wrappers, and other trash with no redeeming value. The figures vary, but residuals account for anywhere from 20 to 40 percent of all waste collected, and they have to be disposed of somehow. For most municipalities, the residuals go to the landfill. With large cities such as Toronto, these are not trivial quantities of trash: Toronto's residuals add up to 400,000 tonnes a year—three times as much as all the garbage Halifax produces annually. Recycling and diversion programs have succeeded in extending the life spans of many landfills, but the reality is that they all eventually fill up. And the process of finding new locations gets only more difficult, as Toronto officials discovered when they began scouting around for a backup landfill in case U.S. politicians carry out their threat to close the border.

European countries have been living with this reality for decades, which is why they've turned to high-tech incineration—also known as thermal processing. Such disposal systems are commonplace and generally accepted in Sweden and Germany, but only a few Canadian cities have opted to take this route (they include Peel, outside Toronto, and Burnaby, in Greater Vancouver). Denmark, a small country with little room for landfills, burns and recycles over 80 percent of its trash. With an incineration rate of 40 percent, Sweden's long-standing environmental strategy involves mandatory packaging requirements, battery collection, and the reuse of incinerated residue in paving material.

It turns out that incineration can actually be used to *improve* air quality. Sound counter-intuitive? Not in Sweden. Since the mid-1990s, Swedish regulators, as well as the European Union, have imposed the world's toughest anti-pollution standards on municipal solid waste incinerators, forcing the operators to retrofit their plants with high-tech scrubbers and other emission-control systems. Most jurisdictions now require municipalities to ensure that heavy-metal-producing garbage, such as spent batteries, is removed from the waste stream before it reaches the incinerators. The result has been a sharp drop in the release of hydrochloric acid, dioxins, and mercury. In 2003, Valfrid Paulsson, the former head of Sweden's environmental protection agency, publicly touted state-of-the-art incineration as a "clean process that is self-paying and profitable for local municipalities. The new techniques developed in the past few years," he said in a controversial interview, "see 95 percent of the toxins being burnt down, while the remaining five percent is taken care of in filters."[15]

While a 2003 opinion poll showed that 70 percent of Torontonians supported high-tech incineration,[16] Canadian environmental groups remain staunchly opposed, their concerns the legacy of the older generation of such plants—including the American "mass burning" facilities of the 1960s and 1970s—which had indisputably serious environmental and health failings. The latest scientific evidence has to be parsed carefully. University of Waterloo researchers showed that modern incinerators produced more acid gas emissions and toxic pollutants—including air-borne dioxins—than landfills. Yet landfills give off higher levels of micro-particles, volatile organic compounds, and water-borne pollutants, including dioxins. "In general, properly designed and operated [incineration] facilities can meet all Canadian environmental regulations," concluded the Federation of Canadian Municipalities in a broad-ranging review of various waste management technologies. "These regulations set limits on the quantities of pollutants that a facility can emit."[17]

The Swedish government knew that older incinerators were responsible for about half of the country's dioxin emissions, but those rates have dropped significantly as the technology improved. More recently, a report on a municipal solid waste incinerator in France found elevated rates of certain cancers in communities downwind of the facility. But the plant had been operating at 160 times the allowable level.[18] And the fact is that landfills exact their own health toll. While a study published in 2000 in the *British Medical Journal* found no congenital birth defects among children born near odour-producing landfills in South Wales, a study published the same year by the *Journal of Environmental Health* determined that landfill workers in Virginia suffered from elevated levels of respiratory diseases because they are exposed to high concentrations of fungi, bacteria, diesel fumes, and heavy metals.[19]

The moral of the story is that we tend to be very selective about what we deem to be an unacceptable health risk. Even though vehicle use and wasteful power consumption can be implicated in hundreds of deaths due to respiratory illnesses, we aren't (yet) banning cars, imposing European-style taxes on fossil fuels, or levying fines against office buildings that leave their lights on all night—all measures that could reduce electricity consumption and improve air quality. Yet some cities remain steadfast in their opposition to high-tech incineration, citing health risks associated with a much earlier generation of technology.

The other primary environmental objection to incineration is the fear that if a city can burn its trash, there will be less incentive to reduce or recycle. But such concerns can be alleviated if municipalities set strict caps on the amount of trash they burn and create aggressive diversion targets. In fact, European jurisdictions have dealt with these precise dilemmas by setting the regulatory bar high enough to address health and air-quality issues, while simultaneously imposing so-called product-lifecycle rules to make manufacturers far more accountable for disposing of the goods they sell. Germany has some of the toughest packaging rules in the world but is also thoroughly committed to high-tech incineration; the two go hand in hand.

There is also a financial case for incinerators, even though they are considerably more expensive to run than landfills. In 1988, the Greater Vancouver Regional District built a high-tech mass burning incinerator at its Cache Creek Landfill. Large enough to process 250,000 tonnes of garbage a year, it now handles 17 percent of Greater Vancouver's total output. The furnaces of such incinerators are surrounded by water-filled pipes that transform the very high internal heat into steam. In the late 1990s, the landfill's owners and a nearby paper recycling firm, Crown Packaging, came up with an innovative arrangement. The company agreed to pay the GVRD 85 percent of the cost of the natural gas it would have used to run its own operation, in exchange for half of the incinerator's steam. A kilometre-long pipe moves the steam between the two facilities. It was the classic win-win: Crown cut its greenhouse gas emissions and its fuel costs, while the GVRD collected an extra $2 million a year in revenues.[20] Four years later, BC Hydro teamed up with the Burnaby Incinerator to use the remaining steam to generate 155 gigawatts of electricity, enough to power 12,500 homes.[21]

Conservation and Alternative Energy

In the 20th century, we built cities with no regard to the way they guzzle energy. But at the dawn of the 21st century, as we face a future of soaring fuel prices and the very real prospect of depleting oil supplies, we need to completely reconsider the relationship between energy and cities. If there is a silver lining to this dark cloud, it is that large urban areas provide tremendous economies of scale for sustainable energy ventures and the emerging alternative fuel technologies that can help make our cities sustainable as well as economically prosperous.

Municipalities must drive these changes. In Toronto, for example, the city's district heating company, Enwave Energy Corporation, in a partnership with a major pension fund, built a deep-water cooling system in 2004, using cold water from Lake Ontario to provide clean air conditioning to downtown office buildings. The City of Toronto, in fact, has been a leader in this area for well over a decade: In 1992, it set up the Toronto Atmospheric Fund with a $25-million endowment, the proceeds of which help fund local greening projects, from homeowner energy audits to retrofits of public buildings. Other cities have followed suit, and much of the federal government's newfound enthusiasm for promoting sustainable cities can be traced to the Toronto Atmospheric Fund's partnership approach.

Such initiatives illustrate how cities can harness their resources to transform themselves into energy innovators as a means of improving air quality. Municipalities, school boards, universities, and other public agencies all operate large fleets—buses, police cars, ambulances, fire engines, garbage trucks, and municipal vehicles. Public institutions have the potential to become large-scale purchasers of green vehicles that run on natural gas, hybrid engines, or other forms of alternative fuels. While earlier generations of hybrids were too expensive for some public agencies, the economics are beginning to change. By 2011, almost 40 models of hybrids will be on the market, including SUVs. Automotive research firm J.D. Power and Associates predicts U.S. hybrid sales—estimated to be 200,000 in 2005—will triple by 2010.[22] And if the price of a barrel of crude continues to soar, those estimates will begin to look conservative. In fact, there is no reason to expect that hybrids will do anything other than follow the path blazed by other new technologies, such as cell phones, DVDs, and laptops: Specialized interest in high-priced early models morphs into broader consumer acceptance, triggering dizzying technological innovation and falling prices. Twenty or maybe even 10 years from now, the traditional combustion engine may seem as antiquated as those boat-like Impala station wagons.

Ottawa, in turn, must do much more to promote the development of alternative clean-burning fuels, such as biodiesel, a diesel substitute that can be refined from soybeans, canola, waste oils, and rendered fats left over from the meat processing industry. While Canada has begun to promote these fuels through tax incentives, it still lags well behind the

United States and Europe. Washington in 1992 passed legislation that aims to increase to 30 percent the proportion of non-fossil-fuel additives to regular gasoline by 2010. Meanwhile, the European Union in 1994 introduced a hefty tax break for biodiesel and more recently approved new fuel standards requiring that all diesel sold on the continent include 2 percent biodiesel.[23] A decade later, Europe was producing two billion litres of biodiesel annually, and that output is expected to rise rapidly. By contrast, North America's entire biodiesel production capacity was 60 million litres as of 2005—just 3 percent of the E.U. market.

Quite apart from such fuel-specific incentives and showy spending programs such as the One-Tonne Challenge, our federal government must begin to think about shifting its entire taxation system to promote sustainable energy. After all, if renewable and alternative energy is genuinely a national priority, then the goods and services related to such types of power should be taxed at a lower rate than traditional fossil fuels.

From an urban perspective, some of the most critical energy decisions will be made by provincial energy regulators. According to a 2005 study on energy, Canada will require an estimated $150 billion in capital investment in its electricity generating system in the coming two decades—to catch up with delayed infrastructure maintenance and the expansion of the supply network. At present, about 60 percent of all electricity generated in Canada comes from clean hydroelectric dams, but almost a quarter is produced by the burning of coal, oil, and natural gas. Ontario historically has been heavily reliant on unreliable nuclear power plants, which continue to demand attention and massive investment. Meanwhile, only a minuscule amount—just over 1 percent of all power generated in Canada—comes from renewable alternatives such as wind and solar power.[24]

Until very recently, Canada's largest electrical monopolies ignored green power suppliers because they had sunk billions into megaprojects such as nuclear plants and hydroelectric dams. Yet there is no doubt that power shortages and the surging popularity of green alternatives have attracted the attention of investors and politicians alike. During the 2004 national election, the federal Liberals promised to invest $450 million in wind and other renewable projects through

2009. Ontario and Manitoba in 2005 agreed to link their electrical grids so some of Manitoba's abundant supply of hydro can flow into energy-starved Ontario. The McGuinty Liberals, meanwhile, are encouraging private investments in wind turbines as part of Ontario's push to expand the production of renewable energy to 2500 megawatts—about 10 percent of the province's capacity—by 2010. Yet such ventures, which continue to compete with nuclear energy, represent just a drop in the bucket, according to the Canadian Wind Energy Association, which maintains that it will be possible to harness 10,000 megawatts of wind energy in Canada by the end of the decade—enough to replace the energy produced by Ontario's coal plants.[25]

Is it possible? The example of Germany suggests that it might be. For well over a decade, German regulators have provided community-based co-ops with long-term, guaranteed rates to give them a financial advantage over private-sector suppliers of power derived from coal- or gas-powered plants. That move spawned investment by hundreds of small organizations. They purchase their equipment from Germany's wind-turbine manufacturing industry, which now employs 45,000 people. The net result is an economic success story. Since 1991, Germany has installed 14,000 megawatts of wind power, equivalent to two-thirds of Ontario Power Generation's entire capacity, including nuclear reactors, coal plants, and Niagara Falls. Across Europe, in fact, wind turbines produce a total of 35,000 megawatts, compared with just 7000 in North America.[26]

The wind revolution could reach directly into the urban environment itself. In Europe and the United States, wind turbine companies are developing small, affordable models that can be installed on rooftops or light standards and hooked into the grid. Increasingly free to pursue new business ventures, Canada's municipal utilities could deploy such turbines throughout large cities to create new supply sources.

Similarly, advances in the conductive materials that go into solar panels will eventually bring down the price of this form of energy. U.S. energy researchers have estimated that panels covering an area the size of Vermont could theoretically satisfy America's electricity needs.[27] Weather-related surges, storage capacity, and transmission continue to represent logistical impediments to solar power. On the other hand, sprawling cities have the potential to solve the other major dilemma, which is available space. After all, large North American cities now feature extensive industrial parks dominated by very large, flat-roofed structures well suited for solar panels. Municipal or provincial policy makers should be developing incentives, planning policies, and building codes designed to encourage builders and landlords to install rooftop panels or wind turbines and hook them into the grid. There is certainly a precedent. In California, environmentally conscious corporations, including Toyota and Target, have already taken this step on their own.

The Eco-City

During the 20th century, a handful of cities amassed enormous wealth because of the fortunes produced by two industries: automobiles and energy. The economies of Houston, Detroit, Calgary, Toronto, and Montreal all boomed thanks to these sectors, whose growth paralleled the evolution of our increasingly car-dependent cities since the end of World War II. Between the 1970s and the 1990s, San José, Seattle, and Austin captured a disproportionate share of the global riches produced by the transistor and information technology revolution, again, because they were home to networks of high-tech innovators and risk-taking investors. In the 21st century, environmentally driven upheavals in energy and transportation will certainly create new fortunes and empires. They will fill the breach when oil and gas prices break through some kind of threshold that forever alters the economics of energy. The question is, which cities are best poised to exploit these looming economic transformations? And will any of them be Canadian?

Public policy will never create a commercial genius, and politicians must take a leap of faith when they fund research. But governments, the private sector, consumers, environmental non-governmental organizations, and universities can join forces to foster a culture of urban environmental consciousness and energy innovation. The latter occurred in Calgary and Edmonton in the late 1980s when the Alberta government set up an energy institute whose far-sighted researchers eventually developed methods for extracting the energy from oil sands.

Will we do the same with renewable or alternative energy, building design, or other areas connected to the task of making our cities more sustainable? Those urban regions where such experimentation is given the most latitude, where the profound challenges of urban sustainability are seen as opportunities rather than crises, will emerge as the economic winners of the 21st century.

Between 1995 and 2000, the number of companies operating in Canada's environmental industries sector grew by an impressive 67 percent—from 4500 to 7500 firms. As of 2000, they represented $14.4 billion in revenues (up from $11 billion five years previous) and boasted an employment base of 160,000 people.[28] Some of that activity has traditionally taken place in heavily industrialized Central Canadian cities such as Hamilton, where factories have had to invest in cleanup and pollution mitigation systems. But beyond the traditional soil remediation and waste management sectors, the environmental sector is becoming a fixture of the new economy, and it will gravitate to environmentally conscious cities such as Waterloo, Toronto, and Halifax.

In Vancouver, the prevailing civic culture shifted from a dependence on resource extraction to the promotion of environmental entrepreneurialism in less than a generation. "It arises out of a historic pre-disposition of people who are into environmental issues to move to the West Coast," remarks Peter Busby, a leading Vancouver architect who designs green condo towers for developers in Las Vegas, San Francisco, and Portland. He predicts Vancouver will become "the premier North American city for businesses focused on environmental and sustainability issues."[29]

The city has become home to hydrogen firms, Ballard Power Systems among them; international engineering outfits specializing in water treatment systems; a green technology testing facility; and think-tanks on sustainable cities. The B.C. government, meanwhile, has begun to introduce key tax-shifting measures designed to encourage environmentally beneficial business activity with financial incentives.

Then there is the link to urban policy. Busby's firm developed an expertise in sustainable architecture because Vancouver has adopted an environmentally conscious vision of its future, which translates into land-use policies that encourage people to live downtown and design standards that push builders to develop green building techniques. Busby points out that Vancouver's traditional elites—the close-knit lumber and mining families—have seen their influence wane since the clear-cutting wars and then the takeovers that resulted in head offices moving elsewhere. The health-oriented and environmentally conscious young people flocking to the city prefer to work in clean sectors such as film production, computer graphics, and anything with a green hue. "When business opportunities arise that relate to the environment," Busby says, "people jump on them."[30] Perhaps one of these entrepreneurs will become the Bill Gates of green energy ... and a Canadian to boot.

THINKING CITIES

L et's pause for a moment to consider how a city globally regarded for its energy and environmental leadership might present itself to visitors. Such a city is naturally a place with a broad public consensus on the importance of transit and compact development. All traffic lights have long-lasting energy-efficient bulbs, public buildings are retrofitted with energy-efficiency heating and cooling systems, and the office towers go dark at night. Its citizens support planning decisions that protect environmentally sensitive land formations and discourage the development of vast, fertilizer-ingesting lawns.

But there is much more. The local utilities compete aggressively with one another to supply green power to consumers. One of them, in fact, has created a novel strategic partnership with a network of suburban businesses, property managers, and retailers to install large-scale solar panels on their buildings. Another is developing a "distributed energy" network that allows it to tap into non-traditional power supplies—from portable generators to hydrogen fuel cells. The universities have chosen to build internationally renowned centres for graduate research in fields such as emerging alternative-energy technologies, green building techniques, and super-lightweight materials geared to making passenger vehicles ultra fuel efficient. What is more, the ethos of our eco-city has captured the imagination of venture capitalists and entrepreneurs, who are partnering with scientists to develop new products and systems—for example, a local infrastructure of hydrogen stations for fuel-cell vehicles—catering to the burgeoning consumer demand for a more energy-efficient urban lifestyle.

Developers and architects compete with one another to create the most energy-efficient residential buildings, and they promote the savings as part of their marketing campaigns. Renovation-minded homeowners retrofit their houses with green roofs—replacing heat-absorbing asphalt or shingles with gardens that help recycle CO_2 and provide natural insulation. Super-compact city cars sell briskly at local car dealers. The municipal government sets ever more aggressive targets for annual bike path construction. One of the city's most successful new retailers is an alternative- and renewable-energy superstore, which not only sells equipment such as solar panels but also provides consulting advice and installation services. It has been directly responsible for a local boom in sales of small-scale wind turbines suitable for the roofs of residential properties. These devices now come in a variety of bright colours and have added a zesty aesthetic to the urban skyline.

Our city proclaims to the world, "Bring your wildest green ideas here. We're interested." More than anything else, though, its environmentally conscious residents enjoy a high quality of urban life. They have moved beyond the grinding, expensive, asthma-inducing business of gridlock and sprawl and instead have come to embrace the social, health, and economic benefits of living in vibrant neighbourhoods with sufficient density to support an abundance of independent retailers, cafés, galleries, theatres, and the energy of a well-used pedestrian realm.

This isn't just a fantasy. Livable, cosmopolitan cities, such as Vancouver, are rapidly emerging as the winners in the post-industrial global market. Why? Because they serve as magnets for the talented researchers, software engineers, artists, and professionals who populate the sectors that are driving the 21st-century economy: fields such as information technology, mass media and entertainment, advanced manufacturing, alternative energy, and biomedical research. Grey matter is the raw material of the post-industrial economy, and the more there is in a particular city, the better its chances. But according to Richard Florida, author of *The Rise of the Creative Class,* talented people gravitate to cities that understand how to create livable, cosmopolitan neighbourhoods. "The Creative Class," he writes, "is strongly oriented to large cities and regions that offer a variety of economic opportunities, a stimulating environment and amenities for every possible lifestyle....

These places offer something for everyone—vibrant urban districts, abundant natural amenities and comfortable suburban 'nerdistans' for techies so inclined."[1]

Florida, a native of Pittsburgh, is a charismatic professor of public policy at George Mason University as well as a consultant with a thriving practice advising cities and other urban organizations. His work on the evolution of the "creative class" and its impact on cities has vaulted him to the forefront of North American urban thinkers. He often cites the influence of Jane Jacobs. Florida's urban philosophy focuses on people and the *quality* of specific places while rejecting the mechanistic characterization of city-regions as economic engines.

Florida recounts how, while researching *The Rise of the Creative Class,* he travelled frequently to cities across the United States and Canada, and around the world—journeys during which he met graduate students, recruiters, government officials, and business leaders. Florida developed a shorthand method for gauging the creativity and openness of the cities he visited. When invited to dinner functions with business leaders, he would ask how to dress. If told to wear a suit and tie, he figured he was in a conservative city with traditional values and an economy to match. If his hosts didn't mind slacks and a sweater, he knew he was in a city that was receptive to the progressive mores of the creative class.

Florida's thesis is that innovative, creative cities—the ones to watch in the coming century—tend to have large gay communities and score high on something he called the Bohemian Index. They are accepting of non-hierarchical and highly flexible corporate organizations, venture capitalists who bet on tech start-ups, and young people pursuing alternative lifestyles (his favourite example is the proliferation of tattoos). In turn, they offer their residents a wide range of intense experiences, which run the gamut from hopping local music scenes to thrilling natural environments. As he observes, "A great city has two hallmarks: tolerance for strangers and intolerance for mediocrity."[2]

These cities, he says, attract the creative class noted above: scientists, artists, software developers, skilled professionals, and so on. A critical mass of such individuals gives rise to the kind of frisson that emerges from local social and professional networks, the presence of leading universities and other higher-learning institutions, and even random interactions in public or semi-public spaces.

The process works in much the same way that certain commercial or industrial areas come to be known for specializing in a particular good—the diamond district in midtown Manhattan or the home-decor district in a post-industrial corner of Toronto. Such clusters exert a gravitational pull, drawing in both retailers and consumers, who go there knowing they'll find the best selection and the best prices. The merchants compete with one another, but they all benefit from the proximity, the rivalry, and the gossipy social networks that develop among them.

This is precisely how week-long theatre, music, craft, visual art, and movie festivals have emerged in recent years as a powerful way of connecting talented people to predominantly urban audiences. Much like the long-established industrial trade fair or the academic conference, these festivals succeed because they bring everyone together in one place at one time—artists, producers, marketers, consumers. The creative chemistry arises from the contacts and interactions that occur in the context of such energized events. Often, they can be traced to a handful of far-sighted and determined people who push hard to put their art on the map.

A current example is Calgary's fast-emerging alternative theatre scene, which offers quirky specialties such as avant-garde puppetry. (Previous examples include Toronto's One-of-a-Kind craft show and the Just-for-Laughs festival in Montreal.) Once such events gather momentum—think of Montreal's jazz festival, the largest of its kind in the world, and the Toronto International Festival of Authors—they morph into something permanent. Their success goes beyond the identification of a particular city with a particular art form. These ingatherings of creative people give rise to the establishment of a creative infrastructure—for example, a hub of production companies or a network of gainfully employed theatre professionals. Dense, cosmopolitan regions also provide the perfect conduit for the spread of interesting new ideas. Malcolm Gladwell, a staff writer for *The New Yorker* magazine, showed in his 2000 bestseller *The Tipping Point* that popular ideas tend to spread through urban populations much in the same way that infectious diseases turn into epidemics. He cites examples such as the birth of an offbeat footwear trend among hip Lower East Side teenagers, and the snowball effect of word-of-mouth endorsements for a novel that became *de rigueur* reading for women's book groups in the San Francisco–Bay Area region and went on to become a national bestseller. "The best way to understand the emergence of fashion trends, the ebb and flow of crime waves, or, for that matter, the transformation of unknown books into bestsellers, or the rise of teenage smoking, or the phenomena of word of mouth, or any number of the other mysterious changes that mark everyday life is to think of them as epidemics," he writes.[3] They are viral and contagious, and, like disease epidemics, require the presence of concentrated populations of people.

These various creative processes feed on themselves and eventually extend beyond urban boundaries. But they seem to take root in cities that can already lay claim to some kind of distinctiveness (a renowned research centre, a physically beautiful setting, a thriving local arts scene), coupled with an urban environment that isn't isolated, insular, and static. Such cities, moreover, have plenty of low-cost "garage" space, says Florida—suitable for upstart companies, artists, and other innovators. It's not a coincidence that the web design industry roared to life in the mid-1990s in a gritty part of lower Manhattan that came to be dubbed Silicon Alley: Even as the World Wide Web was promising to destroy distance and connect computer users all over the globe, the pioneering creators of this medium gravitated to a dense, quintessentially urban environment in which to do their work, because such settings are uniquely conducive to creative thinking, intellectual competition, and the sharing of ideas.

The urban regions that score high on Florida's various indices include Austin, San Francisco, Dublin, Stockholm, and Sydney, but also Toronto, Vancouver, and Montreal. Those that fall short tend to be rustbelt U.S. cities—for example, Buffalo—that never managed to move past their tottering industrial heritage. Florida's framework isn't absolutely watertight; there are high-tech centres that rank low on his immigration index. And some critics have attacked Florida, arguing that he whitewashes the impact of high immigration on the urban labour force. But Florida has countered with a follow-up volume,

The Flight of the Creative Class, in which he argues that the us-versus-them sentiment in post-9/11 America has discouraged high-skilled immigrants and foreign graduate students from settling in the United States. It's a development that has translated into a brain gain in Canada, which he sees as a model for how to manage a cultural mosaic.[4]

As Florida commented in a 2004 essay in the *Harvard Business Review,* "A host of countries—Ireland, Finland, Canada, Australia, New Zealand, among them—are investing in higher education, cultivating creative people, and churning out stellar products, from Nokia phones to the Lord of the Rings movies. Many of these countries have learned from past U.S. success and are shoring up efforts to attract foreign talent—including Americans. If even a handful of these rising nations draws away just 2 to 5 percent of the creative workers from the U.S., the effect on its economy will be enormous. The United States may well have been the Goliath of the twentieth-century global economy, but it will take just half a dozen twenty-first-century Davids to begin to wear it down."[5]

Moreover, Florida and other students of the dynamics of global cities stress that talented people and innovation-oriented investment capital tend to collect in certain urban regions but not others. Florida has vigorously challenged the "flat world" thesis advanced by *New York Times* columnist Thomas Friedman, who argues in *The World Is Flat,* his 2005 bestseller, that globalization and information technology put every place into competition with every other place. He asserts that innovation can now happen anywhere. Not so, counters Florida: "Ideas flow more freely, are honed more sharply, and can be put into practice more quickly when large numbers of innovators, implementers, and financial backers are in constant contact with one another, both in and out of the office. Creative people cluster not simply because they like to be around one another or they prefer cosmopolitan centers with lots of amenities, though both those things count. They and their companies also cluster because of the powerful productivity advantages, economies of scale, and knowledge spillovers such density brings."[6]

In the years since Florida went public with his creative-class theory of urban economic development, cities across North America have rushed to brand themselves as creative centres in a bid to impress the kinds of companies and individuals that are driving these transformations. But this isn't just about slick marketing brochures and economic development schemes with the right buzz words. The sort of urban landscape Florida describes encompasses many complex features—physical, social, cultural, and economic. The members of Florida's creative class seek out novelty, social diversity, and unique experiences as a matter of personal and professional temperament. Uniformity and a dearth of urban stimulation are anathema to the needs of this group. The lesson is that the cities that have set out to attract the members of the creative class must reflect on the richness of the choices they can offer their inhabitants if they genuinely wish to survive and prosper in the economy of the 21st century.

Cities and Civilization

"Creative cities, creative urban milieux, are places of great social and intellectual turbulence, not comfortable places at all."[7] So observes Sir Peter Hall, the eminent British urban historian and planning authority in *Cities in Civilization,* his magisterial account of why certain cities, at certain moments in their history, suddenly became intellectual combustion engines—"cultural crucibles." His list includes classical Athens, early Renaissance Florence, London in the 1600s, Paris in the mid-19th century, *fin de siècle* Vienna, Henry Ford's Detroit, Los Angeles at the dawn of the movie age, and Silicon Valley in the 1960s.

As Canada's largest cities seek their place in the global economic order and internalize Richard Florida's lessons about the creative class, Hall's case studies on the social conditions that trigger so-called golden ages should resonate with urban leaders. In all these cities, a critical mass of artists, innovators, and entrepreneurs collided to produce an explosion of creative output—the artisans and painters of Florence and Paris, the literary and architectural achievements of 16th-century London, and the movies of 1920s Los Angeles. In the laboratories of Stanford University's Palo Alto campus—situated in a sleepy farming area south of San Francisco—in the 1950s and 1960s, a handful of electrical engineers took the new transistor technology developed in the

Bell Labs in New Jersey and refined it, a process that gave rise to what Hall refers to as the "garage entrepreneurs" who fathered the first generation of high-tech firms. They were followed by a cascade of breakaway firms that transformed the Bay Area into the heartland of the digital revolution.

In Paris in the mid-19th century, Hall explains, Napoleon III undertook the modernization of the French state and ordered Baron Georges-Eugène Haussmann to rebuild his capital into a gleaming centre of culture, commerce, and academe. It was a period when there was much new wealth, and the values of this emerging urban class clashed with those of the establishment. That precise confrontation, between conservative old and the progressive or experimental new, plays out in all these case studies to a greater or lesser degree. They were cities experiencing an influx of immigrants and outsiders, who upended the established social order by offering something different. The newly wealthy, in turn, patronized the emerging artists, whose work also represented a break from the past. "Not infrequently it is the recent immigrants, sometimes from the countryside, often from the far distant part of the empire, who provided both the audience and the artists," Hall observes. The Impressionists, he reminds us, were reviled by the critics who appraised their first shows. "Great art is not produced by insiders."[8]

Hall traces a similar dynamic in cities that fathered technological revolutions, such as Detroit, Glasgow (with its ship-building industry), and Berlin during the latter decades of the 19th century, when government officials helped a handful of scientists, including Werner von Siemens, develop new industrial sectors based on innovations in electrical engineering. Many of these cities, Hall notes, evinced a kind of "nervous energy." They tended to be situated in the economic hinterland—smaller urban centres lacking the domination of large, vertically integrated corporations and an old money establishment determined to protect its franchise.

Their social structures, moreover, tended to be more "egalitarian" and less class conscious. "They were not," Hall says, "the leading industrial cities of their day." At the same time, they could offer a rich soil in which innovation-minded entrepreneurship could take root—the presence of skilled workers, ambitious immigrants, and risk-taking entrepreneurs willing to jump on the bandwagon early on. In some cases, as in Berlin, Tokyo, and Singapore, government policy did succeed in spurring the development of an innovation-minded manu-facturing economy. And in the United States in the Cold War era, the massive spending power of the military stoked the engine of the nascent high-tech industry. But, as Hall warns, these cases tend to be the exceptions: "Building innovative milieux is not something that can be done either easily or to order."[9]

If Hall's assessment is accurate, many of Canada's major cities are well positioned to ignite the creative kindling that could vault them to the forefront of the global economy in the coming century. Mass migration is radically changing the social face of our big cities in unpre-dictable and challenging ways. Two decades of transformative advances in communication and information technology have hard-wired our cities to the broader world and altered virtually every aspect of daily life. And since the advent of North American (and soon hemispheric) free trade agreements, our economy has undergone a dramatic geographical shift, from east-west to north-south, and beyond. Our major cities sit on the economic fringes of North America, striving to compete with urban super-regions such as Greater Chicago, the Boston–New York–Washington corridor, and the Los Angeles–San Francisco–Seattle tech-media axis. Montreal fosters economic and cultural ties with France and Europe. Vancouver does business with the Far East and South Asia. Halifax, with its large concentration of academics, increasingly connects itself to New England. And Greater Toronto's export-oriented manufacturers are emerging as winners in the outsourcing boom that has drained blue-collar jobs, especially in the automotive sector, from the U.S. heartland.

The swirling creative tensions Hall describes can be glimpsed in places such as Vancouver, where environmentally conscious young professionals, high-tech firms, Pacific Rim investors, and movie indus-try entrepreneurs have toppled the dominance of the old Anglo fami-lies that controlled the natural resource industries. A generation of affluent Asian immigrants have filled the breech, stepping forward as patrons of the arts and drivers of a refreshing ethos in city building, development, and architecture.

In Halifax and St. John's, threatened a decade ago with death blows to their traditional economic supports (the fishery, the public sector, and defence), offshore oil is pumping cash into the local economy, while a new generation of entrepreneurs, artists, and performers have built exciting opportunities in tourism and entertainment—both of which depend on marketing ingenuity, creativity, acceptance of outsiders, and high-quality urban spaces. As in Vancouver, the clash between the older order and emerging economic actors has coincided with a flowering of cultural and entrepreneurial activity.

Greater Toronto can trace part of its ascendancy to the ongoing exodus of Montreal's talented Anglos. They joined the vast ingathering of immigrants who transformed the once stodgy provincial outpost into North America's fourth-largest urban region—a commercially restless city no longer under the sway of its conservative English-Scottish establishment. In fact, a 2002 study done for the Ontario government by Richard Florida and University of Toronto geographer Meric Gertler found that Toronto, by North American standards, ranks very high when it comes to ethnic diversity and the size of its gay and bohemian communities—evidence of a crucial measure of tolerance, which they consider to be the key precondition for attracting the creative class. They connect these urban social traits, plus Canada's history of support for the arts, to the continental competitiveness of Toronto's tech sector and its other "knowledge intensive economies."[10]

Montreal, in turn, illustrates how the social and cultural forces Florida and Gertler identify can serve as a powerful bulwark against the destabilizing conditions that might otherwise lead a city into a spiral of decline. At one time, Montreal's stock exchange accounted for almost 90 percent of all equity trading in Canada. But decades of on-again-off-again political turmoil, coupled with Toronto's explosive growth since the mid-1970s, spelled the exodus of investment capital and the financial services industry. The city saw manufacturing declines and plant closures because of free trade. Its poverty levels remain high, and the proportion of Montrealers with university degrees continues to lag behind that of Toronto and Vancouver. Still, according to a study by German economist Peter Karl Kresl, Montreal is one of a handful of North American urban centres considered to be "sticky" places; for all its troubles, the city has held onto a substantial number of head offices and large firms and remains a leading centre of research activity in the aerospace and bio-pharmaceuticals sectors. Federal economic development policies have sought to promote trade links with Europe and the francophonie, while the Quebec government's industrial and energy policies built the city's powerful engineering sector.[11] Today, Montreal engineering firms are active around the globe building infrastructure and transit systems in the developing world.

In the meantime, multicultural Montreal was bolstered by its large university sector, its reputation as a sophisticated European-style city, and the steadily growing presence of a thriving arts and music scene. So in 2004, when Montreal officials hired Florida and a local consulting firm to take a measure of the city's creative pulse, the results were encouraging. After Toronto, Montreal has the second-highest percentage of so-called super-creative class individuals (mathematicians, journalists, and so on) of any North American city. "The region's strength is not a single dominant asset but the harmonious balance of diverse technological capability and innovation, available skilled and creative talent and an open and tolerant society," the report concluded.[12] Florida's stamp of approval quickly translated into a plug for Montreal's arts scene in *The New York Times*.

Where immigrants, distinctive urban settings, and artists have carried forward the economies of Toronto and Montreal, the Kitchener-Waterloo-Cambridge region illustrates the intimate relationship between universities and the emergence of strong technology sectors in mid-sized cities situated at a remove from major economic centres. The region, situated in southwestern Ontario's fertile farmland, is home to several post-secondary institutions, but most prominently, the University of Waterloo, which pioneered computer science instruction and co-op placement programs in the 1960s and 1970s. In the late 1980s, the neighbouring cities of Kitchener, Waterloo, Cambridge, and Guelph came together to develop a region-wide economic development strategy focused on bolstering the upstart tech firms—many of them university spinoffs—taking root in the area. Over the next decade, various regional alliances sprang up, eventually linking the so-called Technology Triangle municipalities, universities, tech companies, training firms, philanthropists, and even social agencies focused on dealing with local poverty and community development.[13] Meanwhile, homegrown firms such as Research-in-Motion, which launched the Blackberry text-messaging device, blossomed into internationally known high-tech powerhouses, while their founders reinvested their profits in local environmental and educational initiatives.

This brainy do-it-yourself approach to urban development stands in sharp contrast to the more familiar story of cities and provincial or state governments chasing after multinational firms, using corporate tax breaks as an incentive to persuade manufacturers to build huge factories. As University of Western Ontario political scientist Neil Bradford observes, the story of the Kitchener-Waterloo-Cambridge region shows how concentrated networks of creative people, government officials, and entrepreneurs can rapidly transform cities that hitch their wagon to the innovation-oriented industries of the future. "Rather than simply attempting to lure external private investors or subsidies, local actors were creative and resourceful," Bradford says. "Their input introduced new voices into the policy process and in so doing, helped ensure a better fit between upper level interventions and local circumstances."[14]

Creative Opportunities

There is no magic formula, no policy document with a checklist of corrective actions that can transform a city into the sort of creative, tolerant, innovative place Richard Florida and Peter Hall describe. The creative city isn't just about conspicuous displays of public art and internationally promoted film festivals. Nor is there anything inevitable about the structural dynamics—immigration, the clash of old and new orders, abrupt technological change—described above. Munich and Vienna were ethnically diverse, tolerant, and culturally lively cities at the end of the 19th century. Within just a few decades, marred by world war, economic collapse, and political instability, these cities had degenerated into unstable places that proved to be highly susceptible to Adolph Hitler's fantasies of racial purity. Detroit, as of the 1960s, was not just an urban superpower but a hotbed of American pop culture. Yet, in a brief period, Hall observes, the "hidebound" U.S. automakers lost their pre-eminence to the innovative manufacturing techniques of the Japanese, and the city was doomed. As he remarks, hollowed-out downtown Detroit "is perhaps the first major industrial city in history to revert to farmland."[15]

An enduring culture of urban creativity is, most of all, a way of thinking about the nature of cities and the way fresh or challenging ideas are allowed to flow through their veins. The need to attract outsiders is paramount, which explains why bustling, commerce-oriented, trading cities have played a disproportionate role in human civilization. "Probably no city has ever been creative without continuous renewal of the creative bloodstream," Hall comments.[16] The affluent Asian immigrants and young people who flocked to Vancouver in the 1980s and 1990s brought new approaches to business, networking, architecture, the environment, the arts, and even public education—all of which presented stark and sometimes uncomfortable challenges to Vancouver's clubby status quo.

In Ottawa, likewise, the energetic tech firms and high-flying software entrepreneurs who settled in the suburbs of Kanata and Nepean in the 1990s disrupted the insular environment of a capital city long dominated by civil servants, soldiers, and lobbyists. Writer Charlotte Gray described the social transformation in *Saturday Night* magazine in 2000:

> The number of high-tech companies in the region tripled between 1990 and 1998: it stands at over 1,000 today.... This is the new Canada: neither English nor French is the first language of at least one-tenth of the employees of technology companies. The workforce is composed of twenty- and thirty-year-olds in sneakers and sweatshirts who write the codes, design the programs, found the startups, copyright the ideas, and hustle for venture capital. The elite of this crowd are those who wear iron rings on their little fingers—evidence of engineering degrees and talismans of potential wealth. And the explosion of technology companies has spurred a surge in the glamour services that the techies demand: caterers, party organizers, decorators, fashion designers, landscape artists, top-of-the-line car dealerships, sports bars, and white-limo rentals.

> This is all rather a shock for the federal public service, which has dominated the city since Confederation. Still centred in the downtown

office towers that encircle the Gothic Parliament Buildings, bureaucratic Ottawa is increasingly a reflection of the old Canada—white, bilingual, and aging…. Most government employees are over forty: nearly all the senior executives are over fifty. Now they feel out-muscled in their own city by techie wunderkinds whose work they don't understand and whose values they scorn.[17]

Calgary, built by a closely knit circle of oilmen and ranchers, has also witnessed the emergence of the sort of socio-cultural shifts such as those that shook up Ottawa. The Alberta Energy Research Institute has turned Calgary into a hub of pioneering research into new techniques for oil extraction and refining. A younger generation of Calgary's professional women have begun demanding high-quality daycare services, issuing a challenge to the city's conservative social views. A magazine geared to the city's small but growing gay community was launched in 2003. Even one of the city's most powerful business leaders, the retired CEO of EnCana, Gwyn Morgan, broke the oil baron mould by publicly propounding the need for more sustainable energy sources and instilling a New Age ethos at a company that's been at the epicentre of the oil sands boom cycle.[18]

The influx of high-skilled professionals and immigrants, meantime, has filled the city with talented entrepreneurs, some of whom are branching out from Calgary's traditional economic roots. In 1999, for instance, George Davidson and Bob Christianson, both oil patch executives and Calgary Flames fans, devised a concept that would allow season-ticket holders to sell unwanted seats online rather than to scalpers. Their project begat RepeatSeat, an upstart firm that provides internet ticketing to clients that include sports teams, theatre companies, concert promoters, and business conferences. RepeatSeat provides the clients with software and services that allow them to offer their customers secure online purchasing, using their own brand (e.g., the theatre's name) rather than that of a ticketing agency. Despite its modest public face, the company has found a niche in the middle of a vast industry dominated by Ticketmaster, the U.S.$700-million-a-year California-based agency with the crushing fees, predatory instincts, and a lock on rock concerts. As of 2004, Davidson and Christianson had invested $10 million into their 35-employee company. They have close to 200 clients, ranging from the Flames to New York City's Tribeca Performing Arts Centre—hardly the profile of a firm that traces its roots to the oil industry.[19]

At the same time, the evolution of Calgary's arts scene reveals the increasingly cosmopolitan ethos characteristic of Florida's creative-class cities. The 1980s and 1990s saw bursts of arts spending followed by cutbacks that hurt established cultural institutions. Along the way, though, a handful of independent theatre companies stepped into the breach, carving out an alternative theatre scene from nothing. "When we started," says Mark Lawes, the 39-year-old founder and artistic director of Theatre Junction, "there was a huge opportunity in the market." These new companies understood that young, affluent, and urban-oriented theatre-goers who had travelled abroad were eager to see something new and challenging. What was lacking was theatre space, so Lawes, after a sabbatical in France, put together the $10.5 million needed to buy the Grand Theatre, the city's most venerable downtown theatre, which had been sitting vacant for years. He had returned to Calgary with an entrepreneurial vision of a new theatre—the Grand is now home to a high-end restaurant and is rented out for corporate functions during the Christmas season. For the lobbies and interiors, he hired a leading Montreal design firm that has worked for Cirque du Soleil. The revenues from the tenants subsidize the season, which extends well beyond contemporary theatre into other performance arts, such as modern dance and film. "It's not just a black box. The space is flexible. It's not like walking into a theatre."[20]

Setting the Stage for the Arts

The examples of both Ottawa and Calgary raise the question of how cities foster the kind of environment conducive to the artistic and technological inclinations of the creative class.

Let's begin with culture. To a far greater degree than most people recognize, the presence of a lively arts scene is highly dependent on certain aspects of a city's built form. As Lawes discovered, a fully evolved urban cultural scene requires much more than just landmark theatres, prominent companies, and well-endowed museums. Most artists depend on the availability of work and affordable rehearsal and studio space, as well as access to smaller, low-cost venues in which to perform or display their creations. Independent galleries spring up in derelict industrial districts; their presence can be regarded as a fail-safe indicator of an area's future regeneration, often to the chagrin of the artists who settled in these neighbourhoods. Thriving music scenes, in turn, take root in marginal commercial buildings that can offer large empty spaces—gritty older hotels, vacant warehouses, defunct union halls, even decommissioned churches. Alternative theatre festivals sprout up around similar venues, but also in places where the organizers can rent parking lots or use parks as makeshift performance spaces. The Toronto International Film Festival, now one of the world's largest, traces its roots to a few downtown art house cinemas and the dreams of a handful of film buffs.

The City of Vancouver in recent years adopted a place-oriented arts development policy that allows condo builders to erect higher towers in exchange for establishing arts-oriented commercial spaces, such as the city's modern art gallery, on the ground floors. Toronto, in turn, has become the third-largest live theatre market in the English-speaking world, with long-running musicals and blockbuster shows drawing thousands of tourists and millions of dollars in revenues. The industry traces its origins to a cluster of glamorous old downtown theatres that escaped the wrecking ball in the 1960s and 1970s, while smaller alternative companies sprouted in aging industrial buildings. Although not exactly on the critical cutting edge, the long-running musicals provide an important source of steady work for performers, writers, and backstage personnel, as well as hefty profits for the live theatre companies that bankroll future productions. That's how urban theatrical ecosystems have long functioned in leading cultural centres such as New York and London. It's not a coincidence that Toronto was the birthplace of Soulpepper, an entrepreneurial independent theatre company that has electrified audiences in the 2000s and has succeeded in attracting funds to build its own performance space.

A thriving local arts scene is one of the hallmarks of great cities. And cities that have nurtured the arts reap intellectual and economic benefits as well as cultural ones. Toronto's cultural labour force is now close to 200,000 strong, and the city's arts sector contributes about $9 billion to the local gross domestic product.[21]

But there is an uncomfortable paradox with the arts and big cities: Urban neighbourhoods that evolve into hubs of artistic activity can shoot upscale very quickly. The live-work studios in semi-abandoned industrial buildings get snapped up by condo loft developers. Development pressures can inadvertently eliminate the sort of low-cost commercial spaces that artists require. And the rents of previously affordable galleries or performance spaces creep upward because of gentrification of retail strips.

Skyrocketing housing and studio expenses represent a very real structural dilemma for creative cities. Artists often pay two rents and need other jobs to support themselves. Large urban centres provide the greatest abundance of such part-time or self-employment opportunities. Teaching, for example, is an important source of employment for many visual artists. That means big-city school boards potentially play an important role in not only developing the next generation of artists and audiences but also in sustaining working artists. By investing in the music and art curricula, establishing visiting artists programs, and developing partnerships with private or not-for-profit community arts programs, the local school system can become part of the foundation of a healthy urban cultural milieu.

Yet, even with such employment options, many large cities are unaffordable for artists if the housing market is left to its own devices, as was the case in the loft districts of Soho and Tribeca in New York. Similar pressures afflict Toronto and Vancouver. The exodus of artists isn't all bad news. Small urban centres on the fringes of large cities—Guelph, Peterborough, and Port Hope, all within an hour's drive of Toronto, are good examples—become the beneficiaries, especially if they are home to universities or local colleges.

Large municipalities can help relieve the economic pressures by promoting active and far-flung public art programs—not just the occasional statue, but graffiti murals, rotating subway art displays, poetry on city buses, distinctively designed street furniture in parks, and so on. They must also clear away antiquated zoning rules that prohibit garages or factories from being converted into studio space.

Then there is the issue of artists' housing. In Toronto, an arm's-length municipal agency known as Artscape has built an extensive network of affordable live-work artists' apartments and studios in formerly derelict warehouses. Artscape operates these buildings—some are privately owned, others belong to the city—and has taken an active role in drumming up funds for heritage restoration. Such not-for-profit ventures create a counterbalance to the real estate speculation that invariably follows artists in their quest for low-cost accommodations and studios.

In Montreal, a network of visual artists and craftspeople has sought to push this concept one step further, developing an ambitious not-for-profit Cité des Artistes complex near the harbourfront that will provide about 400 affordable downtown studio lofts but also serve as a destination for the display and sale of their work, as well as studio tours and cafés. Like Artscape's buildings, the lofts will be reserved for artists in financial need. André Paradis, a painter who is the driving force behind Cité des Artistes, points out that the city's once plentiful supply of cheap housing has given way to real estate speculation. While a new generation of Montreal businesspeople recognize the link between culture and urban economic development, Paradis says local government has been slow to follow, having only just created its first culture strategy in recent years. The problem is that municipal leaders embrace Florida's creative-class prescriptions but then approve development plans that push artists out of their garrets. "The Florida approach sees that artists are an asset, not a liability," Paradis remarks. "But does the city have policies in place to encourage artists? Its role is to remove the barriers to make this happen."[22]

The Meeting of the Minds

Alongside their arts scenes, creative-class cities are characterized by a significant and growing presence of knowledge-intensive companies: biotech firms, software and gaming developers, media outfits, and so on. As Peter Hall notes, such cities tend not to be dominated by a handful of vertically integrated giants, but rather are populated by a proliferation of small or mid-sized outfits, many of which may have spun off from one another. They actively invest in R&D and cultivate close relationships to university researchers and their patent commercialization offices. The principals and researchers in these firms tend to find one another, yet, as Florida observes, they must link together in networks that include venture capitalists, merchant bankers, and professional services companies that can provide the sort of financial and managerial expertise necessary to transform entrepreneurial risk takers into established and growth-oriented companies.

These companies are built on ideas, which are a very different sort of raw material than traditional industries rely on. According to Florida, cities that want to attract such firms must pay far closer attention to what Florida describes as human capital. Where once they may have concentrated the bulk of their economic development planning on physical assets, such as highways, ports, and the provision of serviced industrial land, creative cities need to attract and retain innovators, and in ways that go beyond quality-of-life amenities.

Such economic changes call for a completely new way of thinking about urban infrastructure. Take the example of the MaRS Discovery District, a 1.5-million-square-foot, not-for-profit biotech incubator that opened in 2005 in downtown Toronto. In the early 2000s, University of Toronto administrators and the leaders of Toronto's unique cluster of world-beating teaching hospitals began to realize that they were sitting on top of one of North America's most extensive concentrations of biomedical research capability: hundreds of doctors and researchers, working with a foot in academe and another in hospital wards mere blocks away. Philanthropists, corporations, and hospital foundations had bankrolled specialized research institutes geared to fields ranging from inner-city health to osteoporosis. This realization led to the establishment of a partnership between the University of Toronto, its teaching hospitals, and the three levels of government. Together, they put up $450 million for the construction costs of a pair of towering office complexes on either end of the refurbished original wing of Toronto General Hospital. MaRS is equipped with labs, convention facilities, and state-of-the-art digital networks and has begun marketing itself internationally to biomedical R&D firms, venture capitalists, and companies willing to market these discoveries. Moreover, its open design is geared to maximizing face-to-face interactions between all these players—an acknowledgment of the importance of networking in the evolution of knowledge-intensive industries.

How does MaRS fit into the larger urban picture? Since the 1989 ratification of the Canada-U.S. free trade agreement, Canada's manufacturers have thrived while their American counterparts have experienced a loss of industrial jobs to plants to China. But our cities are not immune from such outsourcing trends. That's why our governments, universities, and the private sector need to think strategically about future sources of economic growth if our cities are to retain their prosperity and standard of living. Alberta's decision in the late 1970s to establish an oil sands research institute in Calgary (now known as the Alberta Energy Research Institute) demonstrates the long-term return on such investments. The Kitchener-Waterloo Region has realized the same sorts of dividends from locally driven efforts to translate Waterloo University's research into a thriving high-tech sector. Our municipal leaders have been successful at demonstrating the need to reinvest in municipal infrastructure. But these kinds of city-based public-private-institutional research partnerships will become an ever more important form of infrastructure as our largest cities chart their way into the 21st century.

PLANNING CITIES

Vancouver is an island completely surrounded by envy.
                    —ANONYMOUS, QUOTED IN CHUCK DAVIS,
                    VANCOUVER, THEN AND NOW (2001)

E very year, Mercer Consulting, an international human resources
  consultancy, compiles a ranking of global cities based on a range
of criteria, including social, political, economic, environmental, and
safety features. In 2005, five Canadian cities—Toronto, Vancouver,
Montreal, Ottawa, and Calgary—all ranked in the top 25 for overall
quality of life, and even higher for safety and security. But since the
early 2000s, Vancouver has dominated the top three spots; in 2005,
only Zurich and Geneva fared marginally better.

If liveability has become the lynchpin of post-industrial economic
success in the 21st century, as observers such as Richard Florida have
asserted, our civic leaders would do well to figure out how to plan
urban environments that are relentlessly attentive to improving the
quality of life they can offer their residents. Of all of Canada's large
urban centres, Vancouver's land-use planning policies—a.k.a. "The
Vancouver Model"—are considered to be highly effective for cities
experiencing intense development pressures.

Unlike most of Canada's large municipalities, the City of Vancouver
exercises almost complete control over land-use planning and has
learned to use that power well. As city planner Larry Beasley says,
"We have an unusual attitude about development here. Our attitude
is 'If you don't measure up, we are not afraid to say *No* in this city.'

Many cities are afraid to say *No* to any developer and so they get what they deserve."[1]

The rainy, spectacularly situated West Coast city long derided for its stock hustlers and cultural sleepiness has, in the words of planner Lance Berelowitz, "emerged as the poster child of urbanism in North America"—acclaimed internationally for its topnotch indigenous architecture, its co-op housing movement, its exceptional waterfront public spaces, and its knack for creating friendly but high-density urban neighbourhoods. "In recent years, through a series of locally grown strategies, Vancouver has consciously willed itself into becoming a model of contemporary city-making," writes Berelowitz in *Dream City,* his 2005 exploration of Vancouver and "the global imagination." "Like the most vivid of dreams, the city is reinventing itself...."[2]

Although every city is bound to its own culture and geography, Vancouver's achievement holds vital lessons for Canada's other major cities. "There are no recipes for building better cities, but we can learn a lot from inspiring stories," observes Leonie Sandercock, professor of urban planning and social policy at the University of British Columbia. He attributes Vancouver's success to the combination of several factors, not least of which is a "unique local planning and design culture ... in which not only public sector planners but also designers working for private firms have been socialized into a vision for Vancouver of livability and civility, safety and vitality, and have worked collectively to generate the design and planning tools to create such a city."[3]

Its journey to this exalted status was by no means inevitable. Vancouver is a rail-port terminus city that sprang up on land that had been granted to the Canadian Pacific Railway. In the 1910s, federal money flowed into the construction of grain elevators on Burrard Inlet. Vancouver's harbour commission, established in 1936, enjoyed a jurisdiction that extended all the way to the United States and paved the way for the city's emergence as Canada's largest port, handling B.C. lumber, Alberta sulphur, and Saskatchewan potash.[4] The city's earliest planners drew their inspiration from the Garden City and City Beautiful movements in Britain and the United States. And, as in Toronto, its leafy, comfortable neighbourhoods grew along the city's extensive streetcar network (replaced by trolley buses in the 1950s).

For decades, the City of Vancouver has enjoyed an unrivalled measure of self-determination, guaranteed by a charter that recognizes the municipality's political legitimacy and the rights of its citizens to a voice in determining how their neighbourhoods are planned.

These aren't legal abstractions. In the early 1970s, reform-minded citizens groups successfully blocked plans for a proposed downtown highway at a time when inner-city expressways were carving up urban neighbourhoods across North America. Vancouver, with its intact urban neighbourhoods, today remains the only major Canadian city without one.[5] At the time, local leaders persuaded Ottawa to ante up funds to convert Granville Island, a cluster of industrial buildings on an outcropping of land in False Creek, into a waterfront community. It wasn't always the slam dunk concept it seems today. False Creek at the time was a highly polluted harbour surrounded by crumbling warehouses. A Vancouver alderman wrote off the Granville Island plan as a "crackpot idea." But after city council approved a plan for housing and parks on False Creek, the federally controlled harbour commission agreed not to renew long-term industrial leases on Granville Island.[6] That federal-municipal rapprochement paved the way for the three-decade transformation of Vancouver from a gritty port town into a dramatic waterfront city. During the 1970s and 1980s, the city replaced the decaying industrial buildings along the south shore of False Creek with neighbourhoods, marinas, and public spaces. Granville Island turned into a homey artists' colony with markets, cultural venues, and studios.

The civic focus on the waterfront helped Vancouver secure Expo '86, which was focused on the formerly industrial north shore of False Creek, as well as a defunct pier jutting into Burrard Inlet that was converted into a huge convention and entertainment centre for the event. With the end of Expo, the city embarked on a long-term project to redevelop those lands as well as the former rail yards that dominated the north side of Vancouver's downtown.

What emerged was a homegrown solution founded on a revelation about what to do with downtown redevelopment. In short, Vancouver discovered the secret of Manhattan's unbeatable energy, which is that people live virtually everywhere on the island—it's a 24/7 city, no part of which is entirely vacant at any time of the day or night. Beginning in the late 1980s and 1990s, Vancouver made several critical changes in its approach to land-use planning. It established tough-minded design guidelines to ensure high-quality architecture. Then it laid down an enlightened density-bonusing policy, according to which developers would be allowed to increase the height of their buildings in exchange for a variety of civic amenities. These included heritage protection measures, the provision of space for cultural organizations, and the creation of social housing. The city, moreover, began levying develop-ment charges, using the funds to build high-quality public spaces—landscaped streets, waterfront parks, and a continuous Seawall that have come to define the new Vancouver.

But the lynchpin in the city's transformation involved an epiphany about skyscrapers. Until the early 1990s, Vancouver's central business district, as in most large cities, was zoned for commercial uses. But the office tower boom of the 1980s had dried up. Taking what seemed like a tremendous risk, the city's planners decided to allow high-rise residential development on the peninsula that encompasses Vancouver's core. With the stroke of a planner's pen, once dingy areas on the periphery of Vancouver's downtown turned into forests of architecturally sophisticated condo towers abutting the historic Yaletown warehouses, now a thriving shopping and restaurant district. The city's planning department—which had long nurtured a collaborative approach to development approvals—was able to persuade builders to design narrow-point towers rising out of two- or three-storey pedestals. The result: Over 40,000 people moved into the downtown between 1995 and 2005, and that figure will rise to 120,000 by 2020.[7]

Unlike many of Toronto's gargantuan condo projects, Vancouver's high-rises are designed to respect the public realm. Pedestrians don't walk in windy, shadowed, intimidating canyons but, rather, on care-fully landscaped streets abutted by the townhouses, local stores, and galleries that occupy the pedestals that form the bases of tall, slim towers. "It's very important to have people living next to the street so there isn't that vacuum between high-rises and the street, which is what happens in Toronto," says Arthur Erickson, the éminence grise of

Vancouver architects. "The important thing is that there have been regulations that don't allow a building to go up unless it has those townhouses, which are the eyes on the street."[8]

The layout of the buildings and the streets at their bases, in turn, are conceived to enhance the sightlines to False Creek. And thanks to the city's strategic use of development levies, Vancouver has invested in the 21-kilometre-long Seawall that circumnavigates False Creek, continues around Stanley Park, and then links up the new high-rises and convention centre that are going up on the north shore of the downtown peninsula, an area known as Coal Harbour. This immensely popular public space, which didn't exist two decades ago, is a defining feature of Vancouver's quality of life—the physical by-product of imaginatively conceived and executed planning policies.

Vancouver's newfound sense of cosmopolitanism has prompted local politicians to begin easing up on the web of outdated regulations that restrict nightlife, rules that long ago earned it the sobriquet "No Fun City." The region's self-contained urban planning culture has also equipped Vancouver's citizens with a newfound willingness to tackle the severe social crisis that's played out in the alleys of the Downtown Eastside since the early 1990s. The city's most recent municipal leaders—especially former mayors Philip Owen and Larry Campbell—took considerable political risks by pushing all three levels of government to work in tandem to find ways of helping the homeless addicts who congregate in a few city blocks at the eastern end of False Creek. The resulting tripartite partnership has produced new types of social housing in the area and the opening of North America's first safe-injection site. Vancouver's municipal politicians have succeeded in reframing public concern about concentrated urban poverty and addiction into a debate on how a prosperous city takes responsibility for the plight of its most vulnerable residents without resorting to police bullying and the street-sweeping campaigns that claimed, falsely, to eradicate homelessness in other large urban centres.

With the 2010 winter Olympics looming in Vancouver's future, there is broad consensus that the waterfront is first and foremost a public space; that high-quality buildings pay a dividend to their owners and the city; that there are tremendous urban and environmental benefits from creating high-density downtown residential communities; that developers must invest in the civic realm as part of the cost of doing business; and that local government is best positioned to show leadership and imagination in confronting complex urban social problems. Eschewing a climate of confrontation and bureaucratic intransigence, Vancouver's planners, developers, and residents have been able to locate a kind of equilibrium and focus their collective energy on city building.

WATERFRONT CITIES

The stunning revitalization of Vancouver's waterfront over the past two decades—from a neglected industrial backwater into a focus of the city's urban awakening—is a reminder of one of the most enduring features of urban life, which is the symbiotic relationship between cities and water. Human settlements took root on the shores of major rivers or ports, their earliest residents relying on these bodies of water for sustenance, transportation, trade, and strategic defence. It is impossible to think about rivers such as the Thames, Tiber, Seine, St. Lawrence, Nile, Danube, Charles, and Rhine without considering the historic cities that have evolved on their banks. Natural ports made cities such as New York, Amsterdam, Rotterdam, Halifax, Hong Kong, Toronto, Chicago, San Francisco, and Sydney.[1] These harbours grew in importance with the industrial revolution, as cities throughout North America and Europe built rail corridors, marshalling yards, and warehouse and dockyard facilities on their waterfronts.

During the latter half of the 20th century, those same areas came to be dominated by highways, which replaced rail as the primary form of transportation, both for the movement of goods and the commuters travelling between downtown business districts and suburban bedroom communities. Today, with the enormous volume of manufactured goods being shipped around the globe, ports have once again taken on a vital role in urban economies, but in the form of high-tech container shipping facilities capable of handling massive freighters.

It's one thing to build a large, strategically situated container port with efficient links to surface transportation routes. But the task of deindustrializing and then revitalizing derelict waterfronts involves much more complex and far-reaching decisions that can alter the destinies of cities.

What has become apparent in recent decades is that post-industrial cities face two starkly different choices about how to effect these changes. One leads to privatized waterfronts dominated by controlled-access, view-oriented condo projects and theme-park-style uses such as casinos; the other produces public waterfronts organized around generous open spaces and landmark heritage and cultural venues, supported by mixed-used neighbourhoods. Cities in North America and Europe have been grappling with these transformations for three decades. But as city-dwellers stream back to downtown neighbourhoods, often to be close to the water, there is little debate about which alternative yields the most sustainable, urban-minded waterfronts.

International examples about how to re-envision industrial water-fronts abound. San Francisco was one of the first cities to urbanize its port area, renovating old warehouses and turning docks into marinas abutted by boardwalks linked to the North Beach community. (The 1989 earthquake hastened the process by destroying the elevated Embarcadero expressway that had cut off much of San Francisco's waterfront from the rest of the downtown.) In Amsterdam, with its busy North Atlantic harbour, the City has taken derelict piers and rede-veloped them with rows of high-density townhouses, some sold at market value, others designated as social housing. These projects, facing the stark drama of the harbour, echo the city's architectural vernacu-lar—modern versions of the tight, colourful buildings lining Amsterdam's historic canals. New York City has transformed the old warehouse wharves along the tip of Manhattan into public prome-nades, live-work lofts, and museums. And in London in the past decade, the formerly hardscrabble south shore of the Thames has been the focus of much civic-minded development, including refurbished Victorian warehouses, promenades, and arts facilities such as the rebuilt Globe Theatre.

Chicago provides a case study in how muscular municipal leadership can radically transform a waterfront. In little over a decade, the city converted an old military pier into a waterfront amusement park, bull-dozed a small lakefront airport and turned the property into park land,

and physically shifted a waterfront highway to improve public access to a pair of major museums. In the 2000s, the city decommissioned an old lakeside rail yard and transformed it into a vast new art park, complete with a Frank Gehry–designed bandshell.

Major cultural venues, in fact, belong on valuable waterfront land and have become internationally recognized symbols for some cities, among them Sydney, with its iconic opera house, and Paris, where the French government converted an old railway station on the banks of the Seine into the Musée d'Orsay in the 1980s. But culturally oriented waterfront projects, although *de rigueur* in some European cities, remain the exception in North America. Cities on both sides of the border, fixated as they are on tourism, are much more likely to situate heavily subsidized sports arenas, cavernous convention centres, and theme parks on their waterfronts, despite ample evidence that such self-contained mega-projects are rarely well connected to their surroundings. Since the early 1990s, cash-strapped provincial governments, eager to tap into gambling profits, have hustled to promote waterfront casinos in Montreal, Windsor, Niagara Falls, and Halifax.[2] In 2004, Vancouver joined the rush and approved a large slot-machine complex for a site on False Creek, near B.C. Place. (Toronto remains a holdout.) Much more rare in Canada are bona fide waterfront cultural facilities—the few exceptions being Vancouver's H.R. MacMillan Space Centre; the federally funded Montreal Science Centre, which opened in 2000 in Old Montreal's touristy port district; and a handful of heritage sites on Halifax's historic quays. Toronto wants to build a museum dedicated to the city's diversity and civic spirit on a prime waterfront property, but the project has all the makings of a white elephant.

The broader question focuses on what modern cities want their waterfronts to contribute. Museums? Condos with good views? Parks? It's a difficult question because there is by definition a limited supply of waterfront land, and it's a much-sought-after commodity for two particular industries: developers and tourist operators. There is no question that tourism and downtown residential development play an important economic role in post-industrial cities. But do we rehabilitate our waterfronts for the guests or for ourselves? In Montreal, the recently refurbished port district is almost entirely given over to tourism. By contrast, Vancouver's experience illustrates how visionary planning can foster highly livable, easily accessed, and well-used waterfront spaces that are designed primarily to serve the needs of the city's residents.

Halifax finds itself tugged in both directions. Its waterfront for decades was dominated by a sprawling naval base and ship-building facilities, but these declined significantly due to cuts in Canada's defence budget. During the 2000s, however, thousands of affluent tourists wielding U.S. dollars or euros began arriving by ship to Halifax's dramatic deep-water harbour.[3] They crowd onto Halifax's spacious waterfront boardwalks and explore the core, with its high-end craft shops, stylish restaurants, and thriving arts scene (all of which are located within blocks of the downtown). At the same time, developers have begun building well-designed low-rise condo complexes along the waterfront, thus ensuring that this part of the city doesn't become a tourist monoculture.

Given the relatively rapid transformations that have taken place in Vancouver and Halifax, Toronto's waterfront tribulations represent a stubborn blemish on a city otherwise possessed of a great capacity for building successful neighbourhoods. The same federal program that provided land for Granville Island in the 1970s underwrote the creation of Harbourfront, an ambitious redevelopment venture that was to create waterside public parks and cultural facilities on a series of abandoned quays, to be financed in part by development. In the go-go 1980s, however, a wall of massive condos, apartments, hotels, and even parking garages sprouted along the water's edge. The ensuing development scandal precipitated a royal commission, followed by well over a decade of inaction. Elsewhere, massive developments sprang up on lakefront properties, while the city's few accessible beaches (and the adjacent neighbourhoods) have become increasingly congested. All the while, Toronto's port lands—a vast manmade peninsula once dominated by industrial complexes—lay fallow, despite the area's proximity to some of Canada's most valuable downtown real estate. The latest boondoggle were attempts by aviation entrepreneurs to establish a busy commuter airline on the nearly bankrupt mini-airport that's been located in Toronto harbour since the 1930s.

In 2000, when Toronto was in the throes of a bid for the 2008 Summer Olympics, the three levels of government announced plans to establish a jointly owned waterfront redevelopment corporation, not unlike similar agencies in Manchester, Sydney, and New York. Armed with $1.5 billion in promised public contributions, the new corporation has rolled out plans to build transit-supported mixed-use communities and public spaces on hundreds of hectares of underutilized land along the waterfront—a massive undertaking that will take at least a generation to complete, provided there are no further scandals. Its agenda includes environmental remediation, shoreline naturalization, dragon boat courses, and various visions for replacing the elevated Gardiner Expressway with a network of surface arterials and tunnels.

But progress has been slow in coming because Toronto's waterfront, by contrast to Vancouver's, is highly balkanized, its land subject to the conflicting agendas of numerous public sector bodies and intransigent landowners.[4] While various politicians, including Mayor David Miller, have promised to untangle this bureaucratic knot, no progress has been made. The most problematic waterfront agency of all is the port authority. Established in 1999 to replace the Toronto Harbour Commission,[5] the federally appointed agency—which owns large tracts of land, including the island airport, a small container-handling facility, and a ferry terminal—was given a legal mandate to be financially self-sustaining. But with shipping in long-term decline in Toronto, the port authority has been desperate to squeeze new sources of revenue from its land holdings.

Port authorities in Halifax, Montreal, and Vancouver all face the same revenue pressures. But the ports in Vancouver and Montreal continue to be active and profitable operations, shipping Canadian raw materials and receiving freighters piled high with colourful metal containers that hold every type of import, from toys and electronics to carefully hidden drug stashes and even illegal immigrants. Moreover, their facilities remain physically removed from the most urbanized regions of the waterfronts of these two cities and thus are unlikely to encounter development pressures for decades to come.[6] In Halifax and Toronto, it's a different story. The Halifax Port Authority is pressing ahead with a far-ranging plan to build a giant hotel and convention centre complex on land it owns in the city's predominantly residential south end—a move that is likely to upset the delicate balance of uses that have evolved in recent years on the Halifax waterfront. Similarly, the Toronto Port Authority's bid to establish a busy commuter airline on the island airport was driven primarily by financial expediency rather than by forward-looking urban planning and quality-of-life considerations. With thousands of residents owning waterfront condos, the prospect of deafening jets flying past their windows made no sense. It was a classic example of conflicting uses.

The City of Vancouver hasn't had to fight these bureaucratic battles; nor, indeed, do some of the world's other highly successful waterfront cities. In Sydney, a port city renowned for its waterfront spaces, the Australian state of New South Wales established the Sydney Harbour Foreshore Authority in 1998 and gave the agency a strong mandate to protect waterfront heritage and cultural sites as well as develop and promote the promenades, parks, markets, and museums that have sprung up around the port since the 1970s.[7] An indication of this agency's importance: When the Australian government finds itself with surplus land on the Sydney waterfront—as the defence department did in 2001—the property is transferred to the Authority, whose planners begin the work of extending the city's lively waterfront life to these new parcels.

Cities around the world have demonstrated that waterfronts can be imaginatively remade by agencies with broad mandates, deep pockets, and the power to override the narrow self-interest of waterfront landowners. What is more, these revitalized areas have the capacity to deliver many of the defining features of urban liveability: high-quality open spaces, recreational and cultural amenities, tourist facilities, and high-density residential development. But there is a caveat. Noxious industrial uses and excessive private development at the water's edge are fundamentally incompatible with the growing public desire to reclaim these historic spaces. Only those cities whose leaders and citizens have forged a consensus about these basic principles will succeed in bringing about an urban metamorphosis along the shorelines where their cities first took root.

REMEMBERING CITIES

The city ... does not tell its past, but contains it like the lines of a hand, written in the corners of the streets, the gratings of the windows, the banisters of the steps, the antennae of the lightning rods, the poles of the flags, every segment marked in turn with scratches, indentations, scrolls.

—ITALO CALVINO, *INVISIBLE CITIES* (1972)

When planners, developers, and citizens' groups seek to reinvent derelict industrial waterfronts, we can glimpse one of the most enduring tensions in urban life—the clash between the artifacts of the past and the demands of the future. As cities seek to improve—economically, socially, or aesthetically—it can often entail the demolition of old structures that appear to have lost their relevance, their utility, and, most importantly, their commercial appeal. After all, what good is a crumbling grain elevator on a valuable lakeside property that seems tailor-made for upmarket condos and shops?

This isn't a new problem. The early Christian popes demolished many of the grand pagan monuments of ancient Rome as a means of asserting their own religious dominance. Well over a millennium later, in 1853, Napoleon III acted out a similar impulse when he appointed Baron Haussmann to level vast swaths of slum-ridden medieval Paris and build an efficient, grand city bearing the imprimatur of the Second Empire.[1] Throughout the 20th century, powerful corporate interests, with the blessing of municipal officials, took command of downtown real estate in most large North American cities, razing low-rise historic commercial districts to make way for the skyscrapers that came to symbolize the essence of modern capitalism.

This civic narrative of destruction and rebuilding isn't limited to the rich and powerful. The familiar middle-class enterprise of gutting and renovating older homes can also be seen as a small-scale expression of these same inclinations, which derive from that uniquely human need to imprint our aspirations and tastes on our physical surroundings.

But the urge to destroy struggles with the desire to improve and preserve. In London in the late 17th century, strict building codes—closely regulating external architectural features—were imposed as part of a massive rebuilding campaign following the Great Fire of 1666. (The familiar motivation: The great landlords in central London wanted to see their property values rise.) "For hundreds of years thereafter, the building code ensured that streetscapes throughout London were consolidated as visual compositions," writes Anthony Tung, a former New York City Landmarks Preservation commissioner, in his 2001 tour de force about cities and the epochal challenge of heritage conservation, *Preserving the World's Great Cities*. "Across London's history, this was perhaps the single greatest contribution to the architectural integration of the metropolis."[2] Such urban planning decisions, taken by aristocrats centuries ago, have flown like arrows through time, and today contribute mightily to London's uniqueness.

Canada arrived late to this game. But our urban regions now find themselves competing against global cities that are adding "historic character" to their arsenal of civic advantage. This is about respecting history, creating interesting urban landscapes, and recognizing the potential locked away in apparently derelict industrial structures. In fact, if our governments genuinely want to create livable and aesthetically varied cities, they must find innovative and financially viable ways of protecting all sorts of heritage buildings and older neighbourhoods. There was a time when developers and homeowners would hotly oppose such controls. But as a growing number of successful cities have discovered, there is a compelling case for flexible heritage preservation policies and visionary development that recognizes the commercial potential in old buildings.

For proof, consider the case of Toronto's Distillery District. Between 1837 and 1990, Gooderham and Worts and then a series of corporate successors ran a large distilling operation in a cluster of atmospheric Victorian-era brick and stone factory buildings in the city's southeast quadrant. When the plant ceased operations, it became a popular film location. Then, in 2001, a heritage-minded development group bought the property and transformed it into a pedestrian-only "village" for arts, culture, and entertainment. This former factory quickly transformed into an arts centre, its cobble-stone streets lined with tourists, gallery-hoppers, and theatre-goers. The complex has become the cornerstone of what will become an entirely new downtown medium-density neighbourhood being built on several hectares of contiguous fallow industrial land. This synthesis of old and new testifies to the importance of vision and the opportunities to be had when historic buildings are integrated into transit-oriented downtown development plans that improve urban quality of life, promote culture, and attract tourist activity.

Golden Oldies

Among Canada's largest cities, Montreal has achieved the best track record with maintaining historically relevant buildings and districts. Yet some residents have mixed feelings about the results of the restoration of Old Montreal, says Luc Noppen, Canada Research Chair on Urban Heritage at the Université de Québec à Montréal (UQAM). "Seen from Vancouver, Toronto, Calgary, and Winnipeg, it looks like Montreal has been successful with heritage, but locally, people aren't satisfied."[3]

During the 1960s, the gathering momentum of slum clearance programs and high-rise downtown development schemes triggered backlashes among downtown residents living in 19th-century row houses threatened with demolition. The ensuing controversy kick-started the city's heritage movement. In 1972, the Quebec government enacted the Cultural Properties Act. In 1975, Phyllis Lambert, heiress to the Bronfman empire, founded the Heritage Montreal Foundation. And in 1978, the Société du patrimoine urbain de Montréal was established to transform those once threatened homes into co-ops and non-profit housing associations—an echo of Amsterdam's approach to heritage conservation.[4] Indeed, by the end of the 1970s, with the city's population plummeting in the wake of René Lévesque's election as premier in 1975, Montreal's defiantly pro-development mayor Jean Drapeau "began to recognize the potential of older neighbourhoods for repopulating the inner city," according to Annick Germain and Damaris Rose, professors of urban studies with the Institut national de la recherche scientifique at the University of Quebec.[5]

In 1985, Quebec downloaded heritage protection responsibility to the cities. Montreal has since exercised its considerable authority to protect the heritage character of neighbourhoods such as the Mont Royal Plateau district, using an arsenal of regulatory tools, including strict design guidelines for facades and infill projects. The Plateau "style" has since become an architectural fashion elsewhere in Montreal.

The story of the old city played out somewhat differently. Quebec designated it as a historic area in 1964. Originally, property owners could obtain heritage restoration grants from the Quebec government, but the municipality got into the act after 1985, with the result that over $100 million in public money has been spent to restore the quaint 18th- and 19th-century limestone homes and offices and build underground parking garages.

The area, however, has become the site of a very contemporary form of urban conflict—between the affluent residents of those restored heritage row houses and the tourists who flock to see the old city's cultural attractions. The tourists and those who cater to them ensure that the quaint cobblestone streets are lined with the purveyors of junky souvenirs, overpriced food, and tour buses.[6] But unlike the historic core of Quebec City, Montreal's old city has seen a boom in development activity, with new hotels and entertainment complexes driving out small shops. "It has become a place for the wealthy and tourists," says Noppen.[7]

Outside Quebec, vast amounts of Canada's architectural heritage have vanished in the name of progress—a Canadian version of the damage inflicted by those early popes. Toronto, Calgary, Hamilton, and Vancouver all wiped out much of their historic downtowns in the post-war decades. In the early 1960s, this frenzy of demolition prompted Eric Arthur, a New Zealand–born architect, to pen *No Mean*

City, a paean to the sudden loss of much of Toronto's finest Victorian architecture.[8] His groundbreaking book—the first to articulate the value of that which had been demolished—gave birth to a generation of heritage organizations and programs.

In the 1970s, determined Toronto heritage activists managed to protect and restore hundreds of residential dwellings in historic working-class neighbourhoods such as Cabbagetown, as well as parts of the original blocks of Muddy York, now known as Old Town. They succeeded in persuading council to protect sightlines and enforce height restrictions on development around this area. At the time, the Old Town was derelict. In the late 1970s, the City of Toronto boldly developed a large mixed-income, medium-density neighbourhood nearby, kick-starting the area's residential renaissance. By the 1990s, these heritage and planning decisions were paying handsome rewards, as this neighbourhood—centred at King and Jarvis—evolved into a lively and desirable downtown community distinguished by its heritage character and proximity to downtown amenities, including the historic St. Lawrence Market.[9] The city combined growth and heritage by working out creative development schemes whereby condo builders would be given the right to erect high-rise towers, provided they were well back from the street and that the bases of these buildings fit seamlessly with the surviving 19th-century storefronts that typify the area.

Vancouver succeeded in preserving Gastown, the city's commercial birthplace, but the area functions primarily as a tourist attraction dominated by gift shops and restaurants aimed at bus tours. Calgary, meantime, wiped out much of its historic downtown in a rush to build skyscrapers. So averse was the city to heritage protection that the municipality's 1979 decision to hire a heritage planner was controversial. By the 1990s, however, the city had undergone a sharp about-face in its treatment of historic buildings. "Now, they're considered almost treasures," former mayor Al Duerr said in 1996. "Once, they were a liability."[10]

The city designated Stephen Avenue, a downtown commercial artery, as a pedestrian mall, and rehabilitated many of the buildings along its length. Early-20th-century Beaux Art bank branches became upscale restaurants and concert halls, while traditional two-storey retail buildings found upscale tenants, including book superstores and boutique hotels. Nearby, the grand Hudson's Bay department store, with its arcades and intricate carvings, has been meticulously maintained. At the edge of the core, the city designated an old warehouse district for protection, and its refurbished buildings now attract new-economy tenants such as architects and software firms. The city's heritage revival also included a $9.3-million restoration of the 1911 City Hall and has been fuelled by large donations from its corporate leaders. Today, in fact, the Stephen Avenue Mall is a major tourist attraction, along with the Calgary Stampede.

Still, landmark downtown buildings, including many 1950s and 1960s Modernist structures, continue to face the threat of demolition. In the early 2000s, for example, Winnipeg political leaders promoted the demolition of the historic Eaton's department store downtown in favour of a sports arena. And in Toronto, Maple Leaf Gardens, Canada's temple of hockey, barely avoided demolition when the team moved to the recently constructed Air Canada Centre. The case illustrates how narrow commercial considerations trump heritage and cultural considerations. The Maple Leaf organization, evidently terrified by the prospect of competition, refused to sell the building to the billionaire owner of a minor league hockey team. Instead, Loblaws bought the Gardens and is converting it into a supermarket, retaining little more than the famous Art Deco exterior.

While the building itself will survive, its prosaic new role can only be seen as a lost opportunity. Take the case of the Tate Modern, the contemporary wing of Britain's National Gallery, which opened in 2000 and attracted 20 million visitors in its first half-decade. It resides in a former power plant that had sat abandoned on the south shore of the Thames for decades. "Only ten years ago Sir Giles Gilbert Scott's great building lay opposite St Paul's, dark, unknown, unloved and threatened with demolition," according to a history of the museum's first five years. "Imaginatively converted by Herzog & de Meuron, it was recently voted the capital's favourite building. It has been seen as a symbol of regeneration of life in the capital, and has appeared in feature films, advertisements and novels."[11]

Heritage experts have long recognized that landmark historic buildings are likely to be victims as much of careless policy as of rapacious developers. Many older structures have succumbed to the wrecking ball because parking lots pay lower property taxes than other commercial buildings. In other cases, public institutions fail to step up to the plate when important heritage buildings go onto the market or face redevelopment pressures. Indeed, a 1999 Department of Canadian Heritage study shows that Canada's largest cities have witnessed the demolition of a fifth of their stock of pre-1920s buildings since the 1970s, while the destruction in smaller centres is as high as 40 to 50 percent.[12]

Ottawa has yet to fully internalize such findings. In 2003, Auditor General Sheila Fraser slammed Ottawa for falling behind in its protection efforts and upkeep of hundreds of historic sites, which she found to be "in poor condition." Because of funding cuts, conservation budgets shrank in real terms by 22 percent between 1990 and 2001. She also pointed out that hundreds of federally designated sites enjoy no legal protection because they are owned by private firms, not-for-profit organizations, and individuals.[13] This means that while some national historic sites—for instance, Halifax's Citadel—have been carefully maintained, others, including Toronto's Fort York, owned by the City of Toronto, have been virtually abandoned to the vagaries of development.[14] There is little short-term financial incentive for municipalities to defend historic buildings. Provincial heritage protection rules can be troublingly weak. And the federal government has put Parks Canada, a vast bureaucracy charged with a wide range of responsibilities, in charge of historic sites. Canada, a young country with young cities, still doesn't quite grasp how public consciousness of the past is transmitted through time in the form of historic buildings. As Rollo Myers, a Toronto heritage activist and founder of Citizens for the Old Town, says, "What's missing at the federal level is [Anthony] Tung's idea of 'a culture of conservation.'"[15]

Preservation and Gentrification

When heritage activism became a force in North American cities in the 1960s, the arguments in favour of preserving landmark buildings centred on an emerging urban consciousness about a physical past that was rapidly disappearing.[16] North American cities at the time were steeped in the post-war mindset of large-scale urban renewal and economic modernization. Planners talked about demolishing large tracts of older row housing in favour of new high-rises. Heritage protection was seen as an impediment to growth.

One of the voices who challenged the orthodoxy of the new was Jane Jacobs, who documented the vitality of the tenement neighbourhoods in Greenwich Village. She also made the point that old, unremarkable urban buildings are critically important to the economic well-being of cities because their low-cost structure provides inexpensive space to small retailers, non-profit agencies, artists, and upstart businesses.

Four decades later, in fact, we harbour a much more expansive attitude toward older buildings, heritage and otherwise. Those threatened New York walk-ups are now filled with highly desirable and expensive apartments. And the global travel boom has more than demonstrated the economic relationship between tourism and historic architecture. In 1997, a Rutgers University study proved what European cities have long understood: that it pays to maintain heritage landmarks. Investments in New Jersey's heritage properties, the study showed, had yielded $580 million in direct economic activity, including 9.1 million tourists, more than 10,000 jobs, and $293 million in additional state and local taxes. As the study's author, David Listokin, told *The New York Times,* "There are real dollars to be made in historic preservation."[17] And not just from tourists. Tax credits for the preservation of landmark properties have attracted a flood of private sector investment in the United States, growing from $140 million in 1978 to more than $19 billion in 2001.[18]

Meantime, the public's perception of what constitutes urban heritage has expanded, broadening from a museum-type focus on historically significant landmarks to the recolonization of heritage districts where older (but not necessarily historic) buildings have been pressed into renewed service for contemporary urban uses.

In the 1960s, in San Francisco, Toronto, and other cities, hippies, artists, and adventurous young homeowners began rediscovering the virtues of inner-city neighbourhoods such as North Beach and Yorkville. They renovated aging working-class homes, restoring architectural details that held no interest for renewal-minded planners. New York City led the way. In 1965, Jackie Kennedy persuaded New York City to establish the Landmarks Preservation Commission—an agency of the city government that was to play a critical role in transforming the means by which municipalities can protect the overall character of architecturally distinctive historic neighbourhoods.

Over the next two decades, New York designated 80 neighbourhoods, including SoHo and Tribeca, as historic *districts*. Anthony Tung explains that there is a collective public value to the ambience of such communities, and it transcends the interests of individual building owners. In the years after New York passed its heritage district rules, property owners challenged them in court, arguing that such regulations amount to an uncompensated expropriation of their land holdings. But the courts upheld the regulations and in the process saved much of New York's extraordinary architectural legacy, from Grand Central Station to the majestic apartments of the Upper West Side.

The result is that landowners in historic districts are compelled to adhere to a range of heritage-preserving guidelines governing external features such as windows, historic street lighting, and infill development. "Things in [New York's] mature historic districts just seem to 'look right,'" observes Toronto architect and conservationist Catherine Nasmith. "As you would expect, the buildings are well preserved and commercial signage is felicitous in design. As well, the integrity of architectural detailing is more consistent along the street. For example, windows tend to be multi-paned, air conditioners don't disrupt decorative building features, modern roof-top additions are sympathetic in style (or set back and out of sight), new storefronts are harmonious with old facades, and jarring colours and materials are avoided."[19]

Landmark designation isn't the only tool available to preservationists. In Toronto, in the mid-1990s, the city successfully triggered the renovation of dozens of deteriorating industrial buildings by allowing their owners to turn them into live-work lofts without applying to have their properties rezoned as residential lots. At the time, hundreds of artists were living in illegal apartments in half-abandoned warehouses downtown, and this edict spurred a spectacular rush of private investment, transforming the King-Spadina district into one of the city's hippest communities. Many of these heritage buildings were renovated, while comparably scaled condos went up on vacant lots. The area's attraction lies in its gritty post-industrial character, which arises from streets lined by a generous supply of distinctive early-20th-century factory buildings.

In many big cities, in fact, some of the most desirable—and recession-proof—real estate can be found in core-area heritage districts.[20] According to Robert Shipley, an assistant professor at the University of Waterloo School of Planning, "more than 70 percent of the designated properties performed either at or above the average in their markets, while 40 percent resisted downturns."[21] The irony, however, is that the unique historic ambience of an urban neighbourhood can be destroyed by its own popularity.[22]

New York City's historic district approach is one option, and the result is heritage-driven gentrification coupled with a dramatic increase in the public's awareness of urban architectural heritage. European countries have taken a more holistic view since the mid-1970s, linking heritage protection with other urban planning goals, such as affordable housing. In 1985, the Council of Europe approved the Convention for the Protection of the Architectural Heritage of Europe, which has been ratified by 32 countries. Across Europe, national and local governments now rely on a wide variety of policy tools, including the compilation of registries of historic commercial buildings and the establishment of designated heritage districts, as well as tax incentives and restoration grants. In the Netherlands, various not-for-profit housing organizations bought up and restored decaying historic buildings in Amsterdam that have been put to use providing social housing. Such was the quality of some of these restorations that they could trigger the revitalization of marginalized neighbourhoods. As Tung points out, "An important planning idea had been established: that restoring old buildings as subsidized residences solved several social problems simultaneously."[23]

Some Canadian jurisdictions have begun to recognize the need for more effective heritage conservation policy, especially in the urban context. In 2001, Ottawa introduced a three-year, $24-million fund designed to help commercial property owners pay for heritage restorations. The McGuinty government in Ontario passed important changes to the province's heritage preservation laws in 2005, giving municipalities more power to block demolition applications.

Despite such reforms, many older downtown neighbourhoods with a distinctive ambience continue to lose their historic character because of skyrocketing real estate prices, consumer demand for huge homes, and redevelopment pressures. Builders will throw heritage activists a bone occasionally by offering to preserve a facade, but such concessions do little to ameliorate the crisis of civic amnesia created when speculators demolish our architectural past. While some provinces now allow municipalities to establish formally designated heritage districts and impose standards for restoration and renovations, the neighbourhoods that have taken this step remain the exception and not the rule. The irony, as Tung points out, is that heritage neighbourhoods in New York, London, Paris, and Vienna are "thriving." The point is that private landowners actually benefit when their property rights are restricted by heritage protection rules. But the broader principle behind such measures speaks directly to the way we experience our urban surroundings. "Binding heritage conservation statutes," Tung argues, "establish the idea that the appearance of the public realm is an important societal matter."[24]

Which is something we have lost sight of in our big cities. In an era when so much of what is built in large urban regions is utilitarian, visually deadening, and inward looking, muscular heritage protection laws play a crucial role in reminding us that cities are aesthetic objects and that their appearance is an integral part of our quality of life.

BEAUTIFUL CITIES

At the dawn of the 21st century, the inhabitants of Canada's large cities are waking up to the broader relevance of not just the built heritage but also the city-building potential of high-quality architecture, that most distinctively urban art form.

We live in an era marked by the phenomenon of the internationally acclaimed design superstar. Architects such as Frank Gehry, Daniel Libeskind, Santiago Calatrava, and Sir Norman Foster have their own brands and followings, and their signature buildings are seen to be capable of reviving the fortunes of flagging cities.

Out of the spotlight, a generation of young residential architects has developed specialties in environmentally friendly, energy-efficient building techniques as well as innovative homes squeezed into tight urban spaces. Landscape architects have seen a surge of demand for highly stylized backyards with design features that draw on Japanese techniques. Indeed, there is a growing appetite for international residential design, a reflection of the cultural diversity that characterizes Canada's largest cities.

The owners of large downtown office buildings, meanwhile, have commissioned architects to retrofit lifeless and alienating ground floors with storefronts and external ornamentation that acknowledges the teeming street life on the sidewalk. In the suburbs, the most striking new structures are religious institutions commissioned by ethnocultural communities. Some are exquisitely traditional in their craftsmanship, while others reveal their patron's desire for contemporary forms. In either case, they remind us of the long-standing relationship between architecture and religion, as well as the way immigrant communities are motivated to build gathering places in foreign landscapes.

Many leading hospitals and public library boards commission striking and innovative designs for new wings and branches—an indication that their boards see architectural excellence as an integral part of their mandates. Expansion-minded post-secondary institutions, in turn, have built specialized new research centres and enlarged student residences to accommodate growth.[1] At the University of Toronto, York University, the University of British Columbia, and Simon Fraser University, these campaigns, which were fuelled by ambitious fundraising and development programs, meant the commissioning of showcase architecture. Interestingly, U of T, York, SFU, and UBC have all sought to integrate these new structures into campus-wide master plans that seek to bring the most enduring urban design ideas—accessible buildings, pedestrian-friendly streetscaping, intensification, and the creation of "mixed use" campus neighbourhoods—to the task of institutional expansion.[2]

This renewed urban enthusiasm for high-quality design extends beyond those individuals and organizations commissioning new buildings. Inspired by programs in Europe that showcase local architecture, the City of Toronto's Culture Division and a handful of Toronto design enthusiasts launched Doors Open in 2000. The weekend-long event allows the public to visit distinctive buildings around the city. None of the organizers expected the outpouring of interest that was unleashed by the program. The Doors Open concept quickly spread to the rest of Ontario and has even taken root in New York City.

Perhaps the outpouring of interest in architecture is a reaction to the fact that so much of our urban landscape has been given over to dreary, monotonous commercial construction in which the emphasis is on standardization instead of quality. One big-box shopping mall is indistinguishable from the next. Suburban office parks are filled with tinted glass boxes shorn of any adornment. Looming high-rise condos too often pay little attention to their impact on streetscapes, creating a barren and windswept pedestrian realm. And where pre-war neighbourhoods were constructed incrementally by many individual contractors with their own techniques, today's vast subdivisions are mass produced by a single builder who may offer no more than a handful of models to consumers.

The point is that aesthetic experiences are essential to urban live-ability. By fostering urban placelessness, our cities run the risk of weakening the bonds between residents. Why? Because our shared open spaces—which include parks, squares, and public facilities such as libraries, as well as arterial roads, residential streets, and, somewhat paradoxically, the exteriors of privately owned buildings—become merely functional, rather than social, settings. They are places to pass through rather than experience.

As we've seen in previous chapters, cities must consciously choose to create civic cultures that value environmental sustainability, urban-minded planning, and their own heritage. The same is true with architecture. As with so much else in urban life, the responsibility for creating architecturally sophisticated cities is shared—government can play a more assertive regulatory and financial role. But the onus lies primarily with homeowners, institutions, philanthropists, and developers, and the growing recognition that when cities invest in high-quality design, they'll see both public *and* private benefits.

The Bilbao Effect

The Asper dynasty, created by investor and communications mogul Izzy Asper and passed on to his three children Leonard, David, and Gail, has its roots in one of Canada's most troubled cities, Winnipeg. While their media empire, CanWest Global Communications, remains headquartered in the Manitoba capital, the city has seen, by Canadian standards, an unprecedented degree of inner-city decay. In the early 2000s, the Aspers began plans to shake up Winnipeg by building a dramatic new national human rights museum, to be funded by both private and public cash. To be located at The Forks, a historic downtown park at the junction of the Red and Assiniboine Rivers, the museum will deal with topics such as residential schools and the Charter of Rights. With their close links to the federal Liberals and aggressive lobbying techniques, the Asper family cajoled Ottawa into making a $100-million contribution, plus more funds from the provincial govern-ment and large private donations, for the $243-million project. In 2005, they announced that a 68-year-old Albuquerque architect,

Antoine Predock, had won the international competition to build the museum with a swirling conceptual design that draws visitors up to a torch-like pinnacle. Predock, known for his elemental concrete-and-stone style, has built museums and other civic buildings in the U.S. Southwest and abroad, including Taiwan.

There was little doubt that the project is the Asper clan's attempt at bringing the so-called Bilbao Effect to their troubled hometown. The reference, of course, is to the way Bilbao Guggenheim, a shimmering, hallucinatory structure designed by the Canadian-born architect Frank Gehry, transformed the declining industrial Basque capital into a global tourist destination after it opened in 1997. It was no accident, however, nor the result of just one showy piece of architecture. Rather, the amazing reversal of the city's fortunes was the result of a decade of collaborative strategic planning by Basque and local officials. They were well aware of the long decline of Glasgow—once the world's leading ship-building centre—and recognized the need to make major changes in order to revive the city's economic base in the wake of the decline of the local steel and ship-building industry.

A 1987 urban regeneration plan focused on a shift toward culture, e-commerce, banking, and trade fairs, as well as the establishment of an urban redevelopment corporation to revitalize a stretch of derelict waterfront industrial property. In 1991, Basque officials decided to approach the trustees of the Solomon R. Guggenheim Foundation about participating in their revitalization project with what amounted to a franchise of the iconic New York art gallery, designed by Frank Lloyd Wright. The board embraced the idea. Two years later, Gehry was selected as architect, and the project began securing capital commitments and environmental remediation grants from various public agencies, including the European Union's "urban pilot projects" fund.[3] The result is a testament to the way creative thinking and broad-ranging, high-minded partnerships can produce dramatic urban change. Its success goes a long way to explaining why the architecture critic Raul Barreneche has described the beginning of the 21st century as a "golden age for the museum."[4]

Bilbao isn't the only city to have found creative ways to capitalize on the intimate relationship between showcase architecture, leading cultural institutions, philanthropy, and urban revitalization. During the 1990s, Chicago, a city with a much broader economic base than Bilbao, experienced an outpouring of large-scale reinvestment in several key museums and cultural institutions. These projects, which had a strong architecture and design component, were driven by leading local philanthropists and the advocacy of Chicago's mayor Richard Daley, who pushed major design-conscious civic projects, such as a new millennium lakeside park anchored by a Gehry-built bandshell.

Winnipeg is only the latest city to emulate Bilbao and Chicago. Montreal and Ottawa have seen a flowering of showcase cultural building projects since the late 1980s, ranging from several new museums in the Ottawa-Gatineau region, particularly Douglas Cardinal's Canadian Museum of Civilization, to the forthcoming $1-billion entertainment centre being built with Quebec provincial lottery proceeds for Montreal's Cirque du Soleil.[5]

Toronto's leading cultural venues have also benefited from massive public and private investment in recent years. In the early 2000s, the Royal Ontario Museum, the Art Gallery of Ontario, and the Canadian Opera Company, among others, all secured millions of dollars in federal-provincial infrastructure funding, enough to kick-start ambitious fundraising campaigns intended to underwrite their ambitious expansion schemes.

But it was Royal Ontario Museum president William Thorsell, the former *Globe and Mail* editor-in-chief, who first played the architectural superstar card and thereby succeeded in firing the imagination of politicians and philanthropists alike. He persuaded his board of trustees to run a high-profile international design competition for a major renovation of the museum, arguing that the attention generated by such an exercise would yield the necessary financing. The closely watched and highly publicized contest drew impressive submissions from many prominent architects, including Daniel Libeskind, the wunderkind former musician who built Berlin's arresting Holocaust Museum and went on to design several others. With a jagged, crystalline concept, Libeskind won the job, although his design was met with equal measures of enthusiasm and strident criticism.

Thorsell's strategy was to use a controversial, unconventional, and high-profile design to ignite a broad-based public debate in Toronto about architecture, cities, and culture. He's been nothing if not successful. The city's expansion-minded cultural institutions have put design at the forefront of what they're trying to accomplish—some using classic modernism, others relying on grabby, iconoclastic forms.

But while Toronto is eager to showcase its newfound architectural variety to the so-called archi-tourist market, there is a much more substantial dividend in terms of the city's conception of its own future. Beset by speculative development pressures and a laissez-faire regulatory environment that attaches scant importance to architecture and urban design considerations, Torontonians have awakened to the importance of aesthetics in their urban environment, as well as the role good design plays in mitigating the impact of very large-scale, high-density development on surrounding cityscapes. Architecture is once again on the urban agenda, thanks to visionaries like Thorsell. This important shift in public outlook should trigger planning reforms and give rise to a more mature development culture, one that recognizes the value of structural aesthetics in city building.

Legislating Design

None of this is news to Vancouver, a city with few major cultural institutions and showcase buildings, but an impressive track record in design excellence. How did this come about? Part of the answer is that Vancouver has put in place a development approvals system that includes peer-review design panels, whose expert members grade the architectural and urban form qualities of proposed projects. A thumbs down can send the developer back to the drawing board.

Since the early 1970s, Vancouver officials have made sure that urban design considerations are included in their planning decisions. Developers have to abide by design guidelines—some general, others quite specific—that require them to attend to issues such as the massing of buildings, their relationship to the surrounding structures, landscaping, and the impact on the overall streetscape. The system, according to the urban design analyst John Punter, has been "battle-hardened" by pressure from developers, architects, politicians, and bureaucrats, but results in "consistent medium-to-high quality" development. "It is a system," says Punter, a British academic who has closely studied Vancouver's distinctive planning culture, "that has evolved through a political and professional zeal for reform to establish a more participatory and corporate control process that can deliver contextually sensitive neighbourly development."[6]

Despite its successes, the role of the design panel still generates controversy. Some critics argue that such panels encourage architectural homogeneity and are engaged in the futile task of trying to impose ostensibly objective criteria on the inherent subjectivity of design. These aren't trite objections. Tastes change. Contemporary urban builders and city-dwellers may see aesthetic beauty in old timber-and-red-brick warehouses that were built at a time when their industrial owners would never have guessed at the future uses of these utilitarian structures. Likewise, there are prosaic buildings going up in the current context whose future roles and subsequent alterations we can't even begin to imagine.

Proponents of design review panels point out that architects are trained in a climate of collegial criticism and would not find the process of having their designs assessed foreign. And the net effect is that when architects and their developer clients are required to perform before they can obtain a building permit, the culture begins to shift—a point that designers who work in Vancouver understand from first-hand experience. There, the need to pay attention to urban aesthetics and design has fostered a sense of competition among architects, planners, and builders, who don't want to see their projects turned down by their professional colleagues. It has also transformed the local design community into a sought-after network of architects with a reputation for innovative, high-quality building, many of whom are winning commissions around the world.

What has become apparent in recent years in Vancouver, Toronto, and Montreal is that creating a culture of architecture and design quality requires many ingredients. It depends on a highly collaborative approach to city building that pivots on the strategic leveraging of public funding for important civic structures, both new and historic. It depends on a regulatory framework that encourages development yet recognizes aesthetic and urban contextual considerations, as well as strictly financial factors such as density and height. Most important, such a culture can emerge only from a broad public consensus that cities are much more than just the sum of the privately owned buildings they contain. Cities also encompass the spaces in between, and from this recognition grows our appreciation of the many features that make diverse urban neighbourhoods genuinely, and enduringly, livable.

CONCLUSION:
THE SAFE CITY

*Dull, inert cities ... contain the seeds of their own destruction and
little else. But lively, diverse, intense cities contain the seeds of their
own regeneration, with energy enough to carry over for problems and
needs outside themselves.*

—JANE JACOBS, *THE DEATH AND LIFE OF
GREAT AMERICAN CITIES* (1961)

S ome years ago, a friend from New Mexico came up to visit me in
Toronto. He is my age, and had lived in many parts of the United
States—South Carolina, then Santa Fe, New York City's Lower East Side,
and Colorado. We knew one another because my father and his father
had been classmates in elementary school in Budapest in the 1930s. After
the war, they went their separate ways, and the unpredictable tides of
emigration deposited them on either side of the U.S.-Canada border. Still
friends, these two men traded visits as often as they could, and their
spouses and children developed long-distance relationships.

On this occasion, we found ourselves chatting in a coffee shop,
bantering about university life and beyond, as well as reminiscing.
During the conversation, my friend revealed that at one point during
his youth, he carried an unloaded handgun from time to time, for
self-protection. I was stunned. We had much in common, but I had
never so much as seen a handgun, much less kept one in my possession. Then another thought struck me. If that lineup outside the U.S.
embassy in Vienna, way back in the late fall of 1956, hadn't been

quite so long, or the temperature quite so cold, I would have grown up in America. I, too, might have at times felt the need to carry a gun. It was a disquieting thought.

Of course, my friend's experience was by no means universal. Nor is mine; my parents, having established themselves in Canada in the late 1950s, were able to build up their savings to afford a home in a comfortable middle-class Toronto neighbourhood where there was little overt crime beyond the occasional bicycle theft. For children growing up in the tough neighbourhoods of north end Winnipeg, east end Montreal, or the monolithic public housing complexes in Toronto's northwest suburbs, city life included routine confrontations with crime, racism, police harassment, and poverty.

For the most part, however, Canada's large cities have offered a safe haven for the millions of people who have settled in them. These fast-growing, ethnically diverse urban regions witnessed none of the race rioting that swept through many U.S. cities in the 1960s.[1] In the 1970s and 1980s, metro newspapers in Detroit and Chicago published a front-page running tally of murders in a macabre competition for the title of homicide capital of the United States. Some larger European cities, meanwhile, tolerated or even encouraged the growth of isolated ghettos of marginalized guest workers from Africa, the Middle East, and Eastern Europe—low-income economic migrants whose children were destined to exist in a kind of citizenship limbo.

The general liveability of Canada's large cities is reflected in the national crime rates. Although we become more urbanized with each passing year, there has been a steady reduction since 2000 in break and enters, thefts (except for motor vehicles), assault, and sexual assaults. And while there has been a sharp drop in both property and violent crime in the United States in the 1990s, the homicide rate in Canada's big cities remains significantly lower by comparison with large American cities. Between 1994 and 2003, the murder rate for Canada's 27 largest cities was 1.88 per 100,000 people (see table on the next page). By contrast, in 2001 Detroit ranked at 10.8; Washington, D.C, 7.9; New York City, 7.2; and Buffalo, 6.4.

Yet, we shouldn't be smug. According to Statistics Canada, there was a 12 percent increase in the number of homicides between 2003 and

HOMICIDE RATES PER 100,000 IN CANADIAN CITIES, 1994–2003

City	Rate	City	Rate
Oshawa	0.70	Sudbury	1.76
Waterloo Region	0.96	Hamilton	1.82
London	1.07	Victoria	2.00
St. John's	1.20	Halifax	2.01
Ottawa	1.25	Montreal	2.08
Quebec City	1.25	Edmonton	2.42
St. Catharines	1.35	Saskatoon	2.61
Gatineau	1.51	Vancouver	2.65
Calgary	1.61	Winnipeg	2.86
Toronto	1.73		

Adapted from Statistics Canada, "Homicides by Census Area," *The Daily*, cat. 11–001 (October 6, 2005). Available online at www.statcan.ca/Daily/English/051006/d051006b.htm. Reprinted with permission.

2004, after a steady multi-year decline. Vancouver has been plagued in recent years by a surge in property crime, some of which can be traced to thefts by heroin addicts living in the Downtown Eastside. Winnipeg, Canada's most dangerous big city, has seen a rise in gang activity and arson as its downtown grows ever more derelict. And in Toronto, the proportion of murders that involve illegal handguns soared during the 2000s and became a major election issue in early 2006. A large proportion of both the victims and the accused are black youth living in some of the city's roughest, poorest neighbourhoods—many of them older suburban districts characterized by a dearth of jobs and social services, where gun-toting drug dealers—many linked to organized crime syndicates operating in Jamaica—rule the roost. In fact, drug-related offences have been on the rise across Canada during this decade, and police in many large cities must spend an increasing amount of time shutting down the marijuana grow-ops that have been set up in hundreds of ordinary-looking residential homes.

Crime, of course, is not an inherently urban phenomenon. But urban conditions can give rise to elevated crime rates. Take the situation of gunplay in Toronto. The city's homicide rate has held steady since the early 1970s. But the high-level data don't tell the whole story. In the mid-1970s, about a quarter of all homicides involved firearms; three decades later, the figure has risen to include half of Toronto's murders. Many guns come across the border illegally. The killings, in turn, are more likely to take place in public and fell innocent bystanders who just happen to be in the wrong place at the wrong time. As University of Toronto criminologists Rosemary Gartner and Sara Thompson observe, "The city has become more dangerous for some people and less dangerous for others."

Why? Their explanation is worth quoting at length:

> These changes in the character of the lethal violence in Toronto probably have very little to do with policies and practices of criminal justice agencies … and much more to do with changes over the past ten to fifteen years in social and economic policies and practices that have affected Toronto's educational system, social welfare system, public health system, and the infrastructure and cohesion of local communities…. Young disadvantaged males—and their families—are among those whose lives have been most affected by these policies. To the extent that structural inequalities have created a sense among this group that they are competing with each other for scarce resources within a larger societal context that offers them little hope for the future, violence can become part of a repertoire of behaviours for coping with problems in their lives. Unfortunately, this process has a self-reinforcing element to it, especially among those who, in part because of strained relations with legal authorities, feel outside the law's protection. For example, as violence escalates among young disadvantaged males in certain communities and more young males gain access to guns, it can become a rational choice to carry a gun oneself as protection. This in turn raises the chances that conflicts among males have lethal outcomes and give rise to retaliatory violence, a pattern that was observed in many cities in the United States in the late 1980s and early 1990s.[2]

The point—one this book has returned to again and again—is that when our governments fail to think through the urban repercussions of their actions, particularly those linked to Canada's foundational social policies, the unintended consequences wash unevenly over our cities, eroding that most basic quality of urban liveability: safety.

A society's response to such conditions will reveal much about its capacity to build and sustain 21st-century cities. In many U.S. urban regions, the answer to urban crime has been punitive and reactive: three-strikes laws, aggressive anti-panhandling campaigns, the long-running but futile war on drugs, heightened surveillance and private security, gated communities, tax revolts, public schools that resemble armed camps, gun ownership, and an ideological preoccupation with personal responsibility.

But such solutions ignore the root causes of urban crime, many of which can be traced to economic hardship, social isolation, and poor education. Of course, there are many people who commit crimes that have nothing to do with social conditions. And there are lots of individuals who grow up poor but never resort to crime. Yet, big-city neighbourhoods that are physically alienating, cut off from the urban mainstream, lack decent jobs, and have few community services tend to cloud the horizon for young people. It's easy to understand why, with little hope for the future, some choose drug dealing and gangs— a lifestyle that offers profit, status, thrills, and a sense of belonging. Desperation and grinding hardship invariably breed anti-social behaviour: It's a fact of life.

Toronto's immediate political response to increasing drug-related crime was to put more police in the affected areas, call for tighter border controls to stop firearm smuggling, and lobby for criminal code amendments to establish mandatory minimum sentences for gun possession. At the same time, however, the city's leaders ensured that such law-and-order measures were balanced by proactive policies aimed at improving community safety. In 2004, Toronto mayor David Miller launched a broad-based, long-term campaign to focus attention and resources on a handful of neighbourhoods that had experienced the lion's share of this crime wave.

How has Miller's community safety panel, chaired by Ontario chief justice Roy McMurtry, approached these seemingly intractable issues? As a first step, the provincial government backed away from a zero-tolerance school safety policy that had led to a sharp increase in expulsions, especially among black teens. Criminologists know that kids who have dropped out of the school system are more likely to get involved in gangs.[3] Reducing the dropout rate begins with community-based early learning and parenting programs and extends to collaborative mentoring projects that target high-risk teens in low-income communities, especially those with subsidized housing. Municipalities, school boards, and community organizations, in turn, are improving youth recreation and cultural programs, while industry associations and community colleges have begun to establish apprenticeship programs. The forward-looking goal is to provide the next generation of teens growing up in low-income neighbourhoods with life, education, and career options that counterbalance the seductions of drug dealing and gang life.

Vancouver, in recent years, has adopted a similarly broad-minded philosophy in the way it has tackled the drug tragedy in the Downtown Eastside. Like all port cities, Vancouver has long been a gateway for illicitly imported drugs. By the mid- to late 1990s, the city had become the overdose death capital of North America, and a serial killer was stalking the prostitutes working the rough alleys east of Gastown. A network of community health activists and addicts began pressing the city to change the way it treats substance abuse—to view it as a disease rather than a crime. Two successive mayors—Phillip Owen and then former B.C. coroner Larry Campbell—took up the cause, backing a so-called Four Pillars approach to tackling this kind of urban crisis: prevention and enforcement, but also treatment and harm reduction—the latter meaning the policy of providing addicts with clean needles and a safe place to inject their drugs.

Having moved beyond a punitive philosophy, the city persuaded the upper levels of government and the regional health authority to negotiate a tripartite agreement that involves new affordable housing projects, health and prevention programs, and close cooperation with drug enforcement agencies. The lynchpin of the strategy—and the move that prompted a prickly reaction from Washington's drug czar—was the 2003 opening of a closely monitored supervised injection site where addicts could shoot up in a clinic-like setting with medical personnel in attendance. While such facilities are unheard of in the United States, they exist in many European cities, including Frankfurt. Those safe injection sites—many of which date back to the late 1980s and early 1990s—have succeeded in connecting many addicts with health services, housing, and counselling. There are far fewer overdose deaths. And these facilities have reduced drug activity in public places. With more medical treatment available for addicts who suffer from mental illnesses or have drug-related communicable diseases such as hepatitis C or HIV/AIDS, cities are safer.[4] Toronto has moved to establish a similar approach to urban drug use.

These are difficult and intensely controversial moves, with no guarantee of success. Vancouver was bidding for the 2010 Olympics when the municipality was grappling with the Four Pillars. In fact, Owen, a right-of-centre politician, was removed from his party for backing the Four Pillars plan. And many homeowners in the city are upset about a surge in property crime that they see as linked to the drug crisis. But over the course of half a decade, citizen and police attitudes toward drugs, addiction, and urban poverty have undergone a 180-degree shift. Vancouver public health officials have pointed out that throughout history, human beings have taken psycho-active substances for all sorts of reasons—pleasure, spirituality, medicinal value. Some are illegal, while others bring in huge profits for multinational pharmaceutical companies. A double standard? Campbell, a former narcotics officer who moved from the mayor's office to the Senate, thinks so. He has become a national crusader for the liberalization of our drug laws. "I'd legalize marijuana," he says. "I'd control it, tax the hell out of it and put the money into health care. The growing of marijuana in this province is a $3 billion to $7 billion business. Who is making money off it? Organized crime, that's who. No taxes are being paid. No social benefits are realized."[5]

There's little doubt that prohibition brings with it urban violence and organized crime. If Canada has effectively decriminalized casual marijuana use and allows the sale of pot paraphernalia and home-grow equipment, it only makes sense that the production end should be legalized and then taxed heavily. In fact, a 2004 study by Vancouver's

Fraser Institute, a right-wing think-tank, estimated that by taxing marijuana at the same rate as tobacco, governments would collect about $2 billion a year in additional revenue, not to mention the savings in law enforcement and judicial resources that go toward cycling small time dealers through the courts.[6]

From an urban perspective, moreover, legalization takes the criminality out of grow-ops, gives teens that much less motivation to join gangs, and allows municipalities to regulate how and where the growers can operate. Just as with tightening up penalties for gun possession, such changes in federal criminal laws will have the effect of making our urban neighbourhoods safer places in which to live, work, play, and raise children.

In both Vancouver and Toronto, the political leaders and activists behind such community safety campaigns are showing the rest of us how to think about cities in pragmatic, holistic ways—eschewing short-sighted political or ideological solutions in favour of a more comprehensive philosophy of urban living. An ounce of prevention, as the old saying goes, is worth a pound of cure.

Indeed, the urban agenda that has taken root in Canada's largest cities is all about understanding the critical importance of trying to anticipate how our cities will change as a result of our collective political actions—not just between now and the next election, but over decades and beyond.

The past 15 years should have taught Canadians many such lessons. When we slash spending on education and basic social services, our cities become much harsher and more unforgiving places in which to raise children. When we boost immigration to unprecedented levels without making the necessary investments needed to help these future citizens establish themselves and their families, thousands of newcomers are consigned to the economic and social margins of our large cities. When we allow unfettered market forces to drive urban development, our cities soon begin to buckle beneath the weight of gridlock, sprawl, and declining air quality.

On the other hand, when we promote compact, environmentally conscious, and transit-oriented development, we create the conditions for cities that can boast lively cultural scenes and safe neighbourhoods.

When we forge partnerships between community groups, educators, governments, and businesses, we are better positioned to develop locally driven and imaginative solutions to tough urban social problems—from keeping kids in school to building affordable housing that connects, rather than segregates, its residents and the broader city.

In an era of global trade and immigration, this way of looking at our cities has become ever more important. Our large cities cannot keep the world out, so they must be prepared to take on whatever it serves up. Take the threat of pandemics, such as a human version of the avian flu. Toronto's 2003 SARS scare made the federal government wake up to the links between preventative health policies, cities, and our economy. When SARS hit, only City of Toronto public health officials were ready to move. Today, there is a federal ministry of public health. All three levels of government understand that they must share responsibility for containing urban epidemics, while large publicly funded hospitals have taken up the formidable task of figuring out how to deliver emergency health care in the midst of a fast-moving epidemic.

Likewise, the twinned threats of global terrorism and the sort of immigrant unrest that ignited the *banlieue*—isolated working-class suburbs dominated by public housing projects—surrounding Paris in the fall of 2005 represent stark reminders that the tendrils of geopolitical conflict can extend thousands of kilometres and explode in the middle of large, modern cities.

In London and Madrid, in fact, terrorists chose to target transit and commuter rail operations, yet another piece of proof about the close relationship between urban services and national economies. Can we inoculate our cities against global terrorism? The United States, in the post 9/11 era, has sought to do just that, through draconian homeland security and surveillance measures. Britain isn't far behind, as the streets of its big cities are watched by thousands of closed-circuit video cameras. Canada needs to be vigilant, of course—not just about sleeper cells, but also about how we, as a nation, conduct ourselves on an international stage that looks, with each passing day, more and more like the domestic stage. It's not a stretch to suggest that when former prime minister Jean Chrétien balked at sending Canadian troops to Iraq, he was effectively shoring up the security of Canada's largest cities.

In the wake of the Paris riots, in fact, we arrived at a telling revision of the role of official multiculturalism in the lives of our large cities. Long derided by critics who accused Ottawa of encouraging immigrants to avoid integrating into the Canadian mainstream, ethnic diversity has turned out to be a foundation of our urban stability, rather than an agent of social segregation.

Not all immigration is benign, of course. Local charities with links to Tamil extremist groups, for example, have kept the flame of Sri Lanka's long-running civil war alive in exile, trying to extort funds from members of Toronto's Tamil community.[7]

But these cases remain the exception, not the rule. Like the best and most cosmopolitan ideas about cities, our attitude toward multi-culturalism embodies a subtle but far-sighted understanding of the nature of Canada's urban condition. Which is this: that in a nation of immigrants, we can only coexist in our complex urban settings if we respect one another's ways, listen to one another's ideas, and support our neighbours as they navigate that great distance—both geographic and emotional—between old homes and new homes.

In many ways, our intensely diverse cities have come to resemble grand orchestras, with countless performers playing a breathtaking array of instruments. We may all have a sense of the harmony, the notes we'd like to play, and the solos we intend to perform. But unless we all find a way to agree on a score and then develop a vision of how to collaborate down there in the pit, there can be only noise.

SUGGESTED READING

There is such an abundance of written material about cities in general, and Canadian cities in particular, that it's difficult to know where to begin. What follows is an eclectic selection of books I've found to be useful sources on many aspects of cities, city life, and urban history. Anyone probing further into the topics discussed in this book will invariably uncover many other sources I've missed. But the ones I've listed here can be considered a useful starting point.

Abella, Irving. *A Coat of Many Colours: Two Centuries of Jewish Life in Canada*. Toronto: Key Porter, 2002.

Adams, Michael. *Fire and Ice: The United States, Canada, and the Myth of Converging Values*. Toronto: Penguin Canada, 2003.

Andrew, Caroline, Katherine A.H. Graham, and Susan Phillips. *Urban Affairs: Back on the Policy Agenda*. Montreal and Kingston: McGill-Queen's University Press, 2002.

Aubin, Henry. *Who's Afraid of Demergers?* Montreal: Véhicule Press, 2004.

Berelowitz, Lance. *Dream City: Vancouver and the Global Imagination*. Vancouver: Douglas and McIntyre, 2005.

Bliss, Michael. *Plague: A Story of Smallpox in Montreal*. Toronto: HarperCollins, 1991.

Boudreau, Julie-Anne. *The MegaCity Saga: Democracy and Citizenship in This Global Age*. Montreal: Black Rose Books, 2000.

Calvino, Italo. *Invisible Cities*. Trans. from Italian by William Weaver. London: Vintage, 1997.

Choy, Wayson. *Paper Shadows: A Memoir of a Past Lost and Found*. Toronto: Viking Books Canada, 1999.

Eaton, Ruth. *Ideal Cities: Utopianism and the (Un)Built Environment*. London and New York: Thames and Hudson, 2002.

Florida, Richard. *The Rise of the Creative Class ... and How It's Transforming Work, Leisure, Community, and Everyday Life.* New York: Basic Books, 2002.

Garner, Hugh. *Cabbagetown: The Classic Novel of the Depression in Canada.* Toronto: McGraw-Hill Ryerson, 1950.

Garreau, Joel. *Edge City: Life on the New Frontier.* New York: Doubleday, 1991.

Germain, Annick, and Damaris Rose. *Montréal: The Quest for a Metropolis.* Toronto: John Wiley and Sons, 2000.

Gladwell, Malcolm. *The Tipping Point: How Little Things Can Make a Big Difference.* New York: Little, Brown, 2002.

Hall, Sir Peter. *Cities in Civilization.* London: Weidenfeld and Nicholson, 1998.

Heintzman, Andrew, and Evan Solomon, eds. *Fueling the Future: How the Battle over Energy Is Changing Everything.* Toronto: House of Anansi, 2003.

Hiss, Tony. *The Experience of Place: A Completely New Way of Looking at and Dealing with Our Radically Changing Cities and Countryside.* New York: Alfred Knopf, 1990.

Hulchanski, J. David, and Michael Shapcott, eds. *Finding Room: Policy Options for a Canadian Rental Housing Strategy.* Toronto: CUCS Press, 2004.

Jacobs, Jane. *The Death and Life of Great American Cities.* New York and Toronto: Alfred Knopf/Random House, 1961.

Kunstler, James Howard. *The Geography of Nowhere: The Rise and Decline of America's Man-Made Landscapes.* New York: Simon and Schuster, 1993.

Kunstler, James Howard. *Home from Nowhere: Remaking Our Everyday World for the 21st Century.* New York: Simon and Schuster, 1996.

Landry, Charles. *The Creative City: A Toolkit for Urban Innovators.* London: Earthscan Publications, 2000.

Layton, Jack. *Homelessness: The Making and Unmaking of a Crisis.* Toronto: Penguin Canada, 2000.

LeGates, Richard, and Frederic Stout, eds. *The City Reader.* London and New York: Routledge, 1996.

Lemon, James. *Toronto Since 1918: An Illustrated History.* Toronto: James Lorimer and Company, 1985.

Ondaatje, Michael. *In the Skin of a Lion.* Toronto: McClelland and Stewart, 1987.

Punter, John. *The Vancouver Achievement: Urban Planning and Design.* Vancouver: University of British Columbia Press, 2003.

Richler, Mordecai. *The Street.* Toronto: McClelland and Stewart, 1969.

Rowe, Mary, ed. *Toronto: Considering Self-Government.* Owen Sound, ON: The Ginger Press, 2000.

Rybczynski, Witold. *City Life: Urban Expectations in a New World.* Toronto: HarperCollins Publishers, 1995.

Sewell, John. *The Shape of the City: Toronto Struggles with Modern Planning.* Toronto: University of Toronto Press, 1993.

Smiley, David, ed. *Sprawl and Public Space: Redressing the Mall.* New York: National Endowment for the Arts and Princeton University Press, 2002.

Stoffman, Daniel. *Who Gets In: What's Wrong with Canada's Immigration System and How to Fix It.* Toronto: Macfarlane Walter and Ross, 2002.

Tung, Anthony. *Preserving the World's Great Cities: The Destruction and Renewal of the Historic Metropolis.* New York: Three Rivers Press, 2001.

Ungerleider, Charles. *Failing Our Kids: How We Are Ruining Our Public Schools.* Toronto: McClelland and Stewart, 2003.

Whitaker, Reginald. *Double Standard: The Secret History of Canadian Immigration.* Toronto: Lester and Orpen, Dennys, 1987.

Wickson, Ted. *A Century of Moving Canada: Public Transit, 1904–2004.* Toronto: Canadian Urban Transit Association, 2004.

Wilkinson, Richard. *Unhealthy Societies: The Afflictions of Inequality.* London: Routledge, 1996.

SELECTED
ONLINE RESOURCES

There is a wealth of urban information online, and many excellent websites that function as digital clearinghouses of information and analysis about a range of urban subjects. The following sites and organizations are especially useful.

www.urbancenter.utoronto.ca: University of Toronto's Centre for Urban and Community Studies, which offers a wealth of reports and documents relating to urban issues in Canada.

www.canadascities.ca: Recent developments for hub cities, run by the City of Toronto.

www.conferenceboard.ca: Conference Board of Canada.

www.cric.ca: Centre for Research and Information on Canada, federally run research organization on Canadian demographics.

www.cutaactu.on.ca: Canadian Urban Transit Association.

www.eurocities.org: Network of major European cities.

www.fcm.ca: Federation of Canadian Municipalities.

www.irpp.org: Institute for Research on Public Policy, a Montreal-based think-tank run by Senator Hugh Segal that has in recent years focused its analysis on urban affairs.

www.maytree.com: The Maytree Foundation, run by Toronto urbanist Alan Broadbent, has been at the forefront in recent years of much of the debate on the New Deal, as well as on immigrant resettlement.

www.creativeclass.org: Richard Florida's website.

www.td.com/economics/index.jsp: TD Canada Trust's economics group has evolved into a think-tank of insightful urban analysis; it leads all the major banks in engaging with governments to address city-related issues.

www.childcarecanada.org: The Childcare Resource and Research Unit, University of Toronto's child care and early-childhood development facility.

canada.metropolis.net: Federal immigration policy studies.

www.cprn.com: Ottawa-based think-tank Canadian Policy Research Networks has commissioned an extensive amount of research on cities and social policy, all of it available online.

www.nrtee-trnee.ca: National Round Table on the Environment and the Economy.

www.brookings.edu/index/research.htm: Washington, D.C.–based liberal think-tank the Brookings Institution.

www.vtpi.org: Victoria Transport Policy Institute, run by B.C. transit expert Todd Litman.

ACKNOWLEDGMENTS

This book traces its roots to an unexpected phone call. In early 1995, I was working on an oddball story about a corrupt doughnut franchise for *Toronto Life* magazine. At one point, a source stole my tape recorder and threatened to throw me out of his office. Evidently entertained by the resulting feature, my editor, Angie Gardos, asked if I wanted to cover municipal politics for the magazine. Her faith in my abilities was flattering, as I knew next to nothing about the subject. Despite the learning curve challenges, I wrote *Toronto Life*'s urban affairs column for the next 10 years, a period of unprecedented political turbulence and, therefore, a really great time to be reporting on municipal politics. I simply cannot thank Angie and *Toronto Life* editor-in-chief John Macfarlane enough. It was a fantastic ride.

During those years, I've had the great fortune to get to know and interview some of Canada's leading urban thinkers, policy makers, and politicians. Several became trusted and highly insightful sources, including Peter Tomlinson, Enid Slack, Alan Broadbent, Andrew Sancton, Joe Berridge, Tony Coombes, Annie Kidder, Gord Perks, Ken Greenberg, Phillip Abrahams, Cathy Nasmith, Meric Gertler, Stephen Otto, Anne Golden, and especially Lionel Feldman, who has, over the years, proven to be a wellspring of insider information and highly entertaining urban gossip, and who generously read much of the manuscript. His comments have been an invaluable addition to the text.

Toronto Mayor David Miller and several members of his staff, particularly Andrea Addario, unstintingly provided me with answers to my questions and the time to ask them. They have been a model of political openness and accessibility.

The long-term inmates of the press gallery at City Hall, as well as those who are now out on day parole, were generous and accommodating colleagues. Collectively, they function as the best-informed and most bloody-minded urban think-tank in Canada.

Away from City Hall, I've had the very good fortune to work with many talented editors, including Carol Toller, Ted Mumford, Scott Anderson, John Daly, Gary Salewicz, Gary Ross, Jennifer Bradley Reid, Sarah Murdoch, Paul Wilson, Christian Bellavance, and Derek Weiler.

Outside magazines, I am surrounded by a highly supportive network of family and friends: my mother Eva and my sister Julie; my in-laws Ron and Sybil, Andy and Lori, and Trevor and Robin; The Gang; Jeff and Sylvie; Patty and Paul; Marg Webb, Lisa Keller, Lisa Lifshitz, Romano D'Andrea; and our terrific Regal Road neighbours.

My literary agent, Dean Cooke, demonstrated a zen-like patience with this project—it took me two years to crank out the proposal, but when he finally got it, Dean ran with the pitch and consummated an excellent relationship with Penguin Canada. I am very grateful to Diane Turbide, whose enthusiasm for this book was apparent from the beginning. My editors Jonathan Webb and Judy Phillips provided superb advice on shaping and focusing the final version.

As befitting its theme, this book was written almost entirely in a handful of Toronto coffee houses: various Starbucks, Dooney's, and the weird but comfortable World Class Bakers. None of their respective staff members ever tried to kick me out for loitering or attempted to charge me for the power my laptop sucked out of their walls.

The book quotes the opinions and analyses of dozens of writers, academics, reporters, urbanists, and other sources. But I alone am responsible for its content.

NOTES

Introduction: The New City

1. He said, Toronto "is like New York run by the Swiss." Quoted in *The Globe and Mail's Toronto Magazine,* December 23, 1986.

2. "The Calgary Edmonton Corridor: Take Action to Ensure the Tiger's Roar Doesn't Fade," *TD Economics,* April 2003.

3. KPMG press release, February 18, 2004.

4. "Suburban Nation" is the title of a 2001 polemic about sprawl by the new urbanist gurus Andres Duany and Elizabeth Playter-Zyberk (with Jeff Speck). The exceptions include New York, Boston, San Francisco, Chicago, Portland, Seattle, Austin, Minneapolis-St. Paul, and Denver.

5. There are a few exceptions, including Portland and Minneapolis-St. Paul.

6. Eric Liu, "School De-segregation," *Slate,* August 31, 1996. Available online at www.slate.com/id/1035/.

PART ONE: THE CITY UNDER STRESS

Global Cities

1. Glen Colbourn and Lois Kalchman, "Wexford's last days: 'Fifty-one years of history is a lot to lose. It's painful to see'; Changing demographics sound house league's death knell," *Toronto Star,* January 29, 2005.

2. John Spencer and Michael Hoy, *Parks and Recreation Master Plan* (Brampton, ON: City of Brampton, April 13, 2005).

3. Michael Adams, *Fire and Ice: The United States, Canada and the Myth of Converging Values* (Toronto: Penguin Canada, 2003), 67.

4. Reg Whitaker, *Double Standard: The Secret History of Canadian Immigration* (Toronto: Lester and Orpen, Dennys, 1987).

5. "Focus on Michael Lee-Chin: An Historical Perspective." A short biography of the chair and CEO of AIC Ltd. is available online at www.aic.com/en/PDFs/AIC5042ENG.PDF.

6. Whitaker, *Double Standard.*

7. Daniel Stoffman, *Who Gets In: What's Wrong with Canada's Immigration System and How to Fix It* (Toronto: Macfarlane Walter and Ross, 2002).

8. Don DeVoretz, "Does our immigration model work? YES. It needs fine-tuning but it strikes a good balance, says economist Don DeVoretz," *The Globe and Mail,* December 13, 2005.

9. Infometrica, *Canada's Recent Immigrants: A Comparative Portrait Based on the 1996 Census* (Ottawa: Public Works and Government Services Canada, 2001).

10. Peter Li, *Destination Canada: Immigration Debates and Issues* (Toronto: Oxford University Press, 2003), 162.

11. Grant Schellenberg, *Immigrants in Canada's Census Metropolitan Areas* (Ottawa: Statistics Canada, 2004).

12. Federation of Canadian Municipalities, *Income Gap Study* (Ottawa 2003).

13. Interview with author, March 7, 2005.

14. Cited by Stoffman, *Who Gets In.*

15. Leah Steele, Louise Lemieux-Charles, Jocalyn Clark, and Richard Glazier, "The Impact of Policy Changes on the Health of Recent Immigrants and Refugees in the Inner City," *Canadian Journal of Public Health,* March-April 2002, 118–22.

16. Richard Glazier, Maria Creatore, Andrea Cortinois, Mohammad Agha, and Rahim Moineddin, "Neighbourhood Recent Immigration and Hospitalization in Toronto," *Canadian Journal of Public Health,* May-June 2004, 130–134.

17. Stoffman, *Who Gets In.*

18. Susan McClelland, "Nanny Abuse," *The Walrus,* March 2005, 42.

19. Economic-class immigrants are more likely to settle in Greater Vancouver, whereas Montreal receives proportionally more refugees, according to a 2004 Statistics Canada study on immigrants in census metropolitan areas.

20. Census information compiled by the Canadian Labour and Business Centre, *CLBC Handbook: Immigration & Skill Shortages* (Ottawa, n.d.).

21. Anthony Reinhart, "Drivers struggle to change licensing system," *The Globe and Mail,* June 22, 2005.

22. Don DeVoretz, Brief to the House of Commons Standing Committee on Citizenship and Immigration, February 15, 2005. Accessed at Metropolis Vancouver website, riim.metropolis.net.

23. Naomi Alboim, *Fulfilling the Promise: Integrating Immigrant Skills into the Canadian Economy* (Ottawa: Caledon Institute of Social Policy, 2002).

24. www.capinfo.ca

25. DeVoretz, Brief to the House of Commons Standing Committee, 4.

26. Interview with the author, March 8, 2005.

Greying Cities

1. www.cityfarmer.org/Montreal13.html

2. www.seniors.gov.ab.ca/policy.planning/factsheet_seniors/urban_rural

3. Federation of Canadian Municipalities, *Income Gap Study* (Ottawa 2003).

4. Derek Burleton, "The Calgary-Edmonton Corridor: Take Action Now to Ensure the Tiger's Roar Doesn't Fade," *TD Economics,* April 2003.

5. Lisa Van de Ven, "A cool million in the 'burbs: High end enclaves," *National Post,* December 11, 2004.

6. Peg Tyre, "Seniors and the City; Affluent, Educated Retirees Are Forfeiting a Regular Tee Time in Favour of Loft Living, Opera Tickets and Bistros," *Newsweek,* October 11, 2004.

7. Paula Simons, "Sherwood Park constructing an urban heart for itself: $130-million project will turn ultimate suburb into a vibrant, pedestrian-friendly community centre," *Edmonton Journal,* March 15, 2005.

8. Interview with author, February 24, 2005.

9. Interview with author, January 28, 2005.

10. Interview with author, March 14, 2005.

11. Federation of Canadian Municipalities, *Income Gap Study.*

12. Don Drummond, "A New Paradigm for Affordable Housing: An Economist's Perspective," in *Finding Room: Policy Options for a Canadian Rental Housing Strategy,* ed. J. David Hulchanski and Michael Shapcott (Toronto: CUCS Press, 2004), 217.

13. Tony Ianno, *Creating a National Seniors Agenda: Report of the Prime Minister's Taskforce on Active Living and Dignity for Seniors* (Ottawa: 2004).

14. Ibid.

15. Katherine Harding, "Older and out; A soon-to-be-released report sounds an alarm bell about the number of Toronto seniors who are homeless," *The Globe and Mail,* January 10, 2004.

16. Kevin Fagan, "Homeless seniors helped in Oakland / Unusual center provides long-term care," *San Francisco Chronicle,* January 26, 1994.

17. Harding, "Older and out."

18. Lynn McDonald, Julie Dergal, and Laura Cleghorn, *Homeless Older Adults Research Project* (Toronto: University of Toronto Institute for Human Development, Life Course and Aging, 2004), 2.

19. David Chen, "Need turns aging strangers into roommates," *New York Times,* April 17, 2005,

20. Interview with the author, January 28, 2005.

21. Ian McLeod and Gerry Flahive, *House Calls* (National Film Board, 2004).

22. Interview with author, February 1, 2005.

23. Ibid.

24. Ibid.

25. Lisa Priest, "When seniors turn to violence in their nursing homes," *The Globe and Mail,* November 13, 2004. Moira Welsh, "Nursing homes getting surprise checks; Nursing homes checks tighten; 'We've got a lot more work to do' Smitherman promises changes," *Toronto Star,* January 23, 2004.

26. John Lorinc, "Old: It's the decision you dread: Putting a parent in a nursing home. The choices are so daunting that the whole business is ripe for revolution." *The Globe and Mail Report on Business,* June 2003, 75.

27. McLeod and Flahive, *House Calls.*

Hidden Cities

1. Standing Senate Committee on Aboriginal Peoples, *Urban Aboriginal Youth: An Action Plan for Change* (Final report) (Ottawa 2003), 23.

2. Alan Cairns, *Citizens Plus: Aboriginal People and the Canadian State* (Vancouver: UBC Press, 2000), 123–25.

3. Ibid.

4. Standing Senate Committee on Aboriginal Peoples, *Urban Aboriginal Youth.*

5. Ibid.

6. Ibid.

7. Sara Jean Green, "Then as now, a gathering place," *Toronto Star,* July 17, 1999.

8. Alan Cairns, *Citizens Plus,* 128.

9. Carol La Prairie, *Seen but Not Heard: Native People in the Inner City* (Ottawa: Department of Justice, 1994), 31.

10. Tom Carter, *Literature Review on Issues and Needs of Aboriginal People* (Ottawa: Federation of Canadian Municipalities, 2004).

11. "Self employment on the rise among Aboriginals," *Kitchener-Waterloo Record,* October 27, 2004.

12. Aboriginal Peoples Council of Toronto, *Urban Aboriginal Strategy* (Toronto: n.d.), 6.

13. Graeme Smith, "The death of Neil Stonechild: Judge rejects police version of events on cold night in Saskatoon. But no charges are planned," *The Globe and Mail,* October 27, 2004.

14. Thomas Hayden, "'That is not the image we have of Canada,'" *The Globe and Mail,* March 6, 2004.

15. John Richards, *Neighbourhoods Matter: Poor Neighbourhoods and Urban Aboriginal Policy* (Toronto: C.D. Howe Institute, 2001), 4.

16. Cited in Tom Carter, *Literature Review.*

17. Carter, *Literature Review,* 5.

18. Ibid.

19. La Prairie, *Seen but Not Heard,* xiii.

20. Vancouver/Richmond Health Board, *Healing Ways: Aboriginal Health and Service Review* (Vancouver 1999).

21. Richards, *Neighbourhoods Matter,* 14.

22. La Prairie, *Seen but Not Heard,* 34.

23. Richards, *Neighbourhoods Matter.*

24. Criminal Intelligence Service Saskatchewan, *2005 Intelligence Trends: Aboriginal-Based Gangs in Saskatchewan,* Winter 2005.

25. Carter, *Literature Review,* 13.

26. Vancouver/Richmond Health Board, *Healing Ways.*

27. Standing Senate Committee on Aboriginal Peoples, *Urban Aboriginal Youth,* 75.

28. Standing Senate Committee on Aboriginal Peoples, *Urban Aboriginal Youth,* 1.

Divided Cities

1. Sue Montgomery, "Working poor join lineups: Food banks are the humiliating secret of a growing number of parents who have jobs, but still can't earn enough to put three squares on the table for their children every day," Montreal *Gazette,* October 20, 2004.

2. Jeffrey Reitz and Janet M. Lum, Immigration and Diversity in a Changing Canadian City: Social Bases of Inter-Group Relations in Toronto (Toronto: Department of Sociology, University of Toronto, 2001). Cited in *Falling Behind: Our Growing Income Gap* (Ottawa: Federation of Canadian Municipalities, 2003), 10.

3. Saskia Sassen, "Global," in *The City Reader,* ed. Richard T. LeGates and Frederic Stout (London and New York: Routledge, 1996).

4. Sassen, "New Geography of Centres and Margins," in *The City Reader,* ed. LeGates and Stout, 72.

5. Sassen lecture at Global Cities Speaking Series, University of Toronto, October 27, 2004.

6. John Myles, Garnett Picot, and Wendy Pyper, "Neighbourhood Inequality in Canadian Cities," *Business and Labour Market Analysis* (Ottawa: Statistics Canada, 2000).

7. United Way of Greater Toronto and Canadian Council on Social Development, *Poverty by Postal Code: The Geography of Neighbourhood Poverty—1981–2001* (Toronto 2004).

8. Jane Gadd, "Shelter: The drift to the bottom," *The Globe and Mail,* June 21, 1997.

9. Merrill Cooper, "Housing Affordability: A Children's Issue," in *Finding Room: Policy Options for a Canadian Rental Housing Strategy,* ed. J. David Hulchanski and Michael Shapcott (Toronto: CUCS Press, 2004), 89–113.

10. Naomi Carniol, "Suffering in suburban splendour," *Toronto Star,* August 8, 2005.

11. Gadd, "Shelter: The drift to the bottom."

12. Toronto Campaign 2000, *To 2000 and Beyond: Report Card on Child Poverty in Toronto* (Toronto 2003), 6.

13. United Way of Greater Toronto and Canadian Council on Social Development, *Poverty by Postal Code,* 43.

14. Montreal Public Health, *Annual Report, 2002,* 78.

15. Federation of Canadian Municipalities, *Income Gap Study* (Ottawa 2003).

16. Edmonton Social Planning Council, *Social Policy and the 2004 Civic Election* (Edmonton 2004), 1.

17. UNICEF Innocenti Research Centre, *Child Poverty in Rich Countries in 2005* (Florence 2005).

18. Ibid.

19. In the late 19th and early 20th centuries, many reform-minded planners and architects in England, France, and the United States turned their attention to creating new types of urban neighbourhoods and amenities that would provide families with a respite from the privations of working-class slums. These included the prototypes of the post-war bedroom suburbs as well as modernist high-rises situated away from the urban core. Both remain enduring features of the contemporary urban landscape and our planning orthodoxy, even though the industrial working-class slums that were their inspiration have long since disappeared from our cities.

20. These can take various forms, from the physically secured perimeters of gated communities, which remain relatively scarce in Canada, to more subtle exclusion strategies, such as neighbourhood campaigns to oppose affordable housing, shelters, and basement apartments. In Vancouver, a few entrepreneurial security firms took advantage of mounting concerns over property crime in affluent neighbourhoods by offering up personnel to patrol the streets and shoo away undesirable characters as a way of assisting the police force, hamstrung by an inadequate roster of beat cops.

21. Neil Bradford, *Why Cities Matter: Policy Research Perspectives for Canada.* (Toronto: Canadian Policy Research Networks, 2002), 35.

22. Caroline Beauvais and Jane Jenson, *The Well-Being of Children: Are There Neighbourhood Effects?* (Ottawa: Canadian Policy Research Network, 2003).

23. Clyde Hertzman and Dafna Kohen, *Neighbourhoods Matter for Child Development* (Ottawa: Vanier Institute for the Family, 2003).

24. Cooper, "Housing Affordability: A Children's Issue," 98–99.

25. Richard Glazier, Elizabeth Badley, Julie Gilbert, and Lorne Rothman, "The Nature of Increased Hospital Use in Poor Neighbourhoods: Findings from a Canadian Inner City," *Canadian Journal of Public Health,* July-August 2000, 271.

26. David Alter, David Naylor, Peter Austin, and Jack Tu, "Effects of Socio-Economic Status on Access to Invasive Cardiac Procedures and on Mortality after Acute Myocardial Infarction," *New England Journal of Medicine,* October 28, 1999, 1359.

27. Nicholas Vozoris and Valerie Tarasuk, "The Health of Canadians on Welfare," *Canadian Journal of Public Health,* October 2004, 115–20.

28. Dennis Raphael, Sherry Phillips, Rebecca Renwick, and Hersh Sehdev, "Government Policies as a Threat to Health: Findings from Two Toronto Community Quality of Life Studies," *Canadian Journal of Public Health,* May-June 2000, 181.

29. Richard Wilkinson, *Unhealthy Societies: The Affliction of Inequality* (London: Routledge, 1996).

30. Nancy Ross, Michael Wolfson, James Dunn, Jean-Marie Berthelot, George Kaplan, and John Lynch, "Relation between Income Inequality and Mortality in Canada and the United States: Cross Sectional Assessment Using Census Data and Vital Statistics," *British Medical Journal,* April 1, 2000, 898.

Exposed Cities

1. As a 2001 study by the Toronto Community Foundation noted, "A greater proportion of homeowners versus tenants also increases voter turnout, since municipal governments focus primarily on services related to property." Toronto Community Foundation, *Vital Signs 2001: Municipal Voter Turnout,* available online at www.tcf.ca.

2. Much of the statistical data and many insights in this chapter are drawn from *Finding Room: Policy Options for a Canadian Rental Housing Strategy* (Toronto: CUCS Press, 2004), an outstanding collection of essays on Canada's housing crisis, edited by J. David Hulchanski and Michael Shapcott, both of the University of Toronto, and published by the Centre for Urban and Community Studies at the University of Toronto.

3. Don Drummond, Derek Burleton, and Gillian Manning, "In Search of a New Paradigm," in *Finding Room,* ed. Hulchanski and Shapcott, 18.

4. Ibid.

5. Tom Kent, "Paul Martin's Sugar-Daddy Federalism, Donating to a Favoured Cause—Health Care," *Policy Options,* November 2004, 34.

6. J. David Hulchanski, *Housing Policy for Tomorrow's Cities* (Ottawa: Canadian Policy Research Networks, 2002), 1.

7. Interview with author, February 2, 2005.

8. Interview with author, January 28, 2005.

9. Homelessness is a very visible problem on the downtown streets of Canada's wealthiest metropolis, which has clustered its shelters in a derelict area behind City Hall and just blocks from the luxurious Stephen Avenue eateries and bars that fill up with revellers during the Calgary Stampede. Even

the dormitories of the international youth hostel, once occupied primarily by travellers, now serve as temporary rooms for Calgary's homeless men.

10. Laurie Monsebraaten, "A renter's paradise, a renter's hell; High vacancies not a boon for all tenants: Lack of affordable stock is still a problem," *Toronto Star,* December 6, 2003.

Learning Cities

1. John Ibbitson, "A lesson from Canadian education," *The Globe and Mail,* September 16, 2005.

2. Fernando Cartwright and Mary K. Allen, *Understanding the Urban-Rural Reading Gap* (Ottawa: Statistics Canada, 2002).

3. Christopher Worswick, *School Performance of the Children of Immigrants in Canada, 1994–98* (Ottawa: Department of Economics, Carleton University and Family and Labour Studies, Statistics Canada, 2001).

4. Statistics Canada, *The Daily,* September 18, 2003.

5. William Ouchi, Bruce Cooper, and Lydia Segal, *The Impact of Organization on the Performance of Nine School Systems* (Los Angeles: California Policy Options, UCLA, 2003).

6. Tess Kalinowski, "Kids unprepared for grade 1," *Toronto Star,* November 25, 2004.

7. Les Perreaux, "High-school dropout rates rise in Ontario and Quebec," *The Globe and Mail,* October 11, 2004.

8. Nicholas Keung, "School celebrates racial mix," *Toronto Star,* February 15, 2005.

9. Andrew Duffy, *Class Struggles: Public Education and the New Canadian* (Toronto: Atkinson Fellowship in Public Policy, 2003), 1.

10. Ibid.

11. Editorial, "French training here is a misplaced priority: The reality is, ESL programs face far greater need," *The Vancouver Sun,* March 15, 2003.

12. ESL Consortium, *Growing Diversity: Settlement and Integration Services for Immigrant Children in the New Century* (Vancouver 2002), 2.

13. Heather Sokoloff, "Learning Curve: A Chrétien legacy project aimed at helping Ottawa and the provinces develop academic policy threatens to throw the world of education research into turmoil," *National Post,* April 21, 2004.

14. David Watt, Hetty Roessingh, and Lynn Bosetti, *Educational Experiences of ESL Students Unravelling the Role of English Language Proficiency,* 127.

15. Ibid, 128.

16. Ibid, 130.

17. Richard Brennan, "Minister plotted 'to invent a crisis': Snobelen video spurs angry calls for him to resign," *Toronto Star,* September 13, 1995, A3.

18. Interview with author, February 4, 2005.

19. "Parents from rich Alberta fed up with funding cuts." *Kitchener-Waterloo Record,* March 24, 2003.

20. Caroline Alphonso, "Canada's ranking falls in funding for schools," *The Globe and Mail,* September 14, 2004.

21. Alanna Mitchell, "School Britannia," *The Globe and Mail,* May 1, 2004.

22. People for Education, *Public Education in Ontario's Cities* (Toronto 2003).

23. Education Improvement Commission, *Third Interim Report on the Progress Review of Ontario's New District School Boards* (Toronto: Queen's Printer for Ontario, 2000). Cited in People for Education, *Public Education in Ontario's Cities,* 1.

24. Interview with author, February 1, 2005.

Unbounded Cities

1. Quoted in John Lorinc, "Driven to Disruption: Toronto Used to Be Famous for Its Progressive Transportation Policies," *Toronto Life,* March 2001, 61–64.

2. Canadian Urban Institute, *Smart Growth in Canada* (Toronto 2001).

3. David Gurin, *Understanding Sprawl: A Citizen's Guide* (Vancouver: David Suzuki Foundation, 2003).

4. Ibid.

5. Stanley Brunn, Jack Williams, Donald Zeigler, *Cities of the World: World Regional Urban Development,* 3rd ed. (Lanham, MD: Rowman and Littlefield, 2003), 82.

6. Mark MacKinnon, "A little country, a little high tech: Canadians are becoming more outwardly mobile, moving to greener pastures in 'burbs and tech towns," *The Globe and Mail,* March 8, 1999.

7. Federation of Canadian Municipalities, *Income Gap Study* (Ottawa 2003).

8. Andrew Heisz and Sébastien LaRochelle-Côté, *Working and Commuting in CMA, 1996–2001* (Ottawa: Statistics Canada, 2005).

9. Annick Germain and Damaris Rose, *Montreal: The Quest for a Metropolis* (Toronto: John Wiley and Sons, 2000).

10. If Greater Toronto has become a rocket-powered growth machine, Montreal has seen its fortunes steadily wane since 1975, even with the economic revival of the last decade. In 1967, according to Germain and Rose, the City of Montreal produced an optimistic strategic plan projecting a metropolitan population of 7 million by 2000. Montreal's metropolitan population today is less than half that figure.

11. Germain and Rose, *Montreal.*

12. Anne Swardson, "O, Montreal, city of exodus; secession fears, economy spur decline," *Washington Post,* March 21, 1996.

13. Tu Thanh Ha, "Montreal politicians will try to fill in the doughnut," *The Globe and Mail,* February 25, 1997.

14. Even if they wanted to, municipal councils could do little to oppose the development schemes of large and well-connected developers, who contributed heavily to the Progressive Conservative Party. Changes in the planning legislation meant that developers could rapidly appeal council decisions on development applications to the Ontario Municipal Board, in expectation of a more favourable outcome. The government also watered down its so-called "provincial policy statements"—guidelines pertaining to various facets of planning, such as environmental controls, heritage, and so on. The shift in approach was the stuff of legal fantasies: by changing the phrase "shall be consistent with" to "will have regard to," the government was able to provide its developer allies with a much more *laissez-faire* environment than they had ever enjoyed. From John Lorinc, "The Story of Sprawl," *Toronto Life,* May 2001, 82–86, 88.

15. Derek Burleton, "The Calgary-Edmonton Corridor: Take Action Now to Ensure the Tiger's Roar Doesn't Fade," *TD Economics,* April 2003.

16. Ted Wickson, *A Century of Moving Canada: Public Transit, 1904–2004.* (Toronto: Canadian Urban Transit Association, 2004).

17. National Round Table on the Environment and the Economy, *Environmental Quality in Canadian Cities: The Federal Role* (Ottawa 2003).

18. Pamela Blais, "The Economics of Urban Form." Background paper prepared for the Greater Toronto Area Task Force (Toronto: GTA Task Force, 1995).

19. Mark Winfield, *Smart Growth in Ontario: The Promise vs. Provincial Performance* (Drayton Valley, AB: Pembina Institute, 2003), 4.

20. Gurin, *Understanding Sprawl.*

21. Annette Peters, Stephanie von Klot, Margit Heier, Ines Trentinaglia, Allmut Hörmann, Erich Wichmann, Hannelore Löwel, "Exposure to Traffic and the Onset of Myocardial Infarction," *New England Journal of Medicine,* October 21, 2004, 1721–1730.

22. Eric Miller and Richard Soberman, *Travel Demand and Urban Form: Issue Paper No. 9* (Toronto: Neptis Foundation, 2003), 12.

23. Statistics Canada, *Canadian Community Health Survey: Obesity among Adults and Children* (Ottawa 2005).

24. Lawrence Frank, Martin Andresen, and Thomas Schmid, "Obesity Relationships with Community Design, Physical Activity, and Time Spent in Car," *American Journal of Preventive Medicine* 27, 2 (August 2004): 87–96.

Wasteful Cities

1. Aurora Online with Dr. William Rees. Available at aurora.icaap.org/talks/rees.html.

2. Organisation for Economic Co-operation and Development, *Canada: Environmental Performance Review* (Paris 2005).

3. Jeffrey Wilson and Mark Anielski, *Ecological Footprints of Canadian Municipalities and Regions,* rev. ed. (Ottawa: Federation of Canadian Municipalities, 2005).

4. Earlier generations of planners and politicians understood this dynamic better than do the current lot. In the 1950s, flash floods killed many Torontonians when Hurricane Hazel tore through southern Ontario. In the wake of the disaster, the Ontario government passed legislation establishing conservation authorities, which had a mandate to build reservoirs to ensure that storm water runoff didn't go directly into rivers.

5. Municipal runoff, moreover, is a toxic soup, polluted with dog feces, gasoline, and whatever else tends to be poured into storm sewers.

6. Ken Ogilvie, *Air Water and Soil Quality: Issue Paper No. 2* (Toronto, Neptis Foundation, 2003).

7. Through successive governments, gravel-mining companies operating around the Greater Toronto Area have been able to win approvals for new quarries on agricultural, recreational, and environmentally sensitive land outside the city. Operators are required to put aside a nominal amount for quarry closure and reclamation costs, but they are effectively self-regulating. Ontario's environmental commissioner Gordon Miller has vigorously criticized the government for failing to manage its aggregate resources.

8. Nancy Hofmann, Giuseppe Filoso, and Mike Schofield, *Rural and Small Town Analysis Bulletin: The Loss of Dependable Agricultural Land in Canada.* (Ottawa: Statistics Canada, 2005).

9. Ibid., 8.

10. Dr. Barbara Yaffe, Acting Medical Officer of Health, *Agenda for Action on Air and Health* (Toronto: Toronto Public Health, 2004), i.

11. "Doctors find smog in Ontario more damaging than first estimated: Loss of human life and economic costs from polluted air overwhelmingly high," news release, Ontario Medical Association, June 14, 2005.

12. The figures vary from community to community. According to Ontario's Institute for Clinical Evaluative Studies, Sudbury, Windsor, and northwest Ontario had the highest asthma hospitalization rates between 1994 and 1999, while the rates for Greater Toronto Area and Hamilton were below the provincial average.

13. www.pollutionwatch.org

14. Yaffe, *Agenda for Action on Air and Health.*

15. Ibid.

16. From www.pollutionwatch.org. The website, which provides information on pollution sources, is a collaborative project of Environmental Defence and the Canadian Environmental Law Association.

17. Ibid.

18. Derek Burleton, "Electricity in Canada: Who Needs It? Who's Got It?" *TD Economics,* March 2005.

19. Quoted in Jeff Sallot, "Canada lags on air pollution clean-up compared with U.S., coalition finds," *The Globe and Mail,* October 13, 2005.

20. *Canada: Environmental Performance Review,* 18.

21. Ibid.

PART TWO: HEALTHY NEIGHBOURHOODS, STRONG CITIES

Connecting Immigrants and Good Jobs

1. Statistics Canada, "Longitudinal Survey of Immigrants to Canada," *The Daily,* October 13, 2005.

2. Toronto City Summit Alliance, *Enough Talk: An Action Plan for the Toronto Region,* April 2003, 20.

3. Anne Dawson, "Ontario Liberals line up equalization claim meeting," *Ottawa Citizen,* March 8, 2005.

4. Royal Bank of Canada, *The Diversity Advantage: A Case for Canada's 21st Century Economy,* presented at 10th annual International Metropolis Conference, Toronto, October 20, 2005.

5. Janet Bagnall, "Wasting away: Trained professionals who immigrate to Canada are forced into menial jobs because professional bodies won't recognize their credentials," Montreal *Gazette,* October 1, 2005.

6. John Deverell, "Fighting for the right to work: Immigrant professionals face some high hurdles," *Toronto Star,* December 11, 1989.

7. Elizabeth McIsaac, "Doctor Shortages and the Integration of International Physicians," Maytree Foundation, January 2002 seminar, Toronto. Transcript available online at www.maytree.com.

8. On November 29, 2004, Human Resources and Skills Development minister Joe Volpe announced a $1.6-million grant to the Canadian Aviation Maintenance Council to launch a foreign credential recognition program.

9. Don DeVoretz, *Brief to the Housing Standing Committee on Citizenship and Immigration* (Vancouver: Research on Immigration and Integration in the Metropolis, 2005), 3.

10. Naomi Alboim, *Fulfilling the Promise: Integrating Immigrant Skills into the Canadian Economy* (Ottawa: Caledon Institute of Social Policy, 2003), 1–4.

11. Interview with author, March 8, 2005.

Making Space for Urban Aboriginals

1. Don Langford, "Self-government in three years?" *Winnipeg Free Press,* April 19, 1994.

2. Dan Lett, "Urban Indians get a start," *Winnipeg Free Press,* October 28, 1994.

3. Brian Cole, "Of all the jargon being bandied about these days, none is more...," *Winnipeg Free Press*, July 27, 1996.

4. Sue Bailey, "Chiefs demand Ottawa delay implementing off-reserve election ruling," Canadian Press, November 2, 2000.

5. Standing Senate Committee on Aboriginal Peoples, *Urban Aboriginal Youth: An Action Plan for Change* (Final report) (Ottawa 2003), 23.

6. Interview with author, January 12, 2005.

7. Ibid.

8. Interview with author, January 27, 2005.

9. Bud Robertson, "Aboriginals' needs unmet, nurses say," *Winnipeg Free Press*, May 9, 1995.

10. Vancouver/Richmond Health Board, *Healing Ways: Aboriginal Health and Service Review* (Vancouver 1999).

11. Ibid.

12. Liane Faulder, "How to raise a reader's grades," *Edmonton Journal*, December 7, 2003.

13. Elsie Ross, "Employers Advised to Cast a Wider Net for New Employees," *Daily Oil Bulletin*, March 22, 2005.

14. Ibid.

15. Interview with author, January 12, 2005.

16. Quoted in F. Laurie Barron and Joseph Garcea, eds., "Urban Indian Reserves: Forging New Relationships in Saskatchewan," Purich Aboriginal Issue Series, 1999, 223.

17. Ibid., 264.

Creating Senior-Friendly Cities

1. Tony Ianno, *Creating a National Seniors Agenda: Report of the Prime Minister's Taskforce on Active Living and Dignity for Seniors* (Ottawa 2004).

2. J. David Hulchanski and Michael Shapcott, eds., *Finding Room: Policy Options for a Canadian Rental Housing Strategy* (Toronto: CUCS Press, 2004).

3. "Walking the mall for health," *San Francisco Chronicle*, January 1, 1985.

4. T. Takano, K. Nakamura, and M. Watanabe, "Urban Residential Environments and Senior Citizens' Longevity in Megacity Areas: The Importance of Walkable Green Spaces," *Journal of Epidemiology and Community Health*, December 2002, 913–19.

5. John Lorinc, "City tells intersection guru to hit the road," *The Globe and Mail*, September 25, 2004.

6. Ibid.

7. Kevin McGran, "Gas tax funds power seniors buses," *Toronto Star*, January 6, 2005.

8. Glen Leicester, *Development of the Accessible Transit Strategic Plan* (Burnaby, BC: Greater Vancouver Transportation Authority, 2005).

9. David Foot and Daniel Stoffman, "Toronto That Will Be ... Predictions," *Toronto Life*, January 2000, 84–90.

10. Geoff Ballinger, Jingbo Zhang, and Vern Hicks, *Home Care Estimates in National Health Expenditures* (Ottawa: Canadian Institute for Health Information, 2001).

11. Interview with author, February 18, 2005. See also Marcus Hollander, *Unfinished Business: The Case for Chronic Home Care Services* (Victoria: Hollander Analytical Services, 2004).

12. Ibid., i.

13. Vancouver Coastal Health, *Health Service Redesign Plan 2004/05 to 2006/07* (Vancouver 2004), 27.

14. Merrill Cooper, "Housing Affordability: A Children's Issue," in *Finding Room*, ed. Hulchanski and Shapcott, 89–113.

15. John Lorinc, "Old: It's the decision you dread," *Globe and Mail Report on Business*, June 2003, 75.

16. Ianno, *Creating a National Seniors Agenda*.

17. Lorinc, "Old."

18. Lisa Priest, "When seniors turn to violence in their nursing homes," *The Globe and Mail*, November 13, 2004.

Breaking the Poverty Cycle

1. Edmonton Social Planning Council Fact Sheet, *Welfare and the Cost of Living* (Edmonton, March 2004).

2. Don Drummond and Gillian Manning, "From Welfare to Work in Ontario: Still the Road Less Travelled," *TD Economics,* September 8, 2005.

3. Christa Freiler, Laurel Rothman, and Pedro Barata, *Pathways to Progress: Structural Solutions to Address Child Poverty* (Toronto: Campaign 2000, 2004).

4. Jane Jenson, *Canada's New Social Risk: Towards a New Social Architecture* (Ottawa: Canadian Policy Research Network, 2004), 3.

5. Drummond and Manning, "From Welfare to Work in Ontario."

6. Ken Battle, *Minimum Wages in Canada: A Statistical Portrait with Policy Implications* (Ottawa: Caledon Institute of Social Policy, 2003).

7. Government of Ontario minimum wage fact sheet, available online at www.gov.on.ca/LAB/english/news/2003/03-65f.html.

8. Drummond and Manning, "From Welfare to Work in Ontario," iii.

9. Freiler, Rothman, and Barata, *Pathways to Progress.*

10. Tom Kent, "Paul Martin's Sugar-Daddy Federalism, Donating to a Favoured Cause—Health Care," *Policy Options*, November 2004, 33.

Building Affordable Housing and Mixed-Income Neighbourhoods

1. In 2005, the Liberal government unveiled a $150-million rent supplement program for low-income families. But the amount fell well short of the $500-million-a-year figure recommended by the National Housing and Homelessness Network.

2. J. David Hulchanski and Michael Shapcott, eds., *Finding Room: Policy Options for a Canadian Rental Housing Strategy* (Toronto: CUCS Press, 2004).

3. Don Drummond, Derek Burleton, and Gillian Manning, "In Search of a New Paradigm," in *Finding Room,* ed. Hulchanski and Shapcott, 18.

4. J. David Hulchanski, *Housing Policy for Tomorrow's Cities* (Ottawa: Canadian Policy Research Networks, 2002). Emphasis in original.

5. Decisions to withdraw funding for co-op housing projects have put Canada well behind many industrialized countries, including Denmark, Germany, and Sweden, where such ownership arrangements are a far more accepted form of residential accommodation. It's not just a European phenomenon: In New York City alone, there are 600,000 co-op housing units, compared with about 90,000 in all of Canada. B.C. Institute for Co-operative Studies, University of Victoria, web.uvic.ca/bcics/research/housing/models.html.

6. Lance Berelowitz, *Dream City: Vancouver and the Global Imagination* (Vancouver: Douglas and McIntyre, 2005), 213.

7. John Sewell, *The Shape of the City: Toronto Struggles with Modern Planning* (Toronto: University of Toronto Press, 1993).

8. Homelessness Action Task Force, *Taking Responsibility for Homelessness* (City of Toronto 1999), 173.

9. Ottawa's surplus land is subject to competing bureaucratic and political agendas, and the government's record on using it for affordable housing leaves much to be desired. The real estate—including many former military bases in highly desirable urban locations in cities such as Toronto, Halifax, and Calgary—is transferred to the Canada Lands Company (CLC), which has a mandate to obtain fair market value on property sales. Since it was set up in the late 1980s, CLC's $4.1-billion worth of development deals has led to the construction or rehabilitation of almost 21,000 residential units, of which only 700 qualify as affordable. One of the few recent examples includes a $2.3 million Toronto site transferred to Habitat for Humanity. More typical are the high-end townhouses that went up on a former Canadian forces base in Calgary. *Canada Lands Company Annual Report, 2004–5.*

10. Urban Development Roundtable—Rental Working Group, *Unlocking the Opportunity for New Rental Housing: A Call to Action* (City of Toronto Planning Division 2001).

11. John Punter, *The Vancouver Achievement: Planning and Urban Design* (Vancouver: UBC Press, 2003).

12. In the City of Toronto in the early 2000s, a luxury condominium developer put in an application to tear down an older apartment building whose tenants were largely seniors on fixed income. Council ultimately rejected the application, and its decision survived a legal challenge by the developer. The outcome signalled to the development industry that it couldn't look to the city's plentiful supply of older rental buildings as a source of land for new highrises filled with luxury condos.

Investing in Early Learning

1. Organisation for Economic Co-operation and Development, *Canadian Childcare Report* (Paris 2004), 6.

2. Ibid, 8.

3. Martha Friendly and Jane Beach, *Early Childhood Education and Care in Canada 2004*, 6th ed. From the University of Toronto's Centre for Childcare Resources. Its website offers a clearing house of information on Canada's childcare and early childhood development policies, at www.childcarecanada.org.

4. www.childcarecanda.org

5. John Lorinc, "This package comes with a puzzle; Ottawa's new early-learning funds raise tricky questions for the city's daycare providers," *The Globe and Mail,* February 26, 2005.

6. Cheryl Cornacchia, "Progress in peril, daycares warn: Early childhood education in Quebec has come a long way, offering diverse programs for youngsters. But proposed budget cuts could downgrade a system that has become the country's finest, educators say," Montreal *Gazette,* September 26, 2005.

7. Quoted in Cornacchia, "Progress in peril, daycares warn."

8. Christa Japel, Richard E. Tremblay, and Sylvana Côté, English Summary, "La qualité, ça compte! Résultats de l'Étude longitudinale du développement des enfants du Québec concernant la qualité des services de garde," *Choix IRPP* 11, 4: 45.

9. Not coincidentally, the architect of the Best Start policy and a key figure in pushing Ottawa to develop its own child care strategy is former minister of Children and Youth Services Marie Bountrogianni. She is a highly respected child psychologist from Hamilton who had worked in school boards and health centres before entering politics. She knew, from professional experience, the frustrations many urban parents had encountered when confronting the confusing maze of public services geared to children. Ironically, she was bumped from her cabinet post in mid-2005.

10. Government of Ontario, Ministry of Children and Youth Services, *Best Start: Ontario's Plan for Early Learning and Child Care* (Toronto 2005).

Promoting Diversity and Accessibility in Urban Education

1. People for Education, *Public Education in Ontario's Cities* (Toronto 2005).

2. John Lorinc, "Drop-outs No More," *University of Toronto Magazine,* Fall 2004.

3. Further information about Pathways is available on its website at www.p2e.ca.

4. John Cassidy, "Bloomberg's game," *The New Yorker,* April 4, 2005, 59.

5. Michael Kirst, *Mayoral Influence, New Regimes and Public School Governance* (Philadelphia: Consortium for Policy Research in Education, University of Pennsylvania Graduate School of Education, 2002), 3.

6. Brett Schaeffer, "US Mayor Announces Privatization of Chicago Schools," AlterNet, August 11, 2004, www.alternet.org/story/19469.

7. Comments made at a session of the GTA Forum in Toronto, March 23, 2005.

8. Charles Ungerleider, *Failing Our Kids: How We Are Ruining Our Public Schools* (Toronto: McClelland and Stewart, 2003), 83.

9. Interview with author, January 27, 2005.

10. William Ouchi, Bruce Cooper, and Lydia Segal, *The Impact of Organization on the Performance of Nine School Systems* (Los Angeles: California Policy Options, UCLA, 2003).

11. Interview with author, January 27, 2005.

12. Ibid.

13. Sean Fine, "Edmonton Fights Back," *Education Today,* Fall 2002/Spring 2003.

14. Brian Bergman, "Academy Rewards: An Edmonton School Gives Parents More," *Maclean's,* March 29, 1999, 77.

15. Interview with author, January 27, 2005.

16. Canadian Federation of Students, "Tuition Fees in Canada: A Pan-Canadian Perspective on Educational User Fees," *2005 Fact Sheet* 11, 1. Available online at www.cfs-fcee.ca.

17. Bob Rae, *Ontario: A Leader in Learning* (Toronto: Queen's Printer of Ontario, 2005).

18. Caroline Alphonso, "Canada's ranking falls in funding for schools," *The Globe and Mail,* September 14, 2004.

19. Rae, *Ontario: A Leader in Learning,* 8, 22.

PART THREE: TOWARD THE NEW CITY

Autonomous Cities

1. Cited in Paula Dill and Paul Beford, *Toronto Official Plan* (City of Toronto 2002), 6.

2. Neil Bradford, *Why Cities Matter: Policy Research Perspectives for Canada* (Ottawa: Canadian Policy Research Network, 2002), 29.

3. Quoted in Donald Lidstone, *Assessment of the Municipal Acts of the Provinces and Territories* (Ottawa: Federation of Canadian Municipalities, 2004).

4. Ibid.

5. As an 1891 Supreme Court of Canada ruling stated, municipal corporations are "merely instruments of the senior levels of government for the more convenient administration of local government." Ibid.

6. Bradford, *Why Cities Matter,* 18.

7. Henry Aubin, *Who's Afraid of Demergers?* (Montreal: Véhicule Press, 2004), 20.

8. Robert Bish, "Local Government Amalgamations: Discredited Nineteenth-Century Ideals Alive in the Twenty-First," *C.D. Howe Institute Commentary,* March 2001, Abstract.

9. Ibid., 1.

10. The Silicon Valley, south of San Francisco, is what it is today because a pair of Stanford University graduates, Bill Hewlett and Dave Packard, happened to build their first electronic device in a garage in Palo Alto, which is a few kilometres south of San Francisco.

11. Bish, "Local Government Amalgamations."

12. Making a difficult situation even more complex, the Mike Harris Tories undertook three crucial urban changes at the same time: property tax reform, amalgamation, and a rearranging of local and provincial responsibilities. Queen's Park enacted regulations severely restricting Toronto from raising additional commercial or industrial property taxes. The province uploaded financial responsibility for public education and downloaded all or some financial responsibility for a range of previously cost-shared services, including transit, welfare, and public health. While the Harris government insisted the exchange was "revenue neutral," a 2001 report by the provincial auditor general confirmed that the City of Toronto had incurred almost $140 million in additional costs during the first three years. The city was also forced to pay millions more in costs related to amalgamation, such as severance packages. Smaller Ontario municipalities were given provincial grants to cover amalgamation expenses, but Toronto was given a $200-million "loan."

13. Cited in, Jennifer Lewington, "No easy fix for the city's cash crunch: A new deal on dividing money needed to end budget problems, mayor says," *The Globe and Mail,* June 28, 2005.

14. Aubin, *Who's Afraid of Demergers?*

15. By contrast, Toronto's amalgamation, according to the neo-conservative rhetoric, was all about reducing the payroll. Early in his first term, Mayor Mel Lastman presided over hundreds of layoffs. But over time, the amalgamated city bureaucracy has continued to expand and now exceeds the pre-amalgamation staffing levels.

16. Interview with author, January 20, 2005.

17. Andrew Sancton, *The Governance of Metropolitan Areas in Canada.* Unpublished draft. Submitted to *Public Administration and Development* (London, ON).

18. Ibid., 20.

19. To counter charges of creating yet another level of government, Golden's report urged Queen's Park to eliminate Metro as well as the so-called upper-tier "regional municipalities" of Peel, York, Durham, and Halton, which had been set up in the 1970s to manage growth in the fast-growing bedroom communities outside Metro.

20. Besides world-beating figures such as former New York City mayor Rudolph Giuliani and London's Ken Livingstone, dynamic and energetic mayors have been transforming European cities, including Rome, Berlin, and Paris, according to a May 8, 2005, report in *Time* magazine (international edition): "The reason for this popularity is simple: mayors matter. Leave the grand visions to presidents and prime ministers; mayors are judged by their ability to pick up the trash, get traffic moving, deal with housing and commercial development, control crime, and convince their constituents—as well as tourists and investors—that their cities are best."

21. Thomas Courchene, *Citistates and the State of Cities: Political Economy and Fiscal-Federalism Dimensions* (Montreal: Institute for Research in Public Policy, 2005).

22. Lidstone, *Assessment of the Municipal Acts.*

23. Lynne Koziey, "Taxis should match demand, city," *Calgary Herald,* January 18, 2003.

24. "Top Court will hear taxi case," *Edmonton Journal,* March 20, 2003.

25. City of Toronto Act Taskforce, *Setting the Course for a Strong Toronto* (Toronto: Board of Trade, 2005), 6.

26. Joint Ontario–City of Toronto Task Force to Review the City of Toronto Acts and Other Private (Special) Legislation, *Building a 21st Century City: Final Staff Report* (Toronto: Ministry of Municipal Affairs and Housing, 2005), 3, 4.

27. James Rusk, "OMB changes offer local control," *The Globe and Mail,* December 13, 2005.

28. Besides the undeniably lucrative high-rise condo developments along False Creek, the city has pursued policies such as legalizing second suites to increase the stock of affordable rental housing; the construction of mixed-use, medium-density, environmentally sustainable residential development in an area that will house the athletes' village for the 2010 winter Olympics; redevelopment of railway lands to allow for a consortium of universities to build new technology centres; and the use of heritage preservation policies to encourage the revitalization of the Downtown Eastside, including affordable housing.

29. Interview with author, June 13, 2005.

30. Richard T. LeGates and Frederic Stout, "Introduction," in *The City Reader,* ed. LeGates and Stout (London and New York: Routledge, 1996), 17.

Self-Sufficient Cities

1. Christopher Leo and Lisa Shaw, "What Causes Inner-City Decay and What Can Be Done About It?" in *Urban Affairs: Back on the Policy Agenda,* ed. Caroline Andrew, Katherine A.H. Graham, and Susan Phillips, (Montreal and Kingston: McGill-Queen's University Press, 2002), 119–47.

2. According to Leo and Shaw, Winnipeg's growth rate between 1986 and 1991 was 3.7 percent. By 1996, it had "plummeted" to 0.3 percent. Ibid.

3. As an analysis on municipal voting patterns by the Toronto Community Foundation's Vital Signs 2001 project noted, "Voter turnout is interrelated with poverty issues and the health of the social environment. Canadian studies of federal voter turnout behaviour suggest that youth, low-income or unemployed people, and those with limited formal education are less likely to vote. If these trends are true municipally, vulnerable segments of society are being systematically excluded from the local decision-making process." Available online at www.tcf.ca/vital_signs/vitalsigns2001/index.html.

4. Don Gillmor, "The City Statesman," *Saturday Night,* April 2004.

5. Conference Board of Canada, *A New Deal for the City of Winnipeg* (Ottawa 2004).

6. Federation of Canadian Municipalities, *Early Warning: Will Canadian Cities Compete? A Comparative Overview of Municipal Government in Canada, the U.S. and Europe* (Ottawa: National Round Table on the Environment and the Economy, 2001).

7. Donald Lidstone, *Assessment of the Municipal Acts of the Provinces and Territories* (Ottawa: Federation of Canadian Municipalities, 2004).

8. Enid Slack, "Have Fiscal Issues Put Urban Affairs Back on the Policy Agenda?" in *Urban Affairs: Back on the Policy Agenda,* ed. Andrew, Graham, and Phillips, 309.

9. Municipalities also impose levies on new developments to finance the capital costs associated with urban infrastructure, such as pipes, roads, and parks. But development charges represent a significant source of revenue only for fast-growing suburban cities that are building large subdivisions or office parks on undeveloped land.

10. These gaps survive economic slumps. According to Lidstone, *Assessment of the Municipal Acts,* federal and provincial revenues jumped 16 and 21 percent between 1999 and 2003, whereas municipal income rose only 4 percent—considerably less than the cumulative rate of inflation

11. Enid Slack, *Easing the Fiscal Restraints: New Revenue Tools in the City of Toronto Act,* International Tax Program Working Paper 0507, Joseph Rotman School of Management, University of Toronto.

12. Quoted in John Lorinc, "The Decline and Fall of the Great Canadian Cities," *Saturday Night,* March 17, 2001.

13. Federation of Canadian Municipalities, *Early Warning.*

14. TIFs are permitted in Winnipeg, but the city hasn't made use of them to date.

15. Federation of Canadian Municipalities, *Early Warning.*

16. Transport for London, "Congestion Charging—The 11 Key Numbers" Fact Sheet, available online at www.tfl.gov.uk/tfl/cclondon/cc_fact_sheet_key_numbers.shtml.

17. Federation of Canadian Municipalities, *Early Warning.*

18. Chief Administrative Officer, City of Toronto, *Comparison of Powers and Revenue Sources of Selected Cities* (Toronto 2001).

19. Federation of Canadian Municipalities, *Early Warning,* 5, executive summary.

20. Lidstone, *Assessment of the Municipal Acts.* The $60-billion figure includes an estimated $16.5 billion for water treatment, $6.8 billion for waste water systems, $9 billion for roads, $6.8 billion for transit, and $10 billion for affordable housing.

21. Canada West Foundation, *Foundation for Prosperity: Creating a Sustainable Municipal-Provincial Partnership to Meet the Infrastructure Challenge of Alberta's Second Century* (Calgary 2004), 2.

22. As Auditor General Denis Desautels noted in 1996, federal officials failed to closely monitor the projects and had fuzzy guidelines about what qualified. The result is that about a third of the money was spent on projects that would have been undertaken anyway—meaning that the additional federal dollars simply shifted the financial burden away from the municipalities. In a follow-up report, he said, "the Program is essentially 'running on trust' with little accountability." Auditor General of Canada, *Canada Infrastructure Works Program: Lessons Learned* (Ottawa: Queen's Printer of Canada, 1996). The report is available online at the Auditor General's website at www.oag.bvg.gc.ca.

23. Chief Administrative Officer, City of Toronto, *Comparison of Powers and Revenue Sources.*

24. Under the formula worked out between the Ontario government and the Association of Municipalities of Ontario, 70 percent of the funds would be allocated based on ridership, and 30 percent based on population, a formula designed to ensure the money goes to cities with large transit operations. In the first year, the GTA municipalities of Ottawa, London, Waterloo Region, Windsor, and Hamilton received $138 million, or almost 90 percent of the funding.

25. Speech by Prime Minister Paul Martin at the annual Federation of Canadian Municipalities conference, held June 5, 2005, in St. John's, Newfoundland. As he said, "We are well aware that our major cities face challenges that are very different from those that confront our smaller municipalities."

26. Local Government Bulletin Number 30, September 2002, www.localgovernment.ca.

27. Paul Martin's speech at Federation of Canadian Municipalities annual conference, June 5, 2005, St. John's, Newfoundland.

Compact Cities

1. As of 2005, there were 1500 homes in Cornell, with 10,000 expected by 2015, representing a density of about 4000 people per square kilometre.

2. According to one 2005 analysis, employment in the City of Toronto "peaked" in 1989, at about 1.5 million jobs, and has "languished" ever since. As of 2004, about 100,000 fewer people work in the "416" area than 15 years prior. In the meantime, the lion's share of job creation was taking place in the 905 suburbs around Toronto. In 2002, in fact, the 905 became a "net importer" of labour from Toronto and the rest of Ontario. The following year marked a watershed—the point at which the total employment in the 905 suburbs exceeded the number of jobs in the City of Toronto proper. Joseph Pennachetti, *Enhancing Toronto's Business Climate—It's Everybody's Business* (City of Toronto 2005).

3. Richard White, "Inner city condo projects springing up like clockwork," *Calgary Herald,* January 15, 2005.

4. Jane Gadd, "A housing plan that's just right," *The Globe and Mail,* July 22, 2005.

5. Jack Jedwab, *Gettting to Work in North America's Major Cities and Dependence on Cars* (Montreal: Association for Canadian Studies, 2004).

6. A 1999 opinion poll conducted by Decima Research for the City of Toronto concluded that interest in cycling was growing among both middle-aged boomers and younger residents. The study found that about 400,000 Torontonians use bikes to shop, go to school, or commute to work, and concluded that there was "considerable opportunity" to expand the city's cycling infrastructure. Decima Research Inc., *City of Toronto 1999 Cycling Study: Final Report on Quantitative Research Results* (City of Toronto 2000).

7. With 13,000 post-and-ring bike stands installed as of 2003, Toronto led all North American cities for on-street bike racks, according to the city's Department of Works and Emergency Services.

8. Eva Bordlein, *The Munich Bicycle Development Concept* (Municipality of Munich, n.d.).

9. Canadian Urban Institute, *Smart Growth in Canada* (Toronto 2001).

10. Ibid., 1.

11. During the latter 1990s, Maryland's governor Parris Glendening launched a big smart-growth push, using the state's spending powers to ensure that public money wasn't subsidizing sprawl. He cancelled new highway by-pass projects, rejigged Maryland's $2-billion-a-year transportation budget

to focus on transit, and redirected capital spending on schools, requiring more funds to go into renovating older public schools instead of constructing new ones on the outskirts. But his main achievement was the so-called Priority Funding Areas legislation, which designated urban growth areas throughout the state—mainly cities and heavily developed hubs in suburban areas—and directs a wide range of state-spending initiatives, such as heritage preservation and municipal infrastructure grants, to these regions. Parris Glendening, "Maryland's Smart Growth Initiative: The Next Steps," *Fordham Urban Law Journal,* April 2002, 1493.

12. Canadian Urban Institute, *Smart Growth in Canada.*

13. Mike and Peggy Dobbins, "Sprawl Things Considered," *American City and County,* September 1997, 18.

14. Metro Portland, *The Nature of 2040: The Region's 50-Year Plan for Managing Growth,* available online at www.metro-region.org.

Efficient Cities

1. Andrew Heisz and Grant Schellenberg, *Public Transit Use among Immigrants* (Ottawa: Statistics Canada, 2004); Board of Trade of Metropolitan Montreal, *Public Transit: A Powerful Economic Development Engine for the Metropolitan Montreal Region* (Montreal 2004).

2. Ibid., 15. While the Statistics Canada study didn't offer an explanation for why such a large percentage of public transit users are recent immigrants, the reasons may have to do with the fact that many new Canadians have experienced severe employment difficulties, working in low-paying jobs for longer periods than earlier generations of newcomers. Anecdotal evidence suggests that single-family dwellings in traditionally planned suburban neighbourhoods or high-rises are home to extended families or numerous unrelated individuals living under the same roof. Such conditions suggest lower than average levels of car ownership in otherwise typical suburban settings.

3. The Toronto Transit Commission covers 80 percent of its costs from fares and advertising, making it the most efficient transit operator in North America, well ahead of New York's transit system, which has an efficiency rate of 59 percent. Ted Wickson, *A Century of Moving Canada: Public Transit, 1904–2004* (Toronto: Canadian Urban Transit Association, 2004).

4. Ibid.

5. British Columbia, Alberta, and Quebec now allocate a portion of their provincial gas taxes to municipal transit (British Columbia's is the most generous, at 12 cents per litre). In March 2004, Toronto, Queen's Park, and Ottawa announced a plan to pump $1.05 billion over three years into the Toronto Transit Commission. Later that same year, the McGuinty government promised an ongoing two-cents-per-litre share of the gas tax to municipal transit agencies, divvied up according to a formula based on ridership and

population. The Martin Liberals followed up with their five-year, $5-billion infrastructure program, based on a share of the federal gas tax. In April 2005, the Liberal-NDP budget agreement negotiated by Martin and NDP leader Jack Layton added another $900 million, equivalent to one cent of the federal gas excise tax transfer.

6. Greg Gormick, "The North American Passenger Rail Market," *Railway Age,* March 1, 2005, G1.

7. Todd Litman, *Pay-as-You-Drive Vehicle Insurance: Converting Vehicle Insurance Premiums into Use-Based Charges.* From *TDM Encyclopedia.* Available online at www.vtpi.org.

8. PAYG insurance depends on the installation of devices that can independently track and verify mileage for the insurer. Further complicating the system is the fact that such policies will likely lead to reduced premium revenues from low-mileage customers—an outcome that isn't in the insurance industry's interest. This means that the status quo insurance will in many cases stay in place, absent government regulatory intervention.

9. "Vancouver promotes insurance by the kilometre," CBC News, April 27, 2005.

10. For further information, see the Canadian Urban Transit Association's website at www.cutaactu.ca.

11. Don MacPherson, "Would the Laval metro have cost less? Not necessarily. A private partner would have insisted on a more realistic price estimate to begin with," Montreal *Gazette,* February 5, 2005.

Eco-Cities

1. "Ontario 10-year Outlook Forecasts Power Shortage," *Foster Electric Report,* July 20, 2005.

2. Quebec Ministère des Affaires municipales et de la Métropole, *Planning Framework and Government Orientations, Montreal Metropolitan Region, 2001–2021,* June 2001. Cited in *Environmental Quality in Canadian Cities: The Federal Role* (Ottawa: National Round Table on the Environment and the Economy, 2003), 4.

3. David Owen, "Green Manhattan," *The New Yorker,* October 18, 2004, 111.

4. Caroline Alphonso, "Toronto seeks ways to avoid pollution: Homeowners also urged to keep water system clean," *The Globe and Mail,* May 16, 2000.

5. Newfoundland Design Associates Ltd./CH2M Hill, *St. John's Harbour Clean-up: Phase Two* (City of St John's 2003).

6. Daniel Girard, "Mr. Floatie's turd-world politics: Sewage activist wiped off B.C. ballot. But anti-pollution protest left its mark," *Toronto Star,* October 31, 2005.

7. The technology required to operate municipal solid waste operations has also become staggeringly sophisticated. Transfer stations are equipped with a range of systems designed to separate various types of waste using blowers, magnets, balers, shredders, and rotating drums with filters, as well as manual sorting. But a Federation of Canadian Municipalities waste management study reported that European municipalities tend to be more automated than their North American counterparts. Federation of Canadian Municipalities, *Solid Waste as a Resource: Review of Waste Technologies* (Ottawa, n.d.).

8. Ibid.

9. Don Wanagas, "There is another way," *National Post,* September 30, 2000.

10. According to a study on waste management by the Federation of Canadian Municipalities, residential diversion programs typically succeed in diverting no more than 50 percent of household waste.

11. Michelle Lalonde, "Pollution still pays: City behind target. Quebec should force firms to ante up for recycling costs, DeSousa says," Montreal *Gazette,* May 6, 2005.

12. John Lorinc, "Burning Ambition," *Toronto Life.* November 2004, 81.

13. Toronto Transit Commission, *Operating Statistics, 2004* (Toronto 2004).

14. Richard Gilbert, "Burn, baby, burn: Critics of incinerators make urban analyst Richard Gilbert burning mad. He says shipping away Toronto's garbage doesn't make sense," *The Globe and Mail,* October 22, 2003.

15. Lorinc, "Burning Ambition," 81.

16. Ibid.

17. Federation of Canadian Municipalities, *Solid Waste as a Resource,* 242.

18. Jean-Francois Viel, Patrick Arveux, Josette Baverel, Jean-Yves Cahn, "Soft-Tissue Sarcoma and Non-Hodgkin's Lymphoma Clusters around a Municipal Solid Waste Incinerator with High Dioxin Emission Levels," *American Journal of Epidemiology* 152, 1 (2000): 13–19.

19. H.M.P. Fielder, C.M. Poon-King, S.R. Palmer, N. Moss, and G. Coleman, "Assessment of Impact on Health of Residents Living Near the Nant-y-Gwyddon Landfill Site: Retrospective Analysis," *British Medical Journal* 320, 7226 (January 1, 2000): 19; Panagiota Kitsantas, Anastasia Kitsantas, and H. Richard Travis, "Occupational Exposures and Associated Health Effects among Sanitation Landfill Employees," *Journal of Environmental Health* 63, 5 (December 2000): 17.

20. Bob Brown, "Incinerators Steam Powers Paper Plant," *Waste News,* April 26, 1999.

21. Scott Simpson, "Getting a big charge out of garbage: The GVRD's latest generator is a garbage incinerator that will add some 500 gigawatt hours of power to the grid," *The Vancouver Sun,* April 15, 2003.

22. John Lorinc, "A cleaner future: Just how close are we?" *University of Toronto Magazine,* Summer 2005, n.p.

23. Canadian Renewable Fuels Association, *Biodiesel around the World,* available online at www.greenfuels.org/biodiesel/world.htm#d.

24. Derek Burleton and Priscila Kalevar, *Electricity in Canada: Who Needs It? Who's Got It?* (Toronto: TD Economics, 2005).

25. Canadian Wind Energy Association, www.canwea.ca/en.

26. Michael Parfit, "Future Power: Where Will the World Get Its Next Energy Fix?" *National Geographic,* August 2005, 2–31.

27. Ibid.

28. Organisation for Economic Co-operation and Development, *Canada: Environmental Performance Review* (Paris 2005).

29. Interview with author, January 20, 2005.

30. Ibid.

Thinking Cities

1. Richard Florida, *The Rise of the Creative Class* (New York: Basic Books: 2002), 11.

2. Ibid., 227.

3. Malcolm Gladwell, *The Tipping Point* (New York: Little, Brown, 2000), 7.

4. Richard Florida, *The Flight of the Creative Class* (New York: HarperCollins, 2005).

5. Richard Florida, "America's Looming Creativity Crisis," *Harvard Business Review,* 82, 10 (October 2004): 122.

6. Richard Florida, "The World Is Spiky: Globalization Has Changed the Economic Playing Field, but Hasn't Levelled It," *Atlantic Monthly,* October 2005, 50.

7. Peter Hall, *Cities in Civilization* (London: Weidenfeld and Nicholson, 1998), 285.

8. Ibid., 286.

9. Ibid., 498.

10. Meric Gertler, Richard Florida, Gary Gates, and Tara Vinodrai, *Competing on Creativity: Placing Ontario's Cities in the North American Context* (Toronto: Ontario Ministry of Enterprise, Opportunity and Innovation, 2002), 24.

11. Peter Karl Kresl, *An Outsider's Look at Montreal's Economy* (Montreal: McGill Institute for the Study of Canada, n.d.).

12. Lynn Moore, "City rich with creativity, guru says: U.S. author speaks to board of trade," Montreal *Gazette,* January 28, 2005.

13. Neil Bradford, *Cities and Communities That Work: Innovative Practices and Enabling Policies* (Ottawa: Canadian Policy Research Network, 2003).

14. Ibid., 64.

15. Hall, *Cities in Civilization,* 498.

16. Ibid., 285.

17. Charlotte Gray, "Ottawa Dot Com," *Saturday Night,* March 2000. Reprinted with permission.

18. *The Globe and Mail Report on Business,* "The Power 25," October 25, 2005.

19. John Lorinc, "The niche play: Corporate giants can look awfully intimidating at first, but they can be outwitted by upstarts," *The Globe and Mail,* October 7, 2004.

20. Interview with author, February 4, 2005.

21. Toronto Culture, *Culture Plan for the Creative City* (City of Toronto 2003).

22. Interview with author, February 18, 2005.

Planning Cities

1. Quoted in Leonie Sandercock, "An Anatomy of Civic Ambition in Vancouver: Toward Humane Destiny," *Harvard Design Magazine,* Spring/Summer 2005, 42.

2. Lance Berelowitz, *Dream City: Vancouver and the Global Imagination* (Vancouver: Douglas and McIntyre, 2005), 1.

3. Sandercock, "An Anatomy of Civic Ambition in Vancouver," 43.

4. Patricia Roy, *Vancouver: An Illustrated History* (Toronto: James Lorimer, 1980), 129.

5. Berelowitz describes that fight as part of Vancouver's defining mythology, but points out that the city was able to dodge the expressway bullet because it never had much of a downtown manufacturing sector, nor—as was the case with many U.S. cities—was it required to build inner-city highways during the Cold War to serve military purposes.

6. Roy, *Vancouver: An Illustrated History,* 135.

7. Sandercock, "An Anatomy of Civic Ambition in Vancouver," 36.

8. Interview with author, March 9, 2005.

Waterfront Cities

1. There are exceptions, especially in the United States. When U.S. legislators chose the site of their new capital, they ended up building the city on a swamp, with little orientation toward the Potomac River. Las Vegas, the fastest-growing urban region in the United States, grew up in the middle of a desert, and, like Los Angeles to the west, exists only because of the Herculean engineering projects that redirect water to these populous cities.

2. Windsor's casino enjoys pride of place on the city's riverfront shoreline, beckoning Detroit gamblers to cross the river. Montreal's casino, in turn, opened in 1993 in Parc Jean-Drapeau, an island in the St. Lawrence that had been the site of Expo '67. Montreal was far less successful than Vancouver in redeveloping the Expo lands, and the casino sits in the cavernous former French and Quebec pavilion building. In the case of Halifax, the casino is linked to the downtown by an enclosed above-grade walkway

over a canyon-like stretch of Upper Water Street, the remnant of a half-finished expressway project whose demise saved the city's historic waterfront from destruction.

3. The boom is due to aggressive destination marketing by both the provincial and federal governments in the U.S. northeast, as well as the burgeoning popularity of luxury cruise ships doing circuits along the Atlantic coast.

4. Besides the Toronto Waterfront Revitalization Corp., these include the City of Toronto, the Toronto Economic Development Corporation, Ontario Power Generation, Ontario Place, the Canadian National Exhibition, and the Toronto Port Authority.

5. Established by the federal government in 1911, the Toronto Harbour Commission did more than any other public body to build modern Toronto, conducting massive landfill operations using construction debris that created hundreds of hectares of space for factories and rail corridors. In the 1920s, the commission embarked on a major new harbour area extending out into Lake Ontario. But the decline in shipping traffic rendered it unnecessary, and that peninsula was allowed to grow wild, creating a unique nature reserve known as Tommy Thompson Park.

6. Vancouver's Port Authority has container facilities in two locations: along the south shore of Burrard Inlet, near the city's gritty east end, and at Roberts Bank, a manmade peninsula in the Fraser River delta, well south of the city. A few critics, including the distinguished architect Arthur Erickson, argue that the entire port operation should be consolidated around the Roberts Bank container-handling facility, which has easy access to railways and highways. According to Erickson, such a move would free up another long stretch of the city's waterfront for the sort of redevelopment that transformed False Creek.

7. In the 1970s, the city tried to raze the historic port district known as The Rocks, but residents' groups clashed with bulldozers and prevented the demolition of one of Sydney's oldest neighbourhoods.

Remembering Cities

1. Anthony Tung, *Preserving the World's Great Cities: The Destruction and Renewal of the Historic Metropolis* (New York: Three Rivers Press, 2001). Haussmann ordered the demolition of 27,000 buildings but constructed 100,000 new ones, along with nearly 1600 hectares of parks, 640 kilometres of streets, and 416 kilometres of sewers—an accomplishment described by the distinguished British urban historian Sir Peter Hall as the fastest and most profound transformation of any city in history.

2. Ibid., 280.

3. Interview with author, January 19, 2005.

4. Annick Germain and Damaris Rose, *Montreal: The Quest for a Metropolis* (Toronto: John Wiley and Sons, 2000), 86–91.

5. Ibid.

6. Complicating this picture is the fact the Ottawa has spent lavish sums to rehabilitate parts of the port, literally across the street from the old city. Where the latter is cramped and full of ersatz quaintness, the former is spacious and self-consciously modern.

7. Interview with author, January 19, 2005.

8. In the 1960s, the city was prepared to demolish Old City Hall, built in the Romanesque Revival style by E.J. Lennox, as well as Union Station, the magnificent Beaux Art monument to rail travel designed by John Lyle.

9. The neighbourhood also benefited from an influx of residents who moved into a groundbreaking mid-rise, mixed-income community developed nearby in the 1970s. Conceived during Mayor David Crombie's term in office, the St. Lawrence Community remains one of North America's most successful urban revitalization projects, providing early support for the notion that downtown was a desirable place to live.

10. Alanna Mitchell, "Calgary enters 'renaissance': The city that once willingly razed its history to make room for progress is moving to protect older neighbourhoods and heritage buildings," *The Globe and Mail*, July 22, 1996.

11. Martin Gyford, John Holden, Rt. Hon. Chris Smith, Jon Snow, and Tony Travers, *Tate Modern: The First Five Years* (London: Tate Trustees, 2005), 5.

12. Neville Nankivell, "Preservation by tax incentive," *National Post*, March 20, 2004.

13. Sheila Fraser, Auditor General of Canada, *Protection of Cultural Heritage in the Federal Government* (Ottawa 2003).

14. The site of Canada's defining battle against American expansionism, Fort York was transferred by the federal government to the City of Toronto in 1909. Although declared a national historic site in 1923 and then again in 1958, it barely survived the expansion of the railways and then a major waterfront highway. The Fort grounds have been managed for decades by the City of Toronto, unlike Halifax's Citadel, which is owned and operated by the federal government. The municipality for years failed to invest in properly maintaining the site and has allowed inappropriate development to encroach on it. In the late 1990s, however, local heritage advocates pressed to improve pedestrian access to the Fort district, even as its bastions faced a new threat to its viability as a historic site: the development of extremely large condo towers on nearby industrial land.

15. Interview with author, January 10, 2005.

16. These included Toronto's St. Lawrence Hall, Hamilton's Dundurn Castle, and the City Hall in Kingston. In Toronto's Old Town, the original site of Muddy York, the city itself acquired several buildings of historic relevance,

such as the first post office, a court house, and the home of a prominent newspaper publisher.

17. Rachelle Garbarine, "A new report tells just how preservation pays," *The New York Times,* August 3, 1997.

18. Heritage Canada Foundation Conference Proceedings, *Preservation Pays: The Economics of Heritage Conservation* (Toronto: Heritage Canada Foundation, 2001), 25.

19. Catherine Nasmith, "Lessons from the Big Apple," *The Globe and Mail,* March 12, 2004.

20. Ibid.

21. Heritage Canada Foundation Conference Proceedings, *Preservation Pays,* 13.

22. Residential real estate speculation, in fact, is ripping through neighbourhoods that aren't quite old enough to be considered historic, but whose homes will be deemed to be of heritage value within a decade or two. In Toronto, wealthy homeowners have been tearing down 70- or 80-year-old houses and replacing them with monster homes with little opposition from city planners. Vancouver, by contrast, "has protected most of the best qualities of its late-nineteenth and early twentieth-century suburbs, with their valuable legacy of Craftsman vernacular, their mature treed streets and rich private landscaping," says John Punter, a professor of urban design at Cardiff University in Wales, and author of *The Vancouver Achievement* (Vancouver: UBC Press, 2003), 346. The point is that the unimpeded accumulation of residential demolition jobs undermines the heritage character of middle-class neighbourhoods nearly old enough to be considered historically relevant.

23. Tung, *Preserving the World's Great Cities,* 244.

24. Quoted in Nasmith, "Lessons from the Big Apple."

Beautiful Cities

1. When Ontario started phasing out grade 13 in 2000, a so-called double-cohort of students rolled into the province's post-secondary institutions, forcing all of them to scramble to expand their facilities. Some were forced to lease movie theatres as makeshift lecture halls and snap up rooms in downtown hotels as dorm space.

2. Situated at the western-most tip of the south Vancouver peninsula, the University of British Columbia adopted a "University City" plan that aims to turn the campus into an architecturally progressive "satellite" neighbourhood. Simon Fraser University has also initiated a campaign to develop sustainable and eco-friendly neighbourhoods on its property. Driven by the vision of former president and architecture aficionado Rob Prichard, the University of Toronto has spent the past 15 years redeveloping the empty spaces in its downtown campus and landscaping the internal roadways. Waterloo

University's architectural faculty colonized an old mill building near the centre of Galt in order to spur the revitalization of the town. And York University, located in a northwest Toronto suburb, has been pursuing a plan to impose a traditional street grid on its windswept campus, establish a connection to the subway system, and sell some of its surplus landholdings to developers.

3. Neil Bradford, *Cities and Communities That Work: Innovative Practices and Enabling Policies* (Ottawa: Canadian Policy Research Network, 2003).

4. Raul Barreneche, *New Museums* (London: Phaidon, 2005).

5. In Ottawa, the new museums include The National Gallery of Canada (1988), by Moishe Safdie; The Canadian Museum of Civilization (1989), by Douglas Cardinal; The Canadian Museum of Contemporary Photography (1992), situated in an old railway tunnel between the Chateau Laurier and the Rideau Canal; and the Canadian War Museum (2005), by Moriyama and Teshima/Griffiths Rankin Cook. In Montreal, the Canadian Centre for Architecture, located in a heritage building in the downtown, received a critically acclaimed expansion in 1989.

6. John Punter, *The Vancouver Achievement: Urban Planning and Design* (Vancouver: UBC Press, 2003), 378.

Conclusion: The Safe City

1. The "race riot" that occurred in downtown Toronto in 1992 on the heels of the not-guilty verdict for the Los Angeles police officers who had beat Rodney King to a pulp was little more than a large brawl compared with the conflagration that tore through L.A.'s most troubled inner-city neighbourhoods.

2. Rosemary Gartner and Sara Thompson, "Trends in Homicide in Toronto," in *Research on Community Safety: From Enforcement and Prevention to Civic Engagement,* ed. Bruce Kidd and Jim Phillips (Toronto: Centre of Criminology, University of Toronto, 2004), 38. Reprinted with permission.

3. Scot Wortley and Julian Tanner, "Social Groups or Criminal Organizations? The Extent and Nature of Youth Gang Activity in Toronto," in *Research on Community Safety,* ed. Kidd and Phillips, 58–77.

4. Dagmar Hedrick, *European Report on Drug Consumption Rooms* (Lisbon: European Monitoring Centre for Drugs and Drug Addiction, 2004).

5. Joel Connelly, "Vancouver and Seattle lead world in pot strategies," *Seattle Post-Intelligencer,* July 25, 2005.

6. Stephen Easton, *Marijuana Growth in British Columbia* (Vancouver: Fraser Institute, 2004), 4.

7. Mary Wiens, Joan Melanson, and Piya Chattopadhyay, "Whose Truth?" Toronto, CBC Radio One. Available online at www.cbc.ca/toronto/features/whose_truth/index.html.

INDEX